THE
AWFU
GRAC
OF GOI

THE
AWFUL GRACE
OF GOD

RELIGIOUS TERRORISM, WHITE SUPREMACY, AND THE
UNSOLVED MURDER OF MARTIN LUTHER KING JR.

STUART WEXLER AND LARRY HANCOCK

COUNTERPOINT

Berkeley

Library of Congress Cataloging-in-Publication Data is available.

ISBN: 978-1-58243-830-6

COUNTERPOINT

1919 Fifth Street

Berkeley, CA 94710

www.counterpointpress.com

Interior design by Tabitha Lahr

Cover design by John Yates

Distributed by Publishers Group West

10 9 8 7 6 5 4 3 2 1

We dedicate this work to the Reverend Edwin King. His courage and open mindedness in revisiting the most painful periods of his life, involving violence against him and the murders of his colleagues and friends as they fought for basic human rights, has continually inspired our search for the truth in the murder of Martin Luther King, Jr.

CONTENTS

FOREWORD

During the mid-1990s, while teaching at Hood College, I happened to live only four minutes away from Harold Weisberg, one of the best-known citizen critics of the Warren Commission and giant in the studies of the both the Kennedy and King assassinations. Weisberg had used his legal skills and the Freedom of Information Act to amass a huge document collection, containing some ninety thousand pages of King case files. For a time he served as James Earl Ray's investigator and eventually published his own book on the King assassination.

It was Harold who suggested that I undertake a study of Dr. King's Poor People's Campaign and he gave me free access to the FBI files housed in his basement. I was excited about pursuing a topic that involved a tragic episode in the civil rights movement and I submitted my own Freedom of Information Act (FOIA) request on POCAM (the FBI's designated name for the Poor People's March) to the Justice Department. Justice responded to my request as if I had committed lese majesty—effectively questioning whether I was in the grip of some fantasy life that somehow entitled me access to government documents. The Department of Justice's FOIA section effectively told me to either take a hike or get a lawyer.

Well, I did get a FOIA lawyer and sued for access to the POCAM files. The Friday before the Monday when my case was scheduled for a hearing, Justice capitulated—leaving me with several thousand dollars in lawyer's fees, the money I had planned to use to gain access to the FBI's field office documents which I needed to tell the full story of the Poor People's Campaign. I felt gratified that I had won the battle with Justice, but disappointed because I would be unable to write the most complete story of Dr. King's final project.

I mention this in detail because I can appreciate the effort that the authors of this book put into their work, which is also heavily based in government files. I am also concerned that the entire Freedom of Information Act is under the political gun and that constant government invocations of "State Secrets" is effectively gutting that law and destroying the government transparency it was supposed to produce.

Given my own studies on him, I would recommend that anyone with an interest in the assassination of Dr. Martin Luther King Jr. should have a copy of this work in their library. Wexler and Hancock's book is a major work, grounded in impressive research.

The Awful Grace of God opens by reminding us of exactly what happened in America with the onset of the civil rights movement of the 1950s and 1960s and moves through that period with a focus on violence targeting Dr. King, who had emerged as the symbol of peaceful protest.

Wexler and Hancock demonstrate that officialdom missed the ominous, larger picture in its investigation into the King murder. It failed to deal with the implications of a movement of ideological terrorists who had been waging a campaign of violence, a targeted campaign of bombings and shootings calculated to ignite a state of chaos which would force harsh, repressive measures by the government and in the end actual race war. The ultimate goal of the campaign was to be the literal extermination of both the black race and their alleged enablers—the Jews.

The National States' Rights Party, the White Knights of the Ku Klux Klan of Mississippi, and affiliated leaders of the Christian Identity religious movement were all linked in a plan to ignite a racial Armageddon. In furthering their effort toward a race war, these extremist elements were involved with a series of murder contracts on Dr. King. By 1967, the price on Dr. King's head was up to $100,000 in some offers and news of the bounty was circulating through a number of federal prisons.

Wexler and Hancock make a persuasive argument that James Earl Ray first heard talk of such a bounty while in the Jefferson City prison and that eventually, after months of being on the run and pursuing other options (including fleeing overseas) in Canada, Mexico and the United States, was recruited into a plot against Dr. King when his options and money began to run out in Los Angeles.

The Awful Grace of God presents the view that James Earl Ray was aware of and involved to some extent in the conspiracy against Dr. King. The authors do not pretend to fully resolve Ray's actual role, while considering arguments both for and against his possible act as Dr. King's killer. They also present evidence suggesting that Ray did not go to Memphis knowingly planning to kill Dr. King himself and that a different plan and a different "patsy" were actually in play.

In addition, what the authors do with consummate skill is to dismiss the diversion of "Raoul," a mysterious figure introduced by Ray himself, by making a convincing case that "Raoul" was Ray's own creation, intended to divert guilt from himself as well as from the actual individuals behind the attack. In addition to their examination of "Raoul" the authors also address the allegation that King's murder was the work of elements of the American government—a conspiracy presented in King assassination literature as an alliance of the CIA, and a collection of secret, highly covert military intelligence groups—with the actual assassination alleged to have been performed by or coordinated by military personnel observed and reported in Memphis on the day of the murder.

In March of 1979, the House Select Committee on Assassinations released its report on President Kennedy's and Dr. King's assassinations. The report, submitted to Congress, concluded that the committee found evidence of conspiracy in both cases. The committee requested the Justice Department to accept its findings and open its own investigation. Neither Congress nor the Justice Department chose to act on the committee's findings and recommendations.

The Awful Grace of God is a major contribution by private citizens to throw light on the still-unresolved and paramount issue of who, and with what motive, was actually involved in the murder of America's most renowned and universally admired private citizen of the twentieth century.

—Gerald K. McKnight
Hood College, Professor Emeritus, 2012

INTRODUCTION

On April 4, 1968, a single shot from a .30-06 rifle killed the Reverend Martin Luther King Jr. as he stood on the balcony of the Lorraine Motel in Memphis, Tennessee.

At the time, Robert F. Kennedy was campaigning for the Democratic presidential nomination and learned of King's death as he landed in Indianapolis to deliver a campaign speech to a predominantly black neighborhood. Aides feared a riot, and the chief of police told Kennedy that he could not guarantee his safety, but rather than inciting a riot, Kennedy's brief, heartfelt speech was credited with helping to prevent racial riots in the aftermath of King's assassination and is widely considered one of the best speeches in American history. From the back of a flatbed truck, Kennedy offered the following words:

> In this difficult day, in this difficult time for the United States, it's perhaps well to ask what kind of a nation we are and what direction we want to move in. For those of you who are black—considering the evidence evidently is that there were white people who were responsible—you can be filled with bitterness, and with hatred, and a desire for revenge.
>
> We can move in that direction as a country, in greater polarization—black people amongst blacks, and white amongst whites, filled with hatred toward one another. Or we can make an effort, as Martin Luther King did, to understand and to comprehend, and replace that violence, that stain of bloodshed that has spread across our land, with an effort to understand, compassion, and love.

And then Kennedy quoted his favorite poet, Aeschylus:

Even in our sleep, pain which cannot forget falls drop by drop upon the heart, until, in our own despair, against our will, comes wisdom through the awful grace of God.[1]

We chose "the awful grace of God" as the title for this book because it captures not only the enormous feeling of loss at the death of Martin Luther King Jr., but also the need for an understanding of what happened that fateful day in Memphis. Who murdered King? Was there a conspiracy? What was the motive? And what do the answers to those questions mean for our nation's history and our future? Forty years after King's assassination, we are still looking for that wisdom.

The day following the assassination, while criminal investigations were just beginning, United States Attorney General Ramsey Clark stated to the press that there were no indications of conspiracy in the shooting, "all of our evidence at this time indicates that it was a single person who committed this criminal act."[2] Within two weeks of the killing, the Federal Bureau of Investigation's manhunt had begun to focus on James Earl Ray, an escaped convict with a long history of theft and armed robbery. Ray had never been involved in militant racism, and his history revealed only a single constant— a continuing quest to score big money. At the time of the King shooting, Ray had been on the run for over a year. He had traveled to both Canada and Mexico in unsuccessful efforts to continue his escape overseas. Almost two months to the day after King's assassination, Ray was taken into custody at a London airport.

Both the director of the FBI and the attorney general of the United States singled out James Earl Ray as the lone killer of Dr. King. No motive was ever given for his act. Ray avoided trial with a guilty plea, which he later claimed had been orchestrated by his attorney as the only option for his escaping the death penalty. Ray's own remarks, his lack of any apparent motive, and the fact that he had no personal history of racist activism or connection to racist groups left much of the public with the impression that there must be more to the King assassination, that the story had not been fully told.

That view was solidified by the findings of the House Select Committee on Assassinations (HSCA), formed in 1976 to reexamine the assassinations of President John F. Kennedy, and Dr. Martin Luther King Jr. The committee's report on Dr. King's death was presented in 1978. Their wording was precise; their message clear:

> *The committee believes, on the basis of the circumstantial evidence available to it, that there is a likelihood that James Earl Ray assassinated Dr. Martin Luther King as a result of a conspiracy. . . .*
>
> *The Department of Justice and Federal Bureau of Investigation performed a thorough investigation into the responsibility of James Earl Ray for the assassination of Dr. King, and conducted a thorough fugitive investigation, but failed to investigate adequately the possibility of conspiracy in the assassination.*[3]

The HSCA tried to move beyond the FBI conspiracy investigation, but its resources were limited, its timing perhaps ten years too late. In many instances HSCA investigators were thwarted by the fact that key individuals were deceased. Witnesses who provided reports in 1968 were too frightened to even confirm their original stories, much less expand on them, and named suspects were simply unwilling to talk. And although the HSCA had subpoena power, they lacked the leverage that came with the realistic threat of jail time, perjury charges, or negotiated immunity to get results.

Beyond that, the HSCA inquiry also suffered from some of the same fundamental problems that prevented the FBI from adequately investigating Ray's possible involvement in a conspiracy in the first place. In 1968 and well into the 1990s, many key informant files were held in strict confidence, not available for exchange between individual FBI field offices, not available to local or state law enforcement or prosecutors, and not offered to the

HSCA. Director J. Edgar Hoover had an established policy of not sacrificing informants in civil rights cases that he viewed as being unwinnable in southern courts.

It has only been through a series of successful cold-case prosecutions over the last decade that we have come to realize the extent of such information and its implications for the King investigation. Reports that the FBI produced in the King murder investigation suggest that the local offices had little understanding of the background and associations of the information they produced. Challenges such as compartmentalization of information; the inability to correlate names, aliases, and organizations; and the lack of any of today's data-mining capabilities all fundamentally handicapped individual field offices in the pursuit of leads suggesting any potential conspiracy in the murder of Dr. King.

With access to FBI files and oral histories that only became available over the past decade, with information from successful cold-case prosecutions, and with our own primary source interviews, we are now able to relate a much more comprehensive view of the events that we feel led to Dr. King's assassination.

Part I: The Conspirators exposes an insidious subculture that was united in the goal of killing Dr. King and whose efforts we follow over a period of some five years. It reveals that certain individuals involved in that effort were far more organized, disciplined, and shrewd than had been commonly pictured in existing literature. We trace the efforts of that network by examining several plots against Dr. King, which were deadly serious and, in some cases, quite sophisticated.

The individuals and groups you encounter in this book had indeed been targeting Dr. King for years. They viewed King as the ultimate target because his death represented their best opportunity. Their goal was massive riot and bloodshed, racial violence on a national scale. They wished to kill Dr. King in a dramatic and symbolic manner, a killing that would put an end to any thought of compromise and concessions between liberal white America and an increasingly nationalistic and frustrated black America.

There is no longer any doubt about the existence of such a network or of its ongoing effort to kill Dr. King. What remains are questions about its direct or indirect connection to the actual murder of Dr. King in Memphis, about the role of James Earl Ray, and the possibility of conspiracy in the assassination.

In *Part II: The Accused,* we closely follow James Earl Ray from his escape in 1967 from the Missouri State Penitentiary to the steps that seem to have brought him in touch with an offer he couldn't refuse, an offer that led him to begin stalking Dr. King in Selma, Atlanta, and finally Memphis. We explore a number of bounties offered on Dr. King's life, raising the possibility that James Earl Ray may have been only the final individual to respond to such an offer.

And in *Part III: The Crime,* we examine the possibility that nothing in Memphis actually came about, for either Ray or the plotters, as was intended. And we direct our attention toward investigations and existing FBI documents that might well help resolve the issue of conspiracy once and for all.

If we are right, our conclusions likely point to a group of violent individuals who saw King's murder through the eyes of a much more vengeful God than the one that inspired the slain civil rights figure to continually risk his life in the name of peace and mutual understanding. If the Sermon on the Mount was the religious inspiration for Dr. King, then, for these calculating, violent men, the book of Revelations was the guiding scripture. But their version of the end-times was far different than anything one would hear from most preachers on a Sunday. Their hope was for a race war that would bring on Armageddon itself. For these men, God's grace had run its course, and Bobby Kennedy's soothing words must have seemed like the calm before the awful storm they desired.

PART I
THE CONSPIRATORS

CHAPTER 1

TARGETING MARTIN LUTHER KING JR.

On April 3, 1968, an American Airlines flight from Atlanta to Memphis was stuck at the departure gate. The pilot made a general passenger announcement that the Reverend Dr. Martin Luther King Jr. was on board and that the airline had received a bomb threat. For everyone's safety, they would have to delay their takeoff until all the baggage had been examined.[1]

Only a week earlier, King had arrived late in Memphis to join a protest march for striking African American sanitation workers who were paid lower wages than their white coworkers and who were forced to work in the worst of weather. The protest began to turn violent, and one of the marchers was shot and killed. Now King was returning to deliver a speech at Memphis's Mason Temple, the world headquarters of the Church of God in Christ, and to lead another protest march. As his flight finally departed, Dr. King was once again reminded that his life was continually at risk.[2]

King was booked at the Lorraine Motel in Memphis, sharing a room with his longtime friend Reverend Ralph Abernathy. They had stayed in room 306 so often that it was jokingly referred to as the "King-Abernathy Suite." A thunderstorm brewed that evening as King left for the Mason Temple to deliver an address that would be remembered as one of his greatest—and one that was eerily prescient.[3] As his speech drew to a close, he referred to the day's earlier bomb threat:

And then I got to Memphis. And some began to say the threats . . . or talk about the threats that were out. What would happen to me from some of our sick white brothers?

Well, I don't know what will happen now. We've got some dif-
ficult days ahead. But it doesn't matter with me now. Because I've
been to the mountaintop. And I don't mind. Like anybody, I would
like to live a long life. Longevity has its place. But I'm not concerned
about that now. I just want to do God's will. And He's allowed me
to go up to the mountain. And I've looked over. And I've seen the
promised land. I may not get there with you. But I want you to
know tonight, that we, as a people, will get to the promised land!
And so I'm happy, tonight. I'm not worried about anything. I'm not
fearing any man. Mine eyes have seen the glory of the coming of
the Lord![4]

The next day, April 4, 1968, James Earl Ray, a forty-year-old escaped convict from Jefferson City's Missouri State Penitentiary, rented a room at Bessie Brewer's rooming house, located across the street from the Lorraine Motel. Whether Ray came to Memphis with King's murder as his goal, or whether he was, as he later claimed, manipulated by outside forces to come to Memphis, his name would soon join those of the most notorious criminals in American history. He had brought with him a recently purchased Remington 760 Gamemaster rifle, which would be found within minutes of King's shooting in an alcove of a store adjacent to Bessie Brewer's rooming house.[5]

That fateful day was filled with meetings and phone calls for Dr. King, and he and his circle were once again late—this time for a dinner at the home of his good friend, Reverend Billy Kyles. Kyles was at the Lorraine, hurrying King along. In good spirits, King came out of room 306 onto the balcony and bantered over the railing with Jesse Jackson and others waiting in the parking lot. At exactly 6:01 PM, King was struck by a single .30-06 bullet, and was rushed to Saint Joseph's Hospital, and was pronounced dead at 7:05 PM.[6]

Shortly after the shooting, witnesses saw a man race down the hall of Bessie Brewer's rooming house across the street. In the doorway of Canipe's Amusement Company, Memphis law enforcement officers found a green blanket packed with the Gamemaster rifle, ammunition, and a pair of binoculars, as well as assorted personal items. In his original signed statement, the owner, Guy Canipe, said the package was left there within minutes of the shooting. Police found witnesses who said they saw a white Mustang race away from the curb not far from Canipe's store. The FBI traced fingerprints on the binoculars and other items to James Earl Ray, whose 1967 white Ford Mustang was later found abandoned hundreds of miles away in Atlanta, Georgia.[7]

Eventually James Earl Ray would be captured in England, extradited to the United States, and indicted as the sole killer of Dr. King—based on means and opportunity; but the question of his motive was never adequately resolved, allowing for years of assertions, including by Ray himself, that conspirators had killed King and framed the escaped fugitive. There was no shortage of powerful individuals and violent groups who detested King— from FBI director J. Edgar Hoover to the Ku Klux Klan. Ray's supporters would claim that a massive conspiracy organized by the military and intelligence community killed King. But many of these claims rested on the word of Ray himself, a dubious practice when dealing with a career criminal serving a life sentence.

Others tried to thread the needle, to argue that Ray was a witting participant in a broader conspiracy. Congress, in their late-1970s reinvestigation of King's assassination, argued that Ray was responding to a bounty offer on King made by a group of right-wing businessmen from Ray's hometown of Saint Louis, Missouri.[8] But these businessmen had no record of or connection to violence, including against Dr. King. Those who specifically had a connection to a series of attempts to kill Martin Luther King Jr. before 1968 were dismissed as suspects. These groups had the motive, some argue, but not the sophisticated means to succeed in such a conspiracy, nor did they have the opportunity to collaborate with James Earl Ray. Had investigators looked more carefully, they would have found a good deal of evidence to believe that these groups that had been seriously trying to kill King for almost a decade were, in fact, the best suspects in his actual assassination.

THE MORE THAN NINE LIVES OF MARTIN LUTHER KING JR.

For Dr. King, the April 3 bomb threat was just one more warning. In the thousands of pages of files the FBI collected on Dr. Martin Luther King Jr. there are dozens, if not hundreds, of reported threats against Dr. King's life. Almost all were similar to the plane threat: menacing but harmless. They came mostly by phone, often to newspapers, often anonymously. When law enforcement could trace these threats to their source, they often led to drunks and mentally disturbed individuals. Yet in some cases, such as the January 1956 bombing of Dr. King's home in the midst of the successful Montgomery Bus Boycott, the attempts were far from innocuous.[9] Indeed, from the time of that first bombing until his assassination in 1968, law enforcement investigated serious threats against King, some foiled only by the vagaries of chance.

In one sense, these ongoing public threats simply constituted a constant level of "noise"; Dr. King had no choice but to live with them if he wanted to continue his mission.[10] When asked a question about when he had personally been most frightened, King replied that it had been during a visit to Mississippi. He visit was not only to mourn the victims of the Mississippi Burning murders but also to bring public scrutiny and pressure on law enforcement to pursue justice in what history now calls the Mississippi Burning killings, the brutal slayings of three young civil rights workers. King offered a prayer in which he had said, "O Lord, the killers of those boys may even be within the range of my voice." At that moment, he overheard a big burly sheriff standing near him say, "You're damn right they are."[11]

At the time Dr. King had no way of knowing that the individuals who had killed the young civil rights organizers were associated with the White Knights of the Ku Klux Klan of Mississippi and that the order for their murders had come from its leader, Samuel Holloway Bowers. King had no idea that Sam Bowers had himself targeted King for murder and that Bowers was part of a network that had incited and planned attacks on King over a period of years. King also did not know that a local Mississippi sheriff's deputy would eventually be one of those convicted in the murders of Andrew Goodman, Michael Schwerner, and James Chaney—the three young men for whom King had prayed. As we shall see, King's visits to Mississippi, to bring national attention to these murders and to the 1963 assassination of his National Association for the Advancement of Colored People (NAACP) colleague Medgar Evers, brought King into the crosshairs of committed radicals.

The nature of the radical network that was targeting Dr. King was more national in scope and more united in purpose than has been previously thought. There was a series of systematic attempts on his life by a little-known subculture that was obsessed with King's murder. These efforts to kill King provide the best window into the likeliest conspiracy behind King's murder in Memphis. But when examined in depth for links and commonalities, these plots also reveal a glimpse into a sinister, clandestine movement within American history, one that entwined religious zealotry, reactionary politics, and out-and-out hatred, a story that—if told at all—is often disconnected from the tumult of the 1960s or, just as important, from the twenty-first-century terrorism to which it bears such a close resemblance.

THE FIRST CONTRACT: BIRMINGHAM, ALABAMA, 1958

Alabama was the scene for one of the first serious recorded efforts to kill King, one that came against the backdrop of the heated civil rights battles that engulfed Birmingham, Alabama, in the late 1950s. This plot did not even originally target King but rather the Reverend Fred Shuttlesworth, president of the Alabama Christian Movement for Human Rights, who was arguably even more defiant and strident in his efforts to desegregate Birmingham than King was in Montgomery. Shuttlesworth famously said of the repeated attempts to "dissuade" him (including beatings, bombings, and general harassment[12]), "We mean to kill segregation or be killed by it!"[13] Having seen that the local white establishment, led by Birmingham's notorious commissioner of public safety, Eugene "Bull" Connor, could not deter the indefatigable Reverend Shuttlesworth, the state's Ku Klux Klan sought another avenue to stop him: a contract killing.

For this, they summoned Jesse Benjamin "J. B." Stoner, a Georgia native who supported the Nazis during World War II for their stance on racial purity and anti-Semitism and who was the founder of the new and virulently racist and anti-Semitic National States Rights Party (NSRP) Stoner, who earned national attention for a public feud with Nation of Islam leader Elijah Muhammad (famously telling Muhammad that "you want white blood pumped into your race"[14]), had originally been contracted by local Klan leader Hugh Morris to bomb Shuttlesworth's Bethel Baptist Church.[15] But Stoner offered to include the contract killing of Shuttlesworth and other civil rights leaders, with Dr. King notably at the top of the list. Stoner offered a special reduced rate of $1,500 to kill King and only failed because law enforcement—in conjunction with the FBI—had been running a sting against the Klan and stopped the plot in advance.[16]

BIRMINGHAM AGAIN, 1963

Birmingham continued to be a flashpoint in the civil rights struggle and was the scene for two other attempts on King—one involving another bombing and the other a planned shooting

In the spring of 1963, a large dynamite bomb was thrown at room 30 at the A.G. Gaston Motel where King had set up the headquarters for his efforts to integrate Birmingham's eateries and businesses. An apparent response to countless King-led sit-ins, marches, and protests—efforts that scandalized the local business community into reaching a prointegrationist agreement with King and his aides-the bomb left a five-by-five-foot hole in the motel wall and destroyed two adjacent house trailers. King narrowly escaped death, as he had unexpectedly abandoned plans for a celebration at the motel and had left Birmingham. Law enforcement strongly suspected that the bombing was the work of the Eastview, Alabama, Klavern known as "The Cahaba River Group" or "The Cahaba Boys," a militant KKK subgroup that J. B. Stoner heavily influenced.[17]

Another attempt on King occurred as the nation once again turned its attention to segregationist violence in Birmingham, this time in the wake of the Sixteenth Street Baptist Church bombing that killed four young girls in September 1963.[18]

The four men who reportedly plotted this attempted assassination of King included William Potter Gale, a Californian who organized racist and anti-Semitic paramilitary organizations on the West Coast; Admiral John G. Crommelin, a National States' Rights Party luminary who would one day run as a vice presidential candidate on their national ticket; Sidney Crockett Barnes, a suspected serial bomber who fled a crackdown on racial violence in Florida to settle in Alabama; and Noah Jefferson Carden, a violent racist from Mobile, Alabama.[19] The plotting against King—which involved cooperation with local extremists—actually started just before the Sixteenth Street Church bombing and was among the first plots the House Select Committee on Assassinations (HSCA) considered when Congress reinvestigated the King murder in the late 1970s. The plot apparently continued into 1964, and though details of the exact murder scheme are somewhat sketchy, conversations secretly taped by the Miami Police between Barnes and police/FBI informant William "Willie" Somersett suggest that Carden may have received a rifle from Gale, who hoped that Carden would do the deed. Police even arranged to provide Barnes with a rifle so as to trace it back to the extremist colonel from California.[20]

Birmingham was apparently one of several sites in Alabama considered for a King attack, with Mobile being another preferred location[21]. In fact, the four men even planned a larger wave of statewide violence to lure King to these other areas, notably the sites of the first experiments in school desegregation in Alabama.[22] King may well have been saved from these attempts by another act of violence in Saint Augustine, which drew him to Florida and away from Alabama.

"NOTHING LEFT BUT WHITE FACES . . . ": SAINT AUGUSTINE, FLORIDA, 1964

In 1964, civil rights activist Robert Hayling and others were kidnapped at a Klan rally in Saint Augustine, Florida, beaten unconscious, and nearly burned to death. This drew King and his focus away from Alabama and toward

Florida. In fact, it was King's response to the growing civil disorder in Saint Augustine, Florida, that triggered the next major attempt on his life.

After four sit-in organizers had been badly beaten and guns fired into their homes, Saint Augustine protests degenerated into serious racial violence, extending over several months in 1963 and 1964 as civil rights activists battled against southern reactionaries. Some of this antagonism was stoked by J. B. Stoner and his erstwhile friend the Reverend Charles "Connie" Lynch from California, a minister in a white supremacist church with nationwide reach who, commenting on the four young girls who died in the Birmingham bombing, said that they were not children, but "little niggers . . . and if there's four less niggers tonight, then I say 'Good for whoever planted the bomb!'"[23]

Stoner and Lynch, known as a two-person "riot squad,"[24] consistently followed King and staged counterrallies, where they inflamed white audience members, often to the point of violence. In one Saint Augustine rally, Lynch promised, "There's gonna be a bloody race riot all over this country. The stage is being set for a bloodbath. When the smoke clears, there ain't gonna be nothing left but white faces!"[25] The aftermath of this rally sent nineteen blacks to local area hospitals.

In response to the ongoing violence, Dr. King visited Saint Augustine in May 1964 and announced his support for demonstrations, even telling President Lyndon Johnson that "all semblance of law and nonviolent order had broken down in Saint Augustine."[26] King was tempting fate once again in his trips into Florida. Although little is known as to the exact identities of those who did the deed, a suspected group of Klansmen opened fire on King's rented beach cottage near Saint Augustine, perforating walls and shattering the furniture inside with their bullets.[27] King had been in California at the time, having been warned of plots against his life in Florida.[28]

ENTER THE WHITE KNIGHTS: JACKSON, MISSISSIPPI, 1964

The next reported effort to kill King came in the spring and summer of 1964 and involved a new and very serious group of players in the white supremacist movement, the White Knights of the Ku Klux Klan of Mississippi.

The White Knights formed in the cauldron of anti-integrationist resistance that was Mississippi in the early 1960s. As one of the few states with a majority nonwhite population, Mississippi's white establishment vigorously opposed efforts to give equal rights to minorities. Yet some white Mississippians did not feel that the reactionary moves made by the wealthy White Citizens' Councils and the government-backed Mississippi State Sovereignty Commission went far enough. To some, even the existing Klan regime in the Magnolia State was too passive, and they abandoned their Klaverns in large numbers, coalescing to form the White Knights, led by the devilishly brilliant Samuel Holloway Bowers and eventually becoming the most successfully violent KKK subgroup in the nation. The FBI would connect the White Knights with more than three hundred acts of racial violence, including the Mississippi Burning murders of three civil rights workers and the murder of voting rights activist Vernon Dahmer.[29]

In one 1964 incident, however, FBI reports indicate that the White Knights sought outside criminal help to try to kill King. Specifically, the White Knights contracted with a bank robber and highly respected contract killer from Oklahoma, Donald Eugene Sparks, to eliminate King if he came to Mississippi, as he eventually did in July 1964 in response to the Mississippi Burning murders. According to the FBI sources, Sparks waited at a motel in Jackson, Mississippi, to conclude the deal but backed out of the plot when the White Knights could not raise their promised bounty. Two separate sources described this earlier plot to the FBI after King's murder, but the FBI did only a superficial investigation. Although they found that Sparks was known in White Knights circles, they dismissed the bounty reports because they could not find Sparks's name in any motel registry in Jackson at the relevant time. Beyond having failed to look for any one of his many aliases,[30] they also missed a report in their own files from 1964 that strongly corroborated the story.

White Knights Grand Dragon Billy Buckles told a group of Klansmen (which apparently included at least one FBI informant) that the White Knights were contracting with a criminal to perform an act of violence that would "make the death of Medgar Evers look sick [by comparison]."[31] There are other reports in the FBI files that describe additional King murder plots for June/July 1964, but they presently lack the level of corroboration and specificity available for the Sparks effort in 1964. However, it appears that these later reports convinced at least one very important person that King was in danger. President Lyndon Johnson personally ordered additional federal security for King in response to these Mississippi threats as well as those from Alabama.[32]

In response, one Mississippi sheriff, Lawrence Rainey, openly protested the additional federal guards. Within a matter of weeks Rainey himself would become infamous for his suspected role in the conspiracy behind the Mississippi Burning murders. Rainey had, in fact, been an active member of the Mississippi White Knights when he wrote to the government claiming that his officers—some of whom were later convicted for their roles in the Mississippi Burning murders—could provide all the protection King needed while he was under threat of assassination.[33]

THE WHITE KNIGHTS TRY AGAIN: SELMA, ALABAMA, 1965

An account from the FBI's most trusted inside source on the White Knights indicates that they tried once again to kill King in early 1965. This time the plot was targeted for the state of Mississippi, and the White Knights apparently planned to handle it themselves.

The location was in Selma, where Dr. King had been leading a voter registration drive, without much success. The primary attack was to be by snipers, with a backup plan of rigging a highway bridge with explosives if King escaped the shooting. Advanced word of the attack appears to have come from a deep informant named Delmar Dennis, a minister who had been close to Klan leader Samuel Bowers but who turned on Bowers because of his suspicions of Bowers's patriotism and reservations over the White Knights' excessive violence. The attack did not occur, but only because King's route was changed at the last minute. We are still searching FBI files for further details on this plot.[34]

Dennis's informant file deals mainly with administrative matters related to paying him for his services, and available files on Bowers and the White Knights do not directly mention the plot. But most of the three hundred acts of violence the FBI officially attributes to the White Knights are not directly mentioned in these summary reports, which consist of small vignettes aggregated from local field office files. But in addition to the autobiographical account from Dennis, one of the FBI's most trusted informants, there are strong hints in the FBI files that something bigger was brewing in Selma. Reports emphasize that at this same time, Bowers was questioned for housing explosives in Alabama. This came just as other, simultaneous in format reports show that Bowers was asking his White Knights to bury their weapons in preparation for a future major insurrection. This mystified his followers but is consistent with a larger strategy Bowers contemplated—his belief that a major provocation, such as murdering Dr. King, would result in federal intervention and ultimately a race war.

ATTACK ON THE PALLADIUM: LOS ANGELES, CALIFORNIA, FEBRUARY 1965

On one of the few occasions where an arrest was made in connection with a King plot, right-wing extremist Keith Gilbert was captured in late 1965 trying to evade arrest by fleeing to Canada after authorities found large quantities of stolen dynamite among an arsenal of weapons (including a 60-mm mortar) and right-wing paraphernalia in his Glendale, California, residence. Gilbert had been on the run since February 4, 1965, when he was reported to have been involved in the dynamite robbery that eventually led to his conviction. The robbery came as threats began to pour in that King would be killed on February 25 at the Palladium theater in Los Angeles when he came to speak, in honor of his Nobel Peace Prize. One report in particular, that the entire theater would be destroyed in an explosion, caught the attention of not only authorities but also the local papers.[35]

Authorities received general information that the bombing was to be attributable to the Christian Nationalist State Army, while the day after King spoke, the *Los Angeles Herald Examiner* received information directly tying Gilbert to the threat. The paper reported the six-foot twenty-two-year-old as a racist member of the militant antigovernment group the Minutemen, who was heavily armed and a direct threat to Dr. King (as Gilbert was not yet captured). The report did not highlight the most salient aspect of Gilbert's biography—that he was a committed member of the Church of Jesus Christ Christian whose views on the superiority of the white race would continue to inspire racist extremists on through the 1990s, thanks in part to Gilbert himself.[36] In referring to the failed effort to kill King the day before—probably due to tight security precautions-the paper's source also ominously promised that the mistake would be fixed the next time, when King would be killed with a "high-powered rifle."[37]

THE OHIO PLOT: YELLOW SPRINGS, OHIO, JUNE 1965

In a series of events reminiscent of the Gilbert crime and occurring only a few months later, Daniel Wagner was arrested on suspicion of armed robbery with weapons, including dynamite, that he later testified were to be used in a provocation to "start a civil war within this country" between blacks and whites.[38] Wagner also described two closely connected plots to kill Martin Luther King Jr. and other public officials. The more sensational of these schemes involved Wagner shooting King when he was set to speak at Antioch College in Yellow Springs, Ohio, in June 1965.

Wagner testified to the House Un-American Activities Committee (HUAC) and in a ten-page letter described the plans that ten other men would detonate explosives while attendees fled the shooting. The nineteen-year-old Wagner said Eloise Witte, a bleached-blonde forty-year-old Grand Empress of the Ku Klux Klan in the Cincinnati, Ohio, region, approached him for the plot. The plot failed because Witte could not convince ten other people to join Wagner as a unit.[39] Witte, a rare female in a leadership position within the KKK, denied these reports to HUAC, but a second eyewitness, a young National States' Rights Party member named Richard Hanna, corroborated Wagner's story.

Perhaps the most interesting aspect of Wagner's account to HUAC relates to an earlier plot that inspired Witte to recruit Wagner. Wagner said that when Witte recruited him for her own effort against King, she referred to a recent $25,000 bounty offer on King emanating from the KKK in Georgia.[40] Though this component is close to hearsay, there is some corroboration. First, police did confirm that the dynamite that Wagner and a colleague obtained to spur the hoped-for civil war did indeed come from Klan sources in Georgia, notably from Klan associates of Imperial Wizard James R. Venable.[41] Moreover, Witte's immediate connections were to Venable, who had far-reaching influence as leader of the National Knights of the Ku Klux Klan (NKKKK).

In 1915 Venable's family had supplied the land used for the cross-burning ceremony that launched the modern KKK revival in Stone Mountain, Georgia, where the NKKKK headquarters continued to serve as a symbolic Mecca for the "Hooded Order."[42] In 1965 Venable, a lawyer who with fellow racist J. B. Stoner represented individuals accused of racially motivated crimes (and who shared an Atlanta legal office with Stoner), launched an outreach program to place several additional out-of-state Klans in the Midwest under the umbrella of his organization, including Witte's Klavern.[43] Witte's story, as Wagner related it, of a $25,000 bounty offer is also consistent with the available records. An FBI memorandum of February 8, 1965, from their Atlanta office warned bureau field offices in Mobile, Alabama, and Washington, DC, (locations where King was expected to travel) that Venable was actively involved in organizing plots to kill Dr. King, and other FBI reports from the same period implicate Stoner in those efforts. Venable will eventually be tied into a specific White Knights bounty that will prove to be integral to deciphering the true circumstances behind Dr. King's murder on April 4, 1968.[44]

MANUFACTURING A PRETEXT: THE WHITE KNIGHTS' EFFORTS IN 1966

In two of the previously described assassination attempts, white supremacists planned to take advantage of acts of violence committed in conjunction with King's travels to protest racial injustice. They saw that even attempting to kill King could escalate the violence that could be expected in response to efforts at public integration. In 1966 the White Knights decided to reverse that tactic, performing acts that would lure King to a "kill zone" in Mississippi.

King came to Birmingham in the wake of the Sixteenth Street Baptist Church bombing; he came to Jackson after both the Medgar Evers assassination in 1963 and the Mississippi Burning murders of three civil rights workers in the summer of 1964. Most recently he had come to Mississippi in the wake of the attempted murder of James Meredith, the man who had desegregated the University of Mississippi by being the first black student to apply to and attend the school in 1962 and who in 1966 was leading his March Against Fear to encourage blacks to register to vote despite racist intimidation.[45] That King, as a national figure, would respond in person to well-publicized injustices would be obvious then to anyone who wanted to strike at him. With that in mind, Bowers appears to have conceived of one of the more hideous acts of his violent reign of terror-killing a perfectly innocent black farmer in hopes of luring King into a shooting gallery in Mississippi.

The victim was Ben Chester White, who agreed to help three unassuming white men look for their supposedly missing dog when he entered their car, never to be seen alive again. His body was found battered and riddled with seventeen bullet holes in a creek near a national forest in Natchez, Mississippi. The three men who were arrested-Ernest Avants, Claude Fuller, and James Jones-escaped justice for decades. Jones admitted his guilt and implicated the other men, but Avants's claim that he only shot White's already-dead corpse earned him an acquittal, while Fuller (the accused triggerman) was never even tried. Even Jones (in the face of his own admission) was set free by a hung jury. Justice was only served in 2003, when Avants was finally convicted for his role in the crime. It was at that later trial that previously unreleased FBI documents showed that the three men were members of the White Knights of the Ku Klux Klan and that Samuel Bowers put them up to killing White in hopes of enticing King into a death trap.[46]

AN OPEN CONTRACT: THE WHITE KNIGHTS BOUNTY OFFER IN 1967

The White Knights were not deterred by their previous failures to kill King. Motivated by forces much stronger than just maintaining the culture of Jim Crow, the White Knights appear to have accelerated their efforts to murder Dr. King even as their leading members were finally going to prison for crimes such as the killing of activist Vernon Dahmer.[47]

Driven by the increased scrutiny of law enforcement on a national as well as local level, the White Knights increasingly turned to outsiders for acts of violence. At a time when similar offers appear to have been circulating in a number of different prison systems, a Leavenworth penitentiary prisoner-Donald Nissen-reported being approached by an openly prejudiced fellow inmate with a $100,000 White Knights-sponsored bounty on King's life.[48] The inmate knew Nissen was leaving Leavenworth penitentiary and would make his way to King's home base of Atlanta and told him to contact a series of intermediaries, known in the criminal and intelligence world as "cutouts," to confirm his role, which would involve both scouting King's movements and (if Nissen wanted) actually assassinating the civil rights leader. Nissen remained quiet for fear of upsetting the inmate but revealed the details of the offer to the FBI several months before King was murdered.[49]

There is considerable corroboration for Nissen's story-which includes names of conspirators-and it provides the key to understanding the forces that led to King's death in Memphis. According to the HSCA, similar offers were circulating in the federal penitentiary at Jefferson City, Missouri, and likely caught the attention of a soon-to-be escapee, James Earl Ray, the only man arrested and convicted for King's murder.

TACTICAL SOPHISTICATION

Similarities between the above plots are certainly worth exploring. Notably, the record shows that each of these ultraright groups were more tactically sophisticated than has been commonly assumed. Most of the plots showed a penchant for what intelligence agencies call "plausible deniability." In that context, deniability involves protecting an operation by creating buffers between the "mechanics" who carry out the plan and the higher-ups who plan it-in other words, go-betweens. This allows higher-ups to deny involvement if the plan is discovered before its consummation and also provides buffers in the event a "mechanic" is caught after the deed. Investigators and analysts would have to go through more than one layer of culpable persons before, if ever, they reached those at the top.

In several of these plots, Klan leaders brokered deals with criminals or with out-of-state extremist groups in hopes of insulating themselves from law enforcement scrutiny both before and after the operation. The open King bounty in 1967 illustrates a level of deniability that would have impressed even intelligence professionals and suggests the most persistent group-the White Knights-were learning from their past efforts. This bounty offer extended to criminals who in turn had to contact cutouts before they could be approved for the King assassination operation. The cutouts in that instance may have included a Mississippi businesswoman and even a member of law enforcement, and they appear to have quite effectively served their purpose of concealing the plot from law enforcement after it was reported. The groups trying to kill King were using tactics far different than the brute violence that appeared in magazines and on television screens.

In that sense, these right-wing militant groups also realized the importance of studying the tendencies of their intended victim. At first this seems obvious: If King were coming to stage a public protest, it would seem fitting that his enemies would capitalize on the circumstance and attempt to lull him. But the recorded plots hint at a more sophisticated, evolving effort to target King. Finding and blowing up King's home in 1956 did not take much creativity. Planning a sniper shooting on King's route with a backup plan to bomb him if the sniper shooting failed-as was included in later plots-shows much more attention to detail. The FBI's February 1965 warnings about Venable suggest that the National Knights were plotting against King in several of the cities that he intended to visit. The Ben Chester White murder in 1966 even showed that the White Knights were willing to create an incident in anticipation of King's tendencies to visit and stage protests in order to bring national attention to racial violence. Most notably, the White Knights bounty of 1967 even included provisions (and a payment as part of the bounty) for individuals to carefully watch King in anticipation of his murder.[50]

CONFEDERACY OF CONSPIRATORS

In addition to tactical sophistication, a common thread that weaves together most of the listed attempts is the bonds between the plotters. From plot to plot, there appears to be only one to two degrees separating the prime movers from each other.

Every one of the nine attempts evidencing means, motive, and opportunity-including some of the actual attacks-involved right-wing extremists. Those who, in modern, popular treatments of the King assassination, have chosen to implicate other groups, such as the American intelligence community, therefore have a problem: None of their proposed suspects had any history of trying to kill King. There is no hint of Mafia efforts or attempts by individuals with national intelligence connections to kill King. If the FBI was trying to kill Dr. King (as has been argued by several authors), they could have simply let him die in 1965 in the plot in Selma rather than warn him in advance, as Delmar Dennis indicates in his book.

It would be easy to say that what united those who made serious efforts to kill King was a deep reactionary form of racism, a combination of contempt and fear seen manifested in the brutal beating of peaceful activists at the Woolworth's lunch counter in Jackson, Mississippi. But while this has an element of truth to it, it is also an oversimplification. By 1966 King had achieved almost all his goals in ending de jure racial discrimination and was shifting toward deeper issues of economic and social justice. Killing King remained a top priority for these same people, however, and not as a matter of pure revenge for his past successes. At the planning level of each of the major assassination efforts from 1958 onward were individuals devoted to a hateful Christian denomination led by the Reverend Wesley Swift, who insisted that "pure-blooded whites are the lost children of Israel."[51] They joined Swift in promoting the idea of an apocalyptic race war, and killing King was the best means to that end.

This bond between conspirators can be seen if one simply traces a social network from retired Colonel William Potter Gale, the vituperative racist and anti-Semite from California. One month after reportedly plotting to kill King in Birmingham, Gale addressed a private gathering of extremists at the William Penn Hotel in Whittier, California; attendees included California NSRP leader James Paul Thornton, Atlanta's White Citizens' Council activist Joseph Milteer, and racist evangelist Connie Lynch. Thornton, Milteer, and especially Lynch were close associates of Stoner, and all were devotees-like Gale-of Swift. The Californians Lynch and Gale, while also members of Stoner's National States' Rights Party, were in fact ordained ministers in Swift's Church of Jesus Christ Christian, as was Keith Gilbert.[52] In his church role, Gale was personally invited (by Sidney Crockett Barnes) to administer the memorial services for Kathy Ainsworth, a White Knights terrorist who may have had inside knowledge of aspects of the King murder.[53]

Gale's connection to Mississippi racists likely stemmed from the active part he played in what many historians view as ground zero in the southern counterrevolution against integration and multiculturalism: resistance to James Meredith's admission to and integration of the segregated University of Mississippi in 1962. Gale played a major role in fomenting the one-sided violence that required federal intervention and spurred a proliferation of white supremacist organizations.[54] In fact, documents from the time describe an unknown, out-of-state military figure recruiting veterans across Mississippi into a mysterious more militant racist organization (clearly the White Knights).[55] These references raise the possibility that Gale, who as a World War II officer organized guerrilla operations for General Douglas MacArthur in the Philippines, may have been important in helping to actually form the White Knights.[56]

Georgia Klan leader James Venable's connections to this coterie of radical extremists involve his connection to the California Knights of the Ku Klux Klan (CKKKK). As with Witte's organization in Ohio, the CKKKK was an offshoot of Venable's umbrella organization, the National Knights of the Ku Klux Klan. Venable even spoke to the CKKKK in 1967 at the invitation of its California leader, William V. Fowler, at a common meeting place for Reverend Swift's religious sermons.[57] Fowler, in fact, was a devoted minister in Swift's church.[58] Although Fowler handled the day-to-day operations of the CKKKK, FBI informant reports indicate that Swift had strong and direct influence on the group and that members were told to attend Swift's religious meetings at least once a month.[59]

Venable liked to portray himself as someone above the fray, sympathetic to the political goals of the Klan but ambivalent, at best, to its more radical features. Yet, an informant described Venable as saying, in 1961, that he "did not believe in violence, but the time had come . . . when we have to do it." The comment came after Venable insisted that "Martin Luther King Jr. should have been dead long ago and that he had to be killed."[60] Perhaps Venable's urgency in wanting King killed reflected the same worldview as Swift, for Venable's religious and historical writings make it clear that he shared the same antagonism toward Jews.[61]

The notoriously racist Reverend Swift, for his part, was so close to many of these individuals that he was investigated in connection with their various King plots. The FBI looked at Swift when investigating the Crommelin/Carden/Gale/Barnes plot in the early 1960s, as each of these men were Swift devotees.[62] The FBI even raided Swift's church in connection with the Gilbert plot in 1965.[63] Of course in each instance, the accused men themselves (much less their religious leader) were never actually charged for attempting to assassinate King. And while the FBI may not have looked at Swift in connection to Stoner's plots against King, Swift and Stoner clearly shared a lot in common. Swift kept a flag with a thunderbolt symbol in his office until the day he died;[64] this was the logo for the National States' Rights Party's publication *The Thunderbolt,* a paper that was largely created by Stoner. Swift's ministers were among the most active members of Stoner's NSRP movement.

These cross affiliations between anti-King agitators illustrate the limits of the conventional historical picture of the white supremacist subculture in America. Without question, as HUAC detailed after its investigation of extremist movements in 1967, the Klan and similar groups were highly decentralized even if they were under the umbrella of several different multistate operations such as Venable's National Knights of the Ku Klux Klan.[65] Even within states, much less at the top of the organizations, it was common for infighting-over power and money-to fragment various Klans. That said, within these groups were a subgroup of people who were united by something far more potent and salient than simple resistance to integration. While they had their own separate organizations to run-Bowers with his Mississippi White Knights, Gale with the racist paramilitary California Rangers group, Stoner with the National States' Rights Party-they all subscribed to a religious worldview that captured their imaginations and inspired them to greater and greater levels of violence.

RACISM OR RELIGION?

Much of the investigation into Dr. King's murder has been undermined by a narrow-minded view of what one author called "redneck violence." Under this interpretation, the southern "way of life" came under "attack" in the 1960s, and white supremacists reacted violently. Academic treatments have thus placed Klan and racial violence during the civil rights movement in the category of "vigilante terrorism,"[66] defined as "terrorism initiated by private groups . . . aimed at other private groups in resistance to threatening social change."[67] Others might argue that these attacks were often instigated or abetted by bigoted local law enforcement officials with the consent of local elites and government officials-as in the Mississippi Burning murders-and hence should qualify as vigilante state terrorism.[68]

Scholars and law enforcement have failed to recognize that a religious terrorist network within the white supremacist movement dominated some of these conventional, seemingly autonomous racist groups. In fact, the leaders of some of these extremist organizations were harnessing the raw anger of their rank-and-file members for the purpose of covert religious terrorism. People like Samuel Bowers used Kluckers (rank-and-file Klansmen) to advance a much more ideological agenda, and they did so in a Machiavellian fashion that covered their tracks. Bowers told informant Delmar Dennis that "the typical Mississippi redneck doesn't have sense enough to know what he's doing. I have to use him for my own cause and direct his every action to fit my plan."[69]

White supremacists who plotted to kill King were motivated by a strong religious impulse, and at least some of those in the white supremacist movement in the 1960s should be viewed more as religious terrorists than as political reactionaries. The upper echelons of these groups were motivated by the white Christian separatism espoused by the Reverend Wesley Swift and his Church of Jesus Christ Christian. Swift had founded the Church of Jesus Christ Christian in 1946, and tapes of his white separatist sermons were literally being played at parties of like-minded extremists in places like Jackson, Mississippi, in the early to mid 1960s.[70] The power and reach of Swift's sermons cannot be understated.

Would-be King killer Sidney Crockett Barnes, one of many people across the country on Swift's mailing list, hosted listening "parties" in Mobile, Alabama, that drew attendees from as far away as Miami, Florida. In preaching that Jews were Satan's offspring who manipulated blacks and other races into a communist conspiracy against the white race-God's true "chosen people"- Swift struck three major chords that resonated with extremists like Barnes, especially in the South. In one stroke, Swift gave Christian religious justification for beliefs in white supremacy and for the associated antigovernment communist paranoia appearing in many forms around the country, the latter casting the civil rights movement as a secret Soviet subversive operation. This also had an obvious appeal to those resisting integration as simply a threat to their way of life, giving cover to their violence. At times individuals would start as mere segregationists, only to become sucked into Swift's vortex.

One woman's unfortunate story illustrates the power of Swift's appeal to such people. Married to a mild-mannered man who was concerned, as were many southerners, with the changes wrought by integration, she was worried (but not enough) when he started to listen to Swift's religious sermons. Before long, the husband began to violently insist that she and their children also listen to the tapes. He held listening sessions and meetings in their house, involving some of the most violently racist figures in their state, including Sam Bowers. Eventually the husband joined the White Knights and was investigated for bombings. It reached a point where his wife was forced to escape her husband's grip, with her children in tow, never to rejoin him. Swift's tapes had literally brainwashed her husband and ruined her family in a matter of a few years.[71]

In the opinion of people like this woman's husband, the civil rights movement and the surrounding violence was more than an attack on southern tradition. It was a divine foreshadowing of an end-times race war where God's true chosen people-Anglo-Saxons-would purify the world from the grip of Satan's offspring (Jews) and his minions (blacks and other minorities) This radical variation of Christianity inspired highly devoted followers from around the nation even as the larger white supremacist movement lost its secular motivation following the Civil Rights Act of 1964 and the Voting Rights Act of 1965. They formed something akin to a national militant network under the informal influence of Swift. And while political causes die or evolve with new laws and elections, ideological causes-especially religious causes-can have a very long shelf life.

Martin Luther King, Jr.'s victories for integration had substantially decreased overall Klan membership, and a sharp increase in successful prosecutions and federal surveillance had dramatically reduced what little remained of the white supremacist movement by the late 1960s. But for those who were motivated by religion-and the tapes and sermons of Wesley Swift-this pressure simply changed their tactics, as they increasingly turned to outsiders and core true believers to carry out even more provocative acts of extremism. Unfortunately, law enforcement in the 1960s, not yet attuned to ideological/religious terrorism in general and lacking the resources to deal with issues of conspiracy, was not as discerning as modern counterterrorist units in pursuing the informal Swift network of religious extremists prior to King's murder or in following its trail after April 4, 1968. Modern counterterrorists use advanced data-mining tools to sift through vast amounts of information in hopes of predicting acts of religious terrorism. J. Edgar Hoover's FBI often lacked communication even between field offices, much less with state and municipal police agencies. However, even if data sharing had been perfect, the King investigation suffered in two key respects: It failed to recognize the role that religious fanaticism played in the violence predating King's murder, and thus it also underestimated the sophistication and determination of those groups who would not stop until King was dead. Their obsession with assassinating King would become a holy cause, an act of civil war meant to spark a racial and religious Armageddon.

CHAPTER 2

HOLY CAUSE AND DEVILISH DISCIPLES

In the evening hours of April 4, 1968, as news of Dr. King's assassination spread from Memphis to the entire country, lingering racial animus and frustration incubating from the time of the New York race riot of 1964 through the Newark race riot of 1967 spawned a crescendo of violence. Over the next week, new race riots hammered 125 American cities. More than five thousand fires damaged almost two thousand homes and businesses. Two thousand people were injured, most of them blacks. In aggregate, almost twenty-four thousand people were arrested in what *Time* magazine described as a "shock wave of looting, arson and outrage" that "exceeded anything in the American experience.[1]

Possibly at no other time in United States history had the nation's racial climate been so tense. Anger flared, radicalizing even some of the most committed nonviolent advocates in the civil rights movement. James Meredith, the man who desegregated the University of Mississippi, spoke out in anger: "This is America's answer to the peaceful, nonviolent way of obtaining rights in this country!" Julian Bond, leader of the Student Nonviolent Coordinating Committee (SNCC), said, "Nonviolence was murdered in Memphis last night.[2]

If some in the white supremacist movement cheered the news on April 4, many could not have been pleased with the scale of the federal response. Almost seventy-three thousand Army and National Guard troops were called into service nationwide to help quell the violence, the largest domestic deployment of the national military since the Civil War. Bitter memories of "government intrusion" during Reconstruction, passed down for generations, had helped motivate resistance to federally mandated integration in southern cities like Memphis, Tennessee, and Jackson, Mississippi, just a few years before. Now the nation was closer to martial law than at any time since the 1870s.

But not everyone who openly fought with the National Guard at the University of Mississippi during the Meredith admission were as hostile to federal intervention as is commonly thought. The white supremacist movement was not a monolithic constituency committed to the same goals. Yes, there were those who were in the movement simply to stamp out communism, to resist the changes to their perceived southern way of life, or for motives of pure prejudice. But a cadre of extremists in the upper echelons of some of the most well-led groups shared an extremist commitment to an apocalyptic vision for a race war. To these individuals, the riots from April 4 to April 11 would be as close as they ever came to fulfilling this end-times goal, one that they had been working toward for years. These individuals had not been deterred by the successes of the civil rights movement nor satiated by any prototypes of Richard Nixon's "southern strategy" to win elections below the Mason-Dixon Line by exploiting anti–African American racism. They harnessed what remained of the white supremacist movement and manipulated even their own followers, when necessary, to try to kill Martin Luther King Jr. As we have shown, the influence of these individuals and their religious ideology could be seen in almost every plot and bounty leading to King's murder on April 4, 1968.

A HOLY CAUSE

Understanding the basic religious beliefs of people like Wesley Swift, J. B. Stoner, and Sam Bowers and their religious subculture is critical to fully comprehending both their core motivations and their actions. Wesley Swift's ministry and messages—delivered in services and radio broadcasts, through an extensive audiotape distribution network, and by aides and ministers such as Connie Lynch, William Potter Gale, Sidney Crockett Barnes, and James Warner—helped mold this subculture. It clearly incited militant actions against both blacks and Jews throughout the country. The actions of men such as Sam Bowers can only be understood by realizing that they viewed themselves as zealots, as holy warriors. Theirs was a common crusade, a common tradition, a vision that saw the zealot as a redeemer cleansing the nation of evil by violence that was absolutely necessary to save the nation and ensure its triumphant destiny.[3] Their worldview would be called the Christian Identity movement, and it continues to have an echo in domestic U.S. terrorism to the present day.

The roots of the Christian Identity movement that would eventually come to influence those wanting to kill Dr. King lie in a blend of British Israelism—a Victorian-era view that Anglo-Saxons were the true lost tribes of Israel—and a particularly virulent strain of anti-Semitism put forward in the early 1900s by Howard Rand, an attorney and small businessman in Massachusetts. Rand became a writer and publisher for the movement and was the first to use the term "Christian Identity" in regard to his new religion's views. Rand promoted the belief that God's chosen people were not, as legend would have it, the people self-proclaimed as Jews but a different people entirely, Anglo-Europeans—presumably all white. Followers of his belief proudly proclaimed themselves "Israelites" but most definitely not Jews. They were firm in their belief that the people claiming themselves to be Jews were actually impostors.

This worldview and belief system spread to Canada, where it apparently matured considerably within a group in Vancouver, whose anti-Semitism was especially strong and open.[4] They incorporated much of their developing beliefs in a novel, *When Gog Attacks*, supposedly prophetic of the very near future, published in 1944 by the British Israel Association of Greater Vancouver.[5] Through the story of a fictional British intelligence officer, the true divine history of man is discovered. This revelation, as described by Christian Identity expert Michael Barkun, was that Cain, the descendent of Satan and Eve,

> *founded a secret society to do the Devil's work on earth and had in fact been so successful in this endeavor that everyone on earth with*

the exception of Noah and his family "appears to have come under the control of Satan." Unfortunately, Noah's line was poisoned when Ham married a descendent of Cain's, and thus the "contaminated blood was brought through the Flood." Cain's conspiracy continued on through history, controlled by "certain of the Ashkenazim Jews."[6]

This more militant strain of Christian Identity became more obvious after it spread from Vancouver; the next locus for development of these beliefs was Southern California, particularly the Los Angeles area. The view of Jews as "impostors" became a critical element of Louisiana clergyman and Nazi sympathizer Gerald L. K. Smith's ministry; it also became a central theme of his Christian Nationalist Crusade.[7] Smith became known as the most prominent anti-Semite in America, and much of his outreach was toward the political right.

A good deal of Smith's energy went into agitation against Jews and their purported plan for political conquest and domination of the United States and the world. Smith's contribution to the story of Martin Luther King Jr.'s assassination, however, was the creation of an activist network, not a specific congregation or national church. His message was taken up by many individual ministers, among whom Wesley Swift was the most prominent.

Swift took the strain of anti-Semitism in the Christian Identity belief system to another level. He began to describe Jews as the actual offspring of Satan who carry out his will against the true God.[8] Blacks and other races were pre-Adamite "mud people" whom Jews manipulated in a war against whites. Their fundamental belief that Jews were an evil force, the "quintessence of evil, the literal offspring of Satan," became central to the evolving ministry of Christian Identity.[9] Beyond his "two-seed" theory that posits whites as the true descendants of Adam and Eve but Jews—referred to as Ashkenazim Jews—as descendants of Eve and Satan, Swift's Christian Identity believers distinguish themselves in another, very important regard.[10] They are like many Christian millennialists who believe that the return of Jesus Christ will be preceded by a time of tribulation, one where famines, earthquakes, and wars will plague humanity. But unlike many of those groups, Swift believers do not believe in a rapture that will save the believers from torment by bringing them into the Kingdom of God. Instead, Israelites will remain on earth and be called to violently fight off the evil forces of Satan. That so many Christian Identity believers stockpile weapons and train in armed combat is an obvious extension of this belief.

The activists who followed Swift, both those who could be considered members of his network and others, were motivated by common beliefs and incited by Swift's messages. His followers were part of something that in today's terms we would characterize as a social network, unified by his traveling ministers, his audiotape distribution, and a series of designated couriers. They were affiliated with a number of different racist and reactionary groups such as the United Klans of America and the National States' Rights Party and gathered at regional meetings, bringing with them (often quietly) their apocalyptic goals and agendas. But these sycophants were not in any sense a formal, structured organization, nor did all of them officially belong to any organized Christian Identity congregations.

As perhaps the most compelling proponent of Smith's message, Wesley Swift combined the belief in an eternal struggle between God's people (white Anglo-Saxons) and Satan's (the Jews) with his own well-established racial bias. Smith had been an early and vigorous advocate of the Klan and had reinvigorated Klan activities in Southern California. Swift characterized blacks as the tools of Jewish masters in the cosmic battle; he translated the eternal struggle into a call for white supremacy and a total rejection of civil rights for nonwhites.[11] Anyone not participating in this struggle of good versus evil was sinful and committing an offense against God.

As an extension of that belief, Swift encouraged his ministers and aides toward more political agitation and military preparedness. This was not simply in anticipation of a communist takeover, but in anticipation of the final race war that would bring about Armageddon and God's victory. The message of the final conflict was published in 1963 in William Potter Gale's *The Faith of Our Fathers,* which related contemporary, militant activism against

Jews and blacks as part of a cosmic battle that allegedly began "before the world was made."[12]

The FBI's Project Megiddo, a report on domestic terrorism, provides the following summary of these apocalyptic views of Christian Identity:

> *Christian Identity also believes in the inevitability of the end of the world and the Second Coming of Christ. It is believed that these events are part of a cleansing process that is needed before Christ's kingdom can be established on earth. During this time, Jews and their allies will attempt to destroy the white race using any means available. The result will be a violent and bloody struggle—a war, in effect—between God's forces, the white race, and the forces of evil, the Jews and nonwhites. Significantly, many adherents believe that this will be tied into the coming of the new millennium.*[13]

Around 1962, Gerald Smith broke with Wesley Swift for personal reasons, stating that he felt that Swift had obligations to people who were not cordial to Smith. There is no obvious explanation for this remark, but there is some indication that the two had begun to compete for financial sponsors and that more donors were beginning to favor Swift and swing funding in his direction. This break seems to have occurred at approximately the same time that Swift moved into a much more militant phase, supporting the formation of both the virulently anti-Semitic Christian Defense League and the California Rangers—a secret, underground guerilla force.[14] In 1956 Swift ordained retired army colonel William Gale, who had a number of political, social, and financial connections that were important to Swift's success, and Gale led the paramilitary expansion of Swift's network, possibly with help from an engineer working at Lockheed who became the first president of the Christian Defense League.

It is important to note that no single Christian Identity church or congregation has been proven to have actively translated these beliefs into specific acts of violence. On the other hand, it is a matter of record, supported with criminal convictions, that certain of its ministers and believers did commit violent acts. As Barkun writes in *Religion and the Racist Right,* those individuals formed a "minority . . . [that has] taken Identity beliefs to their logical political conclusions."[15]

A NEXUS FOR VIOLENCE

The man at the center of this violent religious network in the 1960s and a major player in the Christian Identity movement was the Reverend Wesley Swift, working through his Church of Jesus Christ Christian. It was Swift's charismatic leadership and theological ideas that motivated the most committed racists in the fight against civil rights. His ministry espoused extreme racism and anticipated, and hoped to foment, extreme race-related violence.[16] At one point, the minister traveled almost four hundred miles from his home in Lancaster, California, to the state capital of Sacramento to testify against a resolution simply condemning genocide. A survey of many of the most violent civil rights confrontations in 1963–1964 (University of Mississippi, Saint Augustine, Birmingham) shows that Swift's adherents, whom Swift heavily influenced, including Lynch, Stoner, and Gale, were active in inciting militancy and violence in all of them. In Saint Augustine, Florida, for instance, Gale and Lynch joined forces with the local NSRP representative, the Reverend Oren Potito, another Christian Identity minister and president of the Eastern Conference of Swift's Church of Jesus Christ Christian, to stoke the hatreds in that city. They were, like many others, inspired by Swift's weekly sermons that were broadcast over radio, taped, and mailed to his followers across the nation.

The following passage from Swift's "The Seal of God" sermon from 1963 gives a feel for the cohesion and reach of Swift's network.

We got a call very early this morning from the East Coast, and they told us about 12,000 Clansmen [sic] in one meeting and 7,000 in another, and the whole state of Florida is just sweeping back into the state of euphoria. But these events of the last few weeks have helped stir them up until lawyers and judges and professional people are listening. This clergyman who called me said, "Dr. Swift, everyone is playing tapes and they must know, and they are reaching out." And then he gave us an address as to where to send more tapes to help spread the message.

Last evening Connie Lynch spoke to about 7,000 Clansmen in one meeting alone in Florida. So don't think that there is not something going on all over. You can't pick up your newspaper and find out what is going on from one state to another because they isolate this by news control. Not only in Florida, but in Georgia and in Alabama, a great awakening, and they say they expect to see two million clansmen soon, because the movement is unprecedented.[17]

It seems apparent that Wesley Swift was very much committed to the escalation of events in Florida and elsewhere, even as he lurked in the background. The telephone report from Lynch was not unusual. Like Gale, Connie Lynch had joined Swift's Church of Jesus Christ Christian after World War II and spent most of the '50s in California. In the early '60s, he began to hit the road as a traveling parson spreading the message that "all non whites are Satan's children—devil worshipers."[18] By 1963 Lynch had become a full-time traveling representative for Swift, carrying a shared ministry and message from California to the South, personally inciting extreme violence in his travel and public appearances.[19] Lynch was most famous as a comrade-in-racial-agitation with J. B. Stoner. Stoner, Bowers, Gale, and others attended meetings together, exchanged Swift's tapes, and preached the same racist view of Christianity. They formed something akin to a modern-day electronic social network, one that seemingly held, among its other beliefs, some very radical views about Martin Luther King Jr.

TWO DISCIPLES

While Swift had connections to many of the most violent white supremacist organizations in the country, the two that are most relevant and illustrative to a discussion of the assassination of Martin Luther King Jr. are J. B. Stoner's National States' Rights Party and, even more so, Samuel Bowers's White Knights of the Ku Klux Klan of Mississippi. Both men and their groups had, as discussed in chapter 1, attempted to kill King on repeated occasions. Both men and their groups were considered strong suspects at the time of the initial investigation of King's murder in 1968, as well as in 1977 when Congress reinvestigated the crime. And both men and their groups were eliminated from consideration as suspects, in part because of misconceptions about, and ignorance of, their geographical scope, their connections to each other, and their allegiance to the larger Swift network.

That the greater religious goals of each man were lost upon federal investigators, and even academics who examined the Christian Identity movement, is not entirely the fault of the observers. Both Stoner and Bowers sought to hide their greater purpose not only from federal law enforcement but also from their very own members. While using rhetoric that certainly spoke of "saving White Christian civilization," Stoner also admitted that the very name of his group—the National States' Rights Party—was deliberately chosen to obscure its mission. The name had been intentionally selected to create a political image for the organization and to minimize its radical and militant nature. Bowers, for his part, told one informant that he had little respect for his own recruits, whom he viewed as rednecks who could not understand his larger goals; he simply "used them for my cause and direct[ed] every action to fit my plan."[20]

SAM BOWERS, THE MOST DANGEROUS KLAN IN AMERICA, AND "THE PLAN"

Officially formed in late 1963 from disillusioned Mississippi racists belonging to the Original Knights of the Ku Klux Klan, the White Knights of Mississippi became, according to the FBI, the most violent Klan in history, owing in large part to the Machiavellian leadership and vision of its first leader, Sam Bowers.[21] One of Bowers's operatives, Thomas Tarrants, who years later would renounce the Christian Identity belief system and become a mainstream Christian minister, described his one-time leader in hindsight as "indoctrinated, brainwashed . . . absorbed into an ideology that took on the awe of a holy cause, with the sanction of God."[22]

Samuel Holloway Bowers Jr. had been born in New Orleans in 1924. His father was a salesman and his mother the daughter of a wealthy planter.[23] His parents divorced when he was fourteen, and as a teenager he displayed considerable resentment and self-described rage against authority figures.[24] He grew up on the Gulf Coast and was raised in Jackson, Mississippi. Bowers enlisted and served in the navy during World War II as a machinist mate and after the war attended summer sessions in engineering at the University of Southern California in Los Angeles at a time when Christian Identity was first beginning to influence the racist community in that region. Later he attended regular sessions at Tulane University in New Orleans. In the late 1940s, he moved to Laurel, Mississippi, and tried a variety of business ventures before becoming owner of a vending machine operation named the Sambo Amusement Company.[25] Bowers was not married and was not known to have an interest in women. He had a roommate, about which little was known, and seemed to have considerable money and free time.[26] Bowers also used the alias Willoughby Smead on occasion.

The FBI linked the White Knights, under the leadership of Bowers, to an "estimated 10 murders; to the burnings of an estimated 75 black churches; to at least 300 assaults and beatings and bombings." This included the famous Mississippi Burning murders of three civil rights workers in Neshoba County, Mississippi. Often colluding with local law enforcement officials (such as in the Mississippi Burning case), the White Knights would either avoid state prosecution or receive light sentences. Hence it was not until 1998 that Bowers himself was convicted for ordering the killing of voting rights activist Vernon Dahmer, having had his men fire weapons into and firebomb Dahmer's home, nearly killing not only Dahmer (the only one to later perish from burns suffered in the attack) but also his wife and children.[27] Bowers would serve six years of a ten-year sentence for the Mississippi Burning murders in 1968 but received a life sentence for his role in the Dahmer killing, eventually dying himself in prison in 2006. At his trial in 1998, Bowers attempted to mitigate his sentence by calling on representatives from what was otherwise an upstanding community, who testified that Bowers was a generous spirit who taught Sunday school.

Bowers's affinity for Christianity—or his version of it—was never in doubt. He often exhorted his followers to the very same kind of violence that killed Dahmer by appealing to Christian ideals and imagery. Bowers himself actively recruited personnel based on the Swift/Christian Identity message. He was also known to play Swift tapes in social meetings with his key operatives.[28] Bowers had direct personal connections to Swift and his network of followers; Swift's close aide Dennis Mower remarked that he "was on very good terms" with Sam Bowers.[29] Mower's business card was found in the wallet of Bowers's operative (and Swift adherent) Thomas Tarrants upon his arrest for an attempted bombing, and Mower himself acknowledged meeting and working with Tarrants in Los Angeles early in 1968.[30]

More concretely, Bowers's choice of targets in Mississippi speaks to his Christian Identity ideology. By the spring of 1968, Bowers was targeting Jews in Jackson and Meridian, Mississippi, at a pace and magnitude that even exceeded his violence against blacks. This included the bombing of synagogues and the targeting of Jewish leaders. Generally speaking, such anti-Semitism was not a priority for most Klansmen and was felt to be bad for the Klan's populist image. As Jack Nelson details in *Terror in the Night*, Jews had a long history in several southern locations, such as Jackson, Mississippi, and they had reached a long-standing if awkward accommodation between their own history of persecution and the reality of what was facing blacks in the 1960s. While northern Jews, and even some rabbis, challenged this contradiction, many southern Jews were assimilated into the fabric of southern society; Bowers's (and others') decision to attack them outraged many southerners who looked the other way at pre-1964 Klan violence against blacks.

In fact, the waves of attacks on Jews may seem strange even to readers who are familiar only with Klan terror targeting the civil rights movement, with its emphasis on opposing integration and voter rights. But based on his religious worldview, Sam Bowers had continuously run the White Knights with two agendas in mind. The first involved instigating violent actions in opposition to all types of integration and civil rights activities. The second involved stoking a race war in hopes of producing Armageddon. The second agenda was much more covert and carried out by a very select handful of individuals reporting directly to Bowers.

This second agenda was strictly in line with Bowers's religious beliefs and can be clearly seen in his writings. A White Knight tract, "The White Sentinel," described the fundamental war of Christ against Satan and the "synagogue of Satan." It identified the demons of Satan as Jews, Pharisees, and the Jewish temple establishment. In order to bring about God's final victory, His people would have to engage in a final war, "Armageddon," and eliminate Satan's forces. Satan's forces included all his children (the "mongrel races," that is, nonwhites); they would be led in battle by his servants, the Jews. Undoubtedly, given the nature of the enemy, Satan would try first to achieve victory covertly through the advance of communism, itself only a tool of the Jews.[31]

Bowers attempted to explain to his members that there are two types of Klans, those that target "niggers" and those that target Jews, and argued that Jews were more dangerous because they were more insidious and subversive. But Bowers's anti-Semitism was not as appealing to everyday Klansmen as was his anti-integrationist violence against civil rights targets, and he was forced to toe the line between his public comments and his private beliefs.

While he publicly warned his followers of an impending race war and attempted communist takeover, Bowers manipulated his rank-and-file members in a way that could only foment and accelerate this Armageddon. Bowers's efforts in Mississippi often not only inflamed local law enforcement (including the FBI's Jackson, Mississippi, field office) but also risked outright federal intervention. Bowers told FBI informant Delmar Dennis that he manipulated Mississippi's rednecks to "fit [his] plan," which he detailed to Dennis:

> Bowers outlined on a blackboard the overall strategy of which the
> White Knights were merely a part. He said he was trying to create

a race war, and open violence on the part of white Mississippians against native Negro citizens and civil rights agitators. He predicted that Secretary of Defense Robert McNamara would be required to send troops into Mississippi to restore order. Martial law would be declared and the state would be under full dictatorial control from Washington. The excuse for the control would be the race war he was helping to create by engendering hatred among whites in the same manner as it was being fomented by leftist radicals among blacks.[32]

Later, Bowers would say that a strategy of violence "should be carefully planned to include only the leaders and prime white collaborators of the enemy forces. These attacks against selected individual targets should be as severe as circumstances and conditions will permit."[33] Congress would also later investigate Bowers, initially a prime suspect in King's murder, for the Memphis attack based on reports from several informants, all of whom, at least as late as 1978, were too fearful to elaborate on what they knew.

J. B. STONER AND THE NATIONAL STATES' RIGHTS PARTY

A decade before Sam Bowers began his reign of terror in Mississippi, J. B. Stoner, who on at least one occasion offered a contract on Martin Luther King Jr.'s life, was beating the same drum on a march toward Swift's religious dream of a race war. Stoner was born in Georgia in 1924 and orphaned by the age of sixteen. His enculturation into anti-Semitism and racism came during World War II when he apparently figured out a way to communicate overseas with William Joyce, the English radio personality known as Lord Haw Haw. Joyce broadcast pro-Nazi propaganda from Germany into England even as the Blitz turned his native country to rubble.

Having moved from Georgia to Tennessee, where he eventually assumed a position of leadership in a Chattanooga Klavern, Stoner was expelled by the Klan when his anti-Semitism became too much even for them to take. This was not before he had formed his own group, the National Anti-Jewish Party (later to be called the Christian Anti-Jewish Party), whose goals ranged from simply barring Jews from entering North America to, as he told one paper, "making being Jewish punishable by death."[34]

It was in Stoner's capacity in what he sometimes called the "Christian Party" that his animus for blacks became the basis for a heated exchange of letters between him and black separatist Elijah Muhammad, the leader of the Nation of Islam. In one letter, he addressed his remarks to a convention for the Nation of Islam in Chicago in 1957. Stoner quoted amply from the Bible but called Islam a "nigger religion," saying that ". . . only the superior white race is capable of appreciating Christianity."[35] Echoing his sentiments toward Jews, Stoner said that America was "founded by white men for white men" and added that "you have no place in America with your African race or your Islamic African religion."[36] Stoner continued to attack Muhammad and his group as late as 1959, when he offered to send "trained warriors" to help the New York City police commissioner fight the National of Islam, warning the official that he needed to "learn more about that evil genius, Elijah Muhammad, or you will never stop him and his niggers from taking over your city."[37]

It was in 1959 that Stoner, by then a lawyer, became legal counsel for the organization with which he would become most synonymous, the National States' Rights Party (NSRP). Stoner had been one of the founders of the NSRP in 1958, along with Edward Fields, a white activist from Chicago who had moved to Atlanta. [38] Fields and Stoner met at law school and had a long history with each other, beginning with their association in the Christian Anti-Jewish Party in Atlanta, Georgia.[39] The NSRP published its own newsletter, *The Thunderbolt,* edited by Fields and often featuring articles and columns by Stoner. *The Thunderbolt* had gained a circulation of fifteen thousand by the late 1960s, and the party was active in rallies across the United States. The publication would consistently talk about what Admiral John Crommelin, the NSRP's 1960 candidate for U.S. vice president, called the "Hidden Force"—an international Jewish-communist conspiracy that was subverting America. This message resonated with the party's more prominent members, who were among the most militant fundamentalists, racists, and anti-Semites. The party received ongoing endorsements from the ministry of Wesley Swift, and Swift, as mentioned, would keep a flag with *The Thunderbolt*'s symbol in his personal office until the day he died.

But Stoner did far more than simply echo Swift's message—he became a partner in racial agitation with one of Swift's most well-known ministers, Connie Lynch. The two would, in the words of author Patsy Sims, become a "two-man riot squad" in the 1960s, often at counterdemonstrations against King-led protests and marches. They instigated racial violence in Saint Augustine, Florida; Baltimore, Maryland; and Bogalusa, Louisiana, to name a few cities. Often it was Lynch who was doing the rabble-rousing, while attorney Stoner waited in the wings to represent him after the almost inevitable mob violence that followed an NSRP rally. Such was the case in Baltimore, for instance, after Lynch, dressed in his trademark vest made from a Confederate flag, urged a crowd of approximately one thousand people to wage a "war" against the city's black population. "To hell with niggers," Lynch exclaimed, "and those who don't like it can get the hell out of here."[40] As the NSRP rally concluded, "gangs of white youths charged into a predominantly Negro area throwing bottles at Negroes and attacking those they could lay their hands on with their fists." Later Stoner came in to legally represent Lynch and two others who were charged and convicted for inciting a riot and conspiracy to incite a riot.[41]

But Stoner and the NSRP were far more than just a fringe political party with leaders who stoked the flames of racial violence. Other white rights parties of the period, ranging from the Constitution Party to the third party "Dixiecrat" movement, used violent rhetoric that encouraged racial animus but merely as a tool to resist racial integration. But the NSRP, on the other hand, was primarily a front for violent and racist activities. The NSRP provided an organizational structure to recruit individuals who could be screened, selected, and directed toward actual terrorist acts, acts that were as much a part of their agenda as giving speeches and running candidates for office. Stoner himself said that the political machinations of the NSRP were in part a cover for their more militant and violent acts.

Many of the most blatant acts of violence occurred not in Georgia, Stoner's home state, but in Alabama, where the party moved in 1960. Fields and Stoner apparently felt that Birmingham offered the best opportunities for focusing NSRP activities, which involved actions against both Jews and blacks. In line with Christian Identity beliefs, Stoner viewed Jews as the fundamental threat and blacks as their largely unwitting tools; however, both were clearly a danger to "white civilization." Stoner himself described the NSRP as the last hope for saving white, Christian civilization.

Stoner first became influential in Alabama after offering murder contracts on several Alabama-associated civil rights leaders, including Dr. King, in 1958. He had been so eager to conclude the first phase of the 1958 contract that he had acted before the deal was done or payment made. Stoner brought in some of his "boys from Atlanta" and bombed the Reverend Fred Shuttlesworth's church. No money had changed hands, however, and the sting (organized and carried out by local police with support from the local FBI field office) was so obvious as entrapment that the Birmingham district attorney refused to attempt a prosecution.[42]

Reportedly, the sting against Stoner had been carried out not so much to prevent racial violence in Birmingham but instead because well-established local Klansman saw Stoner and the National States' Rights Party as dangerous fringe elements. Stoner was known for his continuing anti-Semitic rants, and he was suspected of having orchestrated a series of bombings targeting Jewish religious centers. An FBI summary report discussed the bombing of the Jewish Temple Beth-El in Atlanta in 1958; its conclusion was that Stoner (as in Birmingham) had not "personally" participated in the attacks but may have sponsored the effort.[43] The Atlanta Temple Beth-El bombing was suspected of being part of an "orchestrated regional bombing campaign" that included schools and Jewish temples in Jacksonville, Charlotte, Miami, and Nashville.[44]

That Stoner avoided prosecution for these events was not surprising. One of the individuals convicted in the crime said that Stoner was always careful to have obvious alibis for any attack in which he had a hand. In the case of the Atlanta bombing, one of the three primary suspects, Chester Griffin, testified that Stoner would supply the bombers with dynamite taken from Anniston, Alabama, but that he would leave Atlanta in anticipation of any bombing. Stoner would flee to Chattanooga so as to have a concrete alibi.[45] Stoner was not convicted for any bombings until the 1980s, although law enforcement was convinced he was the mastermind of many attacks.[46]

It was a combination of both his rabid anti-Semitism and his penchant for extreme violence that made Stoner unwelcome, even among most Klansmen, in Alabama. Local Birmingham Klansmen had even rejected NSRP offers to participate in their violent attacks on Freedom Rider buses of out-of-state activists looking to force integration of public facilities in the South. As violent as their reaction to these "outside agitators" was, the local racists feared that the NSRP would take the extremism to even greater levels. The NSRP was viewed as "poison," and arrangements were made with local police to arrest Stoner and any NSRP members who showed up for the bus attacks (if anyone actually had to be arrested).[47]

But Stoner, like many ideological terrorists, would find others just as committed to his cause and, for that reason, more dangerous than the Klansmen who rejected him. By 1963 his efforts included recruiting and training especially aggressive young members. Stoner himself would commission two motorcades of 150 cars each, full of teenagers led by NSRP-trained operatives, to resist school desegregation efforts in Birmingham in September 1963. At one school, NSRP-trained teenagers led the student body onto the football field for a "spontaneous" demonstration against the arrival of black students. Police stopped one car and confiscated a pistol, a straight razor, a baling hook, and a sawed-off shotgun.

Numerous instances of what at the time appeared to be random racial violence can now be traced to the systematic efforts of the NSRP to radicalize and direct southern teenagers—with only adult members directing these teens behind the scenes. Such teenage violence ranged from the well-photographed harassment of black sit-ins at lunch counters in major southern cities to much more targeted incidents. For example, in Alabama,

an NSRP-affiliated youth physically attacked Dr. King while King attempted
to register at a segregated hotel. In Mobile, Alabama, the NSRP recruited
the then teenaged Thomas Tarrants to lead anti-integration efforts in his
school, and following the success of those activities, Tarrants dropped out
of school to join adult NSRP members in drive-by shootings at the homes
of local black rights activists. Within a short time, Tarrants had been folded
into the nationwide radical network and became one of the most aggressive
terrorists for Sam Bowers's White Knights.

Stoner's behind-the-scenes activities were often overshadowed by the
more visible "redneck violence" so common in the civil rights struggle. Such
violence became intense in Alabama, in May 1963, following one attempt on
King's life by a group that was heavily influenced by J. B. Stoner, and later
in September 1963, following the bombing of the Sixteenth Street Baptist
Church. These events became famous for their scenes of police officers un-
leashing their dogs and firemen spraying their hoses on protestors—even
children. But even as the events on the ground unfolded, religious terrorists,
such as Swift followers William Potter Gale and Sidney Barnes, were finding
ways to piggyback onto the incidents.

In 1963 such efforts included the previously described effort to kill
Martin Luther King Jr., who had first cut his teeth by joining the nonviolent
bus boycott in Montgomery, Alabama, and who famously was arrested for
his efforts to protest the racist conditions in Birmingham. Both efforts in Alabama to kill King failed, and Birmingham ultimately became a victory for
the civil rights protestors and their leaders such as King and Shuttlesworth.

These incidents helped contribute to the climate of chaos in Alabama,
but they did not trigger the race war that Stoner and his cronies desired.
Scenes of Sheriff Eugene "Bull" Connor's dogs attacking young, nonviolent
protestors scandalized the entire South and helped pave the way for the integration of schools and the passage of the Civil Rights Act of 1964, seriously eroding many forms of the most visible and blatant discrimination. The
events of Bloody Sunday in Selma, Alabama, helped support the passage of
the Voting Rights Act of 1965, guaranteeing widespread voting to southern

blacks for the first time since Reconstruction. This two-fisted legal and political assault on Jim Crow, combined with law enforcement's responses to
the extremism in places like Mississippi, did much to weaken and diminish
the Klan and other militant groups.

But ideological terrorism is slower to die than vigilante or other kinds of
terrorism. Increased pressure by law enforcement may reduce membership,
but it can also force rival, fractious, and loosely connected groups of radicals
together in a common cause. Even as the National States' Rights Party lost influence and members to the much less extreme American Independent Party
under the leadership of Alabama's segregationist governor George Wallace,
even as Bowers and many of his closest aides were facing prosecution for
their roles in the Mississippi Burning killings, this process of unification may
have been taking place. While at the apex of its power in 1963, the National
States' Rights Party attracted delegates and created "franchises" in places as
far away as California and even Canada. In 1967, far removed from his zenith
of influence, Stoner would focus his organizing efforts on a new target—
Meridian, Mississippi, the home of the White Knights.

STONER GOES TO MERIDIAN, BUT NOT TO MEMPHIS

Up until 1967, the NSRP had no major presence in Meridian, Mississippi.
But Jackson FBI field office documents on Stoner show that by November
of that year, the racist firebrand was making inroads into the region. Os-
tensibly in town to help with the appeal for seven men convicted for the
Mississippi Burning killings, Stoner expressed an interest in establishing a
unit of his party in the city. He held a series of rallies throughout 1968, using
liaisons in the community who happened to also be the most devoted members of the White Knights of the Ku Klux Klan of Mississippi.[48] These men
included brothers Raymond and Alton Wayne Roberts, Burris Dunn, and
Danny Joe Hawkins and his father Joe Denver Hawkins.[49] These individuals
were suspected of countless acts of racist terrorism on behalf of Sam Bowers
throughout the 1960s. Stoner apparently even advised Raymond Roberts as
to how the White Knights should escalate their efforts in light of a recent

wave of bombings (many committed by a one-time NSRP member). Rather than use one to two sticks of dynamite, an informant reported Stoner as suggesting, "why not use a whole case of dynamite?"[50]

While Stoner's brand of outspoken violence may have appealed to what we will come to designate as "inner-circle" White Knights members, his forays into Meridian met stiff resistance. Even local segregationist conservatives bemoaned the violence that always followed Stoner. Citing the chaos Stoner stoked in Florida and Alabama, on May 31, 1968, *The Meridian Star* published a column that cited government reports condemning Stoner. The column claimed that the NSRP's violent record stained the honor of segregationism [*sic*] and closed by telling Stoner that he was "*definitely* not welcome to Meridian."[51]

But Stoner's group of devoted White Knights were not deterred, and from 1968 on, they continued to press to entrench the NSRP in Meridian. They did so under the auspices of their front organization, the Americans for the Preservation of the White Race.[52] Records show that Dunn, Hawkins, Roberts, and others, such as new Mississippi arrival Sidney Barnes and new White Knight Imperial Wizard L. E. Matthews (he replaced Bowers after Bowers went to prison), met with Stoner and pushed for a NSRP presence in Meridian as late as 1970.[53]

In 1968 the FBI's Jackson field office, involved in an ongoing, virtual war with the White Knights, took note of Stoner's presence and cultivated informants who would report on Stoner. They were particularly concerned about his presence in Mississippi in late March and early April 1968. The entire FBI, in fact, was worried about Martin Luther King Jr.'s upcoming sanitation workers' strike in Memphis, and the Jackson office fully expected that Stoner would be present in Memphis, as he had been at so many King events throughout the South, inflaming the white population in a city that had already seen violence, notably the shooting of a marcher by police officers. It was this violence, only months before King's planned Poor People's Campaign march on Washington, DC, that convinced King to make an unexpected return to Memphis to reassert the efficacy of nonviolent civil protest. But no one would expect J. B. Stoner to advocate for nonviolence, and the Jackson field office placed around-the-clock surveillance on Stoner, anticipating that he would use Mississippi as his home base to counterprotest against King in Memphis.

But for some reason, Stoner never went to Memphis. In fact, the planned second march in Memphis was conspicuous for the absolute lack of any counterrally by segregationists and white supremacists. On the evening King was murdered, Stoner was at a small meeting in Meridian, Mississippi, supposedly to advance his party's agenda. Jackson FBI agent Jim Ingram described the reaction of Stoner's guests to the news of King's murder: "And all of a sudden, this crowd came out in Meridian and started dancing in the streets."[54]

But not dancing in the streets and not in attendance at the meeting were many of Stoner's most faithful advocates from the White Knights. L. E. Matthews, Burris Dunn, Alton Wayne Roberts, and Joe Denver Hawkins were not in the crowd that night. Present were Raymond Roberts and Danny Joe Hawkins. Danny Joe, who was virtually untouchable in terms of criminal prosecutions in Mississippi (he even assaulted an FBI officer without legal repercussions), made certain that local Meridian law enforcement noted his presence that night. He was cited with a speeding ticket, going the wrong way on a one-way street.[55]

In the FBI's eyes, Stoner's presence in Meridian officially cleared him of any involvement in the King murder. Despite the fact that he was their number one suspect, the FBI inexplicably assumed that Stoner, who had offered to kill King in the past, would have to be personally in Memphis to have participated in a conspiracy on King's life. The same thought process—that involvement in King's murder required physical presence in Tennessee—also helped to clear Bowers and other white supremacists such as Sidney Barnes, despite the fact that the FBI had received information from multiple sources suggesting suspicious activity by Bowers and his inner circle in the days immediately before, during, and after King's murder.

Bowers, Stoner, and many of their followers, who were already heading to federal prison for other crimes, would no doubt have considered it laughable that the FBI presumed to think that they would all have shown up in Memphis to carry out an attack. In fact, by using what we call inner-circle groups, the White Knights had actually been able to ratchet up their level of violence while under massive FBI surveillance and interdiction.

Wesley Swift's followers, seeing the waves of race riots that had increased in frequency since 1965, were hoping to use these inner-circle operatives in acts of violence to provoke a federal response with armed soldiers (serving their "Jewish masters") cracking down on rednecks, who would in turn fight back. Joining the fray would be black militants, and this would become a call to arms for other white Christians to join Swift's adherents in a fight to cleanse America. With violence spreading throughout the nation, they hoped this would become the national race war they saw as Armageddon.

What white supremacists got instead were smaller-scale, very intense conflicts between their members and local FBI field agents. It was not the kind of federal response that the Christian Identity believers like Bowers and Stoner wanted, the kind that could become the basis for a race war. To achieve the kind of widespread rioting seen after April 4, to get that kind of federal response, they must have realized that something much bolder than wanton bombings would be necessary. In May 1963, they had already seen the potential of what just such an attempt on King's life could achieve in Birmingham. As a national figure, his influence resonated in every major city. King may have been competing for attention with the likes of militant black leaders such as Stokely Carmichael, but this only enhanced his position as the "ultimate prize" for those in the Swift movement. With King out of the picture as the preeminent voice for nonviolence, one could reason, only those strident voices open to revolutionary violence, such as Carmichael's, would be left to mobilize a black community infuriated with the murder of one of their most cherished leaders. Increasingly desperate to usher in their Armageddon, those like Samuel Bowers would turn to a strategy that had served terrorists well for more than a century, and killing King was the lynchpin in their plans.

CHAPTER 3

PROPAGANDA OF THE DEED

Seen through the prism of religious terrorism, certain of the most militant racist groups' provocative actions—especially their ongoing efforts to kill the Reverend Martin Luther King Jr.—take on new significance. These groups, or at least their subsets, were so violent that they alienated even other Klan organizations. The nation's largest Klan group, the United Klans of America (UKA), headquartered in Alabama, expelled members connected to the National States' Rights Party and actively competed with the White Knights for membership in Mississippi. According to historian Joe Crespino, "UKA leaders actually attempted to adopt a rhetoric and image of nonviolence, to distance themselves from the more militant White Knights."[1]

As a result of their increasingly violent activities, the White Knights and the NSRP lost members by the hundreds to the UKA, and their extreme tactics offended not only the public at large but also local law enforcement. The attorney general in California called the NSRP the most "active and dangerous . . . ultra-right organization" in the state,[2] while authorities in Jackson, Mississippi, launched what one author described as a virtual war on the White Knights of Mississippi.[3] Yet these groups were undeterred, for they believed, as Reverend Swift would promise in one of his sermons in 1964, that the world was "much closer . . . to Armageddon than many people realize."

Grouping religious terrorists into a larger subgroup of ideological terrorists that includes violent anarchists from the late nineteenth and early twentieth centuries and radical Islamic terrorists such as Al-Qaeda in the twenty-first century, expert Christopher Fettweiss notes that in contrast to nationalist terrorists who "kill on behalf of their nation of identity," ideological terrorists have much loftier goals, to change society itself. They see the current state of the world as an "unacceptable condition." Hence they see their acts of provocative violence as necessary to challenge the unacceptable condition with the goal of "'awakening' the masses" in hopes of creating a "better world." To bridge the gap between this unacceptable world and the better world, to awaken the masses, the ideological terrorist places great stock in a strategy first perfected by anarcho-terrorists: "propaganda of the deed."[4]

PROPAGANDA OF THE DEED: PAST AND PRESENT

"A single deed," declared the anarchist Peter Kropotkin, "makes more propaganda in a few days than a thousand pamphlets."Though Kropotkin was speaking in 1881 about his support for the assassination of Tsar Alexander II, his quote gives us insight into many of the most violent (and sometimes seemingly meaningless) attacks carried out by the radical network we are examining. Though on occasion even their own followers failed to understand the grand strategy, leaders like Sam Bowers absolutely grasped the immense leverage provided by the propaganda of the deed. In fact, a study of history through the nineteenth and twentieth centuries reveals that ideological terrorists with limited resources were often forced into exceptionally violent acts of provocation.

Employing the strategy at the turn of the century in America, a loosely networked group of anarchists, known as Galleanists, launched a "mini-war against American capitalism and government" that one author described as "the most extensive, best organized, and carefully planned operation of its type ever undertaken by Italian anarchists."[5] Representing a "true conspiracy . . . involving some fifty to sixty militants,"[6] the Galleanists sent homemade bombs to public officials, launched coordinated bombings in eight different U.S. cities, and famously detonated an explosive on Wall Street in 1920, killing thirty-eight people.[7] These anarchists engaged in such tactics, both in Europe and in the United States, when previous strategies had failed and when law enforcement pressure against them had actually increased. Their example is important to understanding the push for this strategy among certain white supremacists in the 1960s.

Sadly, the same is also true in trying to understand Al-Qaeda in the twentieth century. Journalist Alan Cullison, who fortuitously gained access to Al-Qaeda's internal records on a used computer he bought in Afghanistan after America's invasion in October 2001, noted that that terrorist organization was fractured by internal rivalries and was financially strained in the months leading up to the 9/11 attacks on the twin towers. He added that Al-Qaeda hoped "to tempt the [great international] powers to strike back in a way that would create sympathy for the terrorists."[8] Ironically, Al-Qaeda would be provoking the West into justifying Al-Qaeda's existence and purpose: to fight off Western intrusion. This closely mirrors the motivation of the Galleanist anarchists who hoped their actions would provoke a major overreaction from the powers that be, proving that the state itself was abusive and unnecessary.

For the devotees of Wesley Swift like Sam Bowers, the overreaction they desired of their enemy would be one that confirmed their religious prophecies. Quite simply, it would be the beginning of the race war they desired, the holy beginning of Armageddon for Christian Identity adherents. It would involve provoking large-scale federal intervention in a way calculated to create resentment of it in white Americans, potentially triggered by an act of racial violence. Unable to directly attack the national troops, whites would target the source of the intervention: blacks and Jews. This would create a cycle of revenge and retaliation that would fuel a race war. This is the strategy Sam Bowers outlined, behind the backs of the "rednecks" he was manipulating, to informer Delmar Dennis. It was a strategy that had an obvious appeal for white supremacists and would send a clear message. And it involved violence and assassinations, including attempts on the life of Martin Luther King Jr.

THE PROMISE OF THE DEED: 1963 TO 1964
Birmingham, May 1963

The first attack that demonstrated the potential for violent provocation involved one such attempt on King's life, which came on the heels of violence that had already rocked Alabama for years. Bombings had become routine in Birmingham in the late '50s and early '60s, most often directed toward black churches or blacks and whites who bought or sold property outside the accepted color lines. But despite all the bombing and protests, there had never been major race riots in Birmingham—but that changed in 1963.

In May 1963, a riot followed the coordinated bombings of Martin Luther King's quarters at the A. G. Gaston Motel and the Birmingham home of King's brother, the Reverend A. D. King. The Ku Klux Klan splinter group known as the Cahaba Boys, named after a river south of Birmingham, was responsible for these bombings.[9] *The New York Times* reported in the wake of these attacks that "[r]iots raged out of control for more than three hours" with "50 persons . . . injured, including a policeman and a taxicab driver who were stabbed." *The Times* added, "About 2,500 persons joined the crowds that attacked the police and firemen, wrecked scores of police and private automobiles and burned six small stores and a two-story apartment house."[10] Three thousand federal troops were called in two days later to the outskirts of Birmingham to help quell the growing conflicts between state police officers and the enraged public. President John F. Kennedy even considered federalizing the Alabama National Guard to help stop the attacks, until tensions eventually simmered down.[11]

If an attempted assassination of Dr. King and his brother could unleash such a torrent of violence, the actual killing of another civil rights figure in Jackson, Mississippi, continued to illustrate, to anyone who was paying attention, what a surprising and bold act of violence could accomplish.

The Medgar Evers Assassination, June 1963

The brutal assassination of Medgar Evers on June 12, 1963, might well be viewed as one of the earliest examples of the Mississippi Klan's use of propaganda of the deed. Evers was the Mississippi field secretary for the NAACP who had organized voter registration efforts, encouraged economic boycotts of white-owned businesses that practiced discrimination, advocated for school integration, and pushed for an investigation into the lynching of fourteen-year-old African American Emmett Till. Hours after a ground-breaking national television broadcast by President Kennedy asserting his personal support for new civil rights legislation, Evers was shot in the back with a .30-06 rifle while entering his home in Jackson, Mississippi.

Hints that this was a deliberate act of provocation emerged almost immediately after the shooting. We interviewed Fred Sanders, the lead police detective assigned to the Evers murder investigation, who related an intriguing story about the crowd that formed as he arrived at the crime scene. Sanders says that a white man, who at first appeared to be a reporter, began agitating the crowd that assembled near Evers's home. The man was vociferously urging the crowd to respond with immediate violence. In fact he was so animated and strident that Sanders was concerned about what might result and was compelled to remove the agitator from the crowd and restrain him. Sanders does not know the man's identity and did not officially arrest the individual.[12] Certainly major violence could have erupted immediately in Jackson; instead, it was delayed until Evers's funeral. When it did erupt, it disrupted the relative calm that had been the norm in Jackson for months.

By the time of Evers's funeral, it had been almost a year since the nation focused its attention on the violent confrontation at the University of Mississippi over an attempt to enroll its first black student, James Meredith. President Kennedy had gone on national television at the time of the Meredith fray to appeal for calm, for a measured reaction, and for a retreat from militancy by all parties. Following that, in Jackson, black activism seemed to be on the wane. Even as demonstrations were growing and becoming more numerous around the nation, Jackson's local NAACP meeting attendance was in decline. The trend was clear: "people were dropping away."[13] The NAACP was focused on voter registration, not sit-ins or marches. The energy of the previous months appeared to have become somewhat exhausted. Evers himself was described as looking "very tired."

But Medgar Everss's murder immediately and dramatically changed the entire climate in Jackson. Fear became the order of the day for both whites and blacks. Black protests and demonstrations began to appear immediately, and they were met with police confrontation and aggression. The Evers funeral evolved into a series of spontaneous marches with an even more violent police response, including mass arrests and beatings. The killing of Evers showed that a murder of a nonviolent activist could elicit national attention and create riots.[14]

This disorder came within months of the formal creation of the White Knights of the Ku Klux Klan of Mississippi in December 1963. The man who would emerge as the chief suspect in the murder and who would eventually be convicted for it, Byron de la Beckwith, was, by the middle of the 1960s, a major figure in the new organization. Beckwith was born in Colusa, California, and he claimed that he had been trained from his youth to make war against enemies of the white, Christian republic. Beckwith was also an avowed follower of Wesley Swift and a fanatical believer in Christian Identity. Beckwith became a Christian Identity–ordained minister, routinely introducing himself as an Israelite (not a Jew). Samuel Bowers hosted Beckwith as the principal speaker at a White Knights training meeting where Beckwith claimed responsibility for the sniper shooting of Evers with a .30-06 rifle.[15]

It may well be that Sam Bowers or the White Knights organization did not specifically initiate the Evers murder per se. We should point out that the formal founding of the White Knights of Mississippi did not occur until December 1963, and Beckwith was not a member of record until after Evers's murder. Indeed, Beckwith's son recently claimed to Jerry Mitchell, investigative reporter for the Jackson, Mississippi, *Clarion-Ledger,* that the murder was ordered by the White Citizens' Council in Mississippi.[16] While such groups were formed around the country as "respectable" fronts to oppose desegregation in an outwardly legal way, their connections to violent activity, though rare, was not unheard of, so this is at least plausible.

But such issues are largely technicalities. White Citizens' Council members, such as Noah Jefferson Carden from Mobile, had active connections to extremists in groups like the NSRP, and other members of the council were certainly connected to the Klan. More than one source claims that Beckwith at least implied that Evers's killing was a "Klan project."[17] Whether Bowers himself initiated it, the White Knights would unabashedly claim Beckwith as their own and look upon the Evers assassination as a source of pride for the group. For our study, what matters is the impact of the Evers murder, and what the aftermath implied for the use of other, similarly high-profile attacks.

In that sense, perhaps the most dramatic lesson of Evers's brutal murder was the degree to which it surprised and shocked virtually everyone. It was immediately seen as an extremely violent and sensational action, standing apart from the typical Klan beatings, burnings, bombings, and general harassment that were common in Mississippi at that time. The use of extreme force was also surprising because Medgar Evers was not a militant civil rights activist.[18] As a longtime NAACP staff member, Evers was associated with one of the most conservative civil rights organizations, one which emphasized legal options and working within the system. Although he was passionate about the cause, the official NAACP positions sometimes limited his personal involvement in local integration efforts. However, although Medgar Evers did play a supporting role in the effort to place black student James Meredith in the all-white University of Mississippi, his position was strictly one of nonviolence, even though he knew that he himself was at risk. Whether killing Evers was a Klan action, plotted by Bowers, or the work of Beckwith alone, it showed the potential of bold, violent action for those who hoped for federal intervention and an ensuing race war. The worst was yet to come, however.

Birmingham, September 1963

Riots returned to Birmingham following the Sixteenth Street Baptist Church bombing on September 16, 1963, which killed four young girls and threatened the lives of dozens of other children. That nationally reviled act was actually the fourth bombing in four weeks in Birmingham, following the school desegregation efforts that began in Alabama on September 4, 1963. Black-owned businesses were also set afire not long after the Sixteenth Street Baptist Church bombing. United Press International described the wake as one where "[t]housands of hysterical Negroes poured into the area around the church this morning and police fought for two hours, firing rifles into the air to control them." Two African American teenagers were shot by local police in the aftermath, and twenty others were treated at local hospitals, with "[m]any more cut and bruised by flying debris."[10] President John F. Kennedy did not want to give anti-integrationist icon George Wallace a publicity coup and so, in this instance, deliberately avoided sending federal troops into the Birmingham. But he did send two personal representatives to negotiate a truce between civil rights leaders and city leaders, and he personally monitored the situation closely in the event that troops would be required.

It was only in 1978, when Congress reinvestigated the King assassination, that the public learned that several of Swift's most rabid followers, former admiral John Crommelin, former colonel William Potter Gale, suspected bomb maker Sidney Crockett Barnes, and White Citizens' Council member Noah Jefferson Carden, had traveled to Birmingham before the church bombing. The FBI was suspicious enough at the time to investigate the possibility that Barnes helped with the bomb that killed the four girls. Law enforcement learned that these men apparently plotted further attacks to piggyback on the wave of violence that followed the church attack. One such attack even involved a planned shooting of Martin Luther King Jr. when he came to deliver the eulogy for the four girls.

PROPAGANDA OF THE DEED: LESSONS LEARNED

There are four aspects of the Birmingham bombings and the Evers shooting worth highlighting. The first is the difficulty that federal agencies had in uncovering and prosecuting these crimes. Beckwith avoided conviction until the 1990s, and some of the men connected to the church bombing were not tried until the 2000s. In the case of the A. G. Gaston Motel bombing, certain police officers reportedly assisted with the alibis, and the FBI's key Klan informant in Birmingham, Gary Rowe, personally helped clear the chief participants (he was sleeping with the wife of one of them at the time!).

Rowe's actions demonstrate the conflicted loyalties that many informants harbored.[20] He would, for instance, later be in a car with three other Klansmen who shot and killed civil rights activist Viola Liuzzo in 1965.

The involvement of local police officers—some of whom, in many states, were Klansmen—created additional complications even if the FBI had uncovered a conspiracy. J. Edgar Hoover frequently stopped short of letting deep informants testify at court. With the possibility that any racist law enforcement officer, racist prosecutor, racist juror, or racist judge could derail a prosecution, why risk the informants' lives for a bogus prosecution? Frequently, as in the case of the Sixteenth Street Baptist Church bombing investigation, information that could expose sources and informants was withheld from local and state prosecutors, even years after the crimes.

Robert Chambliss, a main participant in the bombing of the Birmingham church, was not convicted until 1977, when pressure from Alabama Attorney General William Baxley and the media forced the FBI to finally release information that cinched the case. Two other Cahaba Boys, Bobby Frank Cherry and Thomas Blanton Jr., were not even tried until 2001. The FBI's reluctance to expose sources and methods, combined with general problems stemming from compartmentalized information (there were no databases for data mining in the 1960s), meant that a successful conspiracy prosecution for racial crimes was often beyond the grasp of local and federal law enforcement. That problem would become exponential during the investigation of the King murder in 1968, which involved reports from dozens of FBI field offices, sourced to hundreds of active informants.

Secondly, investigating a racist conspiracy was even more difficult when the crimes themselves, as in the 1963 bombings, were sophisticated. Though this was not common to everyday Klan violence, it became, as noted earlier, more frequent as white supremacists turned to smaller and smaller groups to carry out major crimes. These smaller, insulated groups were not nearly as susceptible to informants in the first place, and the crimes themselves were more confusing to investigators. In addition to establishing solid pre-bombing alibis, the "mechanics" in both major Birmingham bombings used diversions and time-delayed bombs. Accounts of the church bombing, for instance, suggest that a fake reported crime helped shift police protection away from the church so that the bombers could plant their explosives.

Thirdly, it is noteworthy that the first Birmingham bombing attack started with a direct effort to kill Martin Luther King Jr., and the second included a plan to escalate the city's violence through a sniper attack by another NSRP devotee. And whether or not they considered the implications of their plans beforehand or learned the lessons afterward, the message from the riots in 1963 was obvious: If an attack was provocative enough, it could fuel the kind of backlash and federal response that could deliver the first skirmishes in their hoped-for race war. If just attempting to kill King could bring President Kennedy to the verge of sending thousands of federal troops into a major American city, what would his actual murder accomplish? Men like Bowers could see the potential for such interventions as escalating to an outright race war.

Without question, many individuals connected to Bowers's White Knights network were on the periphery of the Birmingham attacks, including Sidney Crockett Barnes and William Potter Gale. All these individuals were cross affiliated with each others' organizations and believed in Wesley Swift's teachings; they tried to piggyback on the initial bombings and rioting in Alabama to make it even worse. As such, their actions were consistent with the coordinated escalation of violence common to the anarchist attacks in Europe and the United States—consistent with a strategy of propaganda of the deed. Showing that many of the individuals were experimenting with this strategy is important.

From that perspective, it is worth noting that Dr. King was not just any target but rather was viewed as the "ultimate prize." Serious efforts to kill King, extending from 1958 to 1967, underscore that fact. It may not be an accident that most of those plots developed after 1963. The shift to a strategy of propaganda of the deed may in fact have started after the attempt on King's life in Alabama in May 1963.

Beyond that, we have developed evidence of a heretofore unrecognized plot against King's life in 1964, while he was visiting Jackson in part to fill the vacuum left by the death of Evers. The later murder of Ben Chester White in 1966 clearly shows that the White Knights were not beyond killing someone else in order to lure King into a potential death trap. More than anything, events in Birmingham and Jackson must have suggested to the other zealots in Swift's network that killing civil rights leaders, even just attempting to kill King, had the potential to elicit widespread chaos and violence—the kind that could ultimately lead to their hoped-for religious race war.

As of 1968, these white extremists had not yet reached their ultimate goal—though it was not for lack of effort by Sam Bowers. The pressures that pushed Al-Qaeda and early twentieth-century anarchists to resort to provocative violence were exerting the same effect on Bowers in 1968. During the 1960s, Klan membership had dropped from an estimated forty thousand in 1965 to fourteen thousand in 1968.[21] Massive FBI operations had been highly successful in reducing memberships in Mississippi, Alabama, and Georgia. Many of the most violent radicals were under periodic or ongoing surveillance, the number of informants had skyrocketed, and leaders such as Sam Bowers found their groups fragmented with declining financial resources (a large portion of various Klans' membership dues had been eaten up in defending members charged with racial crimes). Facing prison time himself, Sam Bowers took what would be a counterintuitive measure for rational terrorists with limited goals: He escalated his wave of violence and diversified his range of targets.

Sam Bowers was not a nationalist terrorist with limited ambitions. He was a religious terrorist who saw an America rocked by numerous race riots from 1965 to 1967, a country that must have resembled the America that the Reverend Wesley Swift described in his tape-recorded apocalyptic sermons, which were heard at parties throughout the South. Bowers had been perfecting the propaganda of the deed since 1964 to make Swift's vision a reality. And he would turn to a closed group of elite White Knight members, many of whom shared the same religious views, to carry out his grand strategy, with tactics refined from years of instigating extreme violence.

CHAPTER 4

INNER CIRCLES

"**O**ur God, our Heavenly Guide, as finite creatures of time and as dependent creatures of Thine, we acknowledge Thee as our sovereign Lord," Sam Bowers openly prayed, as he addressed a secret meeting of his fellow White Knights on June 7, 1964, in an abandoned church outside of Raleigh, Mississippi. "Bless us now in this assembly that we may honor Thee in all things, we pray in the name of Christ, our blessed Savior. Amen."[1]

The prayer had finished, but Bowers had only just begun. Outside, in the surrounding woods, security guards checked all the entrants, allowing most of the attendees in with visible firearms. The concern was not weapons but outsiders, and security guards with walkie-talkies circulated throughout the grounds while a half-dozen armed men on horseback patrolled the surrounding woods. Two Piper Cubs flew aerial surveillance and were in touch by radio with men on the ground as Sam Bowers outlined his Imperial Executive Order to the rank-and-file militants. Bowers created the order in anticipation of the summer to come, a summer that he knew would bring activists and national attention to Mississippi, a summer that he told his audience would "determine the fate of Christian Civilization."[2]

This summer, within a very few days, the enemy will launch his final push for victory here in Mississippi. This offensive will consist of two basic salients, which have been designed to envelop and destroy our small forces in a pincer movement of agitation, force by federal troops, and communist propaganda.

The two basic salients are as follows, listed in one-two order as they will be used.

1. Massive street demonstrations and agitation by blacks in many areas at once, designed to provoke white militants into counterdemonstration and open, pitched street battles, resulting in civil chaos and anarchy to provide an excuse for.

2. A decree from the communist authorities in charge of the national government, which will declare the state of Mississippi to be in a state of open revolt, with a complete breakdown of law and order; and declaring martial law, followed by a massive occupation of the state by federal troops, with all known patriotic whites placed under military arrest. If this martial law is imposed, our homes and our lives and our arms will pass under the complete control of the enemy, and he will have won his victory. We will, of course, resist to the very end, but our chances of victory will undoubtedly end with the imposition of martial law in Mississippi by the communist masters in Washington.[3]

After what must have been an alarming prediction to his rank-and-file members, Bowers called them to action:

When the first waves of blacks hit our streets this summer, we must avoid open daylight conflict with them, if at all possible, as private citizens, or as members of this organization. We should join with and support local police and duly constituted law enforcement agencies with volunteer, legally deputized men from our own ranks. We must absolutely avoid the appearance of a mob going into the streets to fight the blacks. Our first contact with the troops of the enemy in the streets should be as legally deputized law enforcement officers . . .

In all cases, however, there must be a secondary group of our members, standing back away from the main area of conflict, armed and ready to move on very short notice, who are not under the control of anyone but our own Christian officers . . . Once committed, this secondary group must move swiftly and vigorously to attack the local headquarters of the enemy, destroy and disrupt his leadership and communications—both local and Washington—and any news communication equipment or agents in the area. The action of this secondary group must be very swift and very forceful with no holds barred . . . It must be understood that the secondary group is an extremely swift and extremely violent hit-and-run group. They should rarely be in action for over one-half hour, and under no circumstances for over one hour. Within two hours of their commitment they should be many miles from the scene of action.[4]

In describing operations at night, Bowers emphasized that

Any personal attacks on the enemy should be carefully planned to include only the leaders and prime white collaborators of the enemy forces. These attacks against these selected, individual targets should, of course, be as severe as circumstances and conditions will permit. No severe attacks should be directed against the general mass of the enemy because of the danger of hurting some actually innocent person. The leaders, of course, are not innocent, and they should be our prime targets . . .[5]

In outlining his master plan to his audience, Bowers was only hinting at part of his agenda. Recall that he was a religious terrorist, leading a group of mostly redneck racists determined to simply preserve the system of white supremacy in the South. The idea that one would provoke an actual federal response would be anathema to these men, brought up to resent the memories of federal "intrusion" during Reconstruction after the Civil War. But Bowers, as he told informant Delmar Dennis, had to manipulate these men for his own ends.

It is thus worth noting that Bowers's prime action that summer did more than just about anything to bring the very federal response he knew these men would oppose. Two weeks after giving this speech, three workers from the Council of Federated Organizations—an umbrella group of civil rights organizations pushing for integration—disappeared in Neshoba County, Mississippi. Found murdered weeks later after one of the largest interventions by the FBI in any state's history, the Mississippi Burning case scandalized the state and infuriated the rest of America; polls showed that 71 percent of Americans favored sending federal troops into Mississippi if events escalated.[6]

This would have been exactly what Sam Bowers wanted. Far from fearing the waves of black violence he warned about in his speech, Bowers and his fellow Christian Identity believers saw in federal intervention the precursor to the end-times, when Jesus Christ would return to earth and usher in one thousand years of utopian peace, in a world occupied exclusively by Anglo-Saxon whites. But Bowers was not entirely deceptive in his message. In arguing for an elite "secondary group" to carry out "swift" "hit-and-run" operations, Bowers was describing an evolutionary step that had already begun in white supremacist organizations around the country. This step involved the forming of elite inner circles, and if reports of one witness are true, one collection of such elite operatives may have been in Memphis on April 4, 1968.

THE TWO FACES OF WHITE SUPREMACY: PUBLIC VERSUS INNER CIRCLE

In her comprehensive overview of the various Ku Klux Klan organizations, *The Klan*, Patsy Sims paints a very clear picture of the two faces of the Klan. Its public face was seen in the Klan titles and regalia—in marches, fund-raising, cross burnings, billboards, and media campaigns. Its public violence was visible in confrontations, mob actions, beatings, and harassment, as well as in spontaneous shootings and murders. That was the sort of violence William Huie, author of *The Klansman*, referred to as typical "redneck" violence. But Sims also described a much more covert, more strategic, and imminently more dangerous face of the Klan, that of the inner circles. It was these small groups of men, five or six in each group, who performed the most serious, planned acts of terror.[7] Their identities were concealed from the Klan as a whole—known only to the top leaders of major white supremacist groups—and on occasion the men had alliances with multiple groups and racist militants (such as members of the National States' Rights Party), allowing them to operate independently and with deniability.

At times these inner groups formed organically, as the inevitable result of the internecine conflicts within and between white supremacist groups. Sims documents countless instances where Klan organizations fragmented, often because of leadership struggles and fights over shady finances or misuses of membership dues. As some Klaverns petered out and others emerged as separate, sometimes nationally known, organizations, money and power were not the only forces driving natural selection in this Darwinian struggle. A very common mutation was the "ideologically pure" group, whose members almost always felt that the previous group to which they belonged was not zealous and not violent enough. Very small in size, these new groups were not only similar in commitment and function to the inner-circle groups but also virtually outsourced in this role to other Klans and similarly intentioned hate groups, such as the NSRP. The practice of outsiders performing acts in other counties, cities, or even states was yet another highly effective tactic in neutering police investigations.

The so-called Cahaba Boys, infamous for the roles they played in bombing the Sixteenth Street Baptist Church and the likely culprits in one of the Birmingham attempts on King's life (for example, the Gaston Motel incident), had evolved into a type of inner circle.[8] Initially the members had been with the Eastview Klavern of the United Klans of America, one of the three major national Klans in the United States. But a rift developed between the UKA and the National States' Rights Party over the latter's extremism—both in the NSRP's commitment to violence and in its zealous anti-Semitism. Some of the Eastview members, notably future Sixteenth Street Baptist Church bombing conspirators Robert Chambliss and Tommy Blanton, shifted their allegiances closer to the NSRP. They met with J. B. Stoner frequently and embraced his ideology.[9] This, in fact, led to their expulsion from the UKA but certainly did not end their commitment to violence.[10]

Naming themselves after Alabama's longest free-flowing river, the Cahaba Boys was a more ideologically driven group that resorted to terrorist acts that scared even the local Alabama Klans. One FBI informant expressed the fear that "the States' Righters [such as the Cahaba Boys] will go out and pull a bunch of bullshit . . . it will fall back on us and we will catch hell for it."[11] Owing to their small size and isolation from mainstream Klans, the Cahaba Boys were able to contract out their services to the NSRP and to other white supremacist groups. According to the niece of one of the key leaders, the group was willing to operate across state lines, making them that much harder to track. Their small size, devotion, and skill[12] (honed through countless attacks from local law enforcement) perfectly positioned the group to participate in the most public and dangerous attacks in Alabama, reportedly including the bombing of Dr. King's room at the Gaston Motel.

Unlike the Cahaba Boys, most inner-circle supremacist groups were deliberately formed subsets of the most well-organized and tightly structured militant organizations. An example of a layered organization with multiple levels of inner circles can be found in a study of the Christian Knights of the Invisible Empire (CKIE), a California group led by Colonel William Gale. In reality, the Christian Knights had been established as the "third front" of a four-front organization.

The public face of the organization was Wesley Swift's Church of Jesus Christ Christian, which was to "have the outward impression of a political-religious group not interested in violence."[13] Faithful and trusted members of the Church of Jesus Christ Christian were recruited for the propaganda efforts of its activist Army of White American Kingdom Evangelists (AWAKE). Tested and trusted members of AWAKE were then selected for membership in the Christian Knights, with the most militant members of the Christian Knights being covertly and individually taken into the "inner den." The inner den would provide the personnel to be used in acts of violence, including murder.[14]

Examples of these inner-circle groups exist in other Klans around the country, notably Imperial Wizard James Venable's National Knights of the Ku Klux Klan, whose Klaverns spanned many states. Venable recruited disaffected members of the more moderate United Klans of America, individuals who wanted more violent resistance to integration efforts, into his inner circle, called the "Black Shirts."[15] It is worth noting that it was members of this elite group who were actively engaged with Daniel Wagner, the young racist from Ohio who claimed that the inebriated leader of Ohio's NKKKK chapter referenced a murder contract from Venable on Martin Luther King's life in 1965. While it is not known if these Black Shirts were in any way connected to that purported assassination plot, it is without question that members of the Black Shirts supplied Wagner with dynamite in Georgia and that he took to Ohio with the unfulfilled hopes of launching a bombing campaign to "start a civil war" in America.[16]

An informant in Swift's ranks, George Harding, revealed the use of inner-circle groups for assassinations. In a FBI report from 1963, Harding describes himself as a strong anticommunist, in sympathy with the overall political and security agenda of the radical right. However, Harding was shocked to find that there were actual preparations in progress to assassinate American political leaders. Harding reported that he had been approached to join an eight-man team that was being formed to assassinate targeted political leaders who were viewed as communist dupes or "fellow travelers."[17] The political orientation of these leaders was liberal enough (or Jewish enough) to mark them as unwitting tools of the communists and therefore a threat to be eliminated. This is consistent with a Miami police-informant report from April 1963 about a meeting of elite figures, devoted to the cause of white supremacy, who secretly discussed deploying strike teams to kill a host of (mostly Jewish) public figures. This meeting, of the Congress of Freedom, was in early April 1963 and included "high-ranking industrialists, bankers, and insurance executives" with "access to great amounts of money." One such figure who could not attend but who sent a representative in his place was Noah Carden, who twice, once in

1963 and once again in 1964, was part of an assassination conspiracy on Martin Luther King Jr.'s life.[18]

The FBI largely dismissed these reports of strike teams. It is clear that the number of teams, and their range of targets (as noted in the Congress of Freedom report), were clearly exaggerated by white supremacist groups for recruitment purposes. But there were inner-circle groups that were common to many major Klan organizations and they closely resembled, and served the same function as, the groups described by Harding. The FBI all but ignored these inner-circle groups, and may not even have been aware of the concept. Instead, they focused their attention on individual members of these elite groups. In Mississippi, this eventually erupted into an outright war between law enforcement and Bowers's operatives, a conflict that may have sparked, as a perverse consequence, a renewed effort to kill Martin Luther King Jr.

SAM BOWERS'S INNER CIRCLE

While there is no "official list" of who was in the White Knights' inner circle, a detailed study of the group from 1967 to 1968 suggests several individuals. These individuals were the most active members of the Americans for the Preservation of the White Race, an organization that the FBI says was a front for the White Knights themselves. These men also had ongoing, direct contact with Bowers. They were also the most frequent lawbreakers among Bowers's Knights, and they happened to be the most ardent supporters of J. B. Stoner's efforts to bring the NSRP to Meridian, Mississippi, between 1967 and 1968.

The White Knights' inner circle likely included Danny Joe and his father, Joe Denver Hawkins (whose entire family was considered among the most open and belligerent racists in Mississippi); Julius (J. L.) Harper, who was the Grand Dragon for the White Knights; Burris Dunn, a cash register–company employee who FBI documents say idolized Sam Bowers; Deavours Nix, the Grand Director of the White Knights' Klan Bureau of Investigation and owner of its most well-known meeting spot (John's Restaurant in Laurel, Mississippi); and L. E. Matthews, a forty-four-year-old electrical contractor widely suspected of being the White Knights' bomb maker. Matthews eventually replaced Sam Bowers as the White Knights' state leader when Bowers went to prison in 1968. The list would also come to include brothers Alton Wayne and Raymond Roberts; teh former convicted for his role in the Mississippi Burning murders.

These individuals were suspects in a rash of violent attacks in the late 1960s, including a wave of bombings and shootings in 1967 and 1968 that were unprecedented both in their numbers (one participant put the number of attacks into the thirties) and in their prime target (Jews). Not surprisingly, it was only when the FBI and local Mississippi law enforcement "turned" some of these individuals into active informants, in the summer of 1968, that inner-circle operatives were forced to lie low and truly violent White Knights activity finally began to dissipate in Mississippi. Before that time, some of these individuals appeared to act with near impunity, with individuals like Danny Joe Hawkins and L. E. Matthews openly defying law enforcement while avoiding successful prosecution. A major reason why these men were able to escape detection, even under intense scrutiny, was because of tactics that Sam Bowers had developed in the previous three years, tactics that may have been used in Memphis on April 4, 1968.

EVOLVING TERROR TACTICS

The individuals connected to the murder of Martin Luther King Jr. had evolved a host of tactics refined by years of contending with pressure from law enforcement. At least three such tactics had become common and are relevant to the possible White Knights' efforts to assassinate Dr. King. These tactics may also have prevented law enforcement from finding a conspiracy in his murder—as they had in a number of previous terror attacks. These tactics included:

"Sitting on Go"

One of the best examples of the White Knights' tactical evolution was the concept of "sitting on go," which was the practice of establishing a target, authorizing action, and defining events that would trigger the act, but making no specific plan or even designating specific individuals to carry out the act. Sam Bowers was well aware of law enforcement efforts to solicit informants. Specific plans might well be compromised. So to avoid that, only the basics of a plot were put in place and pre-authorization given.

When circumstances presented themselves, a single inner-circle member would recruit from a list of vetted personnel, and the act would be immediately carried out, thus giving no time or opportunity for a leak. This tactic was at work in the Mississippi Burning murders of three Neshoba County civil rights workers. In that case, even the location (a dam under construction) in which the bodies would be buried had been identified and scouted months earlier. Individuals not known as officers or members of the White Knights were contacted at the last minute for the actual attack. Sympathetic law enforcement officers had been asked to notify a White Knights member if and when the three civil rights workers, Michael Schwerner, James Earl Chaney, and Andrew Goodman, were taken into custody. The police were then to release them in a fashion in which they could be stalked for the final act.

Of course law enforcement officers sympathetic to the White Knights were never encouraged to be visible members or to participate in "eliminations." And there was considerable "sympathy" among some Mississippi police forces for the White Knights. In 1965 the FBI sent a sixteen-page letter to the governor of Mississippi listing known Klan members in Mississippi law enforcement. In addition to Sheriff Lawrence Rainey and Deputy Cecil Price of Neshoba County, the letter listed sheriffs, constables, and highway patrolmen throughout the state. So common were White Knight members that the FBI had to provide the information in a county-by-county breakdown, in alphabetical order.[19]

Pre-existing Alibis:

The inner circles were quite effective at having alibis arranged for their operatives and for having sources, including police officers, literally on call for such alibis. This was a tactic that stretched back as far as the 1870s and the original wave of Klan violence in response to Reconstruction. In the 1960s, as in the 1870s, the Klans were decentralized into dens or Klaverns for each town or county, with small numbers of men in each operational group. Thus it was easy for members to harmonize their stories and give one consistent but false account to authorities, or to juries at trial.[20] In one variation of such tactics, Klan members would commit a crime using the car from a fellow Klan member who was time-stamped at work. When the FBI obtained license plates from witnesses to the crime, the car would trace to individuals who had rock-solid alibis, because they were indeed at work while their comrades used their cars to commit the crime.

While it is controversial as to whether or not the shooting of NAACP activist Medgar Evers was a Klan act, prosecutors argued that his accused assassin, eventual White Knight and Swift follower Byron de la Beckwith, was protected by a number of false alibi witnesses. Beckwith avoided prison in part because of these witnesses, until a jury in the 1990s apparently recognized it as a fabrication.

Countersurveillance

Countersurveillance refers to keeping tabs on law enforcement before, during, and after the commission of a crime. Beyond their own members and sources within law enforcement, the Klan was notorious for using CB radios to monitor police broadcasts. HUAC cited reports that, in one year alone, the White Knights of the Ku Klux Klan bought almost $800 worth of CB radios (close to $5,500 in today's dollars).[21] Klan use of radio equipment was so obvious during the violence in Saint Augustine, Florida, that the local CB Radio Club wrote a public letter to the local paper complaining that "every time we ride down the street with our aerials waving . . . people turn and look at us like we are criminals."[22] But the radios were more than just a status symbol; they helped the Klan escape from crime scenes. Addressing charges that local law enforcement deliberately avoided investigating racist crimes, HUAC offered the following defense of police:

Klansmen make use of citizens' band radios for communication among themselves. In addition, they have equipment which enables them to intercept police radio calls. By using this kind of communication, with quick means of communication, hot rods, and being in a position to know where police patrol cars are at a given time, they can judge pretty well when and where they can commit an act of violence and have time to make a getaway.[23]

During the Mississippi Burning investigation, when FBI agents located the car belonging to the three victims, they suspected that Klansmen would monitor and quickly report to Klan leadership any calls placed on police radio channels. This forced the FBI agents to locate and use landline telephones to make their reports. Within a few months, the Federal Communications Commission was requested to dispatch technicians to set up a secure radio network for the bureau and to monitor Klan radio transmissions.[24]

Sam Bowers was at the forefront of perfecting and elaborating these three tactics with the White Knights. The White Knights had also begun to use inner circle grouping as early as 1964, and Bowers was the most daring in employing them. It is worth noting that these tactics were designed to help actual operations succeed even under federal and police scrutiny and to help the perpetrators escape justice. To counter them, the FBI and local law enforcement evolved their own set of tactics, aimed less at following up on crimes after the fact and more at preventing them from ever happening. Law enforcement looked to destroy these groups from within, through the recruiting or planting of informants among the group members.

COINTELPRO AND THE EVOLUTION OF BOWERS'S INNER-CIRCLE OPERATIONS

Informants eventually became so common among the White Knights that FBI summary reports cite more than eighty different (unnamed) sources in the same document. This was part and parcel of the FBI's national Counter Intelligence Program (COINTELPRO), a massive effort that also targeted groups ranging from the Black Panthers to Dr. King's Southern Christian Leadership Conference (SCLC).[25]

King had become a thorn in the side of FBI director J. Edgar Hoover. Hoover was obsessed with the idea that King was under the influence of communists and that King's civil rights organization, SCLC, was "communist affiliated." King had also complained about the FBI's failure to protect civil rights protestors in the South, something Hoover felt was a local law enforcement issue not involving federal statutes.[26] Any complaint about the bureau was something Hoover took very personally. His animosity toward King had even led one of his senior agents to send a letter to King exposing purported sexual improprieties. The substance of the letter can be read to imply that King's only honorable choice was to drop out of the civil rights movement—or commit suicide. The details in the letter (and on an accompanying tape recording) were based on alleged sexual liaisons uncovered through COINTELPRO surveillance on the civil rights leader.[27]

Regardless of whom it targeted, COINTELPRO aimed to sow the seeds of internal dissent and paranoia within each organization, creating a parasitic environment where the members would turn on each other. Jackson field office agent Jim Ingram described one somewhat humorous example of this. Having subjected many of the White Knights to ongoing surveillance, Jackson agents recognized that there was more than a hint of truth to the stereotype that Klansmen had a tendency to sleep with each others' spouses. Also recognizing the destabilizing effects this could have on the local members, the agents began leaving anonymous notes in the mailboxes of the two-timed Kluckers. "We know your wife was at so-and-so's house, do you?" the note would read. Before long, Ingram said, Klansmen began to resent and turn on one another.[28]

Though humorous, this kind of creative harassment may, in fact, make light of what was a serious rivalry between the FBI's Jackson field office and the White Knights in Mississippi. The battle between local FBI agents in Jackson and the White Knights of the Ku Klux Klan of Mississippi was probably more intense than any law enforcement confrontation with any Klan group in the nation. Beyond standard COINTELPRO operations, agents physically confronted Klansmen in front of their families. A growing body of evidence suggests that they were willing to import organized crime figures from out of the state to physically abuse and coerce Klansmen into providing information on key crimes.[29] If this seems extreme, one must remember that it came in response to a Klan group that placed senior FBI agents on assassination hit lists, something that was out of bounds even for Mafia leaders. Beyond being the most violent Klan in the country, the Mississippi White Knights treated law enforcement with a disrespect that came from viewing themselves as above the law.

Their arrogance is illustrated by the astonishingly aggressive behavior of Danny Joe Hawkins. Suspected of numerous terrorist bombings, Hawkins's well-known anti-Semitism made him a chief suspect (along with his father Joe Denver Hawkins and fellow White Knight Julius Harper) in the bombing of Mississippi Jewish leader Perry Nussbaum's home in 1967. When two FBI agents followed a speeding Harper in his car, the two Hawkins men pursued the FBI car, eventually forcing it to a stop in a parking lot, at which point father and son held the FBI agents at gunpoint until FBI backup arrived to save the day.[30] Still, Danny Joe Hawkins never went to jail for that confrontation, nor did he go to prison for any one of the numerous bombing efforts of which he was suspected.

Such apparent immunity had become common in Mississippi in the 1960s, reinforcing the hubris of the White Knights. L. E. Matthews, widely suspected of being the White Knights bomb maker (and their eventual Grand Wizard), never even went to trial for planning a bombing. And when White Knights members were tried and convicted, juries sentenced them to shockingly small jail terms. Bowers and White Knight Cecil Price, convicted of having masterminded the murders of the three young civil rights activists in the Mississippi Burning case, received only ten-year and six-year sentences respectively. This created a cycle whereby the FBI would be forced to increase its pursuit of the White Knights, even as the White Knights became more brazen in their violence.

This same cycle of enmity and escalation characterized the confrontation between local law enforcement in the White Knights strongholds of Meridian and Jackson, Mississippi. According to reporter Jack Nelson, Police Chief C. L. Gunn formed two groups to counter the Klan, "one under Sergeant Lester (Gigolo) Joyner and a larger one [that] dressed in black shirts and trousers for its night operations."[31] Nelson continued: "[T]he blackshirts waged their own 'COINTELPRO' of anti-Klan harassment, sometimes going so far as to set off small explosions outside Klansmen's houses or shooting into their homes to intimidate them."[32] In response, the White Knights actually prepared a hit list that included not only Jewish leaders but also Chief Gunn and Special Agent Sam Jennings of the Jackson FBI field office.[33] As late as March 1968, even with prison time pending, Bowers asked Julius Harper to assassinate Roy Moore, the head of the Jackson field office.[34] Before long, the Jackson FBI field office, the local police, and the Anti-Defamation League (alarmed at the violence directed at local Jews) would combine forces to arrange a sting operation with the Roberts brothers, suspected inner-circle operatives who had become FBI informants. The sting uncovered yet another evolution in Bowers's tactics—the use of outsiders to commit his violent deeds.

CHAPTER 5

OUTER RAGE

S am Bowers's strategy of provocation, of propaganda of the deed, of brutal and violent attacks, remained consistent throughout the period in
which he led the White Knights. His tactics sometimes confused his own
general membership, but Bowers himself operated with a larger agenda, using the group's members to his own ends. As time passed, Bowers shared
some of his own theology and insights into that larger agenda with a select
group—local people he knew and could trust to carry out targeted acts of
terror, his inner circle.

Over the longer term, with the need for more extreme provocations in
the midst of increasing FBI and law enforcement pressure on his own inner-
circle members, Bowers was forced to network more extensively and to bring
in outsiders to supplement his elite, core members. His inner-circle operatives were subject to increasingly stringent FBI surveillance as well as outright criminal prosecutions, making violent operations much more difficult.
Bowers himself was one of seven defendants convicted on October 20, 1967,
for the conspiracy to kill Michael Schwerner, Andrew Goodman, and James
Chaney in the Mississippi Burning murders in Neshoba County, Mississippi,
in 1964. Bowers and inner-circle operative Alton Wayne Roberts—the triggerman in the killing of the three civil rights workers—were sentenced to ten
years (of which Bowers would serve six) in December 1967.[1]

But Bowers remained free on appeal bond until he was jailed, in
November 1968, for masterminding the firebombing of the home of black

voting rights activist Vernon Dahmer. Although he was not convicted for Dahmer's murder, Bowers had exhausted his legal appeals for the Mississippi Burning conviction by early 1970 and was transferred to prison that year.[2] However, in the period while he was out on appeal bond and before he went to jail, Bowers was believed to have ordered as many as twenty additional acts of terrorism[3], a wave of violence made possible through the use of outside terrorists who supplemented his remaining inner-circle zealots.

These outsiders were not rank-and-file Klansmen but were, like most inner-circle members, true believers in Bowers's larger agenda and Reverend Wesley Swift's religious aspiration for a race war. Understanding how Bowers used these different subsets of the White Knights, separately and in conjunction with each other, is important, as several of these individuals would be directly and indirectly implicated in Martin Luther King's murder.

Bowers was hardly the first radical to outsource violence—either to other radicals or to professional criminals. As early as 1958, J. B. Stoner was promising Alabama Klansmen that he would bring outsiders from Georgia to Alabama in hopes of killing key civil rights leaders—among them the Reverend Fred Shuttlesworth and Dr. Martin Luther King Jr. The more sophisticated leaders in the white supremacist movement, like Stoner, understood that farming out violence to outsiders frustrated criminal investigators who concentrated their surveillance on local malcontents.

The fact that someone like Stoner would use operatives across state lines also left the true sponsors with solid alibis and no physical connection to the crimes. Had King or Shuttlesworth been killed in 1958, there would have been no shortage of local suspects who wanted both men dead, enough to probably divert and exhaust any investigation before it turned its attention beyond Birmingham. The net effect of using outsiders, especially for a strategic planner like Bowers, was to allow Klan leaders to intensify their violence right under the watchful eye of local and national law enforcement.

That Bowers understood this advantage is obvious from his behavior in the immediate aftermath of the Mississippi Burning killings of the three civil rights workers in Neshoba County, Mississippi. Fearing that intense scrutiny by the FBI would bring new charges and new legal fees, Bowers ordered his rank-and-file members to cease violent actions for several months, while at the same time he directly arranged a bombing of a home being used for civil rights activity in Vicksburg, Mississippi. According to one informant, Bowers justified the Vicksburg attack by saying, "They will not find out who did that one, as I sent someone in from the outside."[4]

Still, outsourcing violent acts to secondary groups of right-wing terror-ists opens the gates to the always-present dilemma of mutual trust. Especially in an environment where the FBI is inserting informants and provo-cateurs into a variety of like-minded organizations to foment rivalries and discord, knowing who is reliable and who isn't trustworthy is vital to the very functioning of a group—particularly to a leader as security conscious and notoriously paranoid as Samuel Bowers. This was the same man who, after all, considered firing every state officer from the White Knights of the Ku Klux Klan of Mississippi so he could be sure the group was free of in-formants.[5]

To navigate this dilemma, Bowers appears to have placed his faith in the power of religious zealotry to guarantee loyalty, turning to two mem-bers of what one White Knight called the Swift Underground. It seems quite likely that the two Swift devotees, Thomas Albert "Tommy" Tarrants III and Kathy Ainsworth, were accepted on the recommendation of extremist and suspected serial bomber Sidney Barnes, who had mentored both individu-als in Mobile, Alabama.[6] In 1967 and 1968, Bowers assigned Tarrants and Ainsworth to work with some of his most trusted operatives in a campaign of violence that rocked Mississippi and confounded law enforcement for months. Tarrants had been a mentee not only of Sidney Barnes but also of local and national NSRP leaders such as Admiral John Crommelin. Part of that mentoring involved Tarrants's indoctrination into the worldview of someone he would later describe as his hero—the Reverend Wesley Swift.[7]

Bowers's use of Kathy Ainsworth as a secondary inner-circle operative was probably even more ingenious. It was rare enough for women to have any kind of serious role in the KKK, but to use one for actual operations was unheard of. That Ainsworth happened to be an attractive elementary school teacher only made her less conspicuous. But Ainsworth was literally raised on Swift's anti-Semitic and racist message. Her mother, Margaret Capomacchia, was a virulent racist who took her daughter from Florida to Alabama to hear Swift tapes at Sidney Barnes's home. Barnes, in fact, walked Ainsworth down the aisle at her wedding (her mother and father were estranged), and Kathy roomed with Barnes's daughter, Bonnie, at college.[8] Eventually, acting for Bowers, Tarrants and Ainsworth would conduct nighttime terror attacks—planting explosives at synagogues and the homes of Jewish residents and civil rights leaders.

Bowers's own penchant for secrecy made the pair of outsiders even more formidable, and they baffled law enforcement with their campaign of violence for months. Bowers himself only met with Tarrants under very guarded and secretive conditions, events that Tarrants says were split between discussing attacks and discussing the teachings of Wesley Swift. Only a handful of Bowers's most trusted members even knew who the two were. And even fewer had direct contact with them.

The White Knights' most direct and ongoing contact with Tarrants and Ainsworth was through Danny Joe Hawkins of Jackson, Mississippi, a dark-haired dockworker who documents describe as becoming more and more open to Swift's message by 1968.[9] Danny Joe Hawkins actually arranged bombings with Ainsworth and Tarrants and was known to use Tarrants's car to do attacks on his own.[10] The younger Hawkins was the primary link to the other inner-circle members, the individuals who had proven themselves as the most trusted members within the White Knights organization itself.

By the summer of 1968, three months after King's murder, a major crack opened into the world of the White Knights' inner circle. The Roberts brothers were facing serious prison time for their role in civil rights violence in Mississippi. Radicalized by informant reports of hit lists on law enforcement officers, and joined by an Anti-Defamation League (ADL) that was justifiably alarmed by the attacks on Jewish targets, a group of policemen and FBI agents promised Alton Wayne and Raymond Roberts reduced sentences and a large cash reward if they would turn on the individuals responsible for the wave of recent bombings in Jackson.

The Roberts brothers agreed, accepting the ADL-provided money, but law enforcement wanted more than just testimony. They had the two inner-circle men play the role of double agents, meeting with Danny Joe Hawkins and Tarrants, pushing the latter two to bomb the home of Rabbi Meyer Davidson in Meridian, Mississippi. Hawkins pulled out at the last minute, and Kathy Ainsworth replaced him. Law enforcement was waiting, according to some with shoot-to-kill orders; as Tarrants went to plant the bomb the night of June 28, 1968, police opened fire, killing Kathy and seriously wounding Tommy.[11] This "Bonnie-and-Clyde" encounter with FBI and police officers stung Bowers at the moment he was heading to prison. Bowers wrote an angry letter to Tom Tucker, one of the police officers who participated in the sting, saying the following:

> *Mr. Tucker, I just do not know what we Christians can do about these Synagogue of Satan Jews other than to oppose them in every possible way and pray for Divine Relief. . . . They try to teach us to love the world, but God's Word Orders us to Love HIM and then also to love our neighbor. The neighbor of a God Loving Christian is obviously any other God Loving Christian. A human animal which resides in a Christian Community . . . is, by its own choice, not the neighbor of a Christian . . . I think it is perfectly obvious to anyone that cares to think about it seriously that Kathy Ainsworth as a Christian, American Patriot, was doing her limited best to preserve Christian Civilization by helping to destroy the body of an animal of Satan's Synagogue, or, failing in that, to terrorize the animal into at least a semblance of submission to God's law.*[12]

It is interesting to note that Bowers's anger did not appear to extend to the wounding of Tommy Tarrants. He barely referenced him at all in the letter, and not by name. Under the original law enforcement plan, Danny Joe

Hawkins was supposed to be one of the victims of this sting operation, and some informed outside observers believe that both Hawkins and Tarrants were not supposed to escape alive. Even the police expressed a measure of remorse at the fact that they had killed a woman and not Hawkins.

For their part, the Roberts brothers boldly returned to Meridian, even after their supposed treachery had been exposed, and flaunted their new money, given to them by a Jewish group, in the presence of men who they supposedly feared would kill them in retaliation.[13] Sam Bowers, the hater of Jews and the man the Roberts brothers feared most, does not to appear to have ordered any attacks on the brothers, who steadfastly refused to testify against him. Bowers was going to prison, leaving the White Knights in the hands of L .E. Matthews, but he still had the power to order "Number 4s," the code word for murders. That he didn't do so against the Roberts brothers, the turncoats whose legal fees had helped drain the White Knights treasury, is strange. Perhaps the reason for Bowers's passivity lies in a mysterious comment he made to an audience two weeks before the betrayal that was bought with money from Jewish interests. Bowers told his followers that "the Jews will finance the White Knights."[14]

If it seems fanciful to speculate that Bowers would somehow use the Roberts brothers as triple agents to set up Danny Joe Hawkins and Tommy Tarrants—along the way pilfering some of the money the ADL provided for the White Knights themselves—it certainly was not beyond his strategic capacity. A bigger problem would be to suggest a reason why Bowers would set up two of his most trusted, covert operatives to be eliminated by law enforcement. While Tarrants's value as a covert operative had clearly been exposed by late May 1968, Hawkins was still, presumably, a valued and dedicated extremist. If Bowers planned such a diabolical move, it may have connected to a story that Kathy Ainsworth's mother would tell a police informant after her daughter's death, a tale that brings the White Knights, and their tactics, fully into the picture of the King assassination.

THE INNER CIRCLE AND THE ASSASSINATION OF
MARTIN LUTHER KING JR.?

At the beginning of August 1968, weeks after the Meridian sting that killed Kathy Ainsworth and wounded Tommy Tarrants, Margaret Capomacchia apparently called on Willie Somersett to get something off her chest. Distraught over the killing of her daughter, Capomacchia told her fellow Floridian, a labor union operative, explosive news. She had inside information on the conspiracy to murder Martin Luther King Jr. four months before, in Memphis.[15]

Capomacchia told Somersett that a group of White Knights from Jackson, colleagues of her deceased daughter, were part of a plot to kill King. She identified the men as having been connected to an upcoming trial in Jackson, Mississippi, for the bombing of a real estate company in that city. From the context of her description of the trial, as well as other identifying information, it is possible to identify the individuals she accused of a King conspiracy: Burris Dunn, Julius Harper, Robert Earl Wilson, and one additional individual, who is still living, and whose identity we will protect. According to Somersett, another individual she implicated, who was not part of the bombing trial in Jackson, was Tommy Tarrants.

Capomacchia said that King was shot once but not from the rooming house bathroom across the street from the Lorraine Motel; rather an assassin killed King from the brush in the same general vicinity as the rooming house. James Earl Ray, the man eventually arrested for the murder, was a patsy, according to Capomacchia's account to Somersett. She added that an inside operative within King's entourage had helped the plot succeed and that a CB radio diversion was used in some capacity to monitor or distract the police after the shooting.

Somersett had been a long-time undercover informant for both the FBI and the Miami Police. In fact, it was Somersett who helped uncover the plot against King, on tape, from Sidney Barnes in 1964. Somersett, not fully clear about what Capomacchia was even saying, and highlighting her emotional distress, reported this information on King's murder to the FBI, who then

reported it to the Jackson field office in Mississippi.[16] The field office investigated the whereabouts of the individuals that Capomacchia accused. The
Jackson agents claimed that all these individuals had alibis on April 4, 1968;
their whereabouts had been verified shortly after King's murder, although
specifics had been given for only one of the accused.[17]

In the meanwhile, Somersett returned to Capomacchia for more information. Her story became clearer and more refined. She focused her charges
of conspiracy on Tommy Tarrants, moving away from the other individuals.
She implied that Tarrants fled Memphis, first to Atlanta, then to North Carolina, where he stayed with an individual phonetically named in the documents
as "Henderson"; upon being forced away by "Henderson" (Tarrants was too
"hot"), the fugitive then went to visit his mentor, Sidney Barnes, in Mobile.[18]
The FBI followed up by interviewing Capomacchia directly, where she denied
knowing any of the people Somersett even named.[19] The FBI itself had soured
on Somersett in the mid-1960s, saying that he ceased providing reliable information, and generally dismissed Capomacchia's account, saying she was
mentally unstable.[20]

In dismissing this story outright, the FBI ignored several key items.
The FBI's alibi accounts seem to ring hollow when one considers that the
Jackson office sent fingerprint records of many of the accused conspirators
to the FBI crime lab on April 16, 1968, in connection with the King investigation. They were among the sixteen names of White Knight terrorists the
Jackson field office felt should be examined as possibly connected to the
King murder.[21] If the Jackson field office had definitively accounted for Capomacchia's alleged conspirators' whereabouts immediately after the King
assassination, why did they ask the crime lab to compare the prints of these
same individuals to prints recovered from the Memphis crime scene?

The FBI also missed obvious evidence that Capomacchia clearly knew
all the individuals she accused. She would, within weeks of this report, move
to Jackson, Mississippi, and openly congregate with them on repeated occasions. In accusing Tarrants specifically, she was accusing someone she personally met at the home of Sidney Barnes. Furthermore, the FBI did learn

that Tarrants had stayed in North Carolina in April 1968, with one J. A. *Hendrixson*, a Swift follower, whose house and land neighbors described as being used for paramilitary training by right-wing extremists.[22] (The area, to this day, is a hotbed for right-wing extremism.) Additionally, the claim that Capomacchia was mentally unstable ignored the obvious fact that her daughter was just killed; a grieving mother is not necessarily a delusional one. More than anything, because they chose to hold this lead in abeyance, and because they dismissed Somersett's report, it is apparent that the FBI never received the most important corroboration of Capomacchia's account: Sidney Barnes gave a very similar story to Somersett just weeks after Capomacchia gave her tale of the King assassination.

Apparently Barnes's account to Somersett went only to the Miami Police Department, who still valued Somersett as an informant. In these reports, Barnes told Somersett that Tarrants did flee to Mobile, just as Capomacchia claimed, several days after King's assassination. Barnes confirmed that Tarrants's car was used in some CB radio operation in Memphis. And he expressed great fear over what Tarrants might say to authorities about this, after Tarrants's capture following the Meridian sting.[23] Earlier reports in the same Miami PD file show that Barnes had approached Somersett about meeting Tarrants even before the Meridian sting, before Tarrants was known to the public as a terrorist bomber.[24]

The reference by both individuals to a CB radio story is fascinating, in light both of Klan tactics and of a documented example of just such an incident in Memphis, immediately after the murder. A famous incident that has been investigated and covered in several books on the King murder involved a CB radio broadcast that diverted investigators from their pursuit of the true killer. Within a half hour of King's murder, police received reports from CB radio broadcasters who were following a fellow operator's distress call. The operator asked that the police be notified that he and fellow drivers were in pursuit of a white Ford Mustang speeding out of Memphis, heading north. This broadcast was later determined to be a hoax. Congress considered the possibility that it was a deliberate hoax, as part of a conspiracy.[25]

For one thing it clearly led the Memphis police away from the direction of a fleeing James Earl Ray (who was racing south in a white Ford Mustang). Moreover the operator, who never identified himself in contradiction to local laws, clearly wanted the police to be notified of this fictional car chase. The reference to the getaway vehicle suggests the operator was monitoring police signals and responding, potentially, with a diversion. While we may never know if false alibis were planned for a King conspiracy (as James Earl Ray was the only man ever charged), and while the evidence for a policy of "sitting-on-go" for the King murder is at best suggestive (Ray apparently stalked King in a number of cities), the CB radio incident is one of the clearest examples of Klan tactics possibly put into practice on April 4, 1968.[26]

The CB radio may have been covered in newspapers at the time, but it was not widely reported[27], and the presence of this component in both Capomacchia's and Barnes's stories suggests two possible interpretations: The stories are independently confirming the same story or the two individuals had coordinated a false story. But Capomacchia herself told Somersett that she was very upset with Barnes and his wife, Pauline, blaming them for her daughter's death. On the surface, the accounts appear to be independent and complementary.

But there are clear problems with the Somersett reports, especially with Capomacchia's story. One of the accused did have a potentially solid alibi recorded in FBI records. He was attending the J. B. Stoner rally in Meridian on the evening of April 4; not only was he identified by watchful agents, but also police had caught him speeding the wrong way on a one-way street right after the event. While it is not clear if he arrived at the Stoner rally at its outset (or later), he would have had to have sped from Memphis to Meridian to get to Mississippi by the recorded time of the ticket.[28]

More problematic for the story was the accusation Capomacchia made against Robert Earl Wilson. He was among a handful of individuals connected to a trial for a real estate office bombing in Jackson. Capomacchia specifically cited that trial as involving the men in the King conspiracy.[29] But Wilson was an FBI informant, who testified against the other individuals on trial. Wilson's betrayal would have been particularly offensive to his fellow White Knights, as he was the individual (before L. E. Matthews) selected to replace Bowers as Imperial Wizard once Bowers went to prison. That he fled Mississippi in 1967 with the wife of one of the accused bombers makes the idea that he would join any of these White Knights in a conspiracy against King that much more improbable.[30]

In fact, what is remarkable about the Capomacchia report is that almost all the individuals she originally accused of the King conspiracy were individuals described in documents as being "on the outs" with Bowers in 1968. Documents show that Bowers suspected Burris Dunn, one of the individuals Capomacchia apparently accused, of being an informant.[31] Another of the accused, Julius Harper, had turned down Bowers's order to kill famed FBI agent Roy Moore in March 1968.[32] If Bowers harbored ill will toward these men as of June 1968, then Barnes and Capomacchia would have been doing him a service in possibly framing these individuals for the King murder or at least causing them a hard time with authorities.

Just as suspiciously, Capomacchia, for all her supposed anger at Sidney and Pauline Barnes, would, within weeks of her report to Somersett, move to Jackson and all but live with the pair. Reports from September 1968 on through 1969 show nothing but mutual admiration between them, and they all actively worked, with associates in the White Knights, to spread Wesley Swift's religious message and J. B. Stoner's political ideas.[33] This suggests that Capomacchia's anger with Barnes was either for show or short-lived— too short-lived, one would suspect, for a grieving mother who supposedly blamed the Barnes couple for her daughter's demise.

The implications of these two suspicious and overlapping accounts are clear. If Capomacchia and Barnes were telling the truth to Somersett, then it would be stunning evidence from individuals with close, personal connections to the White Knights that Bowers's inner-circle operatives, along with Tommy Tarrants, were part of a plot to murder Martin Luther King Jr. This seems unlikely, however, as both accounts are too flawed. Two possibilities then remain: Either Somersett himself was making up stories to tell law enforcement, or Capomacchia and Barnes were part of a concerted effort to use Somersett as a dupe to provide deceptive information to those investigating the King murder.

Both of these possibilities will be explored in the following chapter. Even if it could be proven that Capomacchia and Barnes were using Somersett to frame someone like Tarrants, one could argue that this need not be sinister. Tarrants's life as a violent terrorist was well publicized in newspapers across the country after his capture following the June 30, 1968, nighttime sting that wounded him and ended Kathy Ainsworth's life. Perhaps Capomacchia and Barnes were maligning Tarrants in hopes of discrediting anything he might say that could implicate them in extremist crimes. Barnes, for one, expressed great concern over what Tarrants might say to law enforcement investigators.

To hold truly sinister implications for the King crime, Capomacchia's and Barnes's accounts in August 1968 would have to be part of a consistent effort to frame Tarrants that went back to at least April 1968, and possibly even to late March 1968. On through April 1968, the Tommy Tarrants known to federal authorities was just a racist rabble-rouser from Mobile, Alabama, with a fondness for guns; he had no real criminal record, although he had jumped bond in March in connection with an illegal weapons charge.[34] No one had connected Tarrants to the litany of bombings and shootings for which he now claims credit in public speeches bemoaning his criminal past.[35] Before May 1968, Tarrants was only known as a militant racist—as someone *worth* framing—to those in Wesley Swift's Christian Identity network, to individuals such as Sam Bowers. The person who was terrorizing Jews and blacks in Mississippi from 1967 to 1968 was, as of April 4, 1968, an outsider known to law enforcement only as "The Man."[36] Is it possible "The Man" was indeed framed as part of a conspiracy?

CHAPTER 6

THE KLAN AND "THE MAN"

That was my ambition, to shoot Dr. King. I hated Dr. King.
—Thomas Tarrants III

While writing on the White Knights' 1967–1968 campaign of violence in his excellent book *Terror in the Night* (1993), Pulitzer Prize–winning reporter Jack Nelson all but buried this alleged quote from Tommy Tarrants. Nelson also discovered from Tarrants's testimony that the latter had bought a rifle from Wesley Swift in February 1968 in order to "use it to shoot Martin Luther King, Jr. . . ."[1]

Such a statement would seem to have warranted further attention from a highly regarded investigative journalist like Nelson; however Nelson asked no further questions on the subject of the rifle purchase. By the time Nelson had interviewed Tarrants for the 1993 book, Tarrants had made a dramatic prison conversion from the theology of Christian Identity to evangelical, mainstream Christianity. He even went on to graduate from a credentialed theological seminary and become ordained.[2] So Nelson accepted Tarrants's statement that he was in North Carolina when King was killed.

Nelson's definitive account of a synagogue bombing in Meridian, Mississippi, explains that by April 1968, Tarrants was on the run from agents in the FBI's Mobile, Alabama, field office, who were searching for him on a violation related to illegal firearms possession. Later, in 2007, when asked about the rifle, Tarrants claimed that he had bought it for a totally different purpose and that he had never said that his personal goal was to kill Dr. King. He reiterated that he was in North Carolina when King was killed, and he denied any connection whatsoever to the King murder. He made those remarks in response to the informant reports discussed in the previous chapter, reports implying that he had a role in the King murder.[3]

There is no indication that Tarrants had ever seen the reports in question or other documents that demonstrate that he was among the first persons of interest in Dr. King's murder. When that information was recently presented to Special Agent Jim Ingram, one of the FBI agents who had arrested Tarrants in July 1968 for the attempted bombing of the Meridian synagogue, the former agent was shocked. He responded that, as of April 1968, "he [Tarrants] was not even on our radar."[4] Ingram was specifically referring to a bombshell discovery we made: namely, that Tom Tarrants was somehow one of the earliest persons of interest in the King assassination.

The mystery of how Tarrants's mug shot became one of the first pictures the Birmingham FBI showed to the gun-shop owners that sold the alleged King murder weapon is something that will be examined in the course of this chapter. There are several alternative explanations, including the probability that Tarrants was set up as an unwitting patsy in the King murder.

But to more fully understand the operations of the White Knight inner circle and its terror tactics, we first need to proceed with a more in-depth study of this individual who, for several months in 1967 and 1968, eluded federal investigators who were searching for a violent, racist bomber in Mississippi. Lacking a name, the FBI referred to him simply as "The Man."[5]

GOING RADICAL

Thomas Albert Tarrants III was born and reared in Mobile, Alabama. According to Tarrants himself, he became heavily involved in anti-integration and related activities between the ages of seventeen and nineteen, beginning with an interest in the John Birch Society, then the Klan, and finally involvement with the National States' Rights Party.[6] While in high school, Tarrants became active in opposing school integration. He was suspended because of those activities and at that point began to seek out other militant racists.[7] Tarrants first made contact with local National States' Rights Party members and other Mobile radicals and under their influence became aware of the Christian Identity message of the Reverend Wesley Swift. A NSRP leader in Mobile introduced Tarrants to two "professional radicals" who were part of a very militant group that had first formed in Miami but had been forced out of Florida, settling in locations from Mobile to North Carolina, forming an "underground network."[8]

In particular, Tarrants came to know Sidney Barnes, the man who, in September 1963, plotted to kill King with other radicals. Barnes had an extensive history of militancy in the Miami area and had recently moved from Miami to Mobile. Tarrants found that Barnes shared many of his own racist and anti-Semitic views.[9] He began to visit the Barnes family, listening to tape-recorded sermons delivered by Wesley Swift in his California ministry. It was at Barnes's house where Tarrants first met Kathy Ainsworth in 1966. Ainsworth, a future schoolteacher, was there visiting her college roommate, Sidney Barnes's daughter, Bonnie.[10]

RADICAL NETWORKING

After Tarrants dropped out of high school, he began extended contact with senior leaders of various militant groups. First he visited retired Admiral John Crommelin (a notorious anti-Semite) and spent time on the admiral's estate outside Montgomery, Alabama. Crommelin, you recall, was a senior NSRP officer who would run on their national ticket for vice president in 1960.[11] He was mentioned in FBI reports as having been involved in meetings in the fall of 1963 in which a plot against Dr. King was discussed. The meetings supposedly involved Crommelin, Gale, and Barnes. Crommelin, as the National States' Rights Party's 1960 vice-presidential nominee, must have been a major influence on the young Thomas Tarrants, but he was only the first nationally known militant to mentor him. Following his time with Crommelin, Tarrants described traveling on to NSRP headquarters in

Birmingham, Alabama, to meet with Dr. Edward Fields, the NSRP executive director.[12] We have no details of this meeting; however, Tarrants was clearly impressed by all his NSRP contacts, who generally were not only more militant but also added strong religious and anticommunist beliefs to his developing racism. As he grew to align his worldview more and more with that of men like Fields and Crommelin, Tarrants and his brethren embraced the Reverend Wesley Swift's overarching objective. Tarrants would later tell one author that "our hope and dream was that a race war would come."[13]

Tarrants escalated his radical activities in 1964, participating in drive-by shootings at the homes of local integration figures in Mobile. He described using radios to "monitor police frequencies" during those shootings.[14] As mentioned above, the use of radios for police monitoring was very common among Klan militants. An obvious CB radio antenna was observed on one of the cars that police suspected participated in the Birmingham church bombing. The lone Klansman actually convicted in the Birmingham bombing was known to monitor police radio channels and often would beat them to the scene of reports involving blacks, making citizens arrests and administering pistol whippings.[15]

During one of Tarrants's nighttime excursions to conduct drive-by shootings, he was picked up along with the local Mobile representative of the NSRP; Tarrants was convicted on a firearms charge and was placed on probation until his twenty-first birthday.[16] Tarrants's own account is vague in regard to details of his activities during the remainder of 1964 and into 1966, although he states that by the summer of 1967, at the age of twenty-one, he was personally acquainted with some of the top leaders of the American radical right.[17]

Tarrants's list of personal contacts included a veritable *Who's Who* of the leading racial extremists in America:

- *The head of the National States' Rights Party, Dr. Edward Fields*
- *The Imperial Wizard of the United Klans of America, Robert Shelton*

- *The leader of the Christian Identity movement, Dr. Wesley Swift*
- *The western head of the Minutemen and top Christian Identity aide, Dennis Mower*
- *The Imperial Wizard of the White Knights of Mississippi, Samuel Bowers*

Tarrants lists these contacts in his autobiography, *The Conversion of a Klansman,* written after his early release from prison as he was shifting his ideals to mainstream Christianity. In that same book, he discusses how, after meeting Bowers, he became the "head [of] a small, highly elite terrorist group" that "for nearly a year was responsible for planning the Klan's terrorist operations."[18] Investigative reporter Jerry Mitchell described Tarrants as convincing Bowers, through his persistence and enthusiasm, that only Tarrants could attack desired targets while Bowers and his cadre were under investigation from law enforcement. Bowers accepted the outsider into this new violent role but not without his customary caution. He and Tarrants would meet in secluded forests, where the two would plan attacks and discuss Wesley Swift's latest sermons.[19]

In his book, Jack Nelson states that one of the reasons for Tarrants's effectiveness in White Knight terrorist actions was that he never went to a rally and strictly guarded his identity, disappearing from the area after attacks.[20] This method of operation protected Tarrants from local FBI informants and infiltrators. Both Tarrants and Kathy Ainsworth were violent but unique in their ability to operate in total secrecy; their acts were completely unknown to those around them.[21]

The new terror campaign in which Tarrants became involved included an extended series of bombings, burnings, and shootings at synagogues and the homes of rabbis and Jewish community leaders. The wave of attacks against Jews actually began in North Carolina several months before it started in Mississippi. We do not know the extent to which the two campaigns were coordinated or to what extent Bowers actually influenced both. We do know that there were connections between individuals in both states and that Tarrants actually used a safe house in North Carolina, staying there between attacks in Mississippi.[22]

Nelson argues that the White Knights' shift to attacking Jewish targets was a response to Mississippi Jewish elites' increasing activism in favor of civil rights for blacks. But as the Reverend Edwin King, a leader within the Mississippi Freedom Democratic Party, noted, a number of Jewish leaders were already pushing for black civil rights as far back as 1961.[23] Most of the major civil rights agitation had already succeeded with the passage of major federal acts by 1965. So it would seem unlikely that the shift in Klan targets was revenge on the Jews for shaking off their indifference and pushing for civil rights.

A much more likely explanation is that the Jews were Bowers targets all along, but that the opportunity to attack them did not present itself until 1967. When fighting integration was at the forefront of Klan activities and the White Knights commanded a much larger following in Mississippi, Bowers could not convince his Kluckers to focus their priorities on attacking Jews above blacks.[24] But with his numbers dwindling and his tactics changing to using an inner core of true believers more amenable to Christian Identity beliefs, Bowers could finally attack the "Synagogue of Satan."

With a similar philosophy, based on the ministry of Wesley Swift, Tarrants compared himself to the Arab terrorists in Palestine—the war against the Jews was thus justified any means. Without a doubt, Tarrants was a sincere follower of Wesley Swift, traveling to California to meet and plan with Swift and his lieutenant Dennis Mower in early 1968. Tarrants describes this meeting as including "detailed discussions on ideology, strategy, and tactics."[25] The exact nature of Tarrants's introduction to Swift remains unknown; however, Swift was directly connected to several of Tarrants's NSRP mentors and had been the lead speaker during the NSRP's California recruiting drive in 1963. Connie Lynch, a Christian Identity minister and traveling representative for Swift, was the state organizer for the National States' Rights Party.[26] Sidney Barnes, as a major Swift advocate and eventually a Swift-ordained minister, would also have had channels of communication for introducing

Tarrants to Swift. And Sam Bowers was reportedly well-known to both Swift and Mower; according to information from a Los Angeles FBI informant, Tarrants was directly representing Bowers and the White Knights in the meetings with Swift.[27]

"THE MAN" AT WORK

At first blush, this all sounds rather incredible, but there is ample confirma-tion that a high school dropout, beginning at the age of eighteen, did establish personal relationships with the heads of some of the most radical, violent, and secretive organizations in the country. These men were paranoid about infiltrators, and justifiably so, given the success of FBI infiltration operations against them. But Tarrants became a major operative for the most secretive and paranoid racist of them all, Sam Bowers.[28] Tarrants remarked that at all key meetings with Bowers they would each take separate cars, drive separate routes, walk silently into the densest and most remote parts of a wooded area, and communicate in whispers. If circumstances did not permit that level of secrecy, then the conversation would be made via writing in a notebook that was handed back and forth, and after each exchange the page would be torn out, burned, and flushed down a toilet.[29]

It is also clear from FBI informants and other sources that Tarrants was in contact with the people he had named and that he almost immediately became Bowers's key terrorist operative. Yet, the highly effective informant network the FBI put into place was utterly unable to provide anything on Tarrants's identity, largely because he remained totally separated from Klan activities. He was isolated from local Mississippi Klan members and to a large extent functioned as an outsider, operating from Mobile and a safe house in North Carolina. His status as an outsider is confirmed in an FBI informant report on the White Knight hit squad in which both Tarrants and Ainsworth were described as "members of Dr. Wesley Swift's underground."[30] Beyond that, Tarrants was both effective and efficient, conducting attacks for almost half a year while maintaining virtual invisibility from the FBI, being referred to only as "The Man" in FBI memos.

It was only at the very end of May 1968 that the FBI began to speculate that

"The Man" was someone from Mobile with ties to the Klan in Mississippi.[31] In regard to what "The Man" had been doing, Tarrants's FBI file and eventual conviction indicate he had bombed Jewish and black targets and was suspected in a number of robberies in both Mississippi and Arkansas.[32] In his autobiography, Tarrants does not describe his specific acts of crimes while working with, or for, Bowers and the White Knights—other than the bombing attempt where Kathy Ainsworth was killed and he was captured. Instead he writes about the Jewish terror campaign as being an act of "the Klan."[33] He does describe his arrest, along with Bowers, on a mission to machine-gun a black man's home in Mississippi. This resulted in weapons charges against Tarrants, who would jump bond in March 1968. In a note he penned just one week before Dr. King's murder, on March 28, 1968, he wrote, "Please be advised that, I, Thomas A. Tarrants, have been underground and operating guerilla warfare."[34]

DESPERATE TIMES

By 1968, things had changed substantially for the NSRP, the White Knights, and the militant racist network in general. Much of the change was brought about by the national media reaction and the massive FBI response to the Mississippi Burning murders of civil rights workers Schwerner, Chaney, and Goodman. Following that, there was an equally aggressive bureau response to the terror campaign against Jewish targets that began in fall 1967. On a broader scale, the FBI was in the early stages of a new nationwide initiative targeting a broad range of groups and individuals seen as potentially "subversive." The targets of this operation included black militants, white racists, and a full spectrum of anti–Vietnam War groups. President Johnson had issued special directives broadly expanding the scope of law enforcement and the military, including participation of both national counterintelligence units and regional military intelligence groups in a totally unprecedented level of domestic intelligence collection and surveillance.[35]

In Mississippi, White Knight membership had peaked at five thousand in 1964 but dropped to an estimated fifteen hundred by 1966. Worse yet for Bowers, a significant number of the White Knights' more violent followers had been identified and were facing charges or were suspect as bureau informants.[36] Bowers and seven others had actually been convicted and sentenced to prison in October 1967, and FBI informant roles listed more than four hundred individuals who had provided some level of information. There was widespread discontent over the lack of funds for Klan members' legal defenses. Indeed, that had been an ongoing problem for Bowers since late in 1964. At one point he had proposed suspending bombings and "eliminations" for ninety days to allow the treasury to rebuild.[37] Several of Bowers's earlier cadre, including the Roberts brothers, had apparently split from him, and the FBI was actively soliciting them with deals for information.

The remaining White Knight inner circle was down to a small handful of individuals. Among that handful was Danny Joe Hawkins. But Hawkins was well-known to the FBI; he had been arrested in September 1967 after a confrontation with bureau agents investigating one of the first of the synagogue bombings. The reduced inner circle also included brothers Raymond and Alton Wayne Roberts, eventual informants who would participate in the sting that ended the new Jewish terror-bombing campaign, resulting in the capture of Thomas Tarrants and death of Kathy Ainsworth.[38]

Ainsworth had graduated high school in Florida and received several scholarship offers. She elected to attend the conservative Mississippi College, near Jackson, Mississippi. While attending school there, she shared a room with Bonnie Barnes. It appears that the Barnes family was well acquainted with Ainsworth's mother; they had moved from the Miami area to Mobile, Alabama, in late 1963 and had common associates in Miami. When Ainsworth married in August 1967, her mother, Margaret Capomacchia, selected the honeymoon destination—Christian Identity icon Gerald L. K. Smith's Christ of the Ozarks retreat in Arkansas.[39]

Ainsworth's mother was reported to have very militant racist views and was connected to like-minded individuals, both in Miami and elsewhere.[40] One of Capomacchia's friends owned a farm and house in North Carolina, used by militants from throughout the South.[41] In fact, she appears to have been networked to a wide variety of individuals who had been forced to move away from the Miami area and who settled across the South, from Mobile, Alabama, to North Carolina. Sidney Barnes was one of those individuals.

In 1968 Ainsworth was twenty-six years old and worked as a fifth-grade teacher at Lorena Duling Elementary School.[42] She, like Tarrants, had been heavily influenced by Sidney Barnes, a militant racist and the father of her college roommate. Ainsworth had first met Tarrants in 1966 at the home of Sidney Barnes in Mobile. She shared with Tarrants the common religious and racist views of the Reverend Wesley Swift. Indeed, a card for the Christian Nationalist Crusade, led by the ultraracist Gerald L. K. Smith of Los Angeles, was found in Ainsworth's purse at the time of her death. Ainsworth also carried a calling card from Sam Bowers in her purse.[43] And Sidney Barnes was reported by an FBI informant as saying that Ainsworth was a trusted colleague of Swift's aide, Colonel William Gale.[44] Like Tarrants, Ainsworth was personally connected to many of the leaders of American's radical right.

In the spring of 1968, Tarrants and Ainsworth were extremely important to Sam Bowers, "unique in their ability to operate in total secrecy from those around them,"[45] Bowers had been forced to shift to extremely small cells for terror attacks—only one to two individuals. And in a total break with past operations, Bowers himself personally participated in some of the attacks. He and Tarrants had done one of the first of the Jewish bombings together in September 1967.[46]

In December 1967, the two men were arrested together, with a variety of weapons including a machine gun.[47] This was extremely unusual for Bowers, who for years had never personally involved himself in actual acts of violence. A government informant said that Danny Joe Hawkins was mystified by his decision to accompany Tarrants to a seemingly random shooting, raising questions about his intent. Certain facts of that incident lead us to speculate that Bowers may have been testing Tarrants, having begun to suspect Tarrants as a possible FBI informant. It is interesting that the main charge against Tarrants—possession of an illegal firearm—came as a result of a request from Bowers; the Klan leader asked the arresting officer to get his sweater from the vehicle, at which point the officer discovered the sub-machine gun under the garment.

If Bowers was looking for evidence that Tarrants was a legitimate follower as opposed to an informant, his suspicions may have been raised by the events that followed. Bowers was charged, tried, and acquitted of the firearms charge within three weeks of the arrest; Tarrants, on the other hand, never even found his way into a court on the matter. In March, as noted, charges were brought against him, and, again, he jumped bond; the firearms trial never materialized once Tarrants was arrested for the attempted bombing of the Meridian synagogue. Whether or not Bowers was testing Tarrants in December 1967 or whether or not the disparity in their judicial treatment ignited Bowers's considerable paranoia is impossible to tell. But is relevant when one considers the reasons why Bowers may have chosen Tarrants as a potential patsy for the King murder, a process that may have involved Wesley Swift himself.

As a result of the arrest with Bowers, Tarrants left Mississippi, returned to his home in Mobile, and shortly afterward made a trip to California in March 1968, returning to Mobile later. The trip to California included meetings and planning sessions with Wesley Swift and his aide Dennis Mower.[48] It was on that trip that Tarrants supposedly obtained the rifle previously discussed. Tarrants has never elaborated on the meeting with Swift and Mower, but he did make one further comment about his objectives for the rifle to reporter Jerry Mitchell in an interview in late 2007. Mitchell pointed out that Nelson's book quoted Tarrants as saying that his ambition was to shoot Dr. King, that he hated King. In the Mitchell interview, Tarrants did acknowledge holding those views at the time but pointed out that "a lot of people in the South hated Martin Luther King."[49]

He also acknowledged that he had bought a rifle from Swift, but he stated that the real purpose of the trip was to become acquainted with Swift, to whose sermon recordings he had listened. He described himself as being under the influence of Swift. At the time of the trip to California, James Earl Ray was living in Los Angeles, about an hour away from Swift's church in

Lancaster. Tarrants told Mitchell that he had never met nor heard of Ray.[50]

On March 23, 1968, Tarrants went underground to begin a self-described "guerilla" campaign, committing himself to "military" action. Despite the strongly worded statements in his personal notebook the FBI found, Tarrants wrote in his autobiography that upon going underground he actually went to a safe house in the North Carolina mountains to "relax and wait for the heat to subside." This safe house belonged to a couple who had been "part of the Miami radical group that had scattered throughout the South."[51] Nelson was more specific in his book on Tarrants, describing the house as being near Franklin, North Carolina, and being used by friends of Wesley Swift, whom Tarrants had visited in Los Angeles only weeks earlier. The house was known to the FBI as a base for militants from throughout the South—Mississippi, Alabama, Georgia, and Florida. The FBI also described the woods near the safe house as a site for paramilitary training, including target practice.[52]

Tarrants described staying at the North Carolina house for "several leisurely weeks" and returning to Mississippi only once to meet with Bowers and other key people.[53] His remarks would suggest that he was in or operating from North Carolina during the months of April, May, and most of June (he says that he "spent a great deal of time in North Carolina"),[54] During that time the White Knights' terror campaign continued unabated. Tarrants wrote that he returned to Mississippi only once, in late June, to "coordinate the planning and direct the bombing of Meyer Davidson's house."[55]

In *Terror in the Night,* Jack Nelson tells a different story, describing Tarrants frequently commuting back to Mississippi from North Carolina to machine-gun homes and bomb synagogues. This becomes somewhat open to question because Bowers did have other operatives, including the brothers Raymond and Alton Wayne Roberts, who also conducted bombings, burnings, and shootings in this time frame. The FBI turned the Roberts brothers into informants, and they then pointed the finger at Tarrants for many of the terror acts for which they had been suspected. They would then betray Tarrants to law enforcement, in the sting that would see him wounded and Kathy Ainsworth killed on June 30, 1968.[56]

Tarrants says that he was at the North Carolina safe house when King was killed. Yet somehow, someway, his identity came to the attention of the Birmingham field office of the FBI in connection with King's murder. Within two days of the assassination, the FBI had traced the rifle found in Memphis to a gun shop in Birmingham, Alabama. Agents proceeded to the shop and began to question its staff about the rifle, showing them photos of eight men as possible suspects in its purchase. Seven of the eight men were local Birmingham men; their identities and photographs appear to have come from the local Birmingham law enforcement. The eighth photograph shown was that of Thomas Tarrants—Sam Bowers's as-then-unknown inner-circle terrorist.[57]

The question of why Tarrants would have been one of the first suspects in the purchase of the rifle used to kill Dr. King persists. He had no local history in Birmingham and, according to all available information, supposedly had not yet been identified with any recent racial violence, much less threats against Dr. King. His only arrest history at that time had been as a teenager, for possession of a weapon, and, in late 1967, for the previously discussed arrest with Sam Bowers, again, for possession of a weapon. The FBI did not even show Byron de la Beckwith's picture at the same gun shop for another ten days, even though Beckwith had been widely suspected of the shooting of civil rights leader Medgar Evers in 1963.[58]

The FBI did not give up on Tarrants as a person of interest, even after the gun-shop owners said that he had not been the man who purchased the alleged murder weapon. On April 16, 1968, FBI agents in Los Angeles showed a police sketch of "Eric Galt" to extremist informants in California. Evidence collected in the days following the assassination linked to the Galt name, and the FBI had pictures of the man who used the name. Told by informants that Tarrants had visited extremists on the West Coast in March, the FBI wanted to know if Tarrants looked like "Eric Galt."[59] It was not until April 19 that the FBI realized that Galt was an alias used by James Earl Ray, the man who would one day be caught and convicted for King's murder. This does not change the most salient fact: Law enforcement was pursuing Tarrants as a person of interest early in the King murder, weeks before Tarrants was fingered as the terrorist behind dozens of bombings in Mississippi.

The interest in Tarrants is noteworthy because of how early it developed. It could not have been connected to the report by Margaret Capomacchia— that Tarrants and other White Knights were involved in King's murder— because she did not provide that information to informant Willie Somersett until the very end of July 1968. Nor could it have been connected to the similar report, made by Sidney Barnes, to the same informant, as those reports came after Capomacchia's. That the FBI showed Tarrants's picture in Birmingham within two days of King's murder suggests something more sinister: that Tarrants was somehow implicated in King's murder even before April 4. The file was from Mobile and yet was on call at the Birmingham office before Tarrants was a known commodity for violent crimes; the FBI showed his picture before they showed those of known racist killers— including those in Birmingham itself—at the same gun store. How could his picture take precedence over Thomas Blanton and Robert Chambliss, Birmingham Klansmen who were suspected of trying to kill King in May 1963? Did an informant, in March 1968, suggest that Tarrants—who had just jumped bond in Alabama—was planning to kill King?

The issue is as speculative as it is vital to address. If the chief terrorist for the White Knights of the Ku Klux Klan of Mississippi was implicated in the King murder before King was killed, this would be perhaps the most compelling evidence of a conspiracy behind the civil rights leader's assassination. This would be preassassination evidence linking a group that had a known track record of trying to kill King to the murder. The coincidence would be too much to ignore. This evidence would be compelling whether Tarrants was an actual, would-be conspirator/shooter or whether Tarrants was an unwitting patsy. For if Tarrants was set up, the only group who knew of him and his potential significance was the white supremacists with whom he was acquainted. Tarrants's profile—again, this was before he was connected to any acts of major violence—was too low for any group, such as the CIA or the Mafia, to target him as a patsy. Only his fellow racist zealots would understand that by implicating Tarrants, they were setting up someone who had a clear record of violence that would, presumably, be exposed after he was arrested or killed.

But the evidence that Tarrants was implicated in the King murder before the actual killing in Memphis is only suggestive. Beyond the crucial issue of the timing of the photo showing at the Birmingham gun store, the Mobile FBI field office's reaction to Tarrants's decision to jump bond for the gun charge from Mississippi is strange. At the end of March 1968, the FBI in Mobile appears to have taken Tarrants's fugitive status very seriously. One former Mobile agent, Gerard Robinson, recalled several odd aspects to the FBI's response. Robinson was called in to go to Tarrants's parents' home to aid in the search for the fugitive. This itself was strange to Robinson, because his daily investigative activities focused on the rural outskirts of Mobile and not the city proper. He was only called into city investigations when extra manpower was needed. Additionally, Robinson recalled that he was told to visit the home in search of Tarrants by himself. Robinson stressed that this was a serious violation of rigid bureau protocol; agents were always required to bring a partner when interviewing or searching for a suspect. When a fellow FBI man was unavailable, bureau agents would pay local law enforcement to join their investigation. Yet Robinson was told to search for a potential fugitive, and interview said fugitive's father, with no backup.[60]

Tarrants himself noted, in his autobiography, that he fled Mobile (and went underground) because of an obvious and consistent FBI presence near his home. This is odd because, as noted on many occasions, Tarrants was, at the end of March 1968, largely an unknown. He had been arrested for illegal firearms charges and was known as a belligerent racist in Mobile, but he was far from being a Most Wanted–type fugitive. Yet in the week or two before King's murder, the Mobile FBI—the same office that would provide his photograph to the Birmingham FBI field office for the April 6 photo showing—had an intense interest in him. Were they trying to find Tarrants because they were told he had gone to California to get a rifle to kill King?

Such speculation must be tempered by former Special Agent Robinson's claim that it is not impossible that an everyday fugitive could illicit a serious investigation.[61] But imagining such a scenario would also help explain the very quotes in Jack Nelson's book that raise suspicions about Tarrants in the King crime to begin with. Frustratingly, Nelson provides no footnotes to the statements that Tarrants bought a rifle from Wesley Swift with the intent of killing King or that killing King was his goal. But Nelson gives some clues that may help one decide if this material came from pre-assassination or post-assassination comments. For one thing, Nelson says that the rifle-from-Swift quote comes from Tarrants's testimony. This is important because we can find no example where Tarrants ever testified at any of his trials. Nor is it likely that this came from testimony before Congress, for while Tarrants admitted to reporter Jerry Mitchell, in 2007, that he testified before the House, such testimony is sealed from public view and would not have been available to Nelson. It is, however, common for informant statements, even if they are hearsay, to be cast in direct quotes in FBI reports. Perhaps Nelson saw such quotes and referred to them as "testimony."

We have records covering much of Tarrants's interaction with the FBI after his arrest for the Meridian bombing, including his interviews with FBI agents after the sting. There is no hint of any references to the King assassination. The FBI showed very little interest in Tarrants as a suspect after April 1968, an odd decision if he told them he got a rifle to kill King after he had been identified as a major terrorist for the White Knights of the KKK. This was true even after the Capomacchia reports surfaced. It stands to reason that, if such "testimony" came from informant reports, they were preassassination reports that were, for whatever reason, discounted after April 1968.

Tarrants's own accounts, in 2007, would directly contradict those reports. He has steadfastly maintained that he knew nothing about a plot against King and that he bought a rifle from Swift, but as a means of introduction to the militant minister whom he idolized. Tarrants said this as an evangelical Christian who has devoted his life to the ministry. Jerry Mitchell, whose instincts as a reporter have helped him to win some of the most prestigious awards in journalism, and who is the only person to directly ask Tarrants about the matter, believes Tarrants is telling the truth.[62] If that is the case, it does not devalue the significance of a preassassination report that Tarrants was hunting King, if that is, in fact, what Nelson was citing. On the contrary, the possibility that an informant spread such false rumors about Tarrants just days before the King murder is consistent with what followed the King murder. In other words, Tarrants was very likely being falsely implicated in the King murder in the months that followed his arrest for the Meridian bombing. Specifically, Margaret Capomacchia and Sidney Barnes were almost definitely spreading misinformation when they implied that Tarrants was a conspirator who fled Memphis, hiding out with various extremists, including Barnes himself.

That the Capomacchia/Barnes accounts are part of a disinformation campaign is far less speculative than the idea that sinister informants falsely framed Tarrants in a preassassination campaign. But in establishing an obvious Capomacchia/Barnes deception, it makes the preassassination frame-up more feasible.

That there were suspicious flaws in the Capommachia/Barnes account was discussed at length in the end of chapter 4, but one key issue remains and makes the idea of a post-assassination effort to mislead law enforcement even more tantalizing. This involves the person to whom both individuals told their stories: Willie Somersett. It is very important to stress that, unless Somersett is lying, both individuals called and told very similar stories to the long-time law enforcement snitch. It is thus imperative to analyze two key questions. First, was Somersett lying to the FBI and to the Miami Police when he relayed these stories? Second, if he was being truthful, why would Capomacchia and Barnes choose Somersett for their disinformation campaign?

It is important, in addressing the first question, to note the difference between saying that Somersett was truthful and claiming that the content of his reports were the truth. As with any informant, Somersett could honestly relay deceptive or false material, which he believes to be true. If Barnes and Capomacchia were aware that Somersett was a snitch, then one or both of them could have approached him with the intent to spread disinformation to law enforcement. The evidence indicates that that is precisely what happened in the summer of 1968.

There are many reasons to vouch for Somersett's reliability as an informant on this matter. For one thing, he had no obvious motive to make up these stories. He was implicating a handful of people who operated outside of the Southeast, and thus Somersett likely had little or no contact with them and hence no motive to besmirch them. Somersett made no effort to profit or publicize the Barnes/Capomacchia stories either, even though he had, by that time, achieved a measure of fame. The second reason to support Somersett is the very nature of the reports themselves. Especially in the case of the Capomacchia reports, Somersett raised questions about the reliability of the very story he was reporting. He noted that Capomacchia was very emotional; he stressed that her reports (at least the initial one) was very confusing, to the point that he was unsure he got the details right. If Somersett was attempting to put forth a false story, one would expect that it would show more certainty on his part.

The third reason to believe Somersett is also the reason some would call his story into question: his overall reliability. Recall that Somersett, even as of 1968, remained a prized informant for the Miami Police Department for years. They believed so strongly in him that they paid for him to take the trip to see Barnes and to travel the country in general in hopes of exposing a potential King conspiracy. For part of the 1950s and 1960s, the FBI held the same view of Somersett. They considered him to be one of their most important informants on issues of racial violence.

But starting in the early 1960s, the FBI grew more and more skeptical of Somersett. By 1961, the FBI officially discontinued paying Somersett as an informant but continued to pay attention to reports from the source. By 1966, however, they were receiving reports that seemed farfetched on their face, including one about a plot to kill President Johnson. If they had questioned Somersett's sincerity before, by 1966 they were treating him with kid gloves. This was partly why they treated his accounts from

Margaret Capomacchia with so much skepticism, implying that Somersett was telling tall tales.[63]

If the FBI had taken full stock of Somersett as an informant, their skepticism would have been directed at Capomacchia and not Somersett. What the FBI missed in their treatment of Somersett, both in the King investigation and in general, was that Somersett became a victim of his very own success. What the FBI had seen as a credibility problem with Somersett the man was, in fact, a sign that white supremacists had fingered Somersett as a snitch as early as 1962 and were using him, without his knowledge, to divert and mislead law enforcement. His value to law enforcement as an informant in 1968 would be in exposing the exact reason why he was used to plant false stories on the King murder.

The first evidence that Somersett was compromised as an informant comes in the letters of J. B. Stoner. In a letter he sent to a number of NSRP members, Stoner raised doubts about Somersett and accused him of being a possible informant in 1962.[64] Stoner was a major figure in the white supremacist movement, and his suspicions certainly would have spread to others, likely including Sidney Barnes and Capomacchia. Barnes, in fact, was a victim of Somersett's spying in 1964, which almost definitely reinforced his suspicion that Somersett was disloyal to the supremacist cause.

It was in 1964 that Somersett, on behalf of the Miami PD, surreptitiously taped Barnes speaking about yet another plot against King's life involving many of the same participants in the September 1963 King plot. Notably, Somersett not only got Barnes on record admitting to this conspiracy, but also gave Barnes a rifle (marked by police) to be given to one of the other conspirators. The Miami PD passed this information along to the FBI, as it also included suspicious comments Barnes made in reference to the Sixteenth Street Baptist Church bombing in September of the previous year.[65]

But Barnes had already apparently come to share Stoner's suspicions about Somersett. The FBI documents highlight the fact that Barnes gave Somersett two pieces of obviously false information, one involving a visit from Martin Luther King Jr. and another involving a meeting with an NSRP luminary in Mobile. The FBI itself suspected that Barnes was testing Somersett, and if Somersett had not yet failed the test, the FBI made sure that he did not escape Barnes's skepticism. They proceeded to interview Barnes using information that seemingly could have come only from his meeting with Somersett. Barnes is quoted in the documents as openly suspecting that a snitch was betraying him.[66]

That this all happened in 1964 is significant, for it was after 1964 when Somersett began providing the FBI with so many false, and sometimes bizarre, leads. The FBI appears to have blamed Somersett, when it is clear that anyone who knew Barnes or Stoner—and those would be a lot of the people meeting Somersett—would harbor serious suspicions of the informant. A suspicious mind might choose to ignore Somersett; a keen one might choose to use him as an unwitting proxy to send false information to national and local law enforcement agencies!

That Somersett would have the ears of the most important government agencies became even more apparent by 1967, for this is when Somersett's most famous act of surreptitious tape recording became known to the nation. It was in February 1967 that Florida newspapers began to report on a taped phone conversation between two unidentified individuals, one a Miami police informant, and one a white supremacist. The latter individual made several bold and seemingly prescient predictions about when and how President John F. Kennedy would be killed, including saying that he would be shot from a tall building, with a high-powered rifle. The reports not only went to the FBI, but were also investigated by the Secret Service. The newspapers printed actual quotes from the taped phone conversation, which would have made it obvious to the parties involved that the person doing the recording was Willie Somersett, and the person doing the predicting was Joseph Milteer.[67]

The reports of this taping shocked the nation. It is hard to imagine that Milteer, with his connections to Florida, would have been oblivious to it. If Milteer was unaware of Somersett's betrayal, Somersett did his part to make it more obvious. At a meeting of the National Labor Federation, Somersett called members' attention to newspaper transcripts of the assassination prediction, and then blamed Bobby Kennedy for not having followed up on the lead to protect his brother while serving as attorney general in 1963.[68] The record shows that Milteer, for undisclosed reasons, was not having anything to do with Willie Somersett by 1968. One could only guess why.

All this makes it obvious that Capomacchia and Barnes picked Somersett for the very reason that he was seen as a link to high-end law enforcement investigators. In using Somersett, they could expect the information—really the disinformation—to reach local law enforcement, the FBI, and possibly the Secret Service. Barnes and Capomacchia probably did not know that the past efforts at using Somersett in this regard had already damaged the informant's reputation.

But why frame Tarrants at all? The timing is important and suggestive. They told their stories to Somersett within weeks of the sting in Meridian that, for all intents and purposes, was supposed to kill Tommy (but not Kathy). James Earl Ray would have just been captured for his role in King's murder on June 12, 1968, and no one could guarantee who would say what. If Ray provided evidence of any kind of right-wing conspiracy, a scapegoat may have been needed; conversely, they may have tried to discredit Tarrants—and his ample knowledge of crimes committed by supremacists—before he snitched on his former associates.

Or perhaps something much more sinister was at stake. If they framed Tarrants in August 1968, Barnes and Capomacchia may have been engaging in what spies call a post-assassination effort to mislead law enforcement. This involves telling authorities a partially true story polluted with false information, such as, for instance, suggesting a connection between the White Knights of the Ku Klux Klan of Mississippi and the King murder while falsely implicating an obviously innocent person like Robert Earl Wilson in the crime. When the false aspects of the story are exposed, it discredits even those parts that were real. Authorities throw out the baby with the bathwater and miss a legitimate lead. If that is the case, the Barnes/Capomacchia disinformation effort would be an attempt to move suspicion *away* from Tarrants, but not because Tarrants had guilty knowledge of the King murder. A more dangerous possibility—for Barnes, Capomacchia, and their cohorts—would be if another frame-up was exposed, a preassassination frame-up that failed.

In such a scenario, the effort to frame Tarrants—perhaps leaking to the FBI, in March 1968, the idea that Tarrants had gone to California to get a rifle to kill King—would have *failed* in April, leaving him as a loose end that needed to be eliminated and/or discredited. This is because any law enforcement analysis of a preassassination frame-up of Tarrants would lead to one, and only one, group as King's murderers: the white supremacists who were using Tarrants in terrorist operations. If investigators discovered that Tarrants was framed *before* the King assassination, it would have enormous implications for law enforcement, as he was unknown in April other than to white supremacists; only white supremacists would have framed him. It would show not only a concerted effort to divert law enforcement from solving the King crime but also foreknowledge of King's murder on the part of those who plotted the frame-up. It would be the best evidence of a conspiracy against King in Memphis, and it could explain why, as speculative as it may be, Bowers may have wanted to use the Roberts brothers to set up Tarrants for death by police sting. With Tarrants having survived that sting, Barnes and Capomacchia—both closely connected to the White Knights in Mississippi—may have been employed to run the disinformation campaign that would pollute the investigation and drive law enforcement away from Tarrants and any hint of a preassassination frame-up.

All this is highly speculative, but clearly something is going on here. What is needed to close the circle is first uncovering the reasons for the early and keen federal interest in Tarrants in connection with the King assassination and then seeing if that narrative connects in any way to the later, more obvious attempts to implicate him in the King murder. If the first effort uncovers what we suspect was a preassassination effort to frame Tarrants, then it would constitute very powerful evidence of a white supremacist conspiracy to kill King. Unfortunately, absent additional evidence, closing the circle is not possible at the moment.

But the idea of framing an outside extremist may conform with what newly discovered information suggests was the real conspiracy to murder King. New research suggests that the White Knights were offering a bounty on King's life in 1967. This offer was directed at the kind of criminals with proven track records of professional murders and very little compulsion about whom or what they were targeting. For all the violent activity attributed to the likes of Tarrants and the White Knights' inner circle, it very rarely involved anything like a long-range killing with a sniper rifle. The inner-circle operatives were experts at bomb making, personal whippings, and drive-by-shootings. Having plotted and failed to kill King with bombs and machine guns, Bowers may have found turning to a contract killer a surer bet. The evidence indicates, in fact, that he had already tried and failed to reach members of the most ruthless criminal association in America. But desperation for the end-times apparently raised the stakes and the bounty to levels that no money-hungry criminal could ignore. Such tantalizing offers appear to have been circulating in federal prisons across the country, and they may have reached the ear of the only person ever convicted of killing Martin Luther King Jr.

CHAPTER 7

OUTSIDE OPTIONS AND CONTRACT KILLERS

Any effort to trace a conspiracy in the Martin Luther King assassination must deal with the individual eventually arrested and convicted for King's murder—James Earl Ray. Ray was a forty-year-old fugitive; he had escaped from Missouri State Penitentiary in April 1967. Although he initially pled guilty to the murder, his first remarks in court held open the possibility of a conspiracy, and over the years he would relate an elaborate story of how he had been manipulated as a patsy in the King crime. To date, Ray's supporters (those who believe he is completely innocent of the King crime) have typically worked backward from Ray to conspiracies that have involved agencies of the American government, organized crime, white supremacists, or even individuals within King's own leadership circle.

Ray himself did much to cloud any efforts to connect him with any of these groups. He pleaded guilty in court but only after seeming to correct the judge on the possibility of a conspiracy.[1]

He then quickly recanted the confession and claimed that his lawyer, Percy Foreman, tricked him into pleading guilty.[2] He went on to describe having been framed by a mysterious figure named Raoul,[3] an individual whom no one, until the 1990s, ever claimed to have seen[4], and one whose appearance never stayed the same, even in James Earl Ray's accounts. Most alarmingly, Ray changed his alibi, originally telling author William Bradford Huie that he had picked up Raoul in a white Mustang, fleeing from Bessie Brewer's rooming house, only later to say that he lied to Huie and that he was innocently trying to fix a flat tire at a Memphis service station when he heard the news of King's murder, recognized he was framed, and fled the state of Tennessee.[5] Unable to find any witnesses to such an alibi, and frustrated with Ray's account of Raoul, Huie, and later the House Select Committee on Assassinations, dismissed Ray's alibi and settled on Ray's guilt as a shooter. Huie, who originally thought that there may have been a Klan conspiracy, dismissed the idea that "redneck racists" could have carried out such a plot and argued for Ray's sole guilt, claiming that Ray was out for fame and notoriety.[6]

The HSCA agreed that Ray was the shooter but argued that Ray was, in effect, part of a conspiracy and was motivated by the one thing that always drove his actions: money. Specifically, the congressional committee settled on the likelihood that Ray was responding to a bounty offer circulating in Missouri State Penitentiary, the prison from which he escaped in a bread truck in April 1967. They found a set of links connecting convicts in Missouri State Penitentiary to Saint Louis businessmen who supported reactionary racist presidential candidate George Wallace's American Independent Party; it was those prison inmates who purportedly spoke of a bounty on King's life.[7]

We believe that such an offer could have reached Ray's ears before his escape and that other, similar offers were circulating in the same prison. Ray's own brothers and his past criminal actions attested to the fact that Ray was motivated by money. But as the actual conspiracy to kill King, the Saint Louis businessmen plot is inferior to the conspiracy by the militant network we exposed in previous chapters. The Saint Louis businessmen had no past record of supporting any racial violence. More to the point, though Ray's escape from prison initially took him to his hometown in Saint Louis, his later travels took him to other locales, including Birmingham. His behavior over the course of the next year suggests that he was not responding to any bounty offered for King's murder. Instead, from 1967 to 1968, Ray explored careers ranging from bartending to porn distribution. If he was interested in such a bounty, he was on the outer periphery of such an offer for several months after his escape. As such, the bounty offered by the Saint Louis businessmen may have sparked Ray's initial interest, but the more likely avenue for Ray to enter into a conspiracy to assassinate King is through the network of extremists who had already tried to kill King over and over again.

These groups were evolving tactics that included the use of inner-circle operatives and that eventually led to the use of outsiders, like Tommy Tarrants, across state lines. That such committed terrorists would take the next logical step and reach out to criminals is not surprising. They apparently had done so before, offering a bounty on King to a contract killer whose gang of criminal associates would be known, in law enforcement circles, as the Dixie Mafia. The records indicate that members of this same gang were now being offered a much higher bounty on King's life, at around the same time James Earl Ray was sneaking out of Missouri State Penitentiary.

USING OUTSIDERS

In the previous chapters, we have presented a number of incidents in which outsiders were brought in to commit local crimes of racial violence. In 1958 J. B. Stoner brought his "boys from Atlanta" to bomb a church in Birmingham. Stoner had also offered his services to kill other key civil rights leaders including Dr. King. How much further Stoner's "boys" might have gone is unknown, since the entire affair was stopped short after the first bombing.

Stoner was known to give "bomb training" classes to prospective racist terrorists in Alabama and to have connections with Birmingham's militant outsiders, the Cahaba Boys. Elizabeth Cobbs, a key informant in the Sixteenth Street Baptist Church bombing and a relative of Robert Chambliss, the man eventually convicted for the bombing, writes of hearing that members of the Cahaba Boys would travel to assist groups in other locations and, on occasion, would receive help from members of other groups. They all shared a mutual trust based in the fact that if anyone betrayed those acts, they would be killed. She related that Chambliss would take the family for long weekend drives from Birmingham to remote parts of Alabama, from Mobile to as far as Tennessee. They visited secret storage areas and properties. She noted that some of those sites appeared to contain hidden burials as well. Chambliss himself took a job as a truck driver, and his route took him to Florida, Mississippi, and through southern Alabama. He used the truck to make connections to other like-minded groups and to smuggle weapons and explosives.[8]

Racist outsiders also became an important part of the violence Samuel Bowers's White Knights in Mississippi perpetrated. We related the story of Bowers's use of Thomas Tarrants of Alabama, described as a member of the Swift network, who operated from both Mobile and North Carolina while conducting attacks across Mississippi (and reportedly in other states). As with the Cahaba Boys, and in contrast to the claims made to the HSCA almost a decade later, Bowers's outsiders were willing to perform violence in bordering states. In fact, Delmar Dennis, the White Knight insider who helped the FBI build successful criminal prosecutions against the Mississippi terrorists, told reporter Jerry Mitchell that the White Knights were a group with "national reach."[9] As the wife of one of Bowers's closest associates told us, if King were the target, the White Knights certainly would have no problem operating in Tennessee.[10]

In fact, the very use of outsiders would have insulated militant groups such as the White Knights, from immediate suspicion, even if these outsiders were caught in Memphis. The FBI field office in Jackson did not connect Thomas Tarrants to the White Knights until May 1968, months after Tarrants was caught in a stolen car with an illegal firearm—with Sam Bowers sitting in his passenger seat![11] By the mid-1960s, inner-circle leaders were no longer relying strictly on their own members, or limiting their acts to their own communities. They secured and compartmentalized their operations and, if their use of Tarrants is any indication, did so in part by operating outside their normal geographic base of operations.

Increased and unprecedented federal scrutiny, such as that which occurred during the FBI's Mississippi Burning investigation, only made the inner-circle leaders more brazen in their willingness to use outsiders. Bowers was still able to wage a six-month campaign of terrifying violence while he himself was being investigated, prosecuted, and convicted for the Mississippi Burning killings. He simply relied more heavily on the inner-circle members he could trust (such as Danny Joe Hawkins) and used outsiders such as Thomas Tarrants to avoid scrutiny. Bowers was even willing to use a female elementary school teacher (Kathy Ainsworth) as Tarrants's bomber-in-crime, if it could help bring about his goal for a race war.

With the information now available, there is little doubt that the more sophisticated and cunning members of the militant racist subculture were quite skilled in acting at a distance, using outsiders and establishing layers of separation between themselves and any major act of violence. It would have been extremely naive to expect to catch instigators and organizers personally participating in an attack or even being present in the area of a crime scene. To use those criteria for dismissing a lead, as the FBI did, especially a lead suggesting a conspiracy, leaves a considerable number of unanswered questions.

One of the most significant of those questions is whether or not racist militants might have gone even further outside their own ranks, offering serious murder contracts to career criminals such as James Earl Ray. We believe there is now sufficient information available to demonstrate that such offers were indeed made. In fact, it is now possible to profile the sort of individual who would have been solicited with such offers.

CONTRACTS ON KING

In the first chapter, we reviewed a series of credible threats against Dr. King. Some of those threats involved reports of contracts being offered for King's murder. The FBI made inquiries on such reports, and recently we have been able to obtain fully disclosed copies of some of those investigative reports. We have also been able to locate and interview certain individuals who were involved in these reports, including one of the primary FBI sources. While we cannot confirm that the particular incidents discussed in the following directly resulted in the murder of Dr. King in Memphis, we do feel that they are highly relevant. They illustrate the process and the types of individuals that were being contacted with offers for a bounty on Dr. King's life. They also take us to individuals reportedly associated with the White Knights and with Jackson, Mississippi, names and locations that show up repeatedly in leads provided to the FBI following the assassination in Memphis.

We will now review the details of these contracts in more detail as background to later discussions of the offers that we feel may have drawn James Earl Ray from Los Angeles, California, initially to Selma, Alabama, then to Atlanta, Georgia, and finally to Memphis, Tennessee. Both of the reports we will discuss involved money being offered through individuals in Jackson, Mississippi.

The first was reported by an informant said to be associated with individuals within the White Knights. The individual had no direct, personal involvement with the offer, but related a number of details.

White Knights Offer, 1964

Corroboration that the White Knights were turning to contract killers as early as 1964 came later from information the House Un-American Activities Committee pursued. In their investigation of the Klan, they developed information that the White Knights were approaching an outside criminal for a major but unspecified act within this exact time frame. The report said that at a June 9, 1964, meeting near Jackson, Mississippi,

> Billy Buckles, the Grand Giant, told those assembled that the White Knights of the Ku Klux Klan was sponsoring an ex-convict to do a job in the Jackson area. Buckles claimed that the job was so big it would make the death of Medgar Evers "look sick."[12]

According to FBI informants, in 1964, individuals associated with the White Knights of Mississippi made contact with Donald Eugene Sparks, an individual with an extensive criminal history. Sparks was offered $13,000 to shoot Dr. King during an anticipated appearance in Jackson, Mississippi. Sparks was to use a scope-equipped, high-powered rifle, making it possible for him to shoot at the target from a distance. Sparks, known by his nickname

"Two Jumps," reportedly traveled to Jackson, stayed in a motel there, and surveyed the area for the act. However, no attack had taken place, apparently because the individuals offering the deal could not come up with the cash.[13]

The Sparks offer relies on several different sources, with different patterns of association. One of the sources was William Kenneth Knight, a known associate of Sparks who performed crimes with him in Alabama, Louisiana, and Oklahoma. Knight told the FBI in 1968 that Sparks had spoken about the King contract while the two were fleeing Louisiana after a robbery. Knight described Sparks as a serious individual who hated blacks. Although law enforcement would use Knight as a reliable witness in future prosecutions, they dismissed his 1968 report on Sparks's contract offer because they could not find Sparks's name on a hotel registry in Jackson. The fact that Sparks was known to use aliases apparently did not occur to the FBI's investigators.[14][15]

The FBI found independent corroboration of these rumors about Sparks from a source listed only by his last name: Chambliss. They went a step further and found that known and reliable sources within the White Knights knew Sparks by his nickname and could identify his picture. But despite all this independent information, the FBI never bothered to explore why someone whose primary occupation was home burglary in Oklahoma and Alabama would be known to racist militants in Mississippi.[16]

Many months afterward, the FBI interviewed Sparks, who had been captured on one of many outstanding charges. Sparks told the agents he was not talking and never would talk; his cardinal rule was never to talk to law officers about anything. Years later, when the FBI interviewed him following the King assassination (he was in jail in Alabama at that time), Sparks again refused to talk.[17]

A 1968 FBI summary report also notes that Sparks had eventually appeared on the FBI's Ten Most Wanted Fugitives list. Still, that summary fails to give the full picture of Sparks, including how credible he would have been as a contract killer.[18] Actually, Sparks was an early member of what came to be known, by the late 1960s and especially the early 1970s, as the Dixie

Mafia—something of a misnomer, as they were neither concentrated exclusively in the South nor as centrally organized as the Sicilian Mafia. The most in-depth study of this group may be found in a 1974 intelligence report made under the auspices of the attorney general of Kansas.[19]

Described by one of our sources as "white trash on steroids,"[20] the Dixie Mafia were indeed career criminals, associated through prison contact and often involved in the same types of crimes. They were constantly on the road, and their crimes were often committed far outside their home territories. The Kansas intelligence report suggests that such individuals connected at "safe" restaurants, motels, and clubs. They also kept extensive telephone lists for maintaining contacts; normally the telephone numbers were coded for security purposes.[21] They trusted one another and formed loose gangs with complementary skills, such as safecracking, getaway driving, and check forging. Core members might recruit muscle to help intimidate would-be victims, and other criminal associates could be added to the mix as needed. Their activities ranged from armed robbery and burglary to even murder. They were also active in using violence to shut down disputes, sometimes working in union busting. As described by a Tennessee federal district attorney, experienced members of the group did not take small-time contracts but, for $15,000 to $20,000, would travel wherever necessary and even subcontract, using their prison contacts to get help on jobs.[22]

A number of these individuals started their criminal careers in the high-volume bootlegging business, beginning during Prohibition and continuing in the "dry" states of Oklahoma, Kansas, and Texas after the Twenty-first Amendment repealed the nationwide ban on alcohol. Individuals involved in multistate bootlegging had established their own business network involving transportation, storage, and distribution of the illegal liquor. With the repeal of Prohibition, the players who moved on to other illegal pursuits found themselves with an established pipeline, one very useful in moving stolen goods.[23] It appears that several of them began to develop new businesses, including extremely well-planned burglaries and robberies, often armed robbery of upscale residences (especially those known to have home safes).[24]

The roots of this network were reported to be in the so-called new James gang, led by Jerry Ray James and including Donald Sparks, Rubie Charles Jenkins, and Wayne Padgett, who was based in Tulsa and considered to be the chief organizer for the group's crimes in Oklahoma. Members of the gang were known to travel as far as Georgia and California for their crimes; law enforcement found that they had conducted operations in Kansas, New Orleans, across the Gulf Coast, and in Atlanta.[25] Sparks himself served prison time in Georgia and in Alabama and in 1967 was arrested and taken into custody in Tucson, Arizona, while driving with Jerry Ray James and Wayne Padgett. Rubie Charles Jenkins and Padgett had the same hard-core reputation as Sparks and were reportedly involved in multiple murders.[26] Jenkins, according to one source who refused to be named, kept a burial plot reserved for those individuals stupid enough to cross him.[27]

Indeed, another important point that didn't show up in the FBI report on Sparks and the reported King contract was the fact that Sparks had a considerable reputation as a successful contract killer.[28] While known to be a crack burglar, the Kansas intelligence report credits him with dozens of contract killings, including killings for individuals in New Orleans. The minimum price for those killings (as for other acts such as bombing and arson) was said to be $15,000 to $20,000. We also know that Sparks had been operating in the South during the 1960s, where authorities charged him with three major residential robberies in northern Alabama in 1965.[29]

If the information we obtained is correct, the offer to Sparks did not disappear after the White Knights failed to raise the $13,000 in 1964. Instead, an associate of Sparks, one who may have been involved in the earlier plot, maintained contacts in Mississippi and, three years later, extended a much higher offer to established criminals.

White Knights Offer, 1967

A second reported White Knights contract on Dr. King, also planned for the Jackson area, may well have been an extension of offers first made in 1964. Details of the second offer were reported to the FBI in June 1967.[30] Information was provided to the bureau by a recently released inmate, Donald James Nissen. Nissen had been serving time in the federal penitentiary in Leavenworth, Kansas. Shortly before his release, Nissen was approached by another inmate, LeRoy R. McManaman, who worked with him at the shoe factory in the prison and who knew that Nissen was planning on moving to the Atlanta area, where he had connections for a job. A suggestion was made that there was a standing offer for a large amount of money, up to $100,000, for the murder of Martin Luther King Jr. McManaman told the soon-to-be-released inmate that he could make money simply by observing and reporting on Dr. King in Atlanta, but if he wanted to take it further and perform the killing, there were people available to assist in the murder plot.[31]

If interested, Nissen was to go to Jackson, Mississippi, and contact a woman who was routinely in touch with the individual communicating the offer. She would then introduce Nissen to a federal law enforcement officer and an individual only identified as "Floyd," who would make further introductions; those individuals were insulated from the group making the offer and had the reputation as militants or radical racists. The individuals actually extending the offer were associated with the White Knights of Mississippi; the offer was specifically stated as coming from the White Knights.[32]

Worried that harm might come to him before his release, Nissen was coy, neither refusing nor accepting McManaman's offer. Privately, he was very concerned that he would be associated with any hit on King, and this prompted his decision to speak to the FBI in Texas.[33]

We have had lengthy discussions with Nissen, who has since shifted from a decades-long involvement in crime (primarily robberies) to one dedicated to service to his church and his community. He has confirmed that he did travel back to Atlanta but made no effort to pursue the contract offer. However, while working in Atlanta and traveling to adjacent states including Mississippi, Nissen may have unwittingly been used to transport money related to the bounty offer that McManaman described to him in Leavenworth penitentiary.[34]

In our initial contacts with Nissen, he described and confirmed everything that was contained in the 1967 FBI report—before we discussed it with him or sent him the actual documents. Having simply been told that his name was revealed as a source on the King assassination, he detailed everything he told the bureau. He additionally volunteered another aspect to the story, which, if true, would provide an important lead on the progress of the bounty offer.[35]

Nissen related that a few months after he was released in the summer of 1967, a coworker, Floyd "Buddy" Ayers, approached him in Atlanta with a request to deliver a package to someone in Jackson. As Nissen was working as a traveling salesman, being asked to drop off a package did not strike him as an especially unusual request. So Nissen agreed to drop off the package to a woman at a small Jackson real estate office. Nissen wound up delivering the package to a woman we believe was Sybil Eure, the woman McManaman named as the go-between in Jackson. That he actually delivered the package to Eure is strongly supported by the fact that he correctly described her age and physical appearance to us without the benefit of documents that confirmed his description. Additionally, he carefully pointed out that it was a real estate office run from Eure's home, something also confirmed in documents. The fact that Nissen made the delivery, in the summer of 1967, is important because of what he later found out it contained; Floyd Ayers told him that it included the bounty money on King's life. [36]

Again, Nissen told us that from the beginning he had been fearful of McManaman and consequently had never given him a yes or no answer to the offer. It seems quite possible that McManaman, who knew that Nissen was traveling to Atlanta upon his release, took this as Nissen's tacit agreement to the King bounty and then contacted individuals in Atlanta who could help Nissen.[37] Later, in December 1967, when an FBI follow-up investigation may well have indirectly implicated Nissen as a snitch, a mysterious character confronted and threatened Nissen outside a federal building in Atlanta where he had been meeting his parole officer. Newly married and much alarmed, Nissen left a lucrative sales job in Atlanta and jumped parole with his pregnant wife—only to turn himself in to the FBI after King's murder, fearing for his life.[38]

Two things seem especially revealing in this second, 1967 bounty offer. First, as in 1964, the offer was reported to have been specifically extended by individuals associated with the White Knights of Mississippi. In both cases the offers also specifically involved Jackson, Mississippi. It is striking that the $13,000 offer in 1964 had escalated to $100,000 by 1967, but that may reflect the growing desperation of these militant racists to eliminate King.

The second revealing point is that our research shows that the inmate conveying the bounty offer in the Kansas prison was acquainted with and actually part of the same criminal network as Donald "Two Jumps" Sparks, the individual named in the 1964 White Knights contract. LeRoy McManaman, the Kansas inmate relating the King bounty, had first been arrested in 1940 for transporting $1,000,000 of illegal liquor into the state of Kansas. After his release from that sentence, he received two convictions, one for forgery and another for his 1952 arrest in which he was charged in a series of high-dollar home burglaries. He had not performed the burglaries himself but rather concentrated and organized them. A judge sentenced him to twenty years in prison, but over the protest of the judge, he was given early parole in 1956. Following that he was again arrested for illegal transport of liquor and later, in 1960, arrested for masterminding a car-theft ring that operated throughout Kansas, Oklahoma, and Missouri. His arrest record notes that he traveled constantly and had been arrested in Kansas, Colorado, Nebraska, Oklahoma, and Missouri.[39] McManaman's prison records describe him as a "big-time operator."[40]

The more important point, however, is that one of the individuals involved in McManaman's car-theft ring was Rubie Charles Jenkins, of Tulsa, Oklahoma. Jenkins, along with Sparks, was one of the members of the new James gang out of Oklahoma, and both were reportedly among the earliest and most influential members of a band of criminals that would evolve into the so-called Dixie Mafia of the 1970s.[41] A source who maintained contact with both men and who is one of the nation's leading experts on the Dixie

Mafia says that Sparks and Jenkins were as "thick as brothers."[42] Jenkins, while denying any knowledge of a King bounty, confirmed that McManaman knew and worked together in the same band of Dixie Mafia criminals as Sparks and himself; Jenkins said Sparks knew McManaman and would have trusted him.[43]

McManaman seems to have had some considerable political influence in Kansas and to have become adept at certain legal matters. Kansas newspapers reveal a minor state scandal arising from the fact that he served only three years of a twenty- to twenty-four-year armed-robbery sentence and shortly afterward received a full pardon from the governor.[44] On other occasions he was arrested while still on bond from charges, and in 1964, while out on bond, he crossed state lines to travel to Mississippi. He spent no more than a few months there, living in Jackson with real estate agent Sybil Eure, but apparently established several local contacts. We have no way of knowing whether he heard about the $100,000 offer from local contacts in Mississippi, from his prison letter exchanges with the real estate woman in Jackson, or from his associates among the Dixie Mafia, but all are realistic possibilities.

Just as likely is the possibility that McManaman's connection to the $100,000 offer grew out of his connection to the 1964 plot against King that had involved Sparks. McManaman was, without question, in Jackson, Mississippi, at the same time as the first White Knights bounty offer on Dr. King. That offer involved McManaman's associate from Oklahoma, Donald Sparks. At the time, McManaman was free only on an appeal bond relating to an arrest and charges associated with interstate transport of stolen cars and weapons. His codefendant in the crime was Sparks's close associate and another Dixie Mafia criminal, Rubie Charles Jenkins.[45] A deputy marshal of that period has related that McManaman's travel to Mississippi (while at liberty on an appeal bond from Kansas) would have constituted a federal offense, adding time to his sentence.[46] His mere presence in Jackson while on bond was an even higher risk, given that his previous crimes, appeals, and pardons had already been a topic of considerable controversy in Kansas newspapers.

We are left with the question, what could be important enough to travel to Jackson at that point in time?

The FBI never bothered to ask that question. In fact, the FBI's follow-up investigation into Nissen's lead was as questionable as their original investigation into the 1964 Sparks offer. For one thing, they made no effort to connect McManaman to the Sparks offer, despite the obvious link through Rubie Charles Jenkins. It is unfortunate that the cursory (and therefore dubious) dismissal of the Sparks report in 1965 meant that the FBI never even attempted to draw a connection to it by reviewing old files.

The FBI did go to Leavenworth penitentiary to confirm Nissen's story. In June 1967, they interviewed John May, a prison friend of Nissen's. Nissen had said that he went to May on a suggestion from McManaman; May was an expert machinist who McManaman thought could build a gun for the King murder. While saying that Nissen liked to boast about himself in stories, May confirmed that Nissen had mentioned the McManaman offer on King. May even added that he himself had heard such bounty offers, for $100,000, at bars in North Carolina.[47] In 1967 the FBI paid more attention to May's description of Nissen as a teller of tall tales than to May's confirmation of the existence of a plot to assassinate King. More important, they did not go back to May or reconsider his support for Nissen's story after King was killed.

But if the FBI had paid closer attention to detail when interviewing the key subjects, there was still opportunity to further explore this lead. The FBI interviewed Sybil Eure both before and after the King assassination. In her first account, given in 1967, Eure, a tall, fifty-year-old real estate manager, denied knowing Nissen or anything about a bounty offer on King. She said that a mutual friend introduced McManaman to her in 1964 and that he had a keen mind for real estate; she hoped to go into business with him. The FBI confirmed that she exchanged letters with McManaman and had visited him in prison, and McManaman's prison records show he was considering marrying her.[48] They never asked how it could be that a career criminal with no real experience in selling property could possibly have had a common connection to a respectable real estate agent in Mississippi. In fact, they never even asked Eure to identify the mutual friend who introduced her to McManaman.

The interview of Eure after King was murdered was even more alarming. Eure once again denied knowing or meeting Nissen. But she suddenly had a thought as to why the bounty offer may have stuck in McManaman's mind. She told the FBI that when McManaman was staying with her in Jackson in 1964, she had been closely following the news of the Mississippi Burning killings. When it became clear that Sheriff Lawrence Rainey was connected to the attacks, Eure joked to McManaman that all they needed to do to get $100,000 was to go to Rainey and offer to kill Dr. King, since it was well-known that Rainey had connections to the Mississippi White Knights. At the time, she was struggling with her real estate business and, she claimed, such gallows humor was normal for her. Presumably, the joke was misconstrued by McManaman.[49]

There is only one big problem with Eure's story: In the spring of 1964, when McManaman was staying with her while out of Leavenworth on an appeal bond, the Mississippi Burning murders had not yet happened! Schwerner, Goodman, and Chaney were killed on June 21, 1964. McManaman was back in prison before the Mississippi Burning murders, and it stands to reason that Eure would have cleared this misunderstanding up in the repeated visits and communications she had with McManaman in the years that followed. It defies logic that agents in the Jackson field office, who doggedly investigated the Mississippi Burning case, could not recognize the discrepancy in Eure's testimony. But Eure was described as an attractive, middle-aged woman who ran a respectable business. By her second interview in May 1968, the FBI was still oblivious to the fact that the Klan was not above using pretty women (like Kathy Ainsworth and Sybil Eure), even in terrorist operations.

One would think that the FBI would treat career criminal McManaman with greater scrutiny when they interviewed him, for the first time, in September 1968. But they did not. They did not even confront him with Eure's "joke" about obtaining $100,000 from the White Knights even after he denied knowing anything about a bounty against King. McManaman admitted was not a fan of Martin Luther King Jr., but not much else. He denied even knowing Donald Nissen.[50] Beyond the fact that prison records confirm that they worked together in the Leavenworth shoe factory, there was a bigger problem with McManaman's flat denials.[51] If McManaman did not know Nissen, how could Nissen possibly know the name, occupation, and residence of the woman McManaman intended to marry? The FBI did not ask that question.

One could be more forgiving of the investigation of the package delivery. For one thing, there is no record of this story in any of the accounts Nissen gave to the FBI, especially those he relayed to the FBI in August 1968 after he turned himself in. Nissen insists that he did provide that information,[52] and it is of course possible that his story has been excluded from the record. Perhaps the FBI realized what would happen if they dismissed a report of a King bounty offer before King's murder, only to find out that money had actually been delivered to relevant parties. Given the available facts, we can only speculate. If Nissen's memory is wrong, then the FBI would have had to make a leap of logic to make a connection to Floyd Ayers and the trip to Jackson.

On the surface, all they had was a reference to a first name, "Floyd," in Nissen's original report in June 1967. Notably, this would have been before Nissen had even traveled to Atlanta and before he could have met Ayers. The FBI in Jackson assumed the "Floyd" in Nissen's story was Floyd Gardner,[53] Sybil Eure's brother. Absent a last name, one could not logically dismiss that possibility, but the connection to Floyd Ayers is intriguing for a number of reasons.

For one thing, Ayers had a known connection to James Venable, the Imperial Wizard of the National Knights of the Ku Klux Klan. Magazine articles specifically identify Ayers as an actual Klan member,[54] though Ayers's brother, who neither dismisses nor accepts the possibility of Ayers's involvement in a King conspiracy, says that he simply worked odd jobs for Venable.[55] What is without a doubt is that Ayers, who is described by news sources and by his brother as a very eccentric character, fashioned himself as a Klan member. Both his reputation for telling tales and his desire to have the reputation as a Klan member would actually make him a perfect candidate to be a bagman in the King murder. He would want to please actual Klansmen, and at the same time, he was someone who could be easily dismissed as a kook by fellow conspirators if he actually reported his own involvement in the assassination conspiracy to law enforcement.

There is evidence that he may well have tried to report this involvement in the King crime, or perhaps that he was just as eccentric as reports suggest; in 1968, Ayers falsely posed as an usher at Martin Luther King Jr.'s funeral. Later, he posed as a driver and convinced Martin Luther King Sr. to come with him on a trip to a baseball stadium in Atlanta. At the stadium, a reporter who knew Ayers and his connection to the Klan spotted Martin Luther King Sr. This reporter managed to get King's attention and steer him away from Ayers, who at the time was trying to get King to join him in a remote area of the ballpark, darkened by shadows. The media, without asking Ayers, pushed this incident as a kidnapping attempt by a flamboyant Ayers.[56] One wonders if Ayers, whose brother said he was not a rabid racist, had something he wanted to confess to Martin Luther King Sr. about the death of his son.

If the money for a King bounty connects Eure in Jackson to Ayers in Atlanta, it may explain how the White Knights, strapped for cash, could have hoped to promise $100,000 to members of the Dixie Mafia. New information researcher Lamar Waldron uncovered suggests that large sums of money were being unwittingly collected from union workers in Atlanta and diverted for just such a bounty. Waldron interviewed a confidential source who told him that Joseph Milteer—of Somersett tape recording fame—was ostensibly collecting funds to resist integration in Atlanta; in reality, Milteer was collecting a bounty on King without the knowledge of the auto-factory workers who thought they were simply paying their union dues. Records show that Milteer described himself as an unofficial member of Atlanta's White Citizens' Council, and Waldron says that he was friends with James Venable. Milteer's own records show that he met, on a number of occasions in 1963, with Venable's long-time close associate Calvin Craig. If Milteer's money was funneled through to Ayers, the connection through Venable would be the likely avenue.[57]

Waldron's source said that the connection between the union money and Milteer, who was an independently wealthy and rabid follower of Wesley Swift, was a man named Hugh Spake, who worked at the auto factory. This is where things come full circle. If Waldron's source is credible, Spake received a surprise phone call at the plant on the evening of April 4, 1968, from James Earl Ray, who was at that time fleeing from Memphis to Atlanta. Was Ray looking for his payout? When Ray abandoned his white Ford Mustang in Atlanta after fleeing the Memphis crime scene, it was parked not far from the Lakewood auto plant, where Spake worked; witnesses described Ray as looking at a notepad while leaving the vehicle.[58] Certainly if Ray connects to the extremists who had tried to kill King for years, individuals like Bowers and Barnes, it would likely come through the criminal elements pushing a bounty on behalf of these radicals. The 1964 and 1967 plots show that such efforts were ongoing, and Donald Nissen's story of delivering the actual money indicates that those offers had become very serious in the year leading up to the King murder. But connecting James Earl Ray to such a plot requires an extensive look at his behavior in prison, as a fugitive on the run, and in the month before that fateful day in April 1968.

PART II
THE ACCUSED

CHAPTER 8

"I WASN'T IN IT BY MYSELF"

James Earl Ray was convicted on his own guilty plea in the shooting of Dr. King. The prosecution built an extensive case to show that Ray was the man who had rushed out of a rooming house across from the Lorraine Motel (where King had been shot) only to leave behind a bundle outside a nearby Memphis store including a .30-06 rifle and various personal items with his fingerprints on them. Ray was the man who, using an alias, had bought that rifle in Birmingham, Alabama, only days before the attack in Memphis. Ray had fled from Memphis back to his rooming house in Atlanta and then on to Canada, eventually to London and Portugal as he tried to make his way to Africa. The FBI and Justice Department firmly maintained that Ray was the only person involved in the crime, with no associates or sponsors. Attorney General Ramsey Clark and FBI Director J. Edgar Hoover both issued adamant public remarks that the crime was committed by a single individual and that individual was in custody.

Over time there would be much disagreement with that official government position. Ray himself, after hearing charges read at his trial appearance in November 1968, asked the judge to let him go on record objecting to such remarks by Attorney General Clark and Director Hoover. He specifically objected to the statements that he had acted totally alone, that no elements of conspiracy existed. "Your honor, I would like to say something,"[1] Ray said to Judge Preston Battle, after the judge read the stipulations that he had killed Dr. King. "I don't want to change anything I have said. I don't want to add onto it either. The only thing I have to say is I don't exactly accept the theories of Mr. Clark." When asked to clarify, he said, "I mean on the conspiracy thing."[2]

The judge privately expressed doubts that Ray had acted alone but said that he had accepted the guilty plea because a trial at that point would only have muddied the understanding of the evidence pointing to Ray as the actual killer. The judge's remark reflects a common situation within our legal system. Prosecutors with a clear case against one individual do not want to introduce issues or evidence that might cloud the case with diversions regarding a possible conspiracy.

In turn, defense counsels avoid evidence that would support prior guilty knowledge on their client's part. As an example, in the Robert Kennedy murder case, defendant Sirhan Sirhan's lawyers consciously deferred dealing with any evidence that could have opened the issue of conspiracy, which would have established their client's premeditation and thus increased the probability of a death sentence. Moreover, admission of the defendant's willing participation in conspiracy also tends to undermine an insanity defense, the defense common in obvious cases with multiple witnesses or extremely strong evidence.[3]

ALL ABOUT THE MONEY

Premeditation and motive are indeed fundamental questions in the murder of Dr. King; Ray himself eventually provided a response to both in regard to the King assassination. He claimed that a mysterious figure, known only by his first name, "Raoul," recruited him while in Canada into an illegal cross-border smuggling enterprise; but this operation was really a pretext to manipulate Ray's movements until "Raoul" eventually set up Ray as a patsy in the King murder. According to Ray, Raoul manipulated Ray's movements so it looked as if the escaped convict was stalking King, according to Ray, and he even convinced Ray to purchase the alleged murder weapon in Birmingham. Ray insisted he had no prior knowledge and no involvement in King's assassination; he was an innocent patsy. Unfortunately he offered the Raoul story only days after he had entered and been convicted on a guilty plea, retracted that plea, and proclaimed his total innocence.

Congressional investigations and reporters, such as journalist William Bradford Huie, found a number of conflicts and contradictions in Ray's "Raoul" story, including multiple descriptions of the smuggler's physical appearance. There was no corroboration for Ray meeting "Raoul" or that the latter even existed, so Huie and Congress dismissed the "Raoul" story as fiction. Yet Ray's detractors were still left to consider the question of motive.

The most obvious and intuitive motive —racist hatred for the country's most symbolic civil rights figure—seems unrealistic with regard to what we actually know of James Earl Ray. Ray was definitely not an outspoken or militant racist or a member of any radical group, and he made no racist declarations or claims with regard to the murder. There were a number of indications that he personally held generally racist views and avoided blacks, but that was not uncommon for his time and background. Certainly he had not been a racial militant or participated in racial attacks. In addition, although he used pistols in armed robberies and routinely carried a weapon, his criminal record showed no real history of actually firing weapons. There is no evidence he had ever purchased or owned a rifle other than the .30-06 found in Memphis. Neither is there evidence that Ray was a follower of Christian Identity personalities or any known racial or religious zealot that would have inspired him to personally go hunting Dr. King.

Ray's brothers Jerry and John were definite on the subject: James Earl Ray would not have killed anyone on his own initiative. He might, however, have done it for money. After James Earl Ray was captured, John Ray immediately offered his view that he didn't believe his brother had killed King, but if he had, "it was for a lot of money."[4] Ray's ex-wife, Anna Sandhu (a courtroom artist who married Ray after working one of his later rounds of court appearances in 1977), initially championed his innocence in national media appearances.[5] However, after really getting to know Ray, she changed her mind about both his innocence and his claims. She too became aware of his basic motivation. Any extended investigation of Ray's background confirms that, if nothing else, the individuals who knew him best were in agreement on what had driven James Earl Ray throughout his life: money.

FIRST IMPRESSIONS

Before Ray had even appeared in court, *Look* magazine published a series of articles William Huie wrote on the King murder. Huie had previously written extensively about the Klan and civil rights struggles in the South; he had also taken an early opportunity to contact Ray's first American lawyer and negotiate a deal for Ray's story. Huie was certain that a forty-year-old habitual criminal was unlikely to give true information to legal authorities and even less likely to say anything that would earn himself a murder conviction. On the other hand, Huie figured that in exchange for the promise of money, Ray would provide enough facts for Huie to write some articles. Huie promised he would only be writing about Ray's travels and background and would avoid any details of the crime itself. (In fact, Huie only asked Ray to re-create the day-by-day events of the period from April 23, 1967, to June 8, 1968.)[6] It's likely that Ray agreed for his own protection as well as for the money. Huie's articles allowed Ray a safe way to signal to his conspirators that he was not informing on them. This is why Ray wanted the articles out before the trial—much to the judge's anger.

As previously mentioned, Huie's first article, clearly based on Ray's very earliest confidential remarks to him, presented the scenario that Ray had been recruited into exactly the type of radical racist conspiracy that we have described in previous chapters: "The outline of the plot to murder Dr. King now begins to become visible to me. It may not be visible to my readers because until Ray has been tried, I cannot reveal all that I have found to be true. But from what I know, from what I have learned from Ray and from my own investigative research [the plot's instigators were] calculating men who wanted to use King's murder to trigger violent conflict between white and Negro citizens." Huie went on to state that the murder needed to be done under conditions to create maximum effect, "not while he was living quietly at home ... but at some dramatic moment." And the murder had to be clearly laid at the feet of a white man or men would be easily portrayed as "southerners" and "racists."[7]

Based on Ray's comments to him, Huie's articles also set the stage for Ray's later position that he had been an unwitting patsy, maneuvered by months of covert and sinister contacts with a mysterious individual named Raoul. The *Look* articles allowed Ray to eventually maintain that he was innocent of the actual murder. Taking such a position was very much in character for Ray. All his past crimes and encounters with the law reveal that any acceptance of guilt, even in the face of overwhelming evidence, was just not something James Earl Ray did, ever.

WHO, ME?

In fact, as a habitual career criminal with multiple convictions, Ray so regularly denied anything and everything that he sometimes appeared rather foolish. While in custody in London, Ray had proclaimed to his appointed barrister that he was being mistakenly held: "Look, they have got me mixed up with some guy called James Earl Ray. My name is Ramon George Sneyd. I don't know this Ray guy." But shortly after raising that protest, he asked the same lawyer to contact his brother, Jerry Ray, in Chicago.[8]

Ray's entire criminal career shows signs of cunning and planning but the failure to successfully execute. He committed burglary, armed robbery, and other crimes and on occasion escaped with some of the loot. But often he was captured and arrested. Ironically, he was much better at the crime of escaping prison than at his moneymaking crimes, which repeatedly got him into prison. The other consistent thing about his criminal history was his ongoing ability to totally deny anything and everything potentially harmful to him—even when concrete evidence proved the contrary.

In 1954, for example, Ray had been convicted for burglary in East Alton, Illinois. Security guards noticed a broken side window in a cleaning business, found a suspicious car in an adjacent alley, and removed its distributor (ensuring the car could not be started). Upon entering the cleaners, they saw a figure coming in the window. Chasing the individual off, they found his shoes stuck in the mud outside. Upon returning to the suspicious car, they found the thief had gone back to it but had been unable to start the car, fleeing on foot. The car was registered to James Earl Ray. The next morning, an Alton policeman found a tired, muddy, and stocking-footed Ray walking along the railroad tracks and headed out of town. Despite the obvious evidence, Ray maintained his total innocence, denying the shoes were his, stating he had no idea why his car had been left at the scene of the attempted burglary. When stopped by police in stocking feet, Ray claimed he was simply out on an early morning walk.

Again, in 1959, Ray was involved in a series of armed robberies. Once, while attempting a well-designed plan to rob a Kroger store of the contents of its safe, Ray escaped with his partner but was unexpectedly followed by a brave store employee who observed the two cleverly changing cars. The second car was traced to their rooming house where Ray forcefully resisted arrest. Two loaded revolvers and clothing from the robbery were recovered, as well as the money from the cash register. At the police station, Ray sat with a grin and stated to officers that "I cannot deny it, and I won't admit it." Later he signed a statement admitting guilt but followed that by essentially acting as his own lawyer at the trial, going on the stand and denying everything including all the evidence and his signed statement. The jury took twenty minutes to find him guilty, and the crime earned him a twenty-year prison sentence.

KNOWING WHEN (AND WHEN NOT) TO TALK

It would be dangerous to believe every statement James Earl Ray ever made. On his first trip to prison, he lied about the most routine matters in an interview with a staff psychologist, including information about his father and family, his high school education, and his army service. Contrary to his unexceptional IQ test score of 105, which is referenced in much of the writing on Ray, the prison psychologist's report included an evaluation of Ray indicating superior native intelligence. The psychologist, however, also observed that Ray had an unstable and antisocial personality.[9]

By the time of the King murder, Ray had served thirteen years in four different prisons. He adapted well in prison and obviously learned a great deal about executing crimes. He was a veteran convict possessing years of practice in self-protecting deception and was therefore reluctant to name any accomplices. William Huie was well aware that he was dealing with a seasoned criminal and viewed Ray's experience as a major obstacle to the full truth, assuming any version Ray would provide would be carefully edited.

Unfortunately, many investigators and authors have not displayed the healthy skepticism held by Huie in his dealings with Ray: "I could accept as truth only what I could verify; and verification is often difficult and sometimes impossible,"[10] Far too many seem to have taken Ray's details and elaboration of the role of the mysterious "Raoul" in the King killing at face value, treating Ray as a sincere and willing source, rather than questioning his credibility as a career criminal and experienced convict. Ultimately Ray transferred the entire King murder onto the shoulders of "Raoul."

Huie, the first reporter to actually deal directly with Ray, eventually reached the opinion that "Raoul" was a composite character containing elements of different individuals Ray had indeed met in the period before the King murder but not reflecting any single individual who Ray had actually met or who directed Ray's activities over the many months between his escape and the murder of Dr. King. By the time Huie wrote his third article for *Look,* he had decided that Ray had indeed fired the shot that killed King and that his story of being used as an unknowing pawn in some massive conspiracy was simply not true.[11] In fact, Huie changed the title of his planned book from *They Slew the Dreamer* to *He Slew the Dreamer* for its 1970 publication, dealing strictly with Ray and giving up any attempt to track down individuals that actually might have influenced Ray.[12] The reason for this switch may be that, based on his own personal experience with the average "redneck" Klansman, Huie simply could not conceive of a successful or sophisticated conspiracy emanating from those circles. This forced him to develop a picture of Ray as someone who killed King purely for fame.

Strangely, this image seems actually to be in direct conflict with what Huie had learned about Ray and Ray's activities after escaping prison in 1967. It also seems to ignore Ray's own cunning, developed over decades of crimes and prison time, that can be seen in an objective look at the details of Ray's legal saga over the years. Ray's various appearances in court are covered in detail in many articles and books; however, a few points are highly suggestive.

First, after his capture and while in English custody, Ray requested that his barrister contact Arthur Hanes, of Birmingham, Alabama, to act as his U.S. legal counsel. Hanes was certainly not a nationally sought-after lawyer. He was a former mayor of Birmingham, holding office during some of the most violent of the civil rights protests, including the violent integration confrontations involving Dr. King. Hanes was widely discussed as having backed the excessive police violence ordered by then Chief Eugene "Bull" Connor. And Hanes had successfully defended several Klansmen who had murdered civil rights worker Viola Liuzzo, a housewife from Detroit, shot dead in her car while traveling on a highway between Selma and Montgomery, Alabama.[13] This suggests that either Ray had done some level of advance reading and research on civil rights crimes or that he had received outside advice. Indeed, there were indications that Ray, known to be an inveterate newspaper and magazine reader, was familiar with media coverage of civil rights violence and had made comments about it to fellow convicts.[14]

Secondly, in early October 1968, shortly after being put in custody in England and returned to the United States, Ray invited another lawyer for a visit—one who had openly volunteered to take his case: J. B. Stoner of the National States' Rights Party. Ray did so against the advice of Hanes. No record exists of what the two men may have discussed, or what advice Stoner may have given Ray. Stoner was the only one of Ray's many attorneys for whom Ray did not waive attorney-client privilege when the House Select Committee on Assassinations reinvestigated the crime. Hence when Stoner testified before the HSCA—as someone who many suspected of plotting King's murder—he was not allowed to share private conversations he had with Ray while he was on his defense team.

The visit may have been meaningless; on the other hand, it may have served to reinforce Ray's ideas about what he should, and should not, say in his testimony. Clearly Ray's revelation of the mysterious Raoul's involvement in the killing, and of Ray's having been set up by Raoul as a totally innocent patsy, has to be viewed in light of what Ray likely felt would be in his best, long-term interests. The introduction of "Raoul" certainly served to divert attention from the individuals and groups that would have been the most obvious targets of a broader investigation. And by his own actions, Ray himself ensured that there would be no such broader criminal investigation.

Only thirty-six hours before his trial was scheduled to start, there was an incredible turn of events. First, Ray dismissed Hanes as his attorney, causing a substantial rescheduling. Then, reportedly on advice from his brothers, Ray decided to accept the services of Percy Foreman. And reportedly it was Foreman who had prevailed on Ray to reverse his position and accept the guilty plea. Indeed, four weeks before the start of the rescheduled trial, the judge granted a special hearing on a major new development in the case. It was at this hearing that Foreman entered a plea of guilty, and Ray accepted it before the judge.

Finally, within hours after leaving the courtroom, Ray began drafting a letter to Judge Battle, stating that he had released Foreman and was asking for a postconviction hearing. A second letter requested that his ninety-nine-year sentence be reversed and that a public defender be appointed. Judge Battle, returning from a brief vacation, died of a heart attack. In fact, he was found dead at his desk with Ray's second letter in front of him! Shortly afterward, Ray designated J. B. Stoner as his counsel of record.

All this leaves us with the fact that Ray's very first remarks, both in private and in court, strongly suggest that other parties were associated with the murder of Dr. King. Huie, the first investigating individual to communicate confidentially with Ray, initially wrote that these other individuals had the clear goal of using the murder of King to create a massive provocation and trigger black-on-white violence. But with Ray's introduction of the elaborate "Raoul" scenario, the whole issue of conspiracy became so clouded that Huie, among others, simply gave up on the idea and concluded that Ray had acted strictly on his own. Questions of motive, a lack of legal challenge to the prosecution's evidence, and loose ends suggesting outside influence over Ray were simply left unaddressed. That situation would open the door to years of skepticism and debate.[15]

All this left Ray in a most convenient position. By protesting his innocence, Ray introduced the "real" culprit, painted himself as a simple dupe, and led others to chase his alibi. He also made it quite public that he was not going to say anything or point any fingers toward anyone who might actually do him any harm. That move may have been simply the result of a convict with high native intelligence; on the other hand, it may have been the result of receiving some sound outside advice.

IF IT WASN'T FOR MONEY

Everyone who knew James Earl Ray—his first lawyer, Hanes; the first journalist who had significant contact with him, Huie; and his brothers, John and Jerry—were all initially convinced that Ray would only have become involved in the King murder if he felt there was some large financial gain. It is important to note that the HSCA reached the same conclusion.

For some reason, many King conspiracy writings seem to largely ignore Ray's early history, his full criminal record, and his ongoing quest to score big money. The most detailed coverage of Ray's personal history is given in William Bradford Huie's *He Slew the Dreamer* and Gerold Frank's *An American Death.* Huie's book contains only two chapters on Ray's history; his focus is the events of the year prior to the King assassination. Frank, on the other hand, provides more background on Ray's family history, his early years of factory work, his time in the army, and finally his criminal history.[16] However, in reading Frank's writing on the King murder and his presentation of the evidence for Ray as Dr. King's killer, it is important to note that Frank apparently received an internal endorsement from the FBI and that certain of his remarks about the evidence used in Ray's initial prosecution have become highly questionable.

A memo from FBI Deputy Director Cartha DeLoach to Hoover's second in command, Clyde Tolson, noted that Frank was working on a King assassination book and had asked for the bureau's assistance and that the bureau had an excellent relationship with him. This memo was a follow-up to another internal FBI memo suggesting that it was time for the bureau to choose a friendly, capable author who would prepare a book on the case.[17] Frank himself cites numerous sources and gives ample acknowledgements, but there are no specific references to aid or assistance from the bureau. It also appears that certain pieces of evidence cited in Frank's work, which Frank uses to make a conclusive case against Ray, may not be as clear-cut as originally presented in *An American Death*. We will discuss these issues with the evidence Frank cites and the FBI's crime scene evidence in our own discussion of the murder in Memphis in chapter 13.

Given Ray's family history, his ongoing efforts to score big money are really not surprising. Ray had grown up in an exceptionally poor environment, where simply getting enough money to live was a constant concern. While some members of Ray's own family had held regular jobs and even operated their own businesses, others turned to crime, including theft, burglary, bank robbery, and forgery. But James Earl Ray initially avoided such criminal means and started with a routine factory job, followed by enlistment in the army. In fact, his early years, first when he was working in a shoe factory and later when he was stationed in Germany, were some of his most stable times financially.

In Germany, Ray transferred from the Quartermaster Corps, where he was a truck driver, to the military police (MP).[18] But that duty was a disaster for Ray; the record shows him going AWOL, being confined to quarters, being found drunk in quarters, and going AWOL again.[19] Ray served three months for drunkenness and escaping confinement. It is worth noting that in his 2008 book, *Truth at Last*, Ray's brother John Larry Ray claims that while on MP duty, Ray also participated in the shooting and wounding of a black serviceman. Ray was given a general (rather than honorary) discharge "due to ineptness and lack of adaptability for military service."

John Larry Ray also makes extensive claims that while in the army his brother became associated with the CIA and was subject to mind-control experiments.[20] It appears that document research by Lyndon Barsten, John Ray's coauthor, is largely the source for that CIA scenario, much of it based on speculation about an "unusual" army unit to which Ray was briefly assigned. The book makes a great deal of the proposition that the numerical designation of the unit (the 7892th Infantry Regiment) represented something covert because all "normal" army units were generally designated with only three digits. Also, Barsten was told that the unit was composed of inexperienced and unruly recruits.[21] Actually, the fact that Ray was transferred into the special unit after being repeatedly AWOL, drunk in quarters, and court-martialed suggests that the unit was indeed a indiscriminate, temporary unit that included troublemakers moved out of other units. Fortunately, with the search capabilities and resources available on the Internet, we quickly determined that there was nothing unique about four-digit unit designations in the U.S. Army in Germany during that period and other examples can be located, and thus a less mysterious picture of Ray's army unit service emerges.[22]

Ray's life after his army discharge was largely of one attempt after the other to make money through various criminal acts. That becomes very clear from the information in his FBI files, his arrest and prison records, and extensive interviews done by various authors with his family, cellmates, and former partners in crime. Ray was certainly not fundamentally motivated by anything as esoteric as politics or religion; for Ray, it was all about trying to obtain money. Following his departure from the army, Ray accumulated a record of a dozen petty crimes—burglary, forging money orders, and armed robberies—and was eventually sentenced under the Habitual Criminals Act to twenty years in the Missouri State Penitentiary in Jefferson City.[23]

While in the Missouri State Penitentiary, Ray became a dealer, selling magazines, black market items, and possibly small amounts of amphetamines—whatever he could get his hands on that would move.[24] Estimates are that Ray eventually averaged $200 a month from these sales, sending several hundred dollars to his brother Jerry and having even larger amounts smuggled out to him. One of his later prosecutors estimated that Ray's Missouri State Penitentiary earnings could have netted him several thousand dollars over the five years he spent there. There is considerable argument over how much money Ray might have made in prison, but it is reasonably clear that he did send money out to his brother, taking care to connect with him and obtain funds after his eventual escape.

Still, it seems Ray did have definite political and racial viewpoints although not views strikingly uncharacteristic of his environment. However those views were ones that he and his uncle, Willie Maher, both tried to minimize or conceal after the King murder, since prosecutors might have used them against him to establish motive in the King killing. The reality seems to be that Ray occasionally did make racist remarks and responded positively to others making similar expressions. His participation in such exchanges might well have led to his first hearing about such things as threats against and bounty offers on major black leaders.

WAS RAY THE MAN FOR THE JOB?

Would Ray have been taken seriously as a potential candidate for an offer on Dr. King's life? Did his history match the profile of other individuals who appear to have been told of a bounty offer? Even if he were interested, how credible would Ray have seemed, and how much information might he have been first offered to gauge his interest? The FBI investigation of Ray gives us a detailed picture of his family life, general social and employment background, and some reasonable insight into his views on racial and political matters. In addition, reporter and journalist inquiries have provided considerable elaboration on the FBI's work.

Ray's work experience was limited, but he had held one full-time, legitimate job as a young man. He had worked at the International Shoe Company tannery in Alton, Illinois. That period was a significant improvement in Ray's life, taking him away from the brutal poverty of his earliest years. In Alton, Ray stayed with his grandmother, Mrs. Maher, who helped him get the tannery job. She later served as a primary source for information concerning this period in Ray's life. According to Mrs. Maher, Ray initially spent time with her son, his uncle Willie Maher, but he soon became fast friends with an older man who also worked at the tannery, an older German man named Eric Duncan.[25]

Ray's shop steward later confirmed that the two men were close and spent a great deal of time together, talking "Hitler politics."[26] Initially, Ray's uncle Willie told the FBI that Ray had indeed been very close to an individual who was pro-Nazi and that this friendship had strengthened James Earl Ray's hostility toward both blacks and Jews. This was corroborated by remarks by Ray's brother Jerry, who related that Ray would have preferred to make the United States a country that was all-white, with no blacks and no Jews. Some confirmation of such an attitude comes from Ray's later interest and ongoing efforts to leave the United States for Rhodesia or South Africa, both bastions of racial segregation in Africa.[27] Willie Maher's initial observations about Ray's pro-Nazi friend are well documented; however, Maher later tried to downplay them when interviewed by the HSCA, telling the committee he had never heard Ray utter a single negative remark about blacks.

Other evidence of Ray's general attitude on race is apparent in material gathered during the FBI investigation. In 1955, Ray and a companion robbed a federal post office, and he was sentenced to time in Leavenworth federal penitentiary.[28] Leavenworth was a segregated prison, with whites and blacks housed separately. In general, Ray proved to be a model prisoner; as a result he was approved for work at the prison honor farm. That would have been a much sought-after transfer for less work and greater freedom. But Ray turned down the offer of a transfer. A prison report records that Ray refused "due to the fact that he could not live in an honor farm dormitory because they are integrated."[29]

Given the background of the white population of Missouri State Penitentiary, Ray's feelings would have been relatively common. During his tenure at Missouri State, Ray was reportedly known to several of his fellow inmates as someone who had no use for blacks and who expressed negativity about the more prominent civil rights leaders. Those who expressed matching views were more likely to hear stronger language from Ray, while those who didn't probably never heard him utter any noteworthy remarks about his racial views. Another thing would have made Ray stand out to the racists around him: When Jefferson City integrated its intramural sports, Ray refused to attend the games because the majority of the players were black.[30]

Fellow inmate Cecil Lillibridge probably described Ray most accurately. He said Ray never expressed any particular hatred of Dr. King; he simply disliked blacks in general and the publicity that their leaders were getting. Lillibridge further described Ray as a constant reader of weekly news magazines and felt his major ambition in life was to score a big-money take of $20,000 or $30,000 so he could get out of the U.S. and hide out, possibly in Mexico. It was at Jefferson City where Ray first began to express an interest in Rhodesia as a future destination. Lillibridge did say that Ray sometimes speculated with him about whether or not some splinter group might offer money for the murder of Stokely Carmichael or H. Rap Brown, but he never mentioned Dr. King in such speculation.[31]

Further insight into Ray's attitude on race comes from a nasty and highly visible confrontation he had in early 1968 with a woman in the Jackrabbit bar over prointegration remarks she made. The bartender described Ray dragging her by the hair toward the door and threatening to dump her off in Watts. Her friends broke up the fight, but Ray's behavior led to his being remembered; the integrated bars in L.A. were undoubtedly different from those that Ray habitually frequented.[32]

Individual reports and remarks can always be argued, and some of the reports concerning specific remarks from Ray about Dr. King are questionable. What does seem to be reasonably clear is that Ray was the kind of person who might well have been present in circles where a variety of racist talk could occur, including discussions of bounties on prominent civil rights activists.

Separate from his views on race, Ray's political orientation leaned clearly toward the right. As described above, he had displayed some attraction for Hitler's political philosophy, and according to his brother Jerry, "what appealed to Jimmy in the first place about Hitler was that he would make the U.S. an all-white country, no Jews or Negroes."[33] Much later, in the year before the King assassination, Ray appears to have become a supporter of George Wallace and recruited associates to register to vote and support the Wallace campaign; he identified himself as being involved in Wallace campaign activities when ordering a telephone for his apartment in Los Angeles. He also contacted the John Birch Society in regard to information about emigration to Rhodesia. In communications with William Huie, Ray said that he had made calls and contacts with other ultraright or racist organizations that would look bad for him in the King case; unfortunately he did not specify the names of these organizations.[34]

THE MOTIVATIONS OF JAMES EARL RAY

In summary, it appears that James Earl Ray had been consistently motivated by a fundamental need to make money—at least enough money to allow him to escape the grinding poverty of his childhood. Following his time in the army, he abandoned conventional means and chose to make money by acting outside the law. From 1967 to 1968, he was driven by a new desire to get a larger amount of money, enough to finance his goal of relocating to Rhodesia or South Africa after his escape from prison.

Ray wanted no part of blacks; he opposed integration and the entire civil rights movement. He was not fundamentally driven by racism, but when in the company of like-minded individuals, either in the penitentiary or in bars, he readily expressed racist views and a dislike for "Negroes" and their leaders such as Brown, Carmichael, and King. He was a consistent reader of newspapers and newsmagazines and also gathered information through his many dealings in Missouri State Penitentiary's black market. As a violent offender and convicted armed robber with sympathetic political and racial views, he was a likely candidate to hear talk about a rumored bounty on Dr. King's life.

After King's assassination and Ray's arrest, Ray's acceptance of a guilty plea allowed him to avoid the death penalty while leaving the issue of sponsors and accessories open. The trial judge doubted Ray had acted on his own but felt compelled to accept the guilty plea in order to move forward with the case against Ray. Given that Ray had considerable experience negotiating the criminal justice system and that he had previously used fictitious characters as scapegoats for his crimes, his statements about Raoul must be treated skeptically. Ray consistently told anyone just as much of the truth as he felt useful; he consistently lied about anything that might hurt his own needs or put him at further risk. We feel that Ray created the Raoul figure after the King assassination as a diversion from his actual contacts and to ensure his own safety at the same time. Ray simply would not have directed attention to individuals or groups that might prove personally dangerous to him in prison. Additionally, the Raoul story not only provided an alternative theory (and therefore the sufficient doubt) that could potentially free Ray from conviction, but it also avoided implicating the true conspirators who might still reward Ray (who had as yet failed to collect the bounty for King's life). Given his documented pattern of lying to protect himself, the Raoul story and the details Ray provided about his movements and actions can only be accepted to the extent that they can be independently corroborated.

The 1964 and 1967 bounty offers, discussed in detail in the previous chapter, provide a context in which to consider the idea that James Earl Ray could have become aware of, and eventually responded to, a bounty offer on Dr. King. Both the FBI and a congressional investigative committee documented that such bounty offers were indeed circulating in Ray's last prison, shortly before his own escape. And by early spring 1968, Ray had set up a base of operations in Atlanta—King's hometown. At that point there is specific evidence to indicate that Ray was indeed stalking Dr. King as part of conspiracy, even though his exact intentions and role remain unclear. Regardless, even if he was later set up as a patsy for the shooting in Memphis, as he and his advocates have vigorously claimed, a detailed study of Ray and his activities during both 1967 and 1968 is critical to understanding his recruitment into the King conspiracy.

CHAPTER 9

RAY ON THE RUN

Offers for the murder of Dr. King are a matter of record; we also have reports showing that they were made to habitual criminals including individuals serving extended time in federal prisons. One FBI investigative report on the White Knights' 1967 offer noted that "we have had several instances where persons incarcerated at various times advised that King had a $100,000 bounty placed on his head."[1] But because Ray cannot be considered a reliable or trusted source, we cannot simply turn to him for verification of any bounty offer or role he may have accepted in the assassination of Dr. Martin Luther King Jr.

We do know that Missouri State Penitentiary, where Ray was serving time before his escape in 1967, would have been one point at which Ray could have heard of such an offer. There was a loosely organized militant racist group within the prison; members had worn sheets and killed a black inmate during initial attempts to integrate facilities in 1964.[2] This group could certainly have provided a channel into the prison for information about a bounty offer for King's head.

The House Select Committee on Assassinations seriously investigated one lead regarding a bounty offer that did reach Ray while in prison. That lead traced back to a Saint Louis patent lawyer named John Sutherland. Sutherland was described by associates as a die-hard southerner and Wallace supporter and outspoken in his opposition to integration, civil rights, and the Supreme Court. He founded the Saint Louis White Citizens' Council in 1964 and reportedly served as an advisor to it until his death in 1970. The council had ties to its southern counterparts that were strong supporters of states' rights and segregation.[3] Sutherland was known to have expressed an interest in the NSRP, although the HSCA was unable to trace any specific details of his association with NSRP members.[4] It is known that the NSRP had organized a Saint Louis chapter in 1961, and as of 1966, Missouri had the largest U.S. concentration of active NSRP members.[5] There are also reasons to believe that a King bounty offer may well have been circulated through individuals within the NSRP; we will deal with that possibility in detail in a following chapter.

The HSCA developed considerable evidence to confirm that Sutherland had used an associate, John Kaufman, to contact Russell Byers, a low-level Saint Louis hoodlum, and extend an offer of $50,000 to kill or arrange to kill Dr. King; a "wealthy, secret Southern organization that he would not name" made the offer. The HSCA also located other sources including two attorneys who confirmed that Byers had discussed such an offer. Clearly, Byers was circulating word that a group was willing to pay for King's death. It also turned out that Byers's brother-in-law, John Spica, who was serving a sentence for a contract killing, was jailed in the same cell block as James Earl Ray, and Byers regularly visited Spica at Missouri State Penitentiary.[6]

James Earl Ray admitted that he had gotten to know John Spica, who had worked in the prison. The HSCA interviewed Spica, who distanced himself from Ray and denied any knowledge of a bounty offer. Other inmates advised that the two men were much closer than Spica was admitting.[7]

More important, there is independent corroboration from another inmate named Donald Mitchell for Ray's knowledge of the offer. Mitchell told the HSCA that Ray had mentioned to him, just before Mitchell's release, a deal with people in Saint Louis to collect $50,000 for killing Dr. King. Ray suggested that Mitchell could take the deal for himself if he was interested.[8]

The HSCA also explored various other avenues by which word about the Sutherland offer might have gotten into Missouri State Penitentiary and reached Ray's ears. Its investigation was frustrated by the unwillingness of virtually all the individuals questioned. In the end the HSCA simply concluded that Ray was likely aware of the offer of a major contract on Dr. King by the time that he successfully escaped from Missouri State Penitentiary.

In any event, in April 1967, after two prior attempts, Ray successfully escaped from the Missouri State Penitentiary. His getaway took him to Chicago, back to his former stomping grounds northeast of Saint Louis, and from there directly through Toronto and on to Montreal.[9] In Canada, after failing to obtain credible official identification that would allow him to travel abroad, Ray returned to the United States. Such a route would indicate that Ray was not initially looking toward Atlanta to stalk Dr. King but rather toward Canada for a quick escape overseas.

The work done by the FBI and early investigative reporters such as Huie has taken a great deal of mystery out of Ray's activities in the year preceding the King murder. Huie's inquiries verified a number of the contacts and movements Ray described—sometimes well before the FBI arrived at the same conclusions. But in his revelations to Huie, James Earl Ray also went to considerable length to ensure that some mystery remained.

RAY AND MONEY

Wary of revealing any of his dealings in contraband while an inmate at Missouri State Penitentiary, Ray told Huie that he had saved only $300 at the time of his escape. But Ray very likely accumulated more than $300, having handed over the majority of the surplus to his brother Jerry, who held it for him. In fact, Phil Canale, the state prosecutor for the King case in Memphis, estimated Ray had smuggled out more than $7,000.[10] At one point, Ray's brothers Jerry and John went on record as stating they had handed over various amounts of money to James after his escape, citing figures that were close, in total, to Canale's estimate.[11]

Missouri State Penitentiary officials took great issue with the idea that Ray sold contraband inside the prison or that he was able to generate any serious amount of money through the illegal selling of drugs or pornography to other inmates. They cited official records showing the amount of money legally in his possession, as well as the $210 he sent out and the $242.03 sent to him while in the prison. But interviews with other inmates, which the FBI initially kept confidential, revealed a number of sources who described sales inside the prison and Ray's involvement in the prison's black market, starting with kitchen goods and moving on to minor drugs. In confirmation, Ray's only disciplinary mark at Missouri State Penitentiary related to his being caught carrying contraband including cigarettes, razor blades, and coffee.[12] So, while the amount may be in dispute, there is little doubt that Ray had stashed some money with his brothers, and there is no doubt that it was enough to run the risk of stopping in Chicago long enough to retrieve it after he had managed his prison escape.

After his escape from the Missouri State Penitentiary, Ray stopped in Chicago for several weeks, enough time for him to connect with his brothers and acquire some additional money. Initially, he took a dishwashing job at the Indian Trail Restaurant in the Chicago area for $94 a week, but after a few weeks he received a promotion to a steam table job for $117. He worked for eight weeks and netted approximately $600, while renting a $14-a-week room. Ray waited at the restaurant until his brothers could get in touch and meet to pass on the cash that they had been holding for him. Based on Ray's information, Huie located the restaurant and interviewed the owners. The FBI had failed to do that and, as in several other instances, lagged behind Huie in their own investigation of Ray. The owners recalled that Ray had been a good worker; they had promoted him and seemed content with Ray's performance. But Ray had departed with no notice, shortly after receiving a series of phone calls. His brothers later verified that they were the ones contacting and later meeting Ray.[13]

BACKTRACKING TO SAINT LOUIS

Ray told Huie that he left Chicago with about $450, but he didn't head directly for Canada. Strangely, he headed right back to the Saint Louis area. Given Ray's constant efforts to keep a low profile, it seems rather strange for him (as a recently escaped convict) to head directly back in the direction of Jefferson City. But the Saint Louis area was just across the river from where he had grown up and worked in Alton, Illinois, and was the location of the Grapevine Tavern, which his brother John operated. Certainly his brother's bar might be a location where law enforcement might be expected to be on the lookout for him. But while escaping far away was definitely a priority for Ray, it may be that he first needed more money, names, or contacts to make that happen, and his brother's bar was a familiar and favorable place to start.

The HSCA collected a good deal of information pointing toward the fact that John Ray, who had been previously apolitical, had taken a sudden interest in promoting the Wallace campaign. His bar, the Grapevine, was the center of much Wallace organizing, attracting regular customers (including a number of NSRP members) who were actively campaigning and promoting Wallace for president.[14] And John Ray engaged in transporting individuals to Wallace headquarters to sign them up to vote. In addition, Sutherland (who had initially floated the King bounty) and Kaufman (who mentioned the bounty to several people) were among the strongest Wallace supporters in Saint Louis. Sutherland supported the Wallace campaign financially, paying the salary of one of the American Independent Party staff workers.[15]

John Ray stated that he knew his brother James Earl Ray was a Wallace supporter. Indeed, later, while in California, Ray (who had been even more private and apolitical than his brother) reportedly transported people to the local Wallace headquarters to register them to vote; later those individuals would comment he seemed rather familiar with the place.[16] Interestingly, the reference to his taking people to the Wallace headquarters was the single item in a fifty-six-page "stipulation of fact" that Ray challenged and had removed from his legal record.[17]

All in all, it seems that John Ray's tavern, patronized by so many Wallace supporters, would have been an ideal place for James Earl Ray to encounter gossip about a large cash offer for killing Dr. King. Of course, he may well have encountered nothing more than the same gossip he had heard in prison and figured that pursuing it wasn't his best option. But perhaps

Ray picked up a contact name—just in case. Ray always liked to have a number of options available.

OPTIONS, OPPORTUNITIES, AND RAOUL

It appears that after spending a bit of time in the Saint Louis area, Ray decided that the option of escaping through Canada was simply the best choice for a fugitive convict. There has also been speculation that he may have been tempted by the opportunity to take part in a local robbery across the Mississippi River, in Alton, Illinois, and consequently ended up with the necessary funds (and a compelling reason) to hit the road.[18] The HSCA seriously investigated such speculation. While Ray was in East Saint Louis, the Bank of Alton, just twenty miles away in Alton, Illinois, was indeed robbed by two masked gunmen. They got away with $27,230, so any share of that robbery would have been significant.[19] The HSCA concluded that there was considerable circumstantial evidence to suggest Ray's involvement in the Alton robbery.[20] Among other things, the committee noted that Ray purchased a car and left the Saint Louis area the day after the robbery occurred.

Huie, among others, discounted the possibility that Ray might have teamed up with a local contact for the Alton bank robbery. Still, in making his case, Huie may have overlooked several important pieces of evidence from Ray's background that would have supported Ray's possible involvement. Huie asserted that Ray had never committed a bank or other armed robbery—but in that assertion, he seems to have been unaware that Ray had used a gun in the robbery of several grocery stores in 1959, not to mention that he had committed armed robbery of a London bank while evading capture for King's murder in 1968. Huie also argued that Ray would not have risked a return to prison for such a large score, since Ray had demonstrated the ability to survive with minimal funds while on the lam in Chicago, but that is speculative. Finally, Huie argued that Ray could not have committed the robbery, because he didn't take a large amount of cash on his trip to Canada, but this ignores Ray's known modus operandi of stashing money with his brothers to collect at some later date.

On the other hand, in favor of Huie's assertion that Ray was not involved in the lucrative Alton bank robbery, Ray was so broke when he fled to Europe after the King assassination that he was forced to attempt even riskier robberies in London. Ray himself blamed his final capture solely on his inability to steal more money for his escape. "I should have pulled a holdup, but I didn't. I got on that plane without enough money to go where I intended to go," he told police. If Ray was involved in the Alton robbery, it might well explain his sudden departure to Canada, but we feel that it is simply not possible to resolve the question with the information currently available.

Sorting out the facts concerning James Earl Ray's movements after his escape from Missouri State Penitentiary has never been easy. In Huie's interviews with Ray, whenever Ray was asked about something that made no apparent sense—about where he got money for certain things, or why he spontaneously traveled to certain locations—Ray responded with a single answer: "Raoul." Raoul was Ray's mystery man, recruiting Ray in Canada, giving him money; telling him where to go, where to stay, where to meet; having him buy a rifle in Birmingham; and consequently setting him up as a patsy for the King assassination in Memphis. At first blush, Raoul seemed to be the answer to all the mysteries of the King assassination. Yet, as one becomes more familiar with James Earl Ray, the very existence of Raoul may be better understood in light of Ray's history of creative dissembling.

Ray used the shadowy figure of Raoul to avoid dealing with all questions about his sources of money, ranging from the Alton robbery to his reported marijuana sales in Mexico (interviews in Mexico had revealed that Ray had been in Puerto Vallarta with "a large quantity of marijuana").[21] Ray was open about his travel to Mexico, but, as with the other segments of his travels, he clearly left out a few details. It seemed Ray's initial explanations were all about Raoul. According to Ray, after his escape from prison and his interludes at the Indian Trail Restaurant in Chicago and at his brother's bar in Saint Louis, Ray went to Canada. His goal was to obtain Canadian identification that would enable him to leave for parts unknown, perhaps some racially segregated place in Africa, such as Rhodesia.

But Ray said that Raoul had diverted him, getting him involved in minor smuggling across the Canadian border and then putting him on retainer for future unspecified activities, including smuggling and international gun sales. Raoul offered Ray money up front and the promise of the identification papers that Ray needed. From that point on, Ray asserted, Raoul played the role of puppeteer, manipulating all Ray's future actions. He supplied Ray with money and ordered him to go Mobile, Alabama, but Ray talked Raoul into sending him to Birmingham instead. There Raoul bought Ray a white Ford Mustang and sent him across the Mexican border.

As related by Ray, Raoul eventually called him back to Atlanta and proposed a project involving guns. Ray asserted that he simply took Raoul's money and followed orders.[22] Raoul instructed Ray to shop for and buy a rifle, and when he was dissatisfied with Ray's purchase, it was Raoul who ordered Ray to return the first gun for a .30-06. Raoul supposedly told Ray to meet him in Memphis, thereby setting him up as a patsy. According to Ray, it was Raoul who really killed King, leaving a trail of evidence framing Ray for the murder.

Huie, as well as Ray's first two lawyers, Hanes and Foreman, concluded that Raoul was a construct Ray created to cover "any and all of his contacts and accomplices in crime between July 1967 and April 1968."[23] If the figure of Raoul were a composite, it would certainly explain Ray's constant changes in Raoul's physical description, which varied to include an auburn-haired man, a thirty-five-year-old blond Latino, and a reddish-haired French-Canadian, with complexions that ranged from ruddy and dark to lighter than Ray's own pale skin.

Such prevaricating would be consistent behavior for Ray. He had a history of creating fictional accomplices and, on occasion, placing blame on characters created out of thin air. For example, while under arrest in Las Vegas for vagrancy, Ray created a local character named Bill Holland to explain a roll of silver dollars in his possession.[24] Later, under arrest for a much more serious crime, Ray and a partner created "William J. McBride" to take the fall for a post office burglary. In that case, the fictional character allowed them to successfully claim to have been merely the middlemen who were caught passing stolen money orders, effectively avoiding a federal crime.

Creating Raoul and portraying himself as a dupe through Huie's *Look* articles would have been an effective way for Ray to reassure any real King conspirators who might have viewed Ray as a threat to their anonymity. Ray was insistent that Huie begin publishing newspaper and magazine articles as soon as possible, exposing Huie to the judge's ire but possibly passing on an early signal to others. And it is a matter of record that J. B. Stoner, representing the Patriotic Legal Fund, did contact Ray in London with an offer to finance his defense. Following his extradition to the United States, Ray invited Stoner to a private jail meeting. Such sympathetic support of Ray could be interpreted as evidence of collaboration in the assassination of Martin Luther King Jr. The HSCA explored a variety of leads suggesting that money had been covertly channeled from various Klan members to Ray's defense; however, they could not fully confirm any of those leads.[25]

PUTTING RAY IN CONTEXT

Many researchers, convinced by Ray's statements, see the invisible hand of Raoul and, by extension, a larger conspiracy guiding all Ray's travels in 1967. However, we see Raoul as a red herring that Ray created. He had used similar diversions in previous crimes.

In addition, much of what we see in Ray's travels in 1967, after his escape from Missouri State Penitentiary, fits with Ray's prior history. Ray had formerly traveled to Canada, Mexico, and Los Angeles; he was an old hand at traveling long distances after committing a crime. With only one exception, none of his travels in the year before the King murder, or in his escape afterward, took Ray to places where he had not been in previous years.

For example, Ray had already spent considerable time in Los Angeles after receiving a general discharge from the army. Later, after a 1955 post office break that netted a good number of postal money orders, he and his accomplice took a sixteen-day trip from Memphis to Miami, then to New Orleans, and finally to Kansas City. After an armed robbery of a bar and dice hall in Madison, Illinois, in 1958, Ray drove back through Saint Louis and on to New Orleans. From New Orleans he went on to Brownsville, Texas, where he crossed the border at Matamoros into Mexico. He then obtained a tourist visa and drove from Mexico City to Vera Cruz and on to Acapulco, admittedly doing minor smuggling along the way. By February 1959, Ray was back from Mexico and in Saint Louis again, making a living in petty crimes, including bootlegging. After one of his bootlegging customers was picked up in a car connected to Ray, police raided Ray's grandmother's boarding house. Ray took off for Canada, staying in Montreal for a few months, paying his expenses with the revenue from minor robberies, until he felt the heat was off and he could go back to Saint Louis. Ray would return to many of these cities in the year before and the months following King's assassination.

Although some of Ray's very early crimes seem rather petty, he clearly advanced over time, graduating to armed robberies involving fairly intricate planning. And Ray didn't always get caught in such crimes. We previously related a botched grocery store robbery, but in that same year, Ray and an accomplice had robbed another grocery store in Saint Louis and escaped with $1,200. Even when witnesses identified Ray and his accomplice based on a camera used to record check cashing, the two men managed to remain free. And it is worth noting that in both grocery store robberies, as well as his final London bank robbery, Ray routinely carried and displayed a handgun, committing himself to felony crimes. It is also worth noting that in the botched grocery store robbery, which ultimately landed him in Missouri State Penitentiary in Jefferson City, Ray at first told police "I cannot deny it, and I won't admit it." Later he signed a statement admitting his role but insisted on defending himself in court. And when Ray took the stand at his trial, he denied everything, even rejecting his signed statement. The jury took twenty minutes to find him guilty. Ray drew twenty years in the Missouri State Penitentiary. Ray's accomplice, who had pled guilty, was sentenced to only seven years.[26]

JAMES EARL RAY'S CRIMES AND ESCAPES

Although Ray's actions during the heat of a crime were sometimes spontaneous and less than effective, he did successfully pull off a series of robberies and other crimes. Over the years, his escapes became more thoughtfully planned. If he was not caught at the scene or immediately afterward, he generally managed to stay free for extended periods. He even managed to escape from various prisons, including a state penitentiary.

Strangely, that expertise seems nowhere apparent in the aftermath of the King murder in 1968. There is virtually no indication that Ray had given any thought to an escape after the King shooting. Ray's flight on April 4, 1968, was a pure mess; nothing about it suggests forethought or planning. After the murder in Memphis, Ray fled back to Atlanta, driving backroads for eleven hours, tossing out expensive movie camera equipment, and only taking time to wipe off prints on his car before abandoning it. According to Ray, he had returned to Atlanta to pick up some clothing and remove evidence that might be used to track or incriminate him. But he did that apparently knowing full well he had abandoned a rifle and a whole bag full of his personal possessions outside the scene of the shooting in Memphis, covered with his fingerprints.[27] In Atlanta, he returned to an apartment still containing a number of his possessions, but only partially sanitized the place, wiping fingerprints from various items but leaving maps and various other possessions, including one map with markings that could be interpreted to show that he had been stalking Dr. King in Atlanta.[28] These mistakes appear to be the actions of a panicked fugitive rather than a calculating criminal.

Ray claimed that he consciously left other material for the police to find, including a John Birch Society pamphlet and a couple of pairs of pants that were too small for him. Furthermore, he left a meal receipt showing that he and another person had eaten together in Atlanta. Clearly Ray had not taken any pains to cover his trail before leaving Atlanta in the first place, and he either did a poor job of clearing evidence or intentionally left evidence indicating that he had been in contact with other people immediately before the King murder.[29]

James Earl Ray's record clearly demonstrates that he was experienced at escaping and eluding capture. He was also calculating and cunning, constantly devising options. We will see evidence of this as we trace his travels along the road that finally led to Memphis. We will also see that there is nothing extraordinary about Ray's trips to Canada, Mexico, Los Angeles, and New Orleans in 1967. He had done all that before. But his travel to Birmingham, Alabama, was something strikingly new.

CHAPTER 10

RAY'S LONG AND WINDING ROAD

It seems most likely that Ray's eventual arrival in Memphis can be traced to the talk of King bounties that had been passed among various criminal venues. The FBI and House Select Committee on Assassinations independently confirmed that talk of a bounty offer of a large sum was in circulation within Missouri State Penitentiary, and we have reviewed details of the $100,000 bounty being circulated among the Dixie Mafia. One source provided confirmation that Ray himself was very much aware of the Sutherland offer being circulated in the Saint Louis area. As we follow Ray's travels, we will review other points at which he may have heard such an offer discussed or where he may have made his own inquiries. The possibilities include his brother's bar in East Saint Louis, frequented by Wallace supporters and NSRP members; a bar in Toronto where he may have met a Klan contract bomber from New Orleans; his sojourn in Birmingham where he stayed just fifteen minutes from the NSRP national headquarters; and finally his stay in Los Angeles where he met more Wallace campaign supporters and NSRP members.

While we can't be sure of how his knowledge of a King bounty developed, we can be virtually certain as to what point in time Ray finally started tracking Dr. King. It was after he began to run out of money and made a spontaneous trip from Los Angeles to New Orleans. While certainly not definitive proof, the FBI investigation identified several suspicious phone calls from pay phones where Ray stopped and was seen to use the phone. Among the numbers called are unlisted telephone numbers in Jackson and Laurel,

Mississippi.[1] Reinforcing the FBI's phone inquiry, Ray reportedly received calls from both New Orleans and Atlanta after his return to Los Angeles. And, following those calls, a visitor with a noticeable southern accent arrived in Los Angeles asking for Ray at his rooming house. After that mysterious visit, Ray's own actions leave little doubt that he had committed himself to what we refer to as the "King option."

Huie has noted that the closer Ray's narration got to Memphis, the less reliable it became.[2] But Ray did provide some accurate information about his travels, and there seems to have been a change in his general behavior which suggests a newfound purpose. After his escape from Missouri State Penitentiary, Ray demonstrated considerable patience as well as caution when he took the dishwashing job at the Indian Trail Restaurant outside of Chicago. He did not return to his prior excessive drinking, and he limited his time with prostitutes, demonstrating a great deal of discipline after several years in prison.[3] He was now a man on the run, and he had to be careful. So before he would commit himself to pursuing any bounty on Dr. King, he had a variety of other, less risky options to explore. And the least risky was going far, far away; while working at his restaurant job outside Chicago, he had already written to the Canadian embassy about emigration to Canada.

THE CANADIAN OPTION

On Friday, July 14, 1967, Ray purchased a used car and shortly afterward was on his way to Canada. Ray purchased the car under the name of John L. Rayns (he had used the same name for his job at the Indian Trail Restaurant).[4] Ray used this alias because he actually possessed a social security card in the name of John L. Rayns, and other than his own identity cards, it appears to have been the only U.S. identification he had. By July 17, Ray arrived in Montreal and registered at the Motel La Bourgade under the name John L. Rayns.

The following day, he rented an apartment using the name Eric Starvo Galt, telling the manager he was employed at Expo 67, the International and Universal Exposition being held in Montreal.[5] Ray's use of that name has been discussed at great length by many authors and researchers; some see it as a simply the choice of yet another alias (something Ray routinely did in his travels). After all, he had driven past road signs for the Canadian town of Galt on his way to Montreal. But other researchers and authors are more suspicious and have argued that unknown parties provided the new identity to Ray.[6, 7, 8, 9]

It is clear that Ray's first goal in Canada was simply to acquire what he needed to leave for a foreign country—according to various sources and Ray's own inquiries, a country in Africa, most likely one whose practice of racial segregation fit his own prejudices.[10] But Ray misunderstood the legal requirements for obtaining a Canadian passport, which he would need for international travel out of Canada.[11] His understanding, as illustrated by his actions after the King murder, indicated that he believed that he would need a Canadian citizen to vouch for him in order to get the required paperwork. During his escape after the King murder (but only after taking considerable pains to steal a real identity), an employee at a Canadian travel agency informed him that a sponsor was not a requirement and that the travel agency could sign off on a form which, with a birth certificate, would be all he needed for a Canadian passport.[12] If he had known that, it is highly likely that Ray would have been long gone back in 1967 and never returned to the United States at the time of the assassination.

Because he thought he needed a Canadian sponsor, Ray spent most of his time there in 1967 planning and looking for such a person, in particular a female sponsor. Ray seems to have had no particular interest in women other than his routine use of prostitutes. At the time of his escape from prison, he had no women friends and his relationships with women were limited. But Ray had no problem using women for his own selfish ends.[13]

While in Canada in 1967, Ray went to great lengths to create a new and respectable image in what would be a failed effort to recruit a female patron. He spent hundreds of dollars on new clothes including a tailored suit. Next, Ray (as Galt) booked a stay at a premier Canadian resort, Gray Rocks Inn. At Gray Rocks he met and impressed an attractive Canadian lady.[14] She lived in Ottawa, but she and a girlfriend planned to go to Montreal to visit Expo 67, and so they followed him there, spending a couple of days. He told her he needed to talk to her about something very serious and would come to visit her in Ottawa. Ray would eventually admit that his interest in her was as a potential sponsor for the passport he would need to leave Canada, but for some reason Ray did not follow her to Ottawa for another eleven days.

There is nothing concrete to suggest what Ray actually did during that interval. He later related that he had worked the Montreal waterfront, visiting bars and trying to make contacts to get papers for work on a ship. In one of the bars, he said he met the man he called Raoul and they worked out an arrangement for Ray to make money doing some smuggling across the border from Canada. Independent research has revealed that indeed Ray might have made some interesting contacts, including the possibility that he met a fellow American named Jules Ricco Kimble, a man who shared certain of his opinions and interests—including an interest in making some quick money. That Kimble also performed violent acts on behalf of the Klan makes him an especially suspicious figure.

Toronto Star bureau chief Andy Salwyn made a diligent search for potential Ray connections in the vicinity of the Neptune Bar, a fairly visible hangout in the neighborhood of Ray's Montreal apartment. He located a young lady who said that during that particular summer she had a boyfriend who hung out at that bar. He was from New Orleans and he used the names Rollie and Rolland—and the alias Max Lindsay. The girlfriend told Salwyn that Rollie was an interesting fellow. He had a special radio in his ivory Camaro (which he used to monitor police calls), carried guns in the car's trunk, and made a lot of long-distance calls from her apartment. Later checks would show those calls were to New Orleans and Texas.[15] A second Canadian girlfriend told Salwyn that Rollie had been working at Montreal General Hospital and that she had also telephoned him at a hospital in New Orleans.[16] Could this "Rollie" be Ray's notorious "Raoul"?

In attempting to find out who "Rollie" was, investigation identified a man named Jules Ricco Kimble. Kimble had a very colorful life, going well beyond having a wife in New Orleans and two concurrent girlfriends in Montreal. Kimble's background included Klan activities, suspected drug dealing, and assault. He was also under investigation for attacking black labor leaders targeted by the Klan. The HSCA found corroboration for this information in Royal Canadian Mounted Police files; it indicated Kimble called New Orleans daily, listened to police broadcasts, carried guns, and made racist comments.[17] His wife, in New Orleans, later reported that she had seen guns and explosives in his car.

The HSCA did look into Kimble but ran into a quagmire, largely the result of Kimble's misleading wild tales involving the CIA, spies, and other such intrigue.[18] They were also unable to positively place Kimble in Montreal at the exact time as Ray, although Salwyn had confirmed those dates with Kimble's girlfriend. What does seem to be certain though is that Kimble, who had been arrested on a variety of criminal charges when he returned to his wife in New Orleans, did indeed have significant Klan contacts. In July 1967 he met with four Grand Dragons of the Klan at his home; afterward he disappeared for several days. Other meetings with Klan leaders occurred earlier in February and March 1967.

The HSCA investigation did reveal that Kimble had been arrested in Louisiana for impersonating an officer, aggravated assault, and possession of illegal weapons. His wife told investigators that Kimble used fake medical degrees and other documents to gain employment at a New Orleans hospital and thereby obtain access to controlled drugs.[19] He was being investigated in Louisiana in 1967 by the Louisiana Labor Management Commission of Inquiry for acts of violence against union officers and black labor organizers targeted by the Klan.[20] He was a suspect in the bombings of union officers and other labor-related violence. Later he would be convicted and garner a major federal prison sentence.

Professor Philip Melanson, a respected King assassination researcher, interviewed the Louisiana commission investigator, Joseph Oster. Oster had built an extensive file on Kimble and interviewed his wife at great length regarding Kimble's movements (to the extent that she could track him). The

HSCA had determined that Kimble could not have met Ray in Montreal because they were not there at the same time. Oster, however, documented a far different story, showing that Kimble had traveled to Montreal multiple times in July and August 1967, when Ray was in Montreal.[21] There is no certain proof that Kimble and Ray met each other, but if they did, Kimble's connections in Montreal, New Orleans, and Miami could have proven useful to Ray. If they did not meet, Kimble certainly illustrates the sort of individual Ray could easily have met in the establishments he frequented, the sort of low-level "fences" and smugglers that were apparently easy to find in the bars Ray tended to patronize.

In at least one aspect, Kimble certainly would have been a good match for Ray's "Raoul." Ray talked at length of meeting a fellow in a Montreal bar and entering into a smuggling deal. Kimble had reportedly faked documents to get a hospital job in New Orleans, thereby gaining access to controlled substances. He told his new Canadian girlfriend that he had been involved with narcotics, and she stated that he would sometime disappear for an hour and return with plenty of cash. He reportedly made private plane flights on the weekends, including one to Miami. If Ray did meet Kimble, there is certainly a possibility that Kimble provided him with an opportunity for generating some quick cash.[22] Given the patterns in Ray's behavior, it seems reasonably certain that if he had not made a deal with Kimble, he very likely made one with someone much like Kimble.[23]

In any event, Ray stuck to his option of exiting via Canada and continued to pursue his new lady friend. So next we find him heading to Ottawa to reconnect with her. At first, things were fine. Ray arrived in a good mood, and she gave him a tour of the city. Then they passed the building where she worked. Unfortunately for Ray, it turned out that she was a Canadian government employee at the Department of Transportation. As soon as Ray became aware of that, the relationship cooled. He did not spend the night with her, as he had at Gray Rocks, and she never heard from him again.

As for Ray, he went directly back to Montreal and was on the road toward Chicago the following day. Ray's subsequent behavior suggests that it was at that point that he abandoned his Canadian exit option and that his interest in the King bounty began to surface. While we have no idea of Ray's actual activities following his abortive contacts with his Canadian lady, there is new information suggesting that perhaps he did not drive directly back into the United States.

John Nicol, an investigative reporter for the Canadian Broadcasting Corporation, using never-before-seen Royal Canadian Mounted Police files as well as HSCA documents, established that Ray may have stayed in Toronto before reentering the United States.[24] Previously, Ray was believed to have spent time in Toronto only after the King assassination, during his escape. Nicol additionally established the presence of known NSRP members in Canada who, like many veterans of the NSRP's Birmingham efforts in 1963, had scattered throughout North America to advance the white supremacist cause. Canada, in fact, had its own burgeoning white supremacist movement by the late 1960s, and at least one Klan expert speculated that Ray may have made contact with them.[25] Although one of these men, a native of Canada, had by 1968 purportedly divorced himself from the NSRP, Nicol presented evidence that the HSCA had an intense interest in him and other individuals. Unfortunately, neither the available Royal Canadian Mounted Police nor HSCA files establish the reasons or details of that interest. Did the House or Canadian investigators establish a connection between these individuals and Ray? Could they have been the reason why Ray went immediately to their former base of activities in Birmingham?

BACK IN THE UNITED STATES

It does appear that when Ray crossed back into the United States in August 1967, he was transporting some sort of contraband with him. There has been speculation that Ray might have been given the Galt identity from organized crime sources for the purposes of using Ray as part of a heroin-smuggling network.[26] However, that comes into question since Ray already had a perfectly functional American alias with legitimate identification papers in the name of John Rayns.

Circumstantial corroboration for a smuggling scenario comes from the fact that Ray didn't drive from Canada directly to Birmingham. Using his John Rayns identification, he crossed back into the United States, checking into a motel in Gary, Indiana. And according to Ray himself, he then stopped in Chicago to visit his brother Jerry, where he ditched the car he had purchased, and shortly afterward left on a train to Birmingham, Alabama.[27] It may be that Ray felt there was some risk in the longer-term use of the Rayns name, or it may be that he had simply decided to be cautious and create a unique new alias for himself as soon as he reached Birmingham—which is exactly what he did.

In 1972 George McMillan, author of *The Making of an Assassin*, interviewed Jerry Ray, who said that his brother James Earl Ray had indeed visited him in Chicago, tried to convince him to go into the pornographic movie business, and invited him to go to Birmingham with him, which Jerry Ray declined. James Earl Ray also showed him a large amount of cash and, according to his brother, was also toying with the King bounty option and planned to travel first to Birmingham, because it would be better to go after King or someone from the South. James Earl Ray handed over his car to brother, telling him it was "hot" and that he better get a new set of plates for it, and then he was off to Birmingham, by train.[28]

Later, Jerry Ray denied making those remarks to McMillan and then stated he simply could not recall making such remarks. However, McMillan's original notes of the interview are archived and support the interview as he describes it. And there is circumstantial corroboration in the fact that James Earl Ray did exactly what his brother reportedly stated. Ray relocated to Birmingham and cultivated a new identity as a southerner, that of Eric S. Galt.

INTERLUDE IN BIRMINGHAM

Ray's only explanation for his time in Birmingham was that the mysterious Raoul had asked him to relocate to Mobile, Alabama, but that Ray had talked him into Birmingham instead. (Ray stated that he felt Mobile would be bad for his allergies; also, he preferred a larger town in order to be more inconspicuous.)[29] Neither Mobile nor Birmingham have a significant history as a jumping-off point for smuggling drugs or guns across the border, but both have come up several times in our discussion of the ongoing efforts to kill Dr. King. The idea that Ray had gone to either location in pursuit of people who would know more about a King bounty is speculative. But such speculation becomes more likely when we note that Ray set up residence within a short drive of the National States' Rights Party headquarters office in Birmingham and when we find that Sidney Barnes, of Mobile, later remarked to an FBI source that he himself knew James Earl Ray.[30]

Ray arrived in Birmingham on Sunday, August 25, 1967, still using the name Rayns when checking into the Grenada Hotel. The following day, he would take the first step in establishing a new U.S. identity as Eric Galt, by checking into a rooming house under that name. Ray told the manager at the rooming house that he was taking a long vacation from his recent employment at the Ingalls shipyard in Pascagoula, Mississippi, possibly staying several months.[31] Ray's immediate priority seems to have been to begin establishing a basic "Galt" identity. Two days after checking in as Galt at the rooming house, he rented a safe deposit box. Apparently one use of the box was to stash his other identity documents; he was very sensitive to the risk of having conflicting sets of identification papers in his possession. That would prove to be a reasonable concern, as in June 1968, this discrepancy ultimately led to Ray's capture in London.

Ray's next move was to purchase a sporty used Mustang, get it registered, and then obtain an Alabama driver's license for himself in the name of Eric S. Galt. Ray was not required to present birth or other identification to get the license; he stated on his application that he had been previously licensed in 1962 in Louisiana.[32] Within approximately a week of his arrival in Birmingham, James Earl Ray, also known as John Rayns, was able to present at least minimal paperwork to legally identify himself as Eric S. Galt.[33] That would be the identity he would use for the next several months, during his time in Birmingham, through Atlanta, and all the way to Memphis. Eventually his continuing use of the Galt alias allowed the FBI to quickly track and identify him, based on the registration of the Alabama-tagged Mustang that he eventually abandoned in Atlanta.

With his first priority met, Ray was mobile with enough identification to get through a traffic stop, book a motel room, or cross a border. Then for the next several weeks, Eric Galt did nothing—well, nothing much that we know of. The rooming house manager in Birmingham told the FBI that he was a quiet fellow, spent time alone in the lounge during the day watching television, ate breakfast late to avoid mingling with the other tenants, and otherwise spent a lot of time in his room. Later, there would be a number of witnesses to Ray's activities in Mexico and in Los Angeles; he frequented bars there as he had in Canada. But if he frequented bars in Birmingham, nobody talked about it. He did go out for one known activity: dance lessons. By themselves the dance lessons seem very much out of character for Ray (and he would enroll for another dance course in Los Angeles a few months later), but in combination with another of his options, they make much more sense.

Ray reportedly sold sex magazines in prison, ordered sex manuals while in Canada, reportedly asked his brother about joining him in the pornography business, and, in Birmingham, as Eric Galt, ordered a complete filmmaking system from a company in Chicago. The system included a Super 8 camera, a dual projector, a combination splicing machine, and a twenty-foot remote control—everything one would need to make sex movies, including the ability to film in slow motion and under different types of lighting.[34] Another indicator of what he was doing is the fact that, while in Montreal, he had sent a money order to a manufacturer in California for a compound that would turn regular glass into a two-way mirror.[35] Clearly, with the right subjects, Ray could parlay photography into a less risky income source than armed robbery or, under the right circumstances, use it to blackmail victims in order to raise money in his quest for a Canadian passport and ultimate emigration to Africa.

While in Birmingham, Ray seems to have spent time establishing a Galt identity and focusing on his filmmaking pursuits and his dance and locksmith classes. But does that account for all Ray's time in Birmingham? We simply don't know. We do know that his rooming house was only a short drive to NSRP national headquarters. And the NSRP was very much involved in promoting and raising funds for the Wallace campaign. While in Los Angeles, in December 1967, James Earl Ray visited the campaign headquarters for George Wallace and the American Independent Party (partially staffed by NSRP volunteers); it seems quite possible that he may have done the same in Birmingham.

And if he had gone to a local bar, as was his constant custom, the Birmingham bars were still frequented by the old hard-core racists who had been involved in years of violence, including the 1964 King bombings. While in Birmingham, Ray would have seen regional and national news about the wave of bombings going on next door in Mississippi, as well as in Alabama. He might have seen coverage of the convictions and pending jail sentences for the White Knights in Mississippi. If he turned up any particular information about a bounty related to the White Knights, he most likely also came across newspaper and television coverage of the FBI's massive effort in Mississippi, the trials, and the testimony of informants. If so, that might have raised some flags for the ever-cautious Ray, turning him back to other options.

SHOW ME THE MONEY

In determining how James Earl Ray could have been brought into an ongoing effort to kill Dr. King, we need to reexamine the nature of the offer that would have attracted Ray. Based on Ray's history, two things would be critical: Ray would have to be convinced that there was a significant amount of money in it for him, and he would have to be shown that payment was guaranteed. Racist bar talk was one thing, but for Ray to break through his characteristic caution, he would need to be convinced that people with real money were behind it and that they were using the proper precautions and security for him to elude law enforcement.

For decades, one of the major stumbling blocks preventing investigators from linking Ray to a racist conspiracy to assassinate King was locating a dependable source who could have fronted such a large sum of money.

William Bradford Huie suggested in the first book written on Ray that racist organizations simply did not hire outside people to kill blacks, and even if they would, they didn't have any money. With documents and new research available as of 2010, we now know that Huie was wrong on both counts.

Money was always the first question about purported Klan bounties. The first truly "high-dollar" bounty we find recorded is in the FBI report of a $100,000 bounty on Dr. King in 1965. The story was short on specifics, but it was circulating in North Carolina. Apparently word had been floated at a Klan meeting that "certain parties" had the money and were looking for the right person to accept a contract on King. Unlike the tightly knit White Knights organization in Mississippi, the Carolina Klans were relatively fragmented with several competing leaders. Salisbury, in Rowan County, North Carolina, was a hotbed of violent activity. Another militant group, led by James W. "Catfish" Cole, operated from the Maxton area, and Ed Dawson in Greenville had a reputation for being especially tough.[36] In her epic survey of the Klan, Patsy Sims gives ample evidence of the many factions competing with each other for influence and especially money, because funds were always in short supply. The FBI may have paid little attention to the 1965 bounty talk in their investigation of King's assassination, simply because it seemed virtually impossible that the Carolina Klans had the sort of money mentioned in the report. However, a closer reading of the report suggests that the North Carolina Klansmen in question were simply fronting for certain parties who did have that sort of money.

A second clue contradicting Huie's contention that racist organizations did not have the money to hire outside bounty hunters comes from investigating the late-1966/early-1967 Sutherland offer in Saint Louis. While relatively well-to-do, John Sutherland was not likely to have had $50,000 to back a King bounty, but sources of information about the offer had specifically stated that the money would be coming from "a secret southern organization . . . they had a lot of money."[37] Where and how did Sutherland come across such a secret southern society, and where did they obtain that amount of money?

FOLLOW THE MONEY

Based on investigative work by Atlanta-based researcher Lamar Waldron, we may now have an answer to the question of money, including a source for the gossip in North Carolina, the identity of a secret southern society with a lot of money, and an individual who could have passed the word to both Klansmen in North Carolina and Sutherland in Saint Louis. In *Legacy of Secrecy*, Waldron describes his work with a highly credible Atlanta source who detailed a multiyear fund-raising effort at one of the huge Atlanta automobile factories. The Lakewood, Atlanta, factory employed between seventy-nine hundred and eight thousand United Auto Workers (UAW) members and had been a focus of Klan efforts. One worker at the Lakewood plant was the Imperial Wizard of the Georgia Klan, and estimates were that as many as five thousand Atlanta UAW members belonged to the Klan. The fund-raising started in 1965 and went on every payday for the next three years—right up until the time of Dr. King's assassination.[38]

Waldron's source had been close to the plant worker who participated in the collections at the front entrance of the plant; that individual was routinely joined by Joseph Milteer of Quitman, Georgia, and by one or more professionals from the Atlanta community. The funds were collected for the purpose of opposing integration, stopping residential blockbusting (if one home was sold to a black family, it would dramatically lower the property values in the surrounding area, producing white flight and encouraging other black families to move in), and fighting civil rights activities in general. But Waldron's source reported that some of the most radical and trusted Klan members at the plant were told that the money was really intended to fund the elimination of Dr. King. There is no way to estimate how much money was collected in this effort—it certainly could have been in the tens of thousands of dollars. Apparently the amount was so significant that it had to be hidden by investing a good deal of it in undeveloped mountain property in North Carolina. Properties were held in the names of the principals of this secret group, and those principals spent considerable amounts of their free time in North Carolina.[39]

Joseph Milteer himself was a very special case. Milteer had contacts in Klan groups across the South, including Florida and the Carolinas. He was a recruiter for the National States' Rights Party and had been an officer in their political front, the Constitution Party.[40] He was well acquainted with J. B. Stoner and with Swift's Christian Identity ministry and organization in California. Equally as important, he was an active member of the Atlanta White Citizens' Council, one of a network of White Citizens' Councils stretching across the South—just as John Sutherland was a member of the Saint Louis White Citizens' Council.[41] Unfortunately, there is no hard evidence to tie Milteer personally to Sutherland, but given that Sutherland's wife was from Atlanta, that he was in communication with other White Citizens' Councils, and had shown an interest in the NSRP, such a connection seems imminently possible.

Waldron develops a strong case that Milteer had been searching for individuals to execute a murder contract on King. It became critical for him to fulfill the promises he had made to certain radical and potentially violent people who had participated in raising the funds in Atlanta. The network of fund-raisers needed to demonstrate that they had not been taking money under false pretenses. Initially, Milteer might have assumed he could find Klansman to do the task. But using any of Stoner's "boys from Atlanta" would have been too risky; anyone tied to Georgia racists could be potentially traced back to Milteer or his associates.

Perhaps that explains the fact that the offer was first extended to North Carolina Klansmen, then to a criminal network that could reach out to suitable individuals. It should also be noted that Milteer himself appears to have had connections to some rather mysterious people in a number of states. Investigative reporter Dan Christensen has done virtually the only independent research into Milteer. In a visit to his home after Milteer's somewhat mysterious death in 1974, Christensen found the house had been ransacked. Someone had obviously been through his extensive files and notes. More to the point, Christensen learned that a neighbor had observed men in a truck with Texas license plates carting away boxes from Milteer's home after his death.[42]

BIRMINGHAM AND JAMES EARL RAY, A.K.A. ERIC S. GALT

We believe that the circumstantial evidence corroborated by Ray's remarks to inmate Donald Mitchell and to his brother in Chicago demonstrate that Ray was aware of a substantial bounty being offered for the murder of Dr. King—the same offer that Sutherland's associates had been circulating. However, there is nothing to indicate that Ray personally contacted Sutherland or anyone associated with him or that he received any specific referrals at that point. Ray likely did learn that certain NSRP members had some sort of connection to the offer and that Birmingham would seem a reasonable place to pursue it.

It is quite possible that Ray did make some contact in Birmingham and at least put his name (or rather Galt's) into play for consideration. But there is no indication that anything went further at that point in time. Perhaps the timing wasn't right. It may have taken time to pass along Ray's interest, or perhaps other candidates were higher up in the queue. The secret southern group might not have been ready for a convict on the run . . . yet.

It may have taken much of 1967 for Milteer and his associates to realize that floating offers through select personal contacts just wasn't working and neither were their selective prison-recruiting efforts, which depended on reaching not only an interested party but also one who would be shortly released. The summer rioting of 1967 had been dramatic; the July Detroit riots had left 43 dead, 467 injured, and more than two thousand buildings destroyed. It was the largest American civil disturbance in a single city between the draft riots in New York during the Civil War and the race riots in Los Angeles in 1992. Waldron speculates that the rioting may have escalated pressure on Milteer to make something happen, to take advantage of the growing tension and at least generate an attack on King. He also makes the point that by the end of 1967, Milteer and his associates (much like Sam Bowers and the White Knights) were running out of options.[43]

If Milteer did raise the substantial money Waldron's anonymous source cited, the question would be how that money connects to a White Knights bounty, specifically the one that was making use of outside criminals similar to Ray. Waldron cites work by historian Michael Kurtz, alleging that Milteer had contacts to Mafia kingpin Carlos Marcello in New Orleans. Building on work done by investigative reporter Bill Sartor, Waldron speculates that Milteer was part of a group that paid Marcello to kill King.

We feel that a more likely scenario involves Milteer forwarding the money to his most obvious and known associates: white supremacists. As we have described, Donald Nissen delivered money from Floyd Ayers, a known associate of James Venable, to a Sybil Eure, supposedly the go-between for LeRoy McManaman, the purveyor of the bounty offer in Leavenworth penitentiary, and the White Knights of Mississippi. FBI documents also confirm that Venable and Milteer were personally connected. Given the known associations among these individuals, we can only speculate that bounty money may have gone from Milteer to Venable and on to Ayers to be delivered by Donald Nissen to Eure in Jackson. If Nissen's story is true and it if it does tie Jackson money to Milteer in Atlanta, then Ray would have been in Birmingham only a few months after considerable money was indeed available for a King bounty.

CHAPTER 11

RAY EXPLORES HIS OPTIONS

Ray apparently became restless in Birmingham; he didn't seem to be having much fun—at least according to the folks at the dance studio. But his car tags and driver's license now proved that "Eric S. Galt" was an "Alabama boy" (reinforced with a Confederate sticker on his Mustang). He had figured out what he needed in order to proceed with his plans to produce pornographic movies. The movie equipment had arrived from Chicago on October 4. He was not satisfied with the movie camera that had been substituted and wrote to request a replacement. But Ray was not willing to wait and that same day went out, bought a Polaroid instant camera, and wrote a letter to the dance studio canceling the rest of his lessons. The Polaroid would just have to do for starters. By October 6, he was on the road again. His rooming house manager, Mr. Cherpes, related that just before Ray left, he made a telephone call to Pascagoula, Mississippi, supposedly to verify employment, stating that he was headed there to take a job on a boat. Ray later denied saying that and claimed instead that he had headed to Baton Rouge to try to contact Raoul about a smuggling job.

What Ray really did on his way from Birmingham to Mexico, who Ray really saw, or where he really stopped, remains uncertain. Perhaps he didn't need to stop anywhere at all, since his known activities in Birmingham and his next stops in Mexico demonstrate that he was still pursuing other options. He might have gone to Birmingham in regard to a King bounty, but he was going on to Mexico with something entirely different in mind. And in Mexico, Ray's social life was about to dramatically improve—at least for a few months.

There are a variety of views on Ray's departure from Birmingham, his subsequent sojourn in Mexico in October 1967, and ultimately his move to Los Angeles at the end of 1967. According to Ray, the trip was the result of "Raoul" giving him a little smuggling work to keep him busy while holding him in reserve for some future use. Others have written that Ray's sojourn in Mexico ties in with his recruitment by organized crime as a low-level drug smuggler. Still others present it simply as one more interlude in his decades-long role as an asset for the CIA. Our view is that Mexico tells us a great deal about Ray's personal agenda in 1967: Ray still had an interest in collecting a bounty on King, but it was only one option, not the final one. That stage would not happen until after all the easier options began to run out at the end of 1967 in Los Angeles.

Ray appears to have made a quick and relatively direct trip to Mexico from Alabama, crossing on October 7. He was issued a tourist card as Eric S. Galt when he crossed the border into Nuevo Laredo from Laredo, Texas. Apparently he drove straight on toward Acapulco, staying there for four days in the same hotel as on his first trip there in 1959.

There is sufficient reason to speculate that Ray, in fact, did engage in some cross-border smuggling, both going and coming back from Mexico. Huie felt that he had discovered evidence that a Mexican federal police officer had trailed Ray to his hotel in Acapulco. Huie also discovered that the hotel registration page that should have contained Ray's name suspiciously had a section cut out of it. There was a handwritten explanation at the bottom of the page, suggesting that on October 14 (a week after Ray had entered Mexico), a federal police officer named Ramon del Rio had taken and examined the page. Huie interpreted this as an indication that there had been some suspicion that Ray was involved in smuggling and that he had been the subject of at least a minimal investigation.[1] That might also explain why Ray moved on after only four days; Ray himself said he left because Acapulco was just too expensive. It would be no surprise to find Ray smuggling drugs into Mexico, as he admitted that he had done so on his first trip there years before.

Still, it appears that Ray's primary goals in Mexico were getting into the pornographic film business and exploring options for staying outside the United States. He had been one of the inmates that rented out magazines at Missouri State Penitentiary—most likely not copies of *Time* or *Newsweek*. He was a frequent customer of prostitutes and apparently had reached the conclusion that sex films could be a big money-maker. As Eric S. Galt, Ray moved from Acapulco to Puerto Vallarta, which was still undeveloped and not the tourist haven it would become in future years. He spent three weeks there, first at the Hotel Rio and then at a more expensive beach hotel, the Tropicana. As he had at Gray Rocks in Canada, Ray cultivated an upscale image. He was well dressed, drove a flashy sports car, spent money, and presented himself as an American writer, complete with cameras and a portable typewriter.

THE PORNO OPTION

Ray himself discussed visiting a local brothel repeatedly "on business." He also visited other brothels, establishing a relationship with two prostitutes: first, a girl using the name "La Chilindrina," and then another woman who used the name "Irma La Deuce." Ray spent an extended period of time with Irma, drinking, having sex, sleeping late, and visiting the beach—all a total change in behavior from his previous stops since his prison escape.[2] Ray used Irma as his first photographic test subject. Following a trip to the beach, he asked her to sit in his car, exposing herself with her skirts up. The Polaroid photo turned out poorly, and Ray tore it up; he stopped a few miles later and made a second attempt, but it, too, turned out badly. This seemed to upset Ray, and the next day Irma described him as irritable, complaining of a headache and ready to get into a fight in one of the local bars.[3]

A few days later, Ray showed up drunk at the bar where Irma worked, and she refused to sleep with him that night. She also refused his offer of marriage a day or so later. Ray threatened that he would begin to see the other girls again. That didn't change her mind, so he tried making out with the first girl he met, but that didn't work either. Eventually Ray moved to a more upscale hotel and began visiting a new hotel bar, becoming friends with the bartender there. While out one night hitting the clubs and bars, Ray and his bartender friend met a young girl who caught Ray's fancy. She doubled as a cigarette girl and club photographer and was much more attractive than the prostitutes Ray had first approached. The two men picked up the girl, and Ray began dating her, taking her to the beach, each photographing the other. They spent nights together. He apparently did photo sessions with her as well.[4]

GRASS ON THE BEACH

Ray was clearly taken with the girl and eventually confided to her that he was making good money with marijuana sales. He was buying it on weekends at a nearby resort (Yelapa) and smuggling it back to sell to tourists on the local beaches.[5] Ray wanted her to go with him on his next trip, probably as cover. It turned out that telling her that was a mistake; the girl had a young child and wanted nothing to do with marijuana. She made a clean break with Ray, telling him she could not see him anymore.

His dual rejections and failure to produce any substantial pornography seem to have had a bad effect on Ray, regardless of any of his successes in making money on the side. The fact that Ray had thought it was possible to become a Mexican citizen may explain his bad mood; he did remark in later testimony that one of his reasons for leaving Mexico was that he had concluded he couldn't accomplish anything more in the way of securing permanent residence.[6] That the requirement for citizenship involved more than simply marrying a Mexican citizen seemed to be lost on Ray. His attempts to establish some long-term female relationships, including an actual marriage proposal, would have been for naught.

Ray also might have thought that he could obtain citizenship by getting into business in Mexico. He spent considerable time with a couple of different bartenders and expressed interest in investing in some sort of business. But the best offer he could get was to trade a plot of land for his Mustang; he refused that offer. One of the options Ray more seriously considered was getting into the bar business, which might have actually kept him in Mexico. Bartending was a very portable skill, much like locksmithing. Both were skills that Ray seriously pursued after his escape from Missouri State Penitentiary; they would have served him well if he had made it overseas. During 1967, Ray appears to have put much more effort into activities such as his locksmithing, dance, and bartending courses and his interest in porno film-making than in a King bounty interest. Known to be extremely tightfisted with money, he spent a good deal of what he had on lessons and equipment for these options, hauling the film equipment all the way from Birmingham to Memphis and continuing the locksmithing course even after his arrival in Atlanta. We feel that this is a good indication that Ray was operating as his own man, with his own goals and plans, and was not being "run" by any other parties during 1967.

It's also worthwhile to note that while reading *U.S. News & World Report* in Mexico, Ray happened across an advertisement for immigrants wanted in Rhodesia. Ray wrote off for information but had not received an answer by the time he left Mexico.[7]

SPENDING TIME AND MONEY IN LOS ANGELES

Clearly things had not gone as Ray had hoped in Mexico, and with no path to Mexican citizenship, Ray could not stay forever as a tourist. So, it was back to the United States and on to a city that he had first visited many years before. Ray's initial time in Los Angeles was similar in some ways to his Mexican interlude. At first he seemed to be unconcerned about money and continued to spend at an uncharacteristically high level. He arrived in L.A. on November 19, 1967, and moved into an apartment on North Serrano Avenue. It wasn't a great neighborhood, but it was right off Hollywood Boulevard, a good place to pick up a prostitute or to sell drugs to the hippies. It also provided a number of the all-day bars that seemed to be standard hangouts for Ray.

If the neighborhood sounds like a familiar one for Ray, one of his first acts was extremely uncharacteristic; he had a telephone installed. Ray would testify that he wanted it for job hunting, which he surprisingly did, several weeks later.[8] At first it seemed there would be a delay with the telephone installation, but Ray told the telephone company that he was working with Governor Wallace's American Independent Party and that there was limited time to work at getting Wallace on the ballot. In fact Ray had already called the local Wallace headquarters for information. This new interest in politics was also uncharacteristic for James Earl Ray, just as it had been for his brother back in Saint Louis. We can only speculate whether or not Ray's newfound interest in politics was merely a cover to prospect the rumored King bounty among Wallace supporters. How much contact Ray may have had with members of the American Independent Party and with Wallace supporters is also a matter of speculation. We do know that he took people to the office to register them to vote, and, when questioned, these registrants stated that Ray appeared to be quite familiar with, and at home in, the office. (Ray later denied that.)[9]

At first, Ray's known activities in Los Angeles consisted of spending money, not making it. He booked a series of seven sessions with a Beverly Hills clinical psychologist; the sessions involved hypnosis, and Ray actually used his real name during the sessions. Later the operator commented on Ray's shyness, noted his dislike for blacks, and highlighted Ray's belief that one could use hypnosis simply to look someone in the eye and make them do what he wanted. Ray also spent a good deal of time in bars and engaged in a variety of activities, enrolling in both bartending classes and another series of dancing lessons. The dancing lessons were at an exclusive and expensive dance school. He also took up with Marie Martin, a cocktail waitress and go-go dancer whom he had met in a club, and he seems to have gone to some lengths to establish a relationship with her. He still had his camera equipment and perhaps still had hopes of getting into pornography. Ray knew that Marie had a boyfriend in prison for possession of marijuana and that she had some sort of criminal record of her own back in New Orleans. He met her cousin Charlie Stein, who also had quite a colorful past involving criminal possession of narcotics.[10]

Ray and Charlie Stein would make a much-discussed cross-country round trip to New Orleans in December 1967. It's possible that Ray actually agreed to the trip under a misconception. Marie Martin described her conversation with Ray, saying that it began with her telling Ray that her cousin Rita Stein had a serious problem: She urgently needed to get her two children out of New Orleans before they were placed in a children's home. It seems plausible that Ray accepted the trip because he thought it would involve going off to New Orleans with Rita Stein, or possibly both women. Apparently Martin had asked Ray, "You wouldn't want to drive me down to pick them up, would you?"[11] Marie went on to describe that Ray became extremely unhappy with the fact that he was going to be making the trip with Rita's brother Charlie.

There has been much speculation that Ray's trip to New Orleans was the beginning of his actual involvement in a King conspiracy. Ray himself claimed that the trip was planned and that he was working under Raoul's instructions. Some researchers have suggested that the trip was taken to enable a recruiting meeting. At this point, it is impossible to confirm whether or not Ray actually made the trip strictly with a King bounty in mind, much less whether he might have just restarted some related contacts during the trip. There is some evidence that the trip itself was relatively spontaneous. First, Ray had a session with his psychologist on Thursday morning, December 14, 1967, and as he left he had made another appointment for the following Monday. Second, he also had a previously scheduled dance lesson scheduled for that Monday. When he committed to the New Orleans trip on Friday afternoon, he had to call and cancel both appointments.[12]

Stein and his sister, as well as Ray, would maintain that Stein had never met Ray and had no connection with him other than during the trip. The FBI didn't buy that story; they had reports of Ray's Mustang at Stein's place of work and confronted Stein with the accusation that the trip had been made with the intent of scoring drugs from a source in New Orleans. Stein and his sister denied that, too. In fact, Stein went to great lengths to deny that he was in any way involved with drugs, even though the FBI had reports of young men seen lying in a stupor in his backyard. The FBI was never able to make a case against Stein regarding the New Orleans trip, but it is interesting that the trip seems to have occurred at the same time that Ray had also begun to actively look for legitimate work in L.A. He answered classified ads in the *Los Angeles Times,* applied for a job as a vacuum cleaner salesman, and even tried to get a job as a maintenance man. He placed two ads in the paper, one for restaurant work and one for general labor. Apparently all these efforts were frustrated by the fact that he had no social security card for Eric Galt and was afraid to use his long-established false identity of Rayns and its legitimate identification. His relatively energetic job seeking (compared to earlier stops in Birmingham and Mexico) certainly gives the impression that Ray was beginning to run short of money and that he was looking for any opportunity to generate cash.

Of course it would be no surprise to find Ray using the trip to New Orleans as an opportunity to generate some money based on contacts there. It was not Ray's first exposure to the city; in 1955 he had stopped there during a multistate escape following a theft of postal money orders. In 1958 he had spent time there following the armed robbery of a bar. Ray even admitted he had done some minor cross-border smuggling after the New Orleans sojourn in 1958, as he passed through Texas and crossed the border at Matamoros into Mexico.[13] And, as we will detail in the following chapter, there are a few items that suggest Ray might have used the trip to do some prospecting regarding whether the King bounty was still in play.

After returning from New Orleans to Los Angeles with Charlie Stein and his two little nieces, Ray didn't get any of the legitimate jobs he was seeking, but his spending continued. In fact, January 1968 was extremely busy for Ray. He continued his dance lessons and his locksmithing correspondence course. He also started a series of lessons at the International Bartending School. And Ray seems to have restarted his quest for female film subjects. He joined a swingers club and ran an advertisement in the *Los Angeles Free Press,* seeking "female for mutual enjoyment and/or female for swing session," getting the addresses of several interested parties and sending photos of himself. In support of these efforts, he ordered more sex manuals from Futura Press and a set of chrome handcuffs from a police equipment company in Los Angeles.

It may be worth noting that Ray also subscribed to a mail-forwarding service (only for the month of February 1968) and used that address for the responses to both his *Free Press* advertisement and swingers letters. Ray explained that he didn't want such letters coming to his apartment, but of course the use of an alternate address could also have been useful for other types of confidential correspondence as well. Such mail forwarding would have protected Ray's true location in the event that any letters to or from him had been intercepted. And that would have been a very logical precaution if Ray had started any communication with individuals he might have suspected as being under FBI surveillance or mail monitoring.[14]

And Ray wrote to the Orange County, California, chapter of the Friends of Rhodesia, first with questions and then with a thank-you letter that stated that he anticipated leaving for Rhodesia in November 1969.[15] The letter requested a subscription to the *Rhodesian Commentary*. Ray's consistent and ongoing interest in the racist regimes of South Africa and Rhodesia seems to undermine Ray's own statements that he held no racist views. Yet these were also countries that were commonly described as ideal destinations for criminals wanting to avoid extradition. In any event, it seems clear that Ray still had an overriding interest in leaving the United States for good. He was still a fugitive from the law and, by January 1968, he had been on the run for the better part of a year. Given Ray's conservative nature, he must have begun to wonder how long he could continue eluding law enforcement.

An objective look at Ray's activities in January 1968 shows a continuation of the same sorts of undertakings that he was pursuing for the better part of 1967, going all the way back to his stay in Canada. He wanted to get out of the United States and preferably off the continent. "White" Africa was obviously a preferred destination. He wanted to learn portable skills (bartending, locksmithing), he was not averse to picking up money from the sale of drugs when the opportunity presented, and he certainly seems focused on pornographic films as a moneymaking option. There is no indication of any major change in his behavior, no sign he was tied into a King conspiracy or practicing any more than his routine security precautions. Actually, sending out his photo to a number of women argues against his being involved in anything new or particularly risky. But that was all in January.

Things appear to have changed mightily for Ray in February 1968.

CHAPTER 12

RAY RECRUITED

It appears likely that even before his Missouri State Penitentiary escape in April 1967, Ray knew there were offers on Martin Luther King Jr.'s life. And he was interested. Yet, he chose not to pursue a King bounty as his primary option. His early but abortive attempt to leave North America via Canada demonstrates that. He seems to have returned to an interest in the King bounty after Canada, but he either failed to fully engage with the deal makers or simply didn't get an offer at that point. As can be seen from his various moneymaking schemes, he continued exploring other options while in Mexico and after his move to Los Angeles in November of 1967.

Whether it came from robberies, a cache left from prison contraband sales, or his drug smuggling in 1967, Ray's available funds were clearly drained by the beginning of 1968. He had even tried to earn money by getting "honest" jobs, but those efforts never proved fruitful. And in January, he moved from a reasonably nice apartment (with a private telephone line) into the seedy St. Francis Hotel, in an area of downtown Los Angeles described by one FBI agent as a "den of iniquity, alive with prostitution and drug trafficking."[1]

Ray still possessed the film equipment needed to create pornographic films and began advertising in swinger magazines, presumably for potential participants. He continued to subscribe to his mail-order locksmithing class and even continued his dance lessons. Some have interpreted these activities as evidence that Ray never became involved with a conspiracy at all. While Huie proposed that Ray was spontaneously seized by a desire to make it to the top of the FBI's Most Wanted list, Ray's behavior suggests otherwise. Ray completed his bartending class (he even showed up for the class picture), continued his correspondence locksmithing course (even in Atlanta), and took his film production equipment all the way to Memphis. All this seems strange for someone who had suddenly become obsessed solely with making the FBI Ten Most Wanted Fugitives list. Closer examination of Ray's actions suggest that he simply became increasingly desperate for money and pursued a variety of schemes to quickly raise the funds he needed to get out of the dead end he seemed to have hit in Los Angeles.

In mid-February 1968, things began to change. With no obvious way to pay for it, James Earl Ray suddenly scheduled plastic surgery that would not actually begin until March 5. He stopped his scheduled dance lessons, forfeiting some of his deposit—an anathema for the money-conscious Ray. He declined a bartending job offered to him after his class graduation, though it was exactly the sort of job he had been seeking for the previous two months. At his bartending school graduation, he was heard to remark that he would soon be leaving for Birmingham, Alabama, to visit his brother. He traded his console television to Marie Martin for her portable set, telling her he was returning to the South. And on March 17, he completed a change-of-address form forwarding all his mail to general delivery, Atlanta, Georgia. Notably, he indicated that address would only be good through April 25th.

After his capture, Ray stated that the planned plastic surgery was because he feared that he might show up on the FBI's Ten Most Wanted Fugitives list and he needed to change his appearance.[2] Of course he eventually did make that list, but that would require a much more dramatic crime than any found in Ray's decades-long history of robbery, theft, and fraud. To explain himself, he claimed that he thought his appearance on the FBI's Ten Most Wanted Fugitives list would have resulted from his prison escape in 1967—but surely no career criminal would ever really imagine that a minor prison escape could earn that level of attention from the FBI.

Various authors have written about these "Top Ten" remarks with amusement, picturing Ray as out of touch with reality and possibly not all that bright. Of course that view fails to acknowledge that Ray was absolutely correct; he would indeed be on the Ten Most Wanted Fugitives list within a matter of months. Authors in search of a motive—but not conspiracy—use Ray's statement to define a point at which his ego overcame his caution and he decided to make himself world famous. Others, like Gerold Frank in his book *An American Death,* point to this as a sign that his buried ultraracism, "coming out of the very atmosphere in which Ray grew up and lived," moved Ray to murder Dr. King, trusting that somewhere in the country there must be those who would take good care of him if he rid the world of the black civil rights leader.[3]

With the information now available, we propose that views on Ray's motive such as the Ten-Most-Wanted-Fugitives-list motive Huie describes and I'll-kill-King-and-somebody-will-pay-me-for-it motive Frank suggests were simply incorrect. They do not accurately reflect either Ray's caution, his actions, his desire for money, or, for that matter, the sophistication and reach of the individuals who had been trying to eliminate Dr. King since before 1964. Rather, our view is that Ray's change in behavior in February demonstrates that he was responding to what he felt was finally a truly concrete bounty offer on Dr. King's life. The open questions are how this contact could have been made and why Ray would suddenly have become attractive as a recruit. Since Ray himself would never speak on this subject (and risk his neck admitting premeditation), we are forced to evaluate several options and a variety of circumstantial evidence relevant to these questions.

Ray himself may have unintentionally revealed something germane on the subject. When Huie questioned Ray about his relationship with the John Birch Society (he had requested contact information from them when he was exploring emigration to Rhodesia), Ray told him that he had made contact with other ultraright organizations. In fact, Ray had Huie put that at the top of a list of things that the prosecution might use against him in court. But apparently neither Huie nor anyone else ever explored that particular comment in detail with Ray.[4]

That seems to be a glaring oversight given the most obvious sort of suspects in the King murder. In light of the extended effort to kill Dr. King that we outlined in the early chapters of this book, this oversight becomes even more significant. King was the internationally known moral conscience and voice of the civil rights movement. Whether it was the NSRP, Swift's Christian Identity network, or even the Minutemen, all these groups considered King to be a major threat. They variously saw him as being influenced by the communists, by the Jews, or even by Satan! They made those views public. Given the number of their members and their geographical reach, there certainly was potential for Ray to explore rumors or gossip that these groups might pay to eliminate King. We have shown such offers were definitely in circulation. And for the first time they had the large sums necessary to back up those offers.

As fall of '67 moved into winter of '68, these people with the apparent money and desire to kill Dr. King were, like Ray, becoming increasingly desperate. The lead paragraph for *Los Angeles Times* reporter Jack Nelson's October 23, 1967, article on the FBI's pursuit of white supremacists read, "FBI investigations have cut deeply into Ku Klux Klan membership throughout most of the South and have touched off quarreling among leaders of the nation's largest Klan." Several legal prosecutions were in progress against the Mississippi White Knights and its leader, Sam Bowers, for an attack that killed NAACP activist Vernon Dahmer in 1966. That was after Bowers and others had already just been convicted for conspiracy in the Mississippi Burning killings. Undeterred by his trials or even his conviction, Bowers began to use guerilla-style groups to actually increase the violence in Mississippi, a death-throes reign of terror that did not stop until July 1968. Bowers's White Knights lacked internal sources of money, but they did not lack courage or bravado. In contrast, Milteer's clique in Atlanta appears to have collected sufficient money but was unable to find the right people to put it to use. We submit that these interests aligned by 1967–1968 and eventually found an outside option of their own in James Earl Ray.

We will explore a number of ways in which the "patriot network" (the term Milteer used) might have connected with James Earl Ray. It could have been through his increasing contact with individuals involved in the George Wallace campaign, or through his mysterious (and apparently spontaneous) trip to New Orleans in December 1967. Possibly the connection was made first through telephone calls and then during a visit to Ray at the St. Francis Hotel by a tall man with a southern accent using the alias "James C. Hardin." But however Ray made contact, the evidence suggests that by February 1968, Ray was in touch with individuals who prompted his sudden move to Atlanta in March and eventually took him to Memphis on April 4, 1968.

ON THE TRAIL OF THE KING BOUNTY

The first opportunity for Ray to have resumed his inquires into the King bounty may have come in early December 1967 when the apolitical Ray began to telephone and visit George Wallace's presidential campaign headquarters in Anaheim, California. No one knows the full details of the calls or the reasons for Ray's sudden interest in becoming politically active. But the Los Angeles–area headquarters for the Wallace campaign seem to have attracted a number of right-wing extremists, including another noteworthy volunteer who was extremely well placed in the NSRP, who had worked in the Birmingham NSRP office beginning in 1963, shortly before Ray's arrival in that city, and who (according to an FBI report) continued to be heavily involved in the operations of the Birmingham headquarters even after his own departure for California.[5]

The individual in question had worked alongside violent anti-King radicals J. B. Stoner and his partner Edward Fields in the Birmingham NSRP office. He was from California but had traveled to Birmingham to join the NSRP movement at a time when even the Klan was trying to disassociate from the NSRP. He became involved with recruiting and training young volunteers. Later, he returned to his hometown in California and helped set up the state's first chapter of the NSRP. He spoke at meetings keynoted by national racist figures Wesley Swift and Connie Lynch, and state law enforcement identified him as part of a dangerous and burgeoning right-wing extremist movement in California. In the spring of 1967, having been removed from Wallace's Los Angeles campaign headquarters for distributing NSRP material, the man moved to Atlanta, setting up residence with another active white supremacist who had moved his family to Georgia from Birmingham, Alabama, in February 1967.

In short, a leading NSRP officer who had worked in the Birmingham office just prior to Ray's arrival had moved back to California to become active in NSRP affairs and worked in the same Wallace campaign headquarters that Ray would contact and visit in Los Angeles. Before Ray's visits to Wallace's Los Angeles headquarters, that same NSRP member had moved to Atlanta, Georgia.[6]

If Ray had been probing for names of individuals who might connect him to the King bounty, it might have been the name of just such an individual. This is admittedly highly speculative, but these facts exactly fit the pattern of how such matters worked, how names were passed, and how cutouts were used—just the sort of things that would frustrate any criminal investigation.

An Atlanta FBI informant, Carl Loosier, did indeed alert the FBI about this NSRP individual, specifically in regard to the murder of Dr. King. The FBI began an investigation but suspended it when they determined that the individual in question had not been in Birmingham at the same time Ray was and that there was no evidence to place this individual in Memphis at the time of Dr. King's murder.[7] When the FBI interviewed him, the one-time NSRP activist denied any connection to Ray, and no witness (and certainly not Ray) ever connected the two together. Unfortunately, that was enough for the FBI to close the lead.

We fully realize that attempts to connect the dots in this fashion can be extremely confusing to the reader; the point is that the mode of operation being described perfectly matches the pattern of how the network of extremists we have been discussing throughout the book worked. The individuals involved were very security conscious, either staying continually on the move or, when they themselves were not traveling, using couriers, often passing messages that would have meant nothing at all to those carrying them.

Did Ray stay at rooming house not far from NSRP headquarters in Birmingham simply by chance? Did Ray pick up a name in Birmingham that he decided to follow up on in Los Angeles? Was his sudden interest in the Wallace campaign and its Los Angeles headquarters sincere, given his lack of interest in politics before his arrival in L.A.? Was Ray given a name or a telephone number of a contact in Atlanta or Mississippi? A little more digging into the details of Ray's trip from Los Angeles to New Orleans will point to some answers.

MYSTERIOUS PHONE CALLS AND THE TRIP TO NEW ORLEANS

James Earl Ray's trip to New Orleans represents another possible opportunity for Ray to have tried to connect with a King bounty offer, especially since it would have been a safe meeting place for the fugitive Ray and associates of Sam Bowers's White Knights of Mississippi. Ray made a quick trip to New Orleans in mid-December 1967, but before leaving he dragged his traveling companion, Charlie Stein, to Wallace campaign headquarters, insisting that he register to vote. Stein told investigators that Ray made frequent stops on his trip from Los Angeles to New Orleans and on at least a couple of occasions used pay phones for unknown reasons. Ray himself would admit to making two calls, but only to his brother Jerry.[8]

The FBI rightly assumed that Ray, who was out of Stein's sight on a number of occasions, could have made far more calls than just two. Bureau agents canvassed the route Ray and Stein took to New Orleans and attempted to trace all calls from pay phones during the relevant time period. The available FBI "MURKIN" (MURder of KINg) records lists dozens of numbers that were eventually traced to individuals who were then interviewed and cleared. But there are some interesting gaps in the bureau's call accounting. One of the most mysterious comes from a series of telephone calls made to Mississippi from various pay phones along Ray's route—including calls to the hometowns of some the most committed Klan terrorists in the nation, the White Knights of the Ku Klux Klan.[9]

There are no available details of the results of the FBI's follow-up investigation of these telephone calls to Mississippi. We were able to trace some of the numbers with the help of public librarians from these cities, with two notable exceptions. We learned that one number traced to South Jackson, Mississippi, (home base for a number of White Knights) was unlisted. Likewise, another unlisted number was traced to Laurel, Sam Bowers's hometown and the headquarters of the Mississippi White Knights. As the public librarians noted to us, it was exceptionally rare at that time for telephone numbers to be unlisted. Through additional searches, we were able to identify at least two White Knights who were not listed in the 1967 Laurel, Mississippi, phonebook. Deavours Nix, whose café was reported for strange activity in connection with the King murder, had an unlisted number, as did Percy Quinn, Sam Bowers's attorney. Quinn was the first attorney to visit Thomas Tarrants in the hospital after the abortive Tarrants/ Ainsworth bombing attempt at the end of 1968. Percy Quinn (virtually unknown outside the Laurel area) was also an attorney James Earl Ray sought to serve as his legal counsel.[10] As Ray's trial date neared, Jerry Ray wrote to Ray of the difficulty in reaching Quinn, who worked out of the back room in someone else's home and had no listed telephone.[11] In a recent letter to the authors, Jerry Ray claimed that hiring Quinn was Ray's idea. Obviously, absent further information, we could not possibly say that either of Nix or Quinn's numbers match to a call on Ray's trip to New Orleans.[12]

Many authors have noted that Ray was excessively concerned about investigations into his time in New Orleans and refused to talk when confronted about his time there. Some, like Lamar Waldron, have speculated that Ray must have met with organized crime elements working for New Orleans Mafia kingpin Carlos Marcello. Waldron makes much of the fact that Ray and Stein were involved with procuring drugs and that this would certainly place Ray in Marcello's domain. While the likely (but not definitive) reason for Ray's New Orleans venture included the procurement of some quantity of drugs, it is equally likely that these could have come from criminals, such as Louis "The Mechanic" Smith, who were shifting allegiances to the increasingly influential network of traveling criminals soon to be known as the Dixie Mafia. This loose-knit band of rogues was increasingly at odds with more formal, tightly organized Sicilian crime syndicates, such as the Marcello Mafia in New Orleans. Certainly low-level drug sales would not necessarily catch Marcello's eye, as he was making hundreds of millions of dollars a year from shipping literal barges full of heroin into the ports of New Orleans. It seems more likely that other members of the Dixie Mafia, as the proverbial second fiddles in New Orleans, interacted with Ray. This network's members, such as Donald Eugene Sparks, had inside knowledge of the White Knights' contract offers on King.

If he did not meet with the Dixie Mafia, Ray could have connected with white supremacists in New Orleans, a city within the White Knights' sphere of influence. A 1970s informant report relayed a conversation with White Knights terrorist Danny Joe Hawkins in which Hawkins told the informant that contacts in New Orleans were the primary weapons providers to the Mississippi Klan.[13] Sam Bowers had attended college in New Orleans, and Deavours Nix, the White Knights' intelligence chief, previously worked in New Orleans publishing racist tracts. When police arrested White Knights member and Medgar Evers assassin Byron de la Beckwith (not long after the King assassination), he was reportedly carrying a bomb for an attack in New Orleans, which had been outsourced to the White Knights' contacts there.

In fact, the two possibilities, criminal or Klan recruitment of Ray, are not mutually exclusive. The Dixie Mafia were known to be some of the chief suppliers of weaponry to white supremacist groups. And, as noted earlier, by the summer of 1967, LeRoy McManaman (identified as being a close criminal associate of known Dixie Mafia members) had offered a $100,000 King bounty offer on behalf of the White Knights to an individual known to be leaving Leavenworth penitentiary on his way to Atlanta. When speaking to two sources that were, unbeknownst to him, FBI informants, one of Ray's brothers mentioned the figure of $100,000. The informant report also quotes the brother as saying, "If I was in his position, and had eighteen years to serve and someone offered me a lot of money to kill someone I didn't like anyhow and get me out of the country, I'd do it."[14]

THE ATLANTA/LOS ANGELES/LAUREL CONNECTION

As we detailed in chapter 6, a group of extremists in Atlanta, including Joseph Milteer, may have been raising a pool of money with donations from union members fearful of integration; this money was then diverted for the King assassination. As Ray was enjoying his time in Mexico, months before his move to Los Angeles and then to Atlanta, evidence suggests that these self-described "superpatriots" were also making open, even desperate efforts to recruit potential assassins and accessories to murder King.

One incident described in the 1978 House Select Committee on Assassinations report suggests the kind of desperation that could lead a conspiracy to recruit someone like Ray, someone outside the usual Klan circles and not a professional hit man. Two men, the Powell brothers, who were employed as house painters but who had a reputation for violence, were approached by a friend in an Atlanta bar who told them that an acquaintance could put them in touch with someone with a serious cash offer for killing Dr. King. A few days later the brothers were approached by a man in the bar who showed them a briefcase full of cash ($25,000, Waldron claims) and promised that amount up front plus an equal amount after the murder. The brothers declined the offer but later provided information to the HSCA and passed a lie detector test on their story. However, they eventually refused to give actual testimony, even under subpoena, and replied to threatened contempt charges by saying it was not worth risking their lives.[15] The FBI had not learned about the Atlanta offer until 1976, and upon investigation they were "unable to . . . discredit the story."[16]

A story that echoes elements of the Powell incident and the bounty offer LeRoy McManaman made at Leavenworth penitentiary emerges in documents from the early 1970s.[17] A military officer contacted the FBI with a provocative story about his father, who had been a jailer in the Fulton County, Georgia, system for several years. His father had obtained three signed affidavits from prisoners who claimed that Atlanta businessmen had approached them with a $100,000 bounty offer on Dr. King's life. The father apparently kept this information for protection or possibly even some sort of blackmail scheme against these businessmen.[18] We located the daughter of the Fulton County jailer, who confirmed her brother's story, including references to the prisoner affidavits. She said that she felt her father was killed under mysterious circumstances and that her mother "got rid of" the relevant material (including the affidavits) out of fear.[19] The $100,000 figure in this story is fascinating, as it references the same sum offered in the Leavenworth bounty. Again, according to an informant report, it was the same figure Ray's brother cited as the motivation for Ray's participation in a plot against King.

If $100,000 was raised in the Atlanta area, then it would corroborate Donald Nissen's story that he unwittingly delivered a package of money from Atlanta to a cutout in Jackson, Mississippi. Floyd Ayers, a known associate of James Venable, provided the package to Nissen. Venable personally knew both Joseph Milteer and J. B. Stoner, and he ran the National Knights of the Ku Klux Klan from Stone Mountain, Georgia, just outside of Atlanta.

This southeastern network of radicals had allies on the West Coast, who may have assisted in identifying Ray or connecting him with the individuals offering the King bounty.

There is no doubt that Joseph Milteer's network in the Southeast was well connected to Los Angeles before, during, and after Ray's stay there. Milteer was personally associated with the racist minister Wesley Swift and had visited him in Los Angeles. Milteer was known to talk about Swift and how great a man he was. Milteer was also personally close to both racial agitator J. B. Stoner and a variety of other NSRP members, all of whom were active in the Wallace campaign in 1968.[20] And in 1968, Los Angeles was one of the primary centers of Wallace campaigning, which had, in some fashion, involved James Earl Ray. Connie Lynch, Stoner's comrade-in-racial-incitement, was a minister for Wesley Swift, and the Swift ministry held services and had a number of active followers in the Hollywood area where Ray was staying. One of Swift's other valued ministers and confidantes, William Fowler, created the California Knights of the Ku Klux Klan as a subunit of James Venable's National Knights of the Ku Klux Klan; Venable had spoken to the California Knights as late as 1967 at a venue that belonged to Swift.

Swift and his lieutenants, such as Minuteman Dennis Mower, were also very well connected to the Mississippi White Knights through both Sam Bowers and Thomas Tarrants. Mower is on record as saying he was personally on very good terms with Sam Bowers.

All of this is, of course, circumstantial and proves only that if Ray had expressed an interest in the King "deal" to members of a number of ultra-right groups, his interest could very easily have been passed back to men like Bowers, Stoner, or Milteer—all of whom were in frequent personal contact with their Los Angeles counterparts such as Mower and others previously identified as part of the Swift network, which Milteer described as the "patriot network."

But circumstantial evidence is only persuasive when it fully connects and explains seemingly independent strands of information. In their efforts to find if (and how) Ray may have been recruited into the ongoing effort against Dr. King, the FBI often failed because they themselves did not connect the dots between information held in various files and at different field offices. And they may also have missed something significant in their check of the call records for the lobby pay phone at Ray's apartment house. Former FBI agent William Turner found a potentially important lead missed by the bureau. He had an investigator physically go to Ray's second residence, the low-rent hotel with a telephone booth in the lobby. The investigator photographed the inside of the telephone booth. That photograph showed a brief note, apparently in Ray's handwriting, which listed only a name and a telephone number. The number turned out to be a direct line to a manager at Litton Industries in Beverly Hills—certainly not a common number to be dialed from the pay phone in the lobby of a cheap hotel. Turner noted that Litton Industries operated a shipyard in Pascagoula, Mississippi, and when James Earl Ray had earlier spent time in Birmingham, he had given the name and address of that shipyard, stating he was a former employee.[21] It turns out that due to the perceived loss of jobs to blacks, that particular Pascagoula shipyard was an active hotbed of Klan recruitment, specifically for Bowers's White Knights organization. Unfortunately, whether or not this particular lead might have revealed any long-term channel of communications between Ray and individuals of interest remains a mystery.

While we've explored a number of possibilities as to how Ray may have become entangled with individuals within the radical network seeking Dr. King's murder, so far the available data has provided no definitive answer. But now we turn to yet another possibility—a fascinating but frustrating lead that revolves around a mysterious man using the alias James C. Hardin, who may have been personally involved in Ray's recruitment. While other books mention this lead, most treat the Hardin story as an afterthought.[22] For the first time, with dozens of documents never previously cited, we have been able to determine the real identity of James C. Hardin, based on the FBI's own investigation. Our hope is that with this information, others may add additional background that could help unravel the full Hardin story and its possible connection to Dr. King's murder.

THE MYSTERIOUS JAMES C. HARDIN

During the FBI investigation of the King murder, Allan O. Thompson, the manager of the St. Francis Hotel where Ray was staying, contacted the FBI and told them that he recalled two or three incoming telephone calls for Galt (Ray's alias while living at the hotel) coming from Atlanta and New Orleans. Thompson had heard the caller, who identified himself as "James Hardin," discussing leaving a message for Galt with the telephone operator. Later, in March, an individual using the same name showed up in person and asked for Galt. Thompson felt that he recognized the man's voice as that of the caller; he also commented that the man had a mild southern accent. The FBI did indeed find the name "James Hardin" in a file search—but in their files it was an alias that had surfaced in Jackson, Mississippi; Atlanta, Georgia; and New Orleans, Louisiana. With access to the recently declassified FBI reports of Thompson's original interviews and through additional material obtained through the Freedom of Information Act, we now feel confident that the name Hardin was very likely the alias of an individual with a relatively minor criminal record whose real name was James Wilbourn Ashmore.

Having searched their indices against matches for the alias "Hardin," the FBI sent a variety of photographs (including an old photograph of Ashmore) to Los Angeles for hotel manager Thompson to view. Thompson didn't identify any of the photographs as a perfect match for the "Hardin" who had visited Ray. However, Thompson did point to the photograph of Ashmore, whose features he felt were very similar to Hardin's. Thompson stated that there were minor differences (hair and skin quality), but almost all of them could be attributable to age. Thompson, after all, was being asked to compare a photograph of someone from 1955 to an individual he saw in 1968. A police sketch artist then began work on a detailed composite drawing of "Hardin" based on Thompson's verbal descriptions.[23]

Despite the fact that the motel manager had picked out the photograph of Ashmore as being the closest match to the man who had visited Ray and that Ashmore was known to use the alias Hardin, the bureau apparently did not bother to pursue and interview Ashmore. After extensive searching, we have yet to find FBI documents showing that the bureau followed up this seemingly obvious lead. Nor have we found any documents closing out the lead—an exception to virtually all the other FBI lead inquiries we have researched. What we did find was that the FBI continued to pressure Thompson for more information but only to update the artist's sketch weeks after Thompson had already made the 99 percent identification of an actual suspect photograph!

We obtained James Wilbourn Ashmore's FBI headquarters file through the Freedom of Information Act, and it details a criminal career not far different from Ray's in terms of its consistent low-level theft, fraud, and time spent in state and federal prisons. Ashmore worked throughout the country as a trucker, repeatedly cashing stolen or forged checks. He was arrested numerous times for such activities and once for the interstate transportation of stolen goods. Each time, it appears he got lucky, as prosecutors in different states treated each of his offenses separately, rather than as a collective record of habitual criminal acts. Because of that, his criminal sentences were sometimes short or not prosecuted at all. As an itinerant criminal with time in several prisons, Ashmore fits the profile of someone who might well have had contact with the traveling criminals nicknamed Dixie Mafia. As a former convict who was in and out of various states through his trucking job, he certainly could have been useful to "bigger" criminals, perhaps as a simple courier or cutout. Without further information from the FBI (who have not yet provided us with the requested local field office files on Ashmore) or from his friends and family, we have no specifics on Ashmore's exact movements circa 1968.

So how can we be sure "Hardin" really existed? In another file we found that FBI agent Dennis LeMaster, who had been involved with the background investigation of Ray, indicated that he had doubts as to the hotel manager's veracity. It is true that Thompson mentioned a well-known reward for information on the King crime, but his actions suggest that the Hardin story was far from a simple scam. For instance, Thompson described another individual who had seen and heard Ray in conversation with a man whom Ray referred to as "Hardin" at the Jackrabbit bar.[24] But Thompson steadfastly refused to identify this witness, telling the FBI the fellow wanted nothing to do with them and had only come to Thompson because he wanted to keep his distance. The FBI had to pry information out of Thompson and even considered using a grand jury subpoena to do so; Thompson even disappeared temporarily during their efforts to push for the other individual's name.

Thompson never sought publicity for his story. When after sufficient pressure he did give the bureau the witness's nickname, it proved only that a man with that nickname indeed frequented the Jackrabbit bar that Ray had habitually visited. But, as Thompson predicted, the man definitely wanted nothing to do with the FBI and denied everything except knowing Thompson.

All the information Thompson offered provides valuable corroborating evidence, but of particular note are the origins of the "Hardin" calls (from New Orleans and Atlanta) and the date of "Hardin's" visit to Ray. The telephone calls to Ray came only a couple of months after his trip to New

Orleans, and only days before the reported visit by Hardin. Immediately following the alleged calls and visit from James C. Hardin, on or about March 17, 1968, Ray left Los Angeles and was on his way to Atlanta.

AN OPEN QUESTION

Though we are unable to describe the full or exact sequence of events that took Ray on the road that eventually led him to Memphis, we do know that Ray apparently began an effort to shadow Dr. King's movements. The next three weeks of Ray's travels would start with Ray arriving in Selma, Alabama, on March 22, the same day King was supposed to speak in that city.[25] Ray would then travel on and take refuge in a rooming house in King's hometown of Atlanta, carrying with him a map that included a circle around King's headquarters. While King was calibrating his return trip to Memphis, Tennessee, to rehabilitate his efforts in the Memphis sanitation workers' strike, Ray took a brief detour to Birmingham, Alabama, at the end of March. He bought a rifle, only to exchange it the next day, on the supposed advice of someone he described as his "brother-in-law." Ray did not go to Memphis ahead of King, as he vehemently asserted to law enforcement and others, but first traveled back to Atlanta on April 1 and then immediately followed King to Memphis, where King was shot on April 4, 1968.

Ray's actions would dovetail with what we know from the 1967 White Knights bounty offer to Nissen. Recall that it included two different options for someone wanting in on the plot against King's life, one of which was money to simply track King and case his movements, specifically in Atlanta. Perhaps Ray began his participation with this low-risk option. It would have been very much like the ever-cautious Ray to commit to no more than stalking King, casing key locations in Atlanta, and reporting back to his sponsors. Such a role could have sounded like a very good deal with little risk. When Ray left Los Angeles, stalking Dr. King was his new priority, but he seems not to have been in a particular hurry. Unlike many of his earlier long-distance road trips, Ray took several days to drive back to Alabama and on to Atlanta.

Ray's path first crossed Dr. King's on the night of March 22, 1968, in Selma, Alabama, as King was supposed to speak there that evening. But as often happened, King changed his plans at the last minute and appeared thirty miles away in Camden, Alabama. Initially Ray lied about his Selma stop, saying he had gotten lost between New Orleans and Birmingham. Of course Selma was sixty miles off the freeway between those two cities, so that is at best improbable. When in his interview of him Huie challenged Ray on the Selma stop, Ray finally admitted that he had gone there because of King. But Ray had no weapon other than his pistol at the time, so it seems that the trip to Selma may only have been for observation.

Beyond the tall tale of a sixty-mile accidental diversion to Selma, there is yet another damning lie Ray told about his final trip to Memphis. Ray falsely claimed that he went straight to Memphis after his purchase of a .30-06 rifle at a Birmingham gun store at the end of March, after which he was set up as a patsy for King's murder. According to the evidence, Ray definitely returned to Atlanta before moving on to Memphis on April 3, 1968. Ray steadfastly stuck to his false story, and for good reason: King's decision to return to Memphis at the end of March, to redeem what was supposed to be a nonviolent labor strike, was King's alone. It came only after King had first gone back to his home city of Atlanta. Ray knew that if the public realized that after he had bought the rifle he had returned to Atlanta, just as King did, and then followed the minister on from Atlanta to Memphis, that the coincidence would be too enormous to dismiss. Likewise, Ray knew that if he claimed that he took a direct trip from Birmingham to Memphis—without a stop in Atlanta—it would support the assertion that he was nothing more than an innocent dupe.

So, Ray claimed that he never returned to his rooming house in Atlanta when Reverend King himself had returned to Atlanta. Asked by Congress if he wished to retract his statement that he did not return to Atlanta at the end of March 1968, Ray said in front of the national media, "I know I didn't return to Atlanta. If I did, I will just take responsibility for the King case here on TV."[26] Unfortunately for Ray, investigators produced a receipt that confirmed that he picked up his dry cleaning from the Piedmont Laundry near his Atlanta rooming house on April 1—after the rifle purchase in Birmingham. Along with his lie about the Selma stop, the return to Atlanta remains perhaps the most damning evidence of Ray's stalking of Dr. King.

Of course Ray's explanation was that all his activities of this period were simply due to his following Raoul's orders to get a rifle to show to an international arms smuggler. That, as most of his remarks about Raoul, was nothing but a smoke screen. The .30-06 rifle he eventually purchased was a common (and relatively expensive) hunting weapon, available in thousands of outlets and with no export restriction. The gun-store employees stated that Ray had asked no other questions, particularly ones about the cheap surplus rifles Ray had said were Raoul's real interest. The bottom line is that Ray was an experienced criminal and a very cautious one at that; there is no way that he ended up in Memphis, with a rifle and ammunition, across the street from Dr. King, with no idea at all why he was there. Once he left Los Angeles for the South, James Earl Ray was focused on Dr. King. However, Ray may have been operating in line with a tactic the White Knights of Mississippi had worked to perfect in past crimes. Ray, and any other conspirators, may simply have been "circling the gun."

PART III
THE CRIME

CHAPTER 13

MURDER IN MEMPHIS

The historical treatment of Dr. King's murder in Memphis has solely focus on James Earl Ray. Much of it is based on the prosecution's arguments in Ray's initial trial as well as the conclusions the FBI officially offered. Since Ray himself offered a plea of guilty in that trial, the prosecution's evidence went unchallenged. In addition, the first two books on the murder, William Bradford Huie's *He Slew the Dreamer* and Gerold Frank's *An American Death,* presented Ray as acting completely on his own. In their view, James Earl Ray was a lone gunman who killed the Reverend Dr. Martin Luther King Jr., making him the third assassin of a major political figure of the 1960s. His motive remains a matter of debate—perhaps it was a quest for fame, or perhaps a personal, uncontrolled outburst of racial hatred. But, as far as the history books are concerned, that is the end of the story. It is important to note that the House Select Committee on Assassinations' thorough if imperfect investigation concluded that other parties were involved with Ray.[1]

The explanation for the death of Dr. King is not nearly as simple as one lone racist suddenly deciding that he would travel from Los Angeles, locate Dr. King, buy a rifle, and kill him at the first opportunity. The fundamental problem with that scenario is that it is simplistic and ignores a great deal of evidence. Notably, it does not account for the previous, ongoing efforts to kill King in the years leading up to his assassination. As such, it also dramatically understates both the social and historical significance of Dr. King as one of the most provocative voices for social reform and civil rights.

A single sentence simply naming James Earl Ray as the killer is not acceptable as the full history of Dr. King's assassination. The complete story, exploring all the evidence of a network of conspirators, must be presented, as the historic implications are significant.

FROM SELMA ON TO ATLANTA

The Atlanta map found in his room, with marks indicating the location of King's residence, King's church, and the headquarters of the Southern Christian Leadership Conference was not, as Ray and supporters of his innocence have alleged, simply a map to help Ray find his way around town. True, Ray did collect maps during his travels; however, the markings on the Atlanta map are beyond coincidence. Ray himself told the HSCA that he "could never explain that away to the jury."[2] He had given it a lot of thought and the best he could come up with was that the marks represented restaurants he had visited. This explanation is as absurd as Ray's original story that he had been in Selma, Alabama, at the time King was to speak there simply because he had gotten lost on the freeway to Atlanta, Georgia.

In addition, Ray never explained away evidence of a collaborator in Atlanta. Ray could not explain the receipt for a London broil dinner for two at Mammy's Shanty restaurant in Atlanta.[3] When William Huie confronted him with the receipt, Ray said absolutely nothing.[4] Nor did Ray ever supply a credible explanation for the clothing that did not fit him found in his Atlanta apartment during the police manhunt, or why he had a second key made for his room.

Yet at that point, whatever Ray and unknown others were doing in Atlanta, there is initially nothing obvious about Ray's activities to indicate he was actively working on personally shooting Dr. King. Nor do his activities suggest he had been overwhelmed by some sudden obsession for fame or racial vengeance. For one thing, Ray still had no rifle. Nor did he simply go out and buy one in Atlanta—something easily enough done. Instead, he spent several days driving back and forth from Atlanta to Birmingham shopping for a rifle while still taking the time to purchase a money order and mail it off as continuing payment on his ongoing locksmithing correspondence course. He also took the trouble to notify the U.S. Postal Service that "Eric Galt" had relocated to Atlanta, giving them his new rooming house address and thereby maintaining a paper trail for the exact location of Ray's alias. And after exchanging one rifle for the weapon that would be found in Memphis, Ray took the trouble not only to drive back to Atlanta, but also to drop off some of his clothes at the Piedmont Laundry. After Dr. King's murder in Memphis, Ray would also take the time to return and pick up that same laundry after his overnight drive back to Atlanta! These are hardly the actions of an assassin.

Various authors have given reasons why there was no attack on Dr. King in Atlanta. Gerold Frank wrote that Ray was stalking King, but whenever he saw him in Atlanta, he also saw police protecting King. Frank gives no source for such a remark, and it is generally acknowledged that Dr. King had no special police protection as he traveled between various locations in his hometown. Frank went on to state that Ray chose to strike in Memphis because police protection had not been requested and police were staying away from Dr. King in order not to appear provocative.[5] Yet Frank provides no explanation of how Ray could have anticipated the details of police protection for Dr. King during his return to Memphis (after the violence during his most recent visit), nor does he address why Ray would not have assumed that police protection in the midst of such a volatile environment would have been more pervasive than in the routine environment of King's own hometown.

Actually, in Memphis there were police patrols visible within the immediate neighborhood of King's motel (and Ray's rooming house) including police vehicles in the vicinity of a fire station that Ray would have driven past going to and from his new residence. In fact, police arrived almost immediately at the scene of the shooting. Ray himself sped off in his Mustang no more than a minute or two before police appeared on the street where he had been parked. And, as Philip Melanson, author of *The MURKIN Conspiracy,* points out, "the presence of a security detail could not have prevented the assassination, because it offered no protection against a long-range sniper."[6] Melanson's point is fundamental: If Ray intended to shoot King from a distance, he could have done it as easily in Atlanta as easily as he did in Memphis, especially since he had spent time familiarizing himself with Atlanta.

All in all, Ray's behavior shows no evidence of any concrete assassination plan being in place upon his arrival in Atlanta. We suspect that he was being moved into position, allowed to familiarize himself with Dr. King and the locations he frequented in Atlanta. It is also possible that Ray himself was being observed and tested; after all, he had no history of murder, was certainly not a professional killer, and had no particular experience or skill with a rifle. All parties involved may have been working to decide exactly where and how the strike would be made. It is also quite possible his sponsors were deciding if he would be acceptable for a primary role in the shooting, if he would only be used in a supporting role, or if his role would be that of a fall guy. Certainly there is no sign Ray had been paid any significant amount of money in advance. In fact, he appears to have been so short of cash that he was forced to exchange $700 in Canadian money while in Atlanta.

Another point suggests that there was initially no clear plan of attack for Memphis. There seems to have been no effort to point Ray toward Memphis at the time of the first sanitation workers' strike on March 28. Dr. King's participation in the strike had been scheduled well in advance, there was general anticipation of violence, and it would have been a real opportunity for an attack on Dr. King—one that would generate maximum impact and violent public reprisal. Early on in his work with Ray, Huie had written that, based on Ray's remarks and his own investigative work, the men behind the King murder were "calculating men who wanted to use King's murder to trigger violent conflict between White and Negro citizens." Huie went on to state that the murder needed to be done under conditions that would create maximum effect, "not while he was living quietly at home . . . but at some dramatic moment." And the murder had to be clearly laid at the feet of a white man or men who would be easily portrayed as "southerners" and "racists."[7,8]

We feel Huie's first assessment was quite correct; however, the instigators clearly did not have a well-developed plan in place soon enough to take advantage of the violence of the first march in Memphis. Instead, on March 27, Ray made his first rifle-shopping trip to Birmingham, and on March 28, he was back in Atlanta, mailing off his correspondence course payment.

But there would be a second opportunity to assassinate King in Memphis.

DRAMA IN MEMPHIS

Initially, King's appearances in Memphis in support of the black sanitation workers' strike were not a priority for King. His primary focus at the time was the Poor People's Campaign, which was to culminate in a march on Washington, DC, announced and scheduled for the following summer. Of course providing security would have been an immense challenge for such a gathering, with the federal government pulling out all the stops to prevent any level of violence, especially any violence centered on the person of Dr. King.

Director Hoover and the FBI were already fanning Washington's fears of the upcoming protest, using the opportunity to generate expanded background reports critical of Dr. King. The reports focused as much on King's character as on any legitimate national security concerns and were circulated widely to numerous government agencies. Indeed the FBI director's smear campaign against King had become so obvious that *The Washington Post* ran a story on Hoover alluding to an obvious FBI effort to undermine Dr. King's influence.[9]

It appears that Hoover's obsession was beginning to wear somewhat thin for many people. In January 1968, Attorney General Clark denied an FBI request for bugging the Atlanta Poor People's March project.[10] Not one to be deterred, Hoover issued yet another report on King and sent it to the president, the attorney general, the State Department, the CIA, and a host of military offices.[11] And as part of the FBI's ongoing efforts against King, Director Hoover solicited ideas from various field offices. Responses were relatively mild: The Jackson office wanted to plant news stories about King profiting financially from the Poor People's March, the Mobile office wanted to mail annoying letters to selected King aides to provoke leadership strife, and the Detroit office suggested disrupting bus leases to impede travel to Washington for the march.[12]

King's activities in Memphis, on the other hand, were unanticipated. As of the New Year 1968, Memphis was neither on Dr. King's calendar nor on his mind. But a sanitation workers' strike turned into a civil rights confrontation in March when police violently reacted and attacked some of the participants. One of the local civil rights leaders, the Reverend Billy Kyles, was attending a Ford Foundation ministers' retreat at the time, along with his friend Dr. King. When Kyles heard about the police attack (his own daughter was among those heavily gassed during the march), he mentioned to Dr. King that they might need his support. A few days later, in order to attract national media attention, protest leaders invited several national civil rights figures, including Dr. King, to speak at a rally. Dr. King addressed some fifteen thousand people and, energized by the crowd, spontaneously accepted an invitation to return to Memphis to lead another march, announcing to everyone that he would be coming back to lead them on a protest through downtown Memphis.

Dr. King had altered his future itinerary while he was on the stage speaking. He hoped to be back in Memphis on March 21, but a freak snow storm intervened and he returned instead on March 28. King and his aides had not participated in the planning for the events there, as they normally did for his major appearances.[13] When he arrived he was not told there had already been confrontations at a couple of the larger black schools and that hundreds of students were already challenging police. He came late to join crowds of marchers who had been waiting impatiently all morning. Shortly after the march kicked off, it turned into a series of violent clashes. Some 74 people were injured and 282 arrested. Dr. King himself barely escaped, and police eventually placed him in a well-known luxury hotel, the Rivermont (a "white" hotel), well away from the scene of the protest.

The events of March 28 put Dr. King in a terrible bind. If he could not lead a peaceful march in Memphis, he certainly could not go forward with the Poor People's March in Washington. It was clear to him that he would

have to return to Memphis. On the morning of March 29, King told waiting reporters he would be returning to Memphis to lead another march in
a few days. While King was speaking to reporters, James Earl Ray was driving back from Birmingham to Atlanta, having completed the purchase of a
scope-mounted .30-06 rifle. As of March 28, Atlanta would still have been
a suitable place to murder Dr. King, as it was where he could be found routinely at only two or three locations, and where he had no extraordinary
security. In his hometown, King would have been meeting with aides and
family, distracted by the planning for the march on DC. Focused on showing that nonviolence could still be an effective form of direct action, King
could not have anticipated the type of violence that awaited him on his return to Memphis.

CHANGE OF VENUE

As of March 30, Memphis suddenly became an attractive opportunity for an
attack on Dr. King. It probably seemed a relatively high-risk option for Ray,
who would have been planning on Atlanta as the target city. But that would
not have mattered if he were taking orders from someone else. Apparently,
Ray had been operating with a fair amount of autonomy until April 1. On
March 27, when he visited the Gun Rack in Birmingham, he was already
known to the store staff and had been there on at least one earlier occasion.
He asked lots of questions, especially about the right weapon for long-distance shooting over several hundred yards. When he was offered a .30-06,
Ray rejected it as too expensive—giving the impression that he was the one
making the decision about the potential murder weapon.[14] The gun owner
recalled that Ray had very little appreciation for the intricacies of firearms
and shooting; his questions were ill-informed if not outright ignorant.

Ray returned to Birmingham on March 29, visiting two stores and finally purchasing a .243 rifle with a scope at the Aeromarine Supply Company. He later returned to that store indicating that he needed to exchange
the gun. He explained that his "brother-in-law"[15] had told him that he had
bought the wrong gun and had instructed Ray to get a .30-06 instead.[16] Ray

paid the additional price to get the more expensive weapon and was adamant that he needed it equipped with a telescopic scope as soon as possible.
Ray may still have been unclear as to his exact role in the King conspiracy,
but clearly someone had insisted that Ray go on record as buying a specific
type of weapon, a Remington Gamemaster .30-06 rifle.[17]

The question of why Ray changed his mind on the rifle has remained
a major mystery. Ray, of course, said that Raoul was responsible for the
return and that he made up the story that it was his brother-in-law. Some
authors have speculated that Ray found a defect with the first gun and took
it back. There are two problems with this argument. The first is that, according to the gun-store manager, Ray demonstrated a complete lack of
understanding of guns and weapons when he purchased the .243, raising
questions as to whether or not Ray would have noticed a defect. A more
glaring problem is the fact that Ray returned the .243 for a more expensive
weapon. This was completely out of character for Ray. The return of the
rifle is a strong indication that Ray was working in concert with others. So,
it seems likely that Ray's sponsors felt it was very important that a .30-06
rifle was used.

New research reinforces this explanation. As part of their surveillance
on Sam Bowers, the FBI obtained a full record of his phone calls from the
fall of 1967 to the summer of 1968. During 1967 and 1968, only one call was
made from Bowers's phone to Birmingham, Alabama. That call was made to
an unlisted telephone number during the time of Ray's rifle purchase. Additional research revealed that the number was in the same area of Birmingham as the gun shop and could have been to a nearby pay phone. Research
is still in progress (tracking pay phone listings decades after the fact is a considerable challenge), and access to numbers called from a Birmingham pay
phone is most likely impossible at this late date (there would be no record of
incoming calls to Bowers's telephone). Did James Earl Ray call Sam Bowers
to confirm his gun purchase? Did Bowers return the call and give Ray some
specific instruction about his purchase? It's not something we can confirm,
but the sheer coincidence of a solitary phone call from Bowers's phone to

the proximate neighborhood of the Birmingham gun shop at the time of Ray's purchase is certainly suggestive.

After obtaining the rifle, Ray drove right back to Atlanta, arriving the evening of March 30. Later, he was forced to lie about the return trip to Atlanta, stating instead that he had driven from Birmingham on to Memphis (never explaining why it would take several days to go a few hundred miles). In the end, he was tripped up by a laundry receipt, showing that he had left laundry at the Piedmont Laundry in Atlanta on April 1. Our interpretation of this sequence of events is that when news coverage of Dr. King's planned return to Memphis first appeared on March 30, the conspirators realized that they had a unique opportunity to provoke national unrest by attacking King during the Memphis strike. Ray was contacted in Atlanta and ordered to leave for Memphis immediately. And of course Ray, who would deny that he even knew Dr. King was in Memphis, was also forced to lie about his quick foray into and out of Atlanta—as it suggested that he was taking orders from someone and going to Memphis specifically in connection to Dr. King's visit.[18]

SIEGE MENTALITY IN MEMPHIS

Dr. King was no stranger to Memphis. He had been in the city a number of times since 1958, and the Reverend Billy Kyles was a good friend of his. On the dozen or so occasions when he had previously visited the city, King had generally stayed in private homes but had also used the black-owned Lorraine Motel on occasion.[19] But Memphis in 1968 was not the city that King had known previously. Memphis sanitation workers had been striking ever since two black union members died in an accident as a result of being forced to work during foul weather. The majority of union members were black, and in late February, Kyles had addressed a mass meeting stating that what had begun as a labor issue had become a race issue and that they were "at war" in Memphis.[20] Matters had steadily gotten worse as Memphis police began to use black intelligence officers to monitor meetings and report on protest plans. By March, activists were aware of this practice, and their organizing committee protested to the city council about police strikebreaking. One undercover police officer had been threatened at an organizational meeting and barely escaped serious injury. Ironically, he was rescued by Cornelia Crenshaw, one of the main strike supporters.[21]

During earlier trips to Memphis, Reverend Kyles had personally contacted Memphis Police requesting security for Dr. King. In cooperation, black police officers would be assigned to meet King at the airport. But that sort of relationship no longer existed by April 1968. The subversion of civil rights groups by the police and the FBI had fostered a siege mentality among local organizers. There is little doubt that the FBI's Counter Intelligence Program—the systematic effort to infiltrate and undermine agitators of all stripes—had exacerbated the situation in Memphis. The FBI established its own intelligence sources and used stories about the violence in the sanitation strike to feed its legislative and media campaign against King. In challenging King's competence as a voice for nonviolent protest, the FBI escalated the tension in Memphis through its own actions.[22]

The situation in Memphis was also inflamed by the Klan's threat of a major countermarch. The governor had been notified, and the head of the Memphis police testified at the hearings to block the sanitation workers' march that a confrontation could lead to worse violence than had occurred in Watts or Detroit.[23] Strangely, we have been able to locate no further information on Klan members traveling to Memphis, promoting or assembling there for a countermarch. It appears that none of the usual racist firebrands traveled to Memphis. Rather than finding J. B. Stoner or his compatriots organizing countermarch activities there, we find Stoner traveling to a small meeting in Meridian, Mississippi, the day of the King murder. Surprisingly, the conspicuous and advantageous return of Dr. King to Memphis was marked by the total absence of the hard-core civil rights opponents who had been so visible at similar confrontations over the previous years.

When Dr. King arrived at the airport, members of the march's organizing committee, the Community on the Move for Equality (COME), recognized plainclothes Memphis police officers in the "welcoming" crowd. Organizers openly confronted these black members of police intelligence (including officers Ed Redditt and Willie Richmond) and warned them to stay away from King.[24] Their suspicions of local police at its peak, COME members also decided not to request or accept special police security for Dr. King. Reverend James Lawson contacted Inspector Don Smith, one of the four white senior police officers, and told Smith that the coordinating committee was not interested in arranging special security with the police force.[25]

The breakdown in trust was mutual. Smith honored Lawson's request without confirming this with Dr. King.[26] Notably, none of the plainclothes officers at the airport had a record of cooperation with Memphis's black community, nor had any of the law enforcement personnel present at the airport worked with King's security on previous trips. Certainly the police made no special effort to establish any level of trust, and the situation had only been made worse by using black undercover officers already suspected of being police spies.[27]

Memphis Police testimony also states that an unidentified member of Dr. King's party asked law enforcement to remove any officers from the grounds of the motel itself. It is clear that a tactical detail of three or four police cars was indeed removed from the motel, but only a block away. They were assigned to patrol a four- to six-block perimeter and had no contact with King's aides. In addition, there were no foot patrols in the immediate vicinity of the Lorraine Motel, where Dr. King was shot.[28]

SURVEILLANCE OF KING

Regardless of the lack of coordinated security, a great deal of surveillance was focused on Dr. King and his staff. Detectives Redditt and Richmond were assigned to set up a surveillance post at the Butler Street firehouse, across the street from the Lorraine Motel. There was particular interest in monitoring meetings with some of the most militant young blacks, members of the "Invaders" who had been suspected of having a major role in bringing about the violence associated with the first march.[29] The evening before Dr. King's murder, both of these black intelligence officers were also assigned to cover an organizing meeting at the Mason Temple. The Reverend Malcolm

Blackburn quickly recognized them and warned them that they were about to be pointed out to the entire crowd and were in great danger. He also warned them that it was known that they were spying on Dr. King from the firehouse. Obviously the firehouse surveillance had been exposed.[30]

On the afternoon of April 4, the chief of police called Detective Redditt into a meeting and told him that they had received a threat against a black Memphis officer and that they believed Redditt was to be the target. Redditt was offered protective custody for himself and his family. Redditt declined the special protection but was removed from assignment and driven to his home under the protection of his supervisor, Lieutenant Eli Arkin. Consequently, both Redditt and Arkin were at Redditt's home when the news was broadcast that Dr. King had been shot.[31]

Detective Redditt came to view the threat against him as suspicious, especially because an unknown individual, introduced as being from Washington, had been in the meeting in which the threat had been discussed. Following the assassination, there was considerable suspicion within the Memphis black community that there might have been police complicity in the crime, and these suspicions seem to have led Redditt to question his own removal from the surveillance detail, providing further encouragement for suspicion of police involvement. In his study of the Redditt incident, Philip Melanson observed that Detective Redditt was not actually serving as any sort of security for Dr. King, and in fact none of Lietenant Arkin's intelligence people were doing anything beyond surveillance. Redditt's removal had no direct impact on security for Dr. King, because there was none at the motel. This makes it difficult to see anything in the Redditt incident that would connect him to James Earl Ray or indicate his removal was part of a larger conspiracy to assassinate Dr. King at the Lorraine Motel.

However, suspicions over the Redditt incident were brought to the attention of the HSCA and they spent considerable effort investigating the circumstances of his removal. These investigations have resolved much of the mystery of the reported threat against Redditt, including its source and how it was relayed to Memphis Police.

According to a Memphis Police Department (MPD) report obtained by the HSCA, shortly after 3:00 PM on April 4, Memphis Police Inspector G. P. Tines informed his chief of police that Philip Manuel, an investigator with the Senate Investigating Committee (Senator McClellan's Permanent Subcommittee on Investigations) had contacted him and said that he had himself just received a call from his office in Washington. He had been advised that a committee informant in Mississippi had reported a plan to kill a black police lieutenant in Memphis. The informant had heard talk of the planned attack at a meeting of the Mississippi Freedom Democratic Party (MFDP). Inspector Tines relayed that the Senate committee investigator believed that the threat was directed at MPD Detective Redditt.[32]

A Memphis Police report records Manuel as stating that a memo, with full details and names relating to the plot, was being prepared by Jack Dross, another McClellan committee staff member in Washington, DC. Manuel was scheduled to fly out of Memphis at 5:50 PM and planned to relay further details of the plot that evening, or early next morning. In conjunction with the warning, Inspector Tines had advised the local FBI office, and they indicated they would check into the threat.

That same afternoon, Inspector Tines informed Redditt's supervisor, Lt. Arkin, that following the call from Manuel, the Jackson, Mississippi, FBI office had also been contacted about the reported threat.[33] The FBI related that its own informant had attended the MFDP meeting cited as a source of the Senate committee information. The FBI informant identified certain attendees including militant activist H. Rap Brown. Topics discussed at the meeting included the Mississippi Summer Project and the Washington Poor People's March. The FBI informant further stated that two brothers from Memphis had attended the meeting and remarked about police brutality in Memphis; however, nothing had been said about an attack on Memphis officers, and Redditt's name had not been mentioned.[34]

The FBI also advised Memphis Police that the Mississippi Highway Patrol (MHP) also had an informant at the MFDP meeting and that he had reported discussion of an incident in Knoxville, Tennessee, involving a black police sergeant. That informant had described discussion of a contract on the Knoxville officer. The FBI stated that the MHP had already reported those remarks to the Tennessee Bureau of Investigation (TBI). The FBI did not advise specifically how it came to be in possession of details from a MHP informant, implying that the MHP may have routinely provided informant reports to the FBI. Tines's report went on to speculate that the TBI in Knoxville had called the Senate Investigating Committee office in Washington, who in turn had relayed the plot to the committee investigator in Memphis. In passing the information along, it appears as though the Senate investigator had somehow misinterpreted a specific threat against a sergeant in Knoxville to be a plan to kill a detective in Memphis.

The MPD departmental communications are very specific about the source of the warning assumed to be against Detective Redditt. Redditt had, in fact, become known in Memphis as a police spy due to his ongoing surveillance assignments on the various strike and protest meetings. In addition to Redditt, two black firefighters, Floyd Newsum and Norvell Wallace, stationed at the Butler Street firehouse were also reassigned immediately before Dr. King's assassination. They had both been openly and vocally supportive of the sanitation strike, and Newsum had attended an organizational meeting at the Mason Temple. He had personally confronted Detective Redditt and accused him of spying on the strikers.[35] The HSCA would demonstrate that the information used in the decision to remove the two firemen had actually come from Detective Redditt himself, but in the weeks and months immediately following the assassination, local talk and rumor had combined the removal of Detective Redditt and the black firemen as a single act, wrongly reinforcing the idea of government complicity in King's eventual murder.

When Congress investigated this in the late 1970s, the HSCA located and interviewed the primary informant who had been at the MFDP meeting. The meeting informant stated that he had directly contacted the local Senate investigator and had not contacted anyone in Washington. The informant also specifically stated that he told the Senate investigator that the threat was against a black police sergeant in Knoxville.[36]

One could see this as a simple matter of miscommunication, but the specific mention of Redditt in Memphis leaves that idea open to question. It certainly does not appear to be a case of security stripping—deliberately removing protection from an individual in order to kill him—as security would have done nothing to actually stop a sniper attack. We, however, do feel that the Redditt removal could involve motives that, while not sinister, are not benign either and that connect to the larger efforts to diminish and derail King's socioeconomic reform agenda.

The threat report clearly did sensitize senior Memphis police to potential violence against their officers.[37] At about the same time that information was being exchanged relating to threats against Redditt's life, the Southern Christian Leadership Conference's executive director, Andrew Young, was in a Memphis court, working to get an injunction against King's march lifted by a judge. The First Amendment would normally tilt any court in the direction of Young and the marchers; courts generally require an obvious and clear threat of violence before denying the right to assemble or the right to protest. Thus anyone looking to limit King or prevent the march would have an interest in reporting clear threats against local law enforcement officers.

In addition, we have previously referred to the FBI director's animosity toward Dr. King. Examples of that are presented in other chapters and in some detail in Appendix B. But, as it so happens, the FBI was not the only government entity engaging in such dirty tricks targeting civil rights activists. In fact, the Senate Investigating Committee that employed Philip Manuel in 1968 was known to engage in a variety of tactics intended to undermine civil rights protests and demonstrations. The Permanent Investigating Committee was chaired by segregationist Senator John L. McClellan. By 1969, McClellan had focused his committee (and its investigators) on civil rights groups. As an example of his efforts, just one month after King's death, McClellan had unsuccessfully attempted to use false information (warning of violence and attacks against law enforcement) on Dr. King's Poor People's Campaign to derail its planned march on Washington, DC. In retrospect, it seems likely that the Redditt threat may have been a similar attempt, aimed at raising the perceived threat level for violence during the sanitation workers' strike and at the same time discrediting activist civil rights groups ranging from the MFDP to the Black Panthers. Certainly the misinformation report, sent from the Senate Committee directly to the MPD, was consistent with McClellan's oft-expressed opinion that the civil rights movement was pushing America to the edge of civil breakdown.

LANTERN SPIKE ALERT

In addition to the police intelligence efforts, overall concern about potential violence had risen substantially after the sanitation workers' support march, so the U.S. Army Intelligence and Security Command had declared a Civil Disorder Operation (carried out under a domestic military intelligence program code-named Lantern Spike) in effect, beginning on March 28.[38]

Such action was allowed under a relatively new presidential order; the order called for the army to coordinate with local law enforcement, as well as with the National Guard, in the event of any serious threat of civil unrest. In addition to setting up a local command center, Army Intelligence was also authorized to perform against observations of designated targets.

Following the first march, the Army Intelligence and Security Command directed the 111th Military Intelligence Group to establish a field office in Memphis. On March 28, the commander of the geographic region that included Memphis stationed himself in that city and began to call in personnel from surrounding cities, as well as from Anniston, Alabama, and Atlanta, Georgia. Some twenty-four intelligence personnel were called in, and after the murder of Dr. King, the number was increased. The alert operation continued and was expanded to several southern cities, not ending until April 12.

The official record of this army action is contained in an after-action report, now available for review. The report does mention some field observations but does not give specific detail on the locations of those activities. Given the reports of military personnel at the Butler Street firehouse, it follows that Lantern Spike personnel were very likely involved in direct surveillance of the Lorraine Motel, at least for a time.

It was this volatile combination of tension, arm's-length security, and compromised surveillance surrounding Dr. King and the Lorraine Motel that awaited James Earl Ray upon his arrival in Memphis.

RAY IN MEMPHIS

Exactly how and why Ray ended up at Bessie Brewer's rooming house across from the Lorraine Motel is a mystery[39] Ray himself gave many conflicting details and involved the mysterious figure of Raoul in various ways to further cloud the issue. Certainly Ray did not seem to be following a fixed schedule. He had stayed at the New Rebel Motel in Memphis the night before and arrived at the boarding house across from the Lorraine only a few hours before the shooting. There is evidence that he was settling himself in for at least an overnight stay; he brought in a zipper bag of toiletries, toilet paper, hangers, his radio, and a couple of cans of beer—leaving several hundred dollars of film equipment locked in his car trunk. His actions show no evidence of some tightly planned and scheduled attack. If there was such a plan, it appears Ray was not privy to it.

It is notable that Ray did transport the rifle to Memphis, he did handle it, and his prints were found on it. As an experienced criminal, we can assume that Ray was highly sensitive to leaving prints at any crime scene, and certainly on a significant piece of evidence such as a murder weapon. Ray's prints on the rifle suggest that he was, in fact, simply transporting the rifle under orders. Given Ray's understanding of the use of fingerprints in prosecuting crimes, it is therefore likely that the actual timing of the attack on Dr. King was very much a surprise for Ray.

The official view of the shooting is that Ray waited in the shared boarding house bathroom, observing the Lorraine Motel with binoculars (which he had bought only an hour before). Intuitively this seems improbable as a plan, since it would have involved either continual trips to the bathroom (his room did not have a view of the Lorraine Motel, and he did not examine the room before accepting it) or literally locking himself in there for an indeterminate period of time. This also implies that Ray, an experienced

thief, would not think of surveying the back side of the rooming house beforehand to determine which rooms did have a view of the Lorraine.[40]

We are left with a scenario of Ray watching from the bathroom, possibly ignoring other residents continually knocking on the door, then seeing
Dr. King on the balcony, and sprinting back to his room for his rifle. Locking himself in a common bathroom with a rifle seems equally improbable.
He then took the rifle containing only one shell and positioned himself in
the tub (in a rather awkward firing position) and shot out through the bathroom window, successfully hitting his target. This meant that the success of
Ray's plan relied entirely on the availability of the shared bathroom of a fully
occupied rooming house. (The manager had told him he was getting one of
the few vacant rooms.)[41]

Many authors imply that Ray simply got a break because Dr. King stood
for several minutes on the balcony, talking to people below in the parking
lot. That creates the impression that there would have been plenty of time
for Ray to see Dr. King from the bathroom, make his decision, and perhaps
fetch the rifle (and one bullet). However, the detailed surveillance records,
kept by the observers in the fire station across the way, record that Dr. King
came out of his room at 5:06 PM for little more than a minute. He went back
in, returned to the balcony at 5:59 PM, and was shot at 6:01 PM. Effectively,
King was only on the balcony for approximately three minutes in the hour
before his death.[42]

The only witness who came close to firmly identifying someone like
Ray as being inside the rooming house was Charles Stephens. If Stephens is
to be believed, Ray apparently ran back to his room, sloppily bundled up the
personal possessions intended for an overnight stay into a sheet, slammed
the rifle partially into its box, and hurtled down the rooming house stairs.
Furthermore, Ray's purported escape route was down a flight of stairs to the
sidewalk in front of Jim's Grill, at a time when the place was sure to have
plenty of customers as potential witnesses.

ISSUES OF EVIDENCE

There are numerous difficulties with the above shooting scenario; however, a substantial amount of evidence was assembled to place Ray at the crime scene, to connect Ray to the rifle, and to create a plausible description of the fatal shot having been fired from the rooming house bathroom. But remember, that evidence was never contested in an actual legal prosecution, a venue in which challenge and rebuttals would have been offered. Readers of Frank's and Huie's early books encounter a powerful exposition of the evidence against Ray. Frank writes about a palm print on the wall above the tub, scuff marks in the tub, and an autopsy that traced the path of the bullet and determined that the shot had to be fired from an upper window across the street.[43] He also describes surveys a team of city engineers conducted and writes that for the bullet "to have taken the course taken in [King's] body, it had to have come from the [bathroom] window sill."[44]

The HSCA determined that there had been no probing of the bullet path during the autopsy. The exact position of Dr. King's head at the time of the shooting was uncertain, and the precise path and origin of the bullet could not be traced.[45] Actually, the geometric data was consistent with either the second-floor rooming house windows or the ground-level shrubbery below. Moreover, it turns out the palm print was not matched to Ray, nor were the scuff marks.

Professor Philip Melanson highlights a number of evidentiary issues, including work by the HSCA, that cast doubt on the strength of the original fingerprint identifications. The committee used two different sets of fingerprint experts to reevaluate prints on the rifle, scope, binoculars, newspaper, beer can, and bottle of aftershave. When the conclusions were compared, and the identifications of one expert compared to that of another team of two experts, the committee found that there was no agreement between the two identifications on any of the prints![46] Contrary to initial news stories and even Huie's book on Ray, no palm or fingerprint matches to Ray were found in the prints taken from the common bathroom where he supposedly fired the fatal shot. None of the prints from his rented room were matched to Ray.[47] And the scrape on the bathroom window sill that was touted as evidence of resting the rifle is more than questionable.[48] Witness testimony from individuals in the boarding house varies and is also highly questionable; the only witness, Charles Stephens, who definitively placed Ray at the area of the shooting, was almost certainly too drunk to be credible. Homicide Detective Roy Stephens took the initial statement from Stephens. The detective recalled Charles Stephens as being less than sober, even a couple of hours after the shooting; the detective also recalled Stephens as definitely saying he could not identify the man he saw.[49] Based on Detective Roy Stephens's remarks, it appears that the Stephens's identification of Ray as the man with the rifle became much more definite only over time.

Charles Stephens's accounts were supported in part by a witness who did not have the same credibility problems as he did. Charles Anschutz, another boarder, also reported that he "heard a shot, opened his door, and saw a man fleeing down the hall from the direction of the bathroom." Additionally, and perhaps just as importantly, Anschutz confirmed that he had tried to use the rooming house bathroom, only to find it occupied. Anschutz could not be certain as to how long it took between his two bathroom stops, but Charles Stephens's account suggests that it may have been a while. According to Stephens, Anschutz complained, "Who the hell is in the bathroom?"[50] Anschutz's recollection is important here as well. He said Charles Stephens told him it was the tenant from room 5B, the room James Earl Ray rented under the alias John Willard.

Together, this at least suggests the possibility that Ray had in fact been occupying the bathroom for a long time, with the intention of killing King if the opportunity presented itself. Nonetheless, the issue is clouded by fact that Anschutz could not make a positive identification of Ray, unlike the drunk Stephens, whose reliability many have brought into question. Given these issues, only two things seem certain: the first, that Ray likely did spend some time in the common bathroom; and the second, that the initial case the prosecution presented had a considerable number of holes in it—which only escaped exposure due to Ray's guilty plea and the lack of an aggressive defense.

Another question of evidence, which received little discussion, was the fact that the FBI was never able to determine the source of some of Ray's remaining ammunition. Although there was only a single spent shell in the rifle, there were additional rounds in the bag that he abandoned. The bureau also did not raise the issue of the ammunition. In his book, Gerold Frank simply lists a Peters Cartridge box with nine .30-06 shells, implying all the shells were the same.[51] Some were indeed similar to the hunting round that killed Dr. King; however, the others were military ammunition, full metal jacket rounds with markings suggesting that they had come from belted military ammunition. The gun store where Ray bought his rifle and ammunition stated that they did not carry that sort of ammunition and nothing of the kind shows up on the sales receipt. When asked about the military ammunition, Ray simply claimed he bought it at the same store where he bought the rifle and that there must be a mistake with the receipt.

This is a significant issue. It indicates that Ray may have gotten ammunition from a third party, and it is a known fact that that the Klan often obtained stolen weapons and ammunition from National Guard and Army Reserve units, where belted ammunition would be common. Unfortunately the FBI failed to investigate possible military sources—including White Knight members who served in Mississippi National Guard units that suffered repeated thefts of both weapons and ammunition.[52]

If, indeed, Ray did kill Dr. King, it appears to us to have been a spontaneous shooting, with Ray being in the bathroom, seeing King on the balcony, grabbing the gun, loading a single round, and then firing. Remember King was only on the balcony twice, for only about a minute each time. Ray's activities suggest that he was in Memphis in a surveillance or support role, much the same sort of activity he had begun in Selma and had hoped to perform in Atlanta. Whether a spontaneous act on his part or a response to an order that was not communicated to him in advance, he was left with no choice but to escape as quickly as possible without the chance to remove his prints from the rifle.

Ray certainly seems not to have made a plan or preparations for an escape; over the years he had become relatively good at planning escapes, but there is no sign of that in Memphis. Indeed he only escaped by the skin of his teeth, with the help of a major law enforcement failure to close off escape routes across state lines, as well as a diversionary CB radio broadcast leading police in the opposite direction of his real flight.

RAY'S ROLE: THREE POSSIBILITIES

In light of the material we have presented here, framed in the context of information that we've developed and analyzed relating to the network of militants devoted to the apocalyptic teachings of Wesley Swift, we have reached the conclusion that James Earl Ray was part of a conspiracy to murder Martin Luther King Jr. As to his exact role in an assassination plot, this is less certain, but three logical possibilities emerge from the evidence:

1. Ray heard about a bounty, verified it, and made some level of contact so that he could be assured of claiming his part of the reward if King was killed. He began to monitor King in Selma, became familiar with King's home turf in Atlanta, and bought a rifle. After buying the rifle, he became aware that King would be out in public in Memphis and decided that would be the best place to kill him. He had no specific plan except to get close to King, and circumstances provided him with an opportunity before he had time to plan his escape. As with many of his other previous crimes, he simply reacted on the spur of the moment and his escape was purely a matter of luck.

2. Ray heard about the bounty, verified it, and made some level of contact so that he could be assured of claiming his part of the reward if King was killed. Being naturally cautious, he chose the secondary role of observer and support player, not the role of killer. One of his tasks was to set up an observation post in Memphis; he was also to transport the rifle to be used. However, when presented with the opportunity to shoot King and claim the entire bounty,

he acted spontaneously, as he had in previous crimes, and took the shot. He succeeded but found himself in a very tight position with no prepared plan of escape.

3. Ray was merely playing a supporting role. He was to monitor King, set up an observation post in Memphis, and transport the rifle. However, the conspirators, either with advance knowledge of King's schedule or simply by assuming he would go out in the evening (as he did routinely), were prepared to do the actual shooting, leaving Ray as the patsy with no claim on the money and no escape plan.

NARROWING THE POSSIBILITIES

Based on reported details of Ray's actions following the assassination, plus a good deal of information recently made available, we feel it is now possible to develop a more precise understanding of Ray's role in a King conspiracy. Ray's critical decisions on the day of the crime all suggest that the killing of King was not premeditated. Renting a room only a few hours before the killing, renting room 5B even though it had no view of King's room, and attempting to buy a pair of night vision binoculars when the killing actually took place in relative daylight all suggest that the killing of King was not premeditated. Even the earlier exchange of the .243 for the Remington Gamemaster .30-06 rifle makes little sense if the intention was to shoot King from across the street of the Lorraine Motel. The .243 rifle would have been more than capable of the task on April 4. A .30-06 rifle would only have been needed if the shooting were to be from a greater distance.

In addition, the variety of personal effects Ray decided to take up to his room provided much of the material, including fingerprints, that would have been used against him in court. Given that only an hour or so before the shooting, Ray had taken items including toiletries, underwear, a sheet (he always carried his own sheet and toilet paper into rooming houses), a radio, and even some beer up to his room, it is hard to believe that he had any idea he shortly would be fleeing from the scene of a murder. Beyond that, as an experienced criminal, he took no apparent precautions to avoid leaving prints on the weapon or his personal effects.

The fact that Ray abandoned the rifle and personal effects at the scene is often presented as the only thing that prevented the murder from being the perfect crime, suggesting that it must have been well planned and largely well executed.[53] It is true that within a week of the crime, a laundry mark found on a T-shirt and pair of shorts discovered in the suspiciously abandoned bundle of personal items was traced to the name Eric Galt in Los Angeles. Independently, Ray's abandoned white Mustang had been reported in Atlanta, and a quick check showed it was registered to Eric Galt of Birmingham. Since Ray had been using the Galt identity indiscriminately for almost a year, investigators were able to follow a trail across the country and directly to his room in Atlanta, where more incriminating evidence had been left, including a fingerprint that could be matched to the real James Earl Ray.

Another significant point is that Ray was absolutely unprepared for an escape after the shooting. In fact, he escaped running into police by only a minute or two. By 6:08 PM, a general description of the suspect as a young, well-dressed, white male had been broadcast on police channels, followed at 6:10 by the description of a late-model white Mustang that Ray was driving.[54] The description of the Mustang would gain national media coverage, and ultimately the media reports triggered citizens in Atlanta to bring a recently abandoned white Mustang to the attention of the Atlanta Police Department. Information about the car would lead directly to the Galt alias that Ray had used for the better part of a year and consequently to James Earl Ray.

The fact is that Ray had violated even the most basic precautions for getting away with a crime given that he was an experienced criminal. He had parked a very noticeable vehicle on a street in front of several businesses, including a busy bar and grill. He was observed running down the street, and his car was reported speeding down that street. A general description of Ray and a description of the white Mustang were both broadcast within minutes of the shooting. Ray drove his Mustang all the way to Atlanta, abandoning it with further evidence in the trunk tying him to the crime. Ray certainly knew better than that. He had used cutout cars in prior crimes, making sure that any car reported at the crime scene was dumped and not tied to him. Ray, the experienced criminal, simply did nothing right in his escape from Memphis; it shows no sign at all of planning or preparation. Certainly if Ray had left Atlanta planning to shoot Dr. King, he would have thoroughly covered his trail there before leaving for Memphis. Not only did he not do that, but he also even left laundry in Atlanta.

Ray's uncharacteristically sloppy escape from Memphis leads us to the conclusion that any shooting he might have done there was strictly a spontaneous act. In addition, events in Atlanta (as well as informant reports indicating Bowers's initial unhappiness with the timing of the King murder) suggest that the way the shooting happened was not exactly what Ray's sponsors had in mind. It appears that despite the death of Dr. King, the actual attack did not come together according to any preestablished plan.

Following his extremely narrow escape, Ray drove all night and at 9:00 AM backed his Mustang into a parking spot in a housing complex three miles south of his rooming house in Atlanta. Because he was in a flashy car, was dressed in a suit, and took the trouble to back his car into the parking spot, he was observed in some detail by at least four people. As he walked away from the car, witnesses noted that he was carrying a black notebook with a white piece of paper showing.[55] The notebook never turned up in evidence. From what we know now, that piece of paper probably had one or more important telephone numbers on it.

An eyewitness has revealed to Atlanta-based researcher Lamar Waldron that he observed Milteer's partner Hugh Spake receive a telephone call from James Earl Ray that morning. Spake was working on the assembly line at the Lakewood General Motors factory, and the call came into a common phone, available to all the workers in that area. Spake was on duty, and it was a payday. There is no indication that he was expecting the call or that the call was anything other than a plea for help or money from Ray. Spake was in no position to leave work and didn't. He may have given Ray another number, or he may have called someone for Ray later; Waldron's witness didn't know.[56] There is some reason to suspect that Joseph Milteer may have responded by contacting Ray. A letter recovered from Milteer's home suggests that an associate of his was aware that Milteer had been in Atlanta at the same time Ray was, in the same neighborhood where Ray left his car.[57] If Ray did manage to connect with someone, there is no evidence to show that he was given any significant payoff. Certainly there is no sign that the bounty sponsors were prepared and had cash ready to pay off Ray in Atlanta or that they were set up to provide any special assistance for his escape from that city.

Events in Memphis itself also suggest the idea that Ray literally and figuratively jumped the gun and surprised the conspirators. The hoax CB radio broadcast that lured police away from the direction of a fleeing James Earl Ray occurred some twenty to thirty minutes after the assassination. Gerald Posner, author of *Killing the Dream,* argues that the delay suggests an impulsive action, a simple hoax by someone monitoring police channels; he proposes that any well-prepared conspiracy would have been ready with the diversion immediately after the shooting. But Posner's timing argument against conspiracy makes sense only if the conspirators had somehow anticipated that Ray's white Mustang would be spotted fleeing the scene and that police would immediately obtain that report and broadcast a bulletin with an accurate description of the vehicle. We explore the CB hoax, its investigation, and our assessment of its actual meaning in considerable detail in Appendix B.

After fleeing Memphis, Ray's travel and activities further support the "spontaneous shooting" scenario. One popular view of Ray's escape is that, up until his being taken into custody in London, Ray had moved swiftly and smoothly out of the United States, on through Canada and multiple European countries. That view argues that he had considerable help and support in his escape, obviously being well funded. But we find little evidence to support that view and much that contradicts it.

In fact, Ray was forced to make a last-minute effort to sanitize both his car and his apartment before heading out for Canada. He did a poor job of that, leaving behind key evidence in both locations; there is no indication that he had made any preparations to cover his trail prior to the shooting in Memphis. The only precautions he appears to have taken during the entire period was to buy the rifle in a name other than Galt (he used the name "Harvey Lowmeyer") and to register at the Memphis rooming house under yet another name ("John Willard").[58] Up until the evening before the Memphis shooting, he was still using the Galt name for motel registration. However, he had no counterfeit identification papers for either the Lowmeyer or Willard names, so he had to use the Galt name as he fled the country.[59]

Ray did eventually make it to London (on the cheapest excursion ticket available) and from there on to Portugal. In Portugal he went to the Canadian embassy to have his passport canceled and reissued. Ray's own poor printing resulted in the first passport being issued in the name of Sneya, a misspelling of Sneyd, which did not match his stolen birth certificate. Ray spent time in Portugal, making inquiries into possible mercenary contacts that would get him to one of their colonies. With no luck in that effort, he decided go back to London and try for a Belgium connection of the same sort. On June 8, 1968, as he went back though the London airport, Ray opened his billfold to show a customs clerk his passport, and the clerk noticed that he had a second passport. That was all it took to get the clerk's attention. Upon further investigation, the clerk discovered that "Sneyd" was on the published "Watch for and Detain" bulletin. Ray was taken aside, the fact that he was carrying a concealed pistol taped to his leg undercut his protests, and that was the end of his attempted escape.

Rather than a well-planned and sophisticated escape, we see Ray leaving the United States by bus, having to build his own fake identity in Canada, buying the cheapest possible ticket overseas ($340 round-trip excursion to London), and then making his way to Portugal where he fruitlessly tried to make contact with companies who provided mercenaries for service in Africa, apparently hoping they would employ him and provide the transportation and paperwork to get him there. With only $840, Ray could have flown directly to Rhodesia and at least been safe from extradition, but apparently he didn't have that relatively modest amount. Even if he had made it back through London to Brussels, what would have become of him is unclear. Certainly he didn't have the money to play tourist forever. In fact he was so desperate for money that he was forced into multiple robbery attempts in London, finally stealing $240 from a London bank. When he was taken into custody at the airport, Ray had a total of $143 on his person.[60]

RAY AND CONSPIRACY

We conclude that James Earl Ray was not in Memphis because of his ego nor because of his own racist agenda. There is simply nothing in his prior history, nor in the period after his escape from Missouri State Penitentiary, that supports that view. Ray had no social or political agendas; for him, life was about survival and an ongoing need for money. Some of the early authors rejected the idea of conspiracy; although they acknowledge that Ray might have heard rumors about money being offered for King's life, they simply could not conceive of a group of conspirators who might have contacted Ray. They could not conceive of Klansmen paying for a killing, or using outsiders or criminals as paid assassins. They could not imagine Ray contacting anyone who had plotted against King in 1967 and who would still be plotting against the civil rights leader in 1968.[61]

These things were not only possible, but also actually did occur. A network of radical racists had plotted against Dr. King for many years, evolving their plans and tactics over time. Many attacks had been planned, some aborted and some failed. However, the goal remained, and the efforts were ongoing. In most cases the conspirators successfully insulated themselves from any association with the various assassination attempts, letting others do their work. And in doing so, they all became expert at constructing diversions, working through cutouts, and establishing solid alibis. They would always be somewhere else when the violence occurred. We also have new information suggesting that some of them did indeed have the resources to raise the large amounts of money necessary for a bounty on King's life.

It seems probable that the money raised by the Milteer clique in Atlanta became the source of the high-dollar offer for Dr. King's assassination, which was first rumored in North Carolina and then showed up in select locations including Jefferson City and Leavenworth penitentiary. Ray heard about the offer in Missouri State Penitentiary after his escape in 1967, and he very likely heard more gossip about it at his brother's Grapevine Tavern in Saint Louis. He continued onto Canada to escape North America, but when his exit strategy failed, he returned to the United States with two new interests: getting into pornographic filmmaking and pursuing the big money offer on Dr. King. He headed for Birmingham, creating a new "Alabama boy" identity, getting ready for the porno business, and very likely making inquiries about the King offer. We have no way of knowing whether he made any contact with conspirators in Birmingham, for at that time the folks with the money may have been hesitant to deal with a convict on the run. With more and more criminal prosecutions putting these individuals behind bars, these people were desperate. So was Ray.

By February 1968, Ray's changed behavior indicates that contact was likely made with those plotting to assassinate King. We cannot claim to know what part of the offer he accepted, but it appears that he may have only agreed to participate in surveillance and support. But something unplanned happened in Memphis, something for which neither he nor his sponsors were prepared. Ray apparently tried to contact them during his escape, but he certainly received neither the money nor the support that he needed. In the end Ray was left largely to his own resources and with no real exit strategy.

Ray conspired to kill Martin Luther King Jr. He did go to Memphis knowing that Dr. King was going to be attacked. It appears unlikely to us that he initially planned to shoot Dr. King himself. But we also feel it is unlikely that the shooting of Dr. King occurred exactly as its instigators planned. For this reason, an open-minded investigation of King's murder even in 1968 should have exposed this plot.

CHAPTER 14

AFTERMATH: MISSED EVIDENCE AND CLOSING ARGUMENTS

" Devilish" Nix is what the black woman called him, when she spoke to agents of the FBI's Dallas field office on April 22, 1968. Devilish because he had a habit of pushing the waitresses at his Mississippi restaurant into acts of prostitution after business hours. Devilish because he beat employees. Devilish, perhaps, because if the woman was telling the truth, Deavours Nix, one of Sam Bowers's closest aides, may have had an active role in arranging the murder of Martin Luther King Jr. just two and half weeks before.[1]

The woman—Myrtis Ruth Hendricks, a.k.a "Jitterbug" was one of the cooks who worked for Nix at John's Restaurant in Laurel, Mississippi, a known hangout for the White Knights and for Sam Bowers. After her first day on the job in December 1967, Nix had forced Hendricks to have sex with him and was aggressively pushing her into a life of prostitution. For this reason, she and her boyfriend, Thomas McGee, also an employee at the restaurant, had moved out of Laurel to Abilene, Texas. McGee joined Hendricks at the Dallas FBI field office offering moral support but expressing great fear at the harm that would come to them and their remaining friends and relatives in Mississippi if their names were leaked.[2] The details of Hendricks's story of suspicious activity at John's Restaurant from April 2 to April 4, 1968, were captured in the original report from Dallas to FBI headquarters:

> On April Two, last, [Hendricks] overheard Nix say "I got a call on the King," but did not hear any more of the conversation. On the

evening of April 3, last, two men, neatly dressed, with short, stocky builds, came to Nix's place where she started to work at three p.m. and worked nights. While going to the bathroom, she observed a rifle with a telescopic sight, in a case in Nix's office. Later, the two men took the rifle and a long box, which took three men to carry out, and put them in a sixty-four maroon Dodge with a fake "continental kit" on the back.

On April Four, last, while on duty, she overheard Nix receive a telephone call on his phone which is close to the kitchen. After this call, Nick said, "Martin Luther King is Dead." This was before the news came over the radio about the murder. [Emphasis added][3]

The Dallas report was forwarded to FBI headquarters, which in turn forwarded the lead to the Jackson field office for investigation. In separate files, the Jackson office appears to have developed some suggestive corroboration for Hendricks's story. Several informants placed both Bowers and Nix at John's Restaurant in the days leading up to and including the evening of April 4, 1968. One, in particular, told the FBI that that he saw Bowers and Nix privately meet with two unknown individuals in Nix's office on the evening of April 3, 1968, with Bowers later telling one of them that "you are the only one that has enough sense to do this."[4] Rather than see this as partial support of Hendricks's story, the FBI used it to refute her claims. They simply noted that the informant said he had not seen any weapon in the office or seen a weapon transported to a vehicle.[5] The problem with that interpretation was that Hendricks had made no specific claim as to the time of the rifle story, and she had worked that day from the late afternoon through the evening. The informant and Hendricks may simply have been describing two closely related but different episodes. More to the point, the FBI missed what may have been a bombshell, contained in the summary file on Bowers:

On April 5, 1968, [Jackson Informant] T-2 advised that while in John's Cafe that morning, he saw Sam Bowers and told him that he did a good job the previous night (making reference to the killing of MARTIN LUTHER KING, JR.). Sam Bowers remarked that he carried Billy Roy Pitts up to Memphis and that "poor Billy Roy" did not know what they were up to, but they got King shot.[6]

At first glance, this seems like Sam Bowers must have been joking. Bowers himself had witnesses to place him in Mississippi when King was shot. Moreover, Pitts was a turncoat, who was cooperating with the FBI in their prosecutions of Bowers and other White Knights for the killing of activist Vernon Dahmer in 1966.

On the other hand, there may have been more truth to the remark than was immediately apparent. In separate files related to the Dahmer case, other informants note that Bowers's underlings were still in active contact with Billy Roy Pitts at the time of the King assassination.[7] A "limited hangout" in which Bowers could implicate a White Knights deserter to throw suspicion off his involvement—and the involvement of anyone in his inner circle—would be consistent with what we feel White Knights associates Sidney Barnes and Margaret Capomacchia were doing to Thomas Tarrants several months after the crime.

Other documents suggest that Bowers, always paranoid about informants but brilliant in his tactics, was playing an active game of disinformation. Reports of his comments after the assassination have him telling one informant that he "would not have had King shot at this time" and blaming "the feds" for the shooting.[8] At the same time he said this to one informant, another informant reported that he was openly celebrating King's death.[9]

The Hendricks account should have been the canary in the coal mine that pushed investigators into a serious reconsideration of Bowers as a suspect in the King murder. With Bowers in their sights, a bureau that collated and cross-referenced the material could have developed a powerful circumstantial case for a conspiracy to murder King—not just against Bowers but also against key members of the Swift network described in this book. But circumscribing the FBI were major obstacles—procedural, structural, and cultural—that all but guaranteed failure.

FAILURE TO LAUNCH

As the FBI was receiving strange reports about Sam Bowers's behavior at John's Restaurant on April 5, its investigation was actually pointing it in the direction of a conspiracy, an angle that it would explore with some vigor but relinquish too easily. Up until April 19, 1968, the immediate investigation of physical evidence and witness testimony in Memphis suggested to the bureau that there, in fact, were three coconspirators in the King murder: John Willard, Eric Galt, and Harvey Lowmeyer. Willard was the individual who rented room 5B at Bessie Brewer's rooming house across the street from the Lorraine Motel, in the general direction from where witnesses heard the fatal shot. Witnesses inside the rooming house said an individual they believed was renting that room had fled down the stairs immediately after the shooting. Agents had identified Galt canvassing motels in Memphis; he had stayed at the New Rebel Motel in Memphis but checked out of the motel not long before King was shot. More important, Galt was noted as driving the kind of white Mustang witnesses described as fleeing the vicinity of the King shooting. An abandoned white Mustang was found in Atlanta, Georgia, on April 9, and it was traced to an Eric Galt of Alabama. Clothing in the package found outside Canipe's Amusement Company also traced to an Eric Galt, this time in Los Angeles. But the rifle wrapped in the same green blanket had a serial number that allowed authorities to trace the gun to a Birmingham gun store, where investigators learned that a Harvey Lowmeyer had purchased the weapon. Even though Attorney General Ramsey Clark told the press, in the midst of rioting that was rocking the country, that only one person had committed the King murder, Hoover had kept some options relatively open.

But on April 19, 1968, that all changed, as the FBI crime lab determined that fingerprints collected from the weapon and the abandoned car matched the same individual: escaped fugitive James Earl Ray. Combined with picture identifications and handwriting analysis, it became obvious to the FBI that Willard, Galt, and Lowmeyer were all aliases of James Earl Ray, whose prison radio was also found among the items in the green blanket.[10] This represented a critical juncture in the investigation of the King assassination. From that point forward, the FBI began to dismiss or minimize the possibility of a conspiracy in Dr. King's murder.

The timing of this discovery and the resulting focus on Ray was most unfortunate, as some of the most important conspiracy leads emerged just after this date. Those leads included the Hendricks story about Deavours Nix and the mysterious events at John's Restaurant provided to the Dallas field office on April 22. But perhaps just as important, it was after April 19, 1968, that FBI headquarters finally began to seriously consider and collate past attempts on King's life. On April 24, 1968, the FBI reported the results of a thorough examination of the more than sixteen thousand pages of material in Martin Luther King Jr.'s file.

Holding information that dated back to the early 1960s, this file contained reports of dozens of threats on King's life. While many are of the known alcoholic-makes-a-veiled-threat variety, others included accounts that could have pushed the FBI in the direction of the subculture of religious zealots who had plotted to kill King for years. The April 24 report included references to reports from 1964 suggesting the White Knights were considering "taking action" against King in Mississippi, reports of James Venable and J. B. Stoner's effort in 1965 to kill King, reports about Swift devotee Keith Gilbert's efforts to kill King by blowing up the Palladium in Los Angeles, and the report from Donald Nissen of a $100,000 bounty offer on King's life originating with the White Knights of the Ku Klux Klan of Mississippi.[11] Separately, on the same day, a message sent from Oklahoma to FBI headquarters detailed an informant account from 1968, supported by independent reports from 1965, of a contract on King's life the White Knights offered to Dixie Mafia killer Donald Sparks that fell through in 1964.[12]

The only major plot that had been reported to the bureau before April 19 was the one Miami Judge Seymour Gelber provided to the FBI in 1964 and reviewed again on April 15, 1968.[13] That report related to the attempts by Sidney Crockett Barnes, retired Admiral John Crommelin, Mobile White Citizens' Council member Noah Carden, and retired Colonel William Potter Gale, to murder King in Birmingham in September 1963, when he came to eulogize the victims of the Sixteenth Street Baptist Church bombing. Perhaps more than any other, it was the investigation of this very early conspiracy lead that provided the glue that would unite almost all the previous attempts on King under the umbrella of Wesley Swift's Christian Identity message. The Los Angeles FBI field office was even directed to investigate Swift's possible connection to the Birmingham plot, as all four men were ardent followers of the minister's Church of Jesus Christ Christian.[14]

Perhaps that additional investigation would have shed light on Swift's influence on Gilbert, Stoner, and Bowers. But when the FBI lab established the link between James Earl Ray and Eric Galt, eliminating the initial idea of multiple conspirators physically in Memphis, J. Edgar Hoover issued a directive to several field offices, notably Memphis, Birmingham, Los Angeles, and Mobile, to "hold all leads in abeyance concerning whereabouts and activities of various individuals, including Dr. Wesley Swift, in view of the present information concerning suspect Galt."[15]

The same kind of thoughtful, diligent, and inspired investigative work that had helped the FBI link Ray to the Memphis crime seems to significantly diminish in the investigation of conspiracy leads after April 19, especially leads to suspects who produced alibis for being nowhere near Memphis at the time of the shooting. FBI headquarters held in abeyance lead after lead. The subsequent investigation of a conspiracy angle could best be described as superficial and disjointed.[16]

For example, the FBI seems to have dropped the ball when it came to evidence pointing to Donald Sparks. Though they had received reports from 1968 that Donald Sparks was contracted to kill Dr. King, though they had seen independent reports from Mississippi corroborating this plot, and though they had a reliable source within the White Knights who identified Sparks by his picture and knew his nickname, the FBI nonetheless dismissed the existence of this contract offer. They didn't follow up this lead because they could not find records of Sparks's name in any Jackson, Mississippi, motel registries, and because one of the plot informants linked Sparks to a separate murder of another major criminal, John Dillon, in a way that the FBI found troubling. But the FBI also knew, from their own manhunt for Sparks when he was on their Ten Most Wanted Fugitives list, that he used many different fake names and aliases, so the fact that his name was not on a motel register should have been no surprise. Moreover, local authorities in Oklahoma received word that some of Sparks's closest associates (and possibly Sparks himself) were implicated in the Dillon murder. Nonetheless, this lead, like many others, died.[17]

Perhaps the most shocking example of a superficial investigation came when the Jackson field office reinterviewed Sybil Eure in connection with her possible role as a cutout in the later bounty offer on King in 1967. Recall that Sparks's criminal associate, LeRoy McManaman, approached Donald Nissen at Leavenworth penitentiary and told Nissen that Eure was the person to contact if Nissen wanted to participate in the plot against King and collect some of the $100,000 bounty. Having already interviewed Eure in June 1967, Jackson agents reinterviewed her in May 1968. Eure changed her story, saying that she recalled joking to McManaman about a bounty on Martin Luther King Jr. in the wake of the Mississippi Burning murders in 1964; McManaman, she implied, must have simply misunderstood the joke. The FBI did not address the fundamental problem that she could not have told this joke to McManaman while he was living with her in Jackson, because he was back in federal prison by April 1964.[18] The Mississippi Burning killings, a crime that had consumed the Jackson field office like few others, a case that had only just consummated in the convictions of several White Knights in October 1967, did not occur until June 1964. It defies explanation that the agents did not notice this flaw. But this and other matters—such as how a real estate businesswoman from Mississippi shared common associations with a major criminal operator from Kansas—were never explored.

This is not to say that the failure to dig deeply into a conspiracy connected to Swift followers like Bowers was entirely the result of FBI negligence; a big part of the problem was structural. Evidence for the kind of conspiracy detailed in this book was littered over four different streams of files, each containing hundreds to thousands of pages of material. Each field office conducted its own separate investigation into the King murder and produced detailed reports of their investigations in their own local records. Separately, each field office had ongoing investigations of known and suspected criminals, such as Sam Bowers and Sidney Barnes, that predated, ran concurrently with, and postdated the King investigation. As noted before, the FBI also had a lengthy security file on Dr. King himself, which included details of many murder threats on Reverend King's life. Finally, and most important, there was the FBI central headquarters' MURKIN file, which was used to centralize and coordinate the King assassination investigation across the fifty-plus field offices. But the FBI failed to adequately coordinate this enormous amount of information across functional lines.

Key details for investigators were left out as information in field office files was often communicated to headquarters in abridged form, and vice versa. A key detail related to the Nissen investigation—that in 1967, his cellmate, John May, corroborated the McManaman story, does not appear to have every made its way into the MURKIN central headquarters file. The Jackson field office had this report in a separate non-MURKIN field office file, and it also appeared in the security file on King at FBI headquarters, but it was never apparently shared with MURKIN investigators, and thus never passed on to other field offices. It was lost in the process of truncating and summarizing information.[19] The information that would have connected Sparks to McManaman—specifically their close connections to Rubie Charles Jenkins—would have likely come from non-King-related Oklahoma field office files on Jenkins; that information was never shared. Information from 1964 showing that the White Knights had considered contracting out to criminals for a major, unknown operation was in separate field office files (on the White Knights of the Ku Klux Klan of Mississippi) in the Jackson office, and this material never found its way into the King investigation files either.

Leads and details were considered in isolation from each other rather than in their totality, and thus leads appeared weaker than they actually were. This lack of correlation between leads and data was horizontal—between the four lines of records—as shown above. But it was also vertical over time in the same set of records. FBI headquarters was well aware of both the Sparks plot and the McManaman plot. The similarities could have raised questions forcing investigators to reconsider the merits of both. But once the Sparks plot was superficially dismissed by the end of April 1968, it was not even referenced in May as the Nissen bounty came under closer scrutiny. This problem of vertical analysis, of failing to connect leads over time, was magnified by what may have been the single biggest flaw in the FBI's investigative approach.

The FBI simply refused to consider the possibility that white supremacists who had alibis on the day of the assassination could have plotted a conspiracy against King across state lines. Once they learned that J. B. Stoner was not in Memphis on April 4, 1968, the FBI dismissed the man they initially thought of as their chief suspect.[20] They eliminated Sidney Barnes from consideration because neighbors saw him in Mobile.[21] They dismissed Sam Bowers for the same reason, as he was in John's Restaurant in Laurel, Mississippi. After April, the names Bowers, Barnes, and Stoner all but disappear from any serious examination of a possible conspiracy in the King murder. They do not reappear until after James Earl Ray's arrest in London and his extradition to the United States after June 8, 1968. That is when the FBI missed their second chance to investigate a conspiracy involving Swift zealots.

THE LAST CRITICAL JUNCTURE

Two simultaneous stories presented one last opportunity that could have led the FBI to investigate a conspiracy on King's life planned by Wesley Swift's devotees.

The first story was really a culmination of the manhunt for Donald Nissen, whose report in 1967 to Dallas FBI agents about a $100,000 King bounty represented the last alleged major plot in the investigative record. The FBI had been hunting Nissen since they learned that he had jumped parole before the King assassination and was on the run. Nissen had a wife, a new baby, and a steady job as a book salesman when the FBI learned that he was missing since before King's murder. This raised obvious concerns for the FBI, who reinterviewed Sybil Eure and searched frantically for Nissen. Nissen contacted the FBI at the end of July and agreed that if Arizona-based FBI agent G. Wayne Mack, whom Nissen knew and with whom he was comfortable, would handle his arrest, the fugitive would turn himself in. Mack agreed, and Nissen turned himself in in Saint Louis in August 1968.

Mack debriefed Nissen, and his report shows that Nissen fled Atlanta in December 1967, shortly after Nissen said he was threatened outside a federal building by an unknown individual whom he felt was connected to McManaman. This individual accused Nissen of being an informant and warned him against future cooperation with law enforcement. Nissen later told us that he remembered the windows of his vehicle were shot out at this time, though this is not reflected in Mack's report. Nissen told Mack he was scared to tell parole officials about this threatening individual because McManaman had told Nissen, while they were together in Leavenworth, that a federal law enforcement officer was involved in the King bounty plot. Having explained his decision to flee Atlanta, the reports show that Nissen reasserted the original story he told the FBI in Dallas about the Leavenworth offer but provided no additional information about a King plot.[22]

It does not matter whether or not Nissen's account to us—that he told Mack about unwittingly delivering the package of bounty money to a real estate office in Mississippi in the summer of 1967—is a case of faulty memory or not. That Nissen met Eure and delivered a package is established independently by the fact that Nissen could describe the woman (tall, late middle age) and the real estate office (run out of a home rather than an office building) without the benefit of records that confirm his accuracy. Whether Mack learned of the delivery and sanitized it from the record or whether Nissen deliberately chose not to tell him (for fear of the legal ramifications) is irrelevant, because the story should have spurred a reconsideration of the possibility of a White Knights plot against King. The simple fact that Nissen was threatened for his cooperation and scared enough by the that threat to jump parole and risk returning to prison should have triggered a reevaluation of the Nissen story. But the FBI had already accepted Eure's story about the "bounty joke" without challenging her claims. They did not realize that in their own files was confirmation of the original Nissen account from Leavenworth inmate John May. They considered but apparently failed to appreciate the fact that their investigation of criminal contracts on King revealed "several instances where persons incarcerated at various times advised that King had a bounty of $100,000 on his head." Instead, the final word for the FBI on the matter was their first interview of LeRoy McManaman in September 1968, an interview in which they never even confronted the Leavenworth criminal about Eure's supposed joke (while recording that he anticipated marrying Eure after his release), an interview in which they accepted McManaman's claim that he never knew Nissen (despite Nissen's intimate knowledge of McManaman's personal life), an interview in which they simply accepted McManaman's denial of any involvement in the King crime at face value.

While Donald Nissen was reminding the FBI about a $100,000 bounty offer from the Mississippi White Knights on the life of Martin Luther King Jr., a bounty being extended to career criminals, the FBI was hearing another story involving a conspiracy of White Knights. This was Margaret Capomacchia's story to informant Willie Somersett, explained in detail in the first section of this book. Capomacchia pointed the finger not at criminal operatives, but at members of Sam Bowers's inner circle and Tommy Tarrants, the outsider Bowers used to carry out a wave of violence. The FBI dismissed the content of the story, based largely on the fact that they could supposedly account for the whereabouts of every one of the accused on April 4, and because one of the accused, Robert Earl Wilson, clearly would not have participated in a plot with the others. They dismissed the source of the story as well, describing Capomacchia as too "mentally unstable" for her information to be of value, and because they, unlike the Miami Police Department, had classified informant Somersett as having marginal value.

The FBI was right to dismiss the content of the story, but they should have seriously considered the source of the tale, specifically Margaret Capomacchia. Had they investigated her story any further, they would have heard the story that Somersett was relaying (to the Miami Police Department) from one of her associates, Sidney Barnes. Barnes, who Capomacchia involved in her own account, confirmed key aspects of Capomacchia's obviously misguided story to Somersett. That alone should have raised eyebrows, as Barnes was independently confirming an obviously false story. What's more, separate criminal files on Barnes would have shown that the extremist had already planted false information with Somersett in the past. This was in connection with the second plot by Barnes, Carden, and Gale on King's life, in 1964, a plot detailed in files on Barnes that were never shared at any level in the King assassination investigation. The FBI recognized in 1964 that Barnes was testing Somersett by providing him with nuggets of false information; it also noted how suspicious Barnes became of snitches after his experience with Somersett. In short, the FBI should have been seriously questioning both whether and why their informant was being called into the homes of extremists and presented with detailed, false stories about a King assassination conspiracy. But the FBI never received the other reports from Somersett, nor did they reexamine Barnes's files in any depth. And of course they noted that Barnes was in Mobile on the day King was shot, so he could not possibly have had any involvement in a King conspiracy.

Those same independent files on Barnes, as well as separate files on Capomacchia, reveal other relevant information. Specifically, they show that from August onward, Barnes and Capomacchia both moved to Jackson, Mississippi, where their most frequent and ongoing associations were with each other and members of Sam Bowers's inner circle. This should have raised the clear possibility that Capomacchia and Barnes were trying to lead the FBI in the wrong direction by planting disinformation with their dupe, Willie Somersett, and that these efforts were possibly connected to the White Knights.

The juxtaposition of the Barnes/Capomacchia accounts and the Nissen story reveal something significant: At the same time Nissen was pointing the FBI in what appears to be the right direction, Capomacchia and Barnes were poisoning the well. If the FBI had viewed these leads in their totality and not in isolation, they could have pursued the reasons for the Barnes/ Capomacchia disinformation campaign while reconsidering the possibility of a White Knights bounty on King. The fact of a disinformation campaign conducted by White Knights associates would have made any reevaluation of Nissen's account that much more tantalizing. In particular, it would have raised the question of why Capomacchia and Barnes both implicated Tommy Tarrants. The FBI might have then looked at the striking fact that Tarrants was a King assassination suspect in early to mid April, before the bureau had connected him to any violence in Mississippi, much less to any activity in Birmingham, Alabama. This, in turn, could have pointed the FBI toward a preassassination frame-up of Tarrants by the one group of people who did know about his reputation for violence: white supremacists. But the early investigation of Tarrants was detailed in separate field office MURKIN files in Birmingham and Los Angeles, and not in the FBI central headquarters MURKIN files. The compartmentalization of leads and information fundamentally hindered a serious investigation.

While they certainly would not have intended to take advantage of the weaknesses in the FBI's investigation, Capomacchia and Barnes may have benefited from them. If their goal was to dispel any consideration of White Knights' involvement in the King assassination by telling a part truth, it may have worked. It is worth noting that, despite the Nissen account, the FBI never seriously investigated Capomacchia and Barnes's White Knights friends as suspects after August 1968, nor were J. B. Stoner or Barnes himself, two individuals who had tried to kill King in the past.

By this time, it is worth noting again, the FBI was actively supporting what was a local prosecution of James Earl Ray. The Memphis district attorney was gearing up to present a case to a Tennessee judge and a Tennessee jury. Any conspiracy by itself complicates a criminal prosecution, but a conspiracy to murder across state lines makes matters even more difficult when the victim is not a federal officer. It would have complicated issues of jurisdiction and extradition and would have made coordination between prosecutors and investigators more difficult. But in 1968, developments in the application of federal law made this concern moot.

Increasingly, federal prosecutors in the Civil Rights Division of the Justice Department were becoming more and more adept at using Title 18 Section 241 of the United States Code to convict groups of conspiracy. This component of federal law states the following:

> *If two or more persons conspire to injure, oppress, threaten, or intimi-*
> *date any person in any State, Territory, Commonwealth, Possession,*
> *or District in the free exercise or enjoyment of any right or privilege*
> *secured to him by the Constitution or laws of the United States . . .*
> *They shall be fined under this title or imprisoned not more than ten*
> *years, or both; and if death results from the acts committed in viola-*
> *tion of this section or if such acts include . . . an attempt to kill, they*
> *shall be fined under this title or imprisoned for any term of years or*
> *for life, or both, or may be sentenced to death.*[23]

Indeed attorneys at the United States Department of Justice had recently, in October 1967, successfully prosecuted several Klansmen, including Sam Bowers, for conspiring to kill the three civil rights workers in the Mississippi Burning case.

Attorneys in the Civil Rights Division of the Department of Justice were increasingly applying creative and broad interpretations of what qualified as a constitutionally protected activity—the "right or privilege" part of the criminal code—to mount federal conspiracy prosecutions against the Klan. They did so in the Mississippi Burning case; they did so earlier with the murder of civil rights worker Viola Liuzzo in Alabama in 1965; and they did so with the murder of black World War II veteran Lemuel Penn in 1964 in Georgia.

The Justice Department had gained a tremendous amount of experience in navigating and collating the FBI's investigative records, handling FBI informants, and seeing through the smoke screens the Klan set up—the use of false alibis and other obstructionist tactics—to prevent successful prosecutions. And the Justice Department was becoming more and more adept at developing the narrative of conspiracy, tracing though mazes of coincidences and circumstantial inferences to weave together prosecutions that could successfully convict even those individuals, like Sam Bowers, who were smart enough to keep a safe distance from their crimes.

It is prosecutors—not investigators—who are focused on establishing issues of motive and, in the case of a conspiracy, aligning the behavior of the actual perpetrators with suspicious activity on the part of other potential plotters. In the case of Ray, more than one witness told investigators that Ray was motivated by money and that bounty offers on King were circulating in Missouri State Penitentiary before Ray's escape in April 1967. They often connected to amorphous groups like the KKK or unnamed southern businessmen. Donald Nissen's story, albeit in a separate federal prison, linked a bounty to the Mississippi White Knights, a specific group with a documented history of trying to kill King. Starting in 1967, this group was increasingly interacting with the National States' Rights Party through J. B. Stoner, another individual who had tried to kill King; and when Ray failed to escape North America through Canada, he traveled to Birmingham, the most publicized haven of violent NSRP activity in the United States, and rented a rooming house just fifteen minutes away from the NSRP's headquarters at 1865 Bessemer Road.

If Nissen's story was true, Ray arrived within weeks of the bounty money being transferred from Atlanta, Georgia, to Jackson, Mississippi. The evidence is fuzzy as to how and when Ray was recruited into a specific plot against King, but after his sojourn in Mexico and move to Los Angeles at the end of 1967, the apolitical fugitive suddenly started making contacts at the California headquarters for racist third-party presidential candidate George Wallace. It is known that at least one radical extremist with connections to Milteer,

Stoner, and Swift had once worked at that campaign office. Whether Ray was seeking out this individual (who had moved to Atlanta) or found others to reach, it is impossible to tell. Ray never adequately explained it, and investigators for the FBI, much less for Justice, never really asked.

In any event, starting March 17, 1968, Ray abandoned other potential vocations (porn, bartending) and avocations (dancing) right at the time that he was running out of money; he began to follow King's movements throughout the Southeast. In stalking King, especially in following him to Atlanta, Ray was fulfilling one role Leroy McManaman propositioned in his bounty offer to Nissen. It was also in Atlanta where Ray appears to have eaten with another individual at Mammy's Shanty, a restaurant that researcher and Atlanta native Lamar Waldron says was a hangout for racist types.[24] The FBI never pieced this together, but perhaps a Justice Department investigation could have.

Certainly, an open-minded Justice Department investigation could have seen what Ray did at the end of March 1968 in Birmingham as representing not only one of the most telling signs of a conspiracy but also one of the most intriguing potential links to Sam Bowers. Showing an obvious lack of knowledge of guns, Ray purchased one rifle on March 29. A regular at the gun store said Ray seemed so lost that he was "out of place."[25] Yet the frugal Ray returned on March 30 and exchanged the weapon for a highly regarded but more expensive rifle, the .30-06 Gamemaster whose bullets shared the same basic characteristics as the fatal round removed from Dr. King. Ray told the staff that his "brother-in-law" told him to make the trade. No one has ever hinted that Ray's actual brother-in-law, Carol Pepper, was connected to a King plot, and no one at the rooming house recalled seeing Ray with anyone else, including his real brothers. If someone with knowledge of guns did insist on the weapons exchange, it is worth noting that March 29, 1968, was the only time, over the course of many months, that someone at Sam Bower's company, Sambo Amusement, called Birmingham, Alabama. While it is uncertain who made the call and to where, the records show that it was to an unlisted number that appears to have been located just minutes

from the Aeromarine Supply Company, where the gun was traced.[26] The
FBI should have done additional investigation to establish this more clearly
and followed up with interviews of Bowers and Sambo employees; but the
records of the Birmingham call come from separate Jackson files on Bowers
and never made it into the MURKIN FBI headquarters file. Perhaps the a
prosecutor at the Civil Rights Division could have made the connection—
and forced a follow-up investigation —where the FBI did not.

Any prosecutor would (and the Memphis prosecutors did) focus on
Ray's actions immediately after the gun purchase—the quick return trip to
Atlanta and his travels to Memphis—as key to any conviction of Ray. Even
Ray admitted that this coincidence was devastating and denied it—in the
face of clear contrary evidence—to the day he died. As noted earlier in the
chapter, at the same time Ray was making these adventures, in the days
immediately leading up to King's murder, witnesses described Sam Bowers
and one of his top aides acting very suspiciously at John's Restaurant. To the
FBI, Sam Bowers's presence at John's Restaurant on April 5 was a reason to
exclude him as a suspect. Who knows how the Justice Department, whose
experience with Klan conspiracy trials made them leery of alibis on many
levels, would have done with something like the Hendrix story?

Even if one adopts one of the scenarios we present—that Ray, contrary
to his assigned role as a "caser," shot King to collect a larger share of a bounty,
surprising other conspirators and forcing all parties (including Ray himself)
to scramble—it would not absolve Bowers and company of guilt in a federal
conspiracy case. For such a charge only requires that parties to a murder actively plan and intend on killing King, regardless of how such a plan actually
played out. As the murder was planned outside of Memphis, federal lawyers
could have prosecuted someone like Bowers under federal laws.

But if the law permitted the Justice Department to pursue such a case,
if the Civil Rights Division had already demonstrated the ability to develop
a conspiracy argument especially against racists in civil rights crimes, why
didn't they do so? After all, the FBI was and is the chief investigative unit for
the Department of Justice and their attorneys. Part of the problem was that

Attorney General Ramsey Clark, who, having seen the riots that were destroying dozens of America's cities, assured the press on April 5, 1968, that only one man had killed Martin Luther King Jr., would later admit this was premature and done to pacify the public. But his statements would obviously circumscribe the behavior of any of his subordinates, who, if they did pursue a conspiracy case, would effectively be publicly embarrassing their boss if it came to fruition with a prosecution.

But is questionable whether or not the Justice Department could have uncovered a conspiracy, even on their best day, even if they had an interest in doing so, for J. Edgar Hoover was making sure that was all but impossible.

Hoover hated Attorney General Clark. It was Clark who had terminated Hoover's ongoing wiretapping program against Martin Luther King Jr. According to Hoover biographer Curt Gentry, Hoover considered Clark to be a "jellyfish" or a "softie" when it came to crime.[27] To Hoover, Clark was the worst attorney general he had ever worked with. Congress reviewed Hoover's interaction with Clark's Justice Department as part of the House Select Committee on Assassination's reexamination of the King murder in 1978. In their "Staff Report on the Performance of the Department of Justice and the FBI," the HSCA found that Director Hoover had personally ordered that certain instructions from the attorney general be ignored so that the "course and direction of the investigation remained exclusively in the hands of the FBI."[28] The staff report concluded that the FBI investigation reflected "arrogance and independence of various personnel" and "poor and counterproductive relationships between the bureau and lawyers at the Justice Department." It also noted that Director Hoover's lack of respect for Attorney General Clark had become an attitude "more or less" universally held within the bureau.

The HSCA staff report comments that Hoover himself directed that details of the FBI investigation be filtered from the reports sent to the Justice Department and that only high-level summary information on the status of the investigation be provided. The hope for a serious, separate investigation of Barnes, Stoner, and Bowers did not emerge until almost a decade after the murder, with the emergence of the HSCA in 1976.

The Watergate scandal had raised serious doubts about the motives and machinations of the government, and the steady efforts of independent researchers to raise questions about the Martin Luther King and John F. Kennedy assassinations had forced a critical mass in public opinion, leading to the formation of the select committee. But while it represented a clear improvement over the original, deficient, FBI investigation, the HSCA was also flawed, for reasons both within and beyond their control.

PICKING UP THE PIECES

In many ways, Congress's investigation showed the potential that existed in 1968 for uncovering the truth, had the Justice Department been a clearinghouse for all the relevant information in the FBI's records. In 1978, the HSCA reviewed all four of the major file threads the FBI produced, cross-referencing the central and local MURKIN records, the distinct files dedicated to dangerous individuals and groups, and the security file on Martin Luther King Jr. at FBI headquarters. After collating that information, they conducted follow-up investigations and interviews, much like the Justice Department would have done in 1968 and 1969.

Hence, when it came to J. B. Stoner, Congress took the possibility of his involvement far more seriously than did the FBI, dedicating an entire subsection of their final report to the militant extremist. They did not accept the idea that Stoner must have been innocent because he was not present in Memphis on April 4, 1968. They found the fact that Stoner came to represent James Earl Ray and that he also employed Ray's brother in his political campaign far more suspicious than did the FBI. The HSCA conducted secret, executive interviews with Stoner and apparently confronted him with contradictions in his public statements. Notably, they found it troubling that Stoner openly boasted that he had information related to a conspiracy in the King murder but that he would not disclose this relevant data to their committee.[29]

Congress also reexamined the possibility that the White Knights were involved in the King assassination, and gave that research angle far more credence than the original FBI investigators had.[30] They specifically cited the

FBI's failure to investigate the White Knights as a group that "demonstrated both a propensity for violence and a clear antagonism toward Dr. King."[31] It was Congress who was first able to show how the separate Jackson field office reports on Bowers's and Nix's activities in John's Restaurant provided corroboration for the Hendricks story. They reinterviewed Hendricks, who denied the substance of her testimony, but only after expressing fear of a reprisal from her former boyfriend, Thomas McGee; it was McGee who told the FBI in 1968 that he was afraid of retaliation from the Klan if Hendricks's story became public. When Congress approached the other informants who corroborated aspects of Hendricks's story, they also refused to cooperate.[32]

Sidney Barnes refused to cooperate, too. The HSCA gave renewed attention to Barnes's involvement in the September 1963 plot against King involving Carden, Gale, and Crommelin. It was one of the few plots detailed in their final report. But when it came time to interview Barnes about these matters, he steadfastly refused to be interviewed.[33]

This illustrates a clear weakness in the HSCA investigation of the King murder. Congress has some subpoena power, but resisting such efforts or lying to Congress does not carry the same kind of consequences as one would face in confronting the Department of Justice and a possible grand jury investigation. Even if one does cooperate or comply with a congressional subpoena, it is incredibly rare for charges of perjury to result from false testimony to such a committee. One can simply wait out a select committee, which is formed by Congress for only a specified amount of time and with a limited budget.

As a shrewd attorney, Stoner would have been more aware of this advantage than anyone, but his status as a one-time attorney for Ray gave Stoner even more cover, for he was protected by the cloak of attorney-client privilege. James Earl Ray waived this protection for all his other attorneys. But Ray refused to do so for Stoner, meaning that the extremist could not testify about his personal exchanges with Ray, even before a secret, executive session of Congress. This was suspicious enough for Congress to call attention to Ray's exceptional treatment of Stoner in their final report.[34]

The limits of their budget and subpoena power meant that the HSCA continued to suffer from the flaws of the original FBI investigation in 1968, even as they criticized the FBI for those flaws. (Budget and time constraints, for instance, prevented the HSCA from interviewing Deavours Nix or Sam Bowers.) Yes, the HSCA castigated the FBI for the silly notion that someone would have to be in Memphis to participate in a conspiracy. But the reality was that unless they could conduct serious interviews with the likes of J. B. Stoner, the HSCA was still left with an FBI investigation that cleared the racist lawyer based on his whereabouts. The same was true for Barnes and Bowers; if the original FBI investigation was limited, so too was any effort to build on that investigation, especially if follow-up interviews were hampered by uncooperative witnesses.

The willingness to widen the scope of the investigation by cross-referencing the various streams of files the FBI produced could only take the HSCA so far. Without the sophisticated data-mining capabilities that exist today, the likelihood of missing information was significant. If the HSCA even learned about the Nissen story, much less took the account seriously, it does not show up in their final report, and the HSCA never approached Nissen. There is no mention of the Dixie Mafia and individuals like Donald Sparks or LeRoy McManaman in the HSCA report. The HSCA investigated information from Willie Somersett, but their report focused on a different angle: the claim by Somersett's intelligence contact in the Miami Police Department, Lieutenant Charles Sapp, that Somersett provided information about King's murder in the days immediately prior to the crime in Memphis.[35] The final HSCA report makes no mention of Somersett's informant reports on Capomacchia or Barnes, which implicated the White Knights in King's homicide. Although the Barnes material was not provided to the FBI in 1968, journalist Dan Christensen quoted from Somersett's reports to the Miami Police Department in a series of articles at the same time. Christensen leaves out Barnes's name but identifies Tarrants as the person whose car was used in a radio diversion in Memphis.[36]

Administrative records show the HSCA was interested in Tommy Tarrants but do not disclose why; in any event, it appears as if the FBI destroyed
their Mobile field office file on Tarrants just before Congress became interested in the one-time terrorist.[37] It was that file that contained the picture
of Tarrants that the FBI showed the employees of the gun store in Birmingham; that his picture was included at all, and before the FBI showed photos
of other known racist killers, is a mystery the HSCA also failed to explore.
Tarrants says the HSCA interviewed him,[38] but his name does not appear
in HSCA's final report. As someone who was on the verge of being released
from prison after turning from Christian Identity theology to mainstream
Christianity, Tarrants would have been an invaluable source on right-wing
Christian extremists. He had personal connections and interactions with
Barnes, Bowers, Carden, Crommelin, and key members of the Minutemen
and the National States' Rights Party, all of whom the HSCA investigated in
connection with the King murder. Of course, disclosing Tarrants—someone
who had just turned against what these violent individual stood for—by
name would have been dangerous to the new convert. Most of these individuals were still alive and could pose a threat to him. Lacking the cooperation
of many of these extremists but limited by the FBI's premature decision to
clear them of a conspiracy based on their alibis, the HSCA dug deeply into
the separate sets of files compiled on these individuals and their groups; this
material was independent of the King crime and connected to investigations
into other violent acts and conspiracies.

The HSCA deserves credit for thoroughly examining this material. But
the files on these individuals and groups were housed in dozens of field offices across the country. If any of these extremists moved or did business
in a different state, if any of the groups had affiliates in a different region of
the country, FBI field office investigations were opened and files were created. It is not clear that the HSCA had access to, for instance, the Jackson
field office file on Sidney Barnes or the Birmingham field office file on the
White Knights of the Ku Klux Klan. In the case of Barnes, the Jackson file
not only details his extensive connections to the White Knights—something

the HSCA left for a footnote in their final report—but also shows that the Jackson office thought he was an active bomb maker for Klan groups.[39] Most relevantly, Barnes's Jackson file also included the Mobile field office reports showing that Barnes possessed and intended to deliver a rifle to Noah Carden as part of the plot on King's life in 1964, a plot that was not even mentioned in the HSCA report. Perhaps most intriguingly, the Jackson field office file on Barnes includes an exchange between Barnes and one of L. E. Matthews's associates, Elaine Smith, in 1969, where Barnes is reported to have bragged that he "knew James Earl Ray."[40] If the HSCA learned of any of this, they left it out of their report.

Instead, the HSCA relied on new interviews with unnamed sources to all but clear Barnes, Bowers, and others. One source, who claimed to have personal relationships in 1968 with Barnes, Carden, and Crommelin, insisted that he did not know of any plot against King's life. This same source said that Barnes was all bark and no bite and that he would talk about violence but never participated in any actual crimes. If the HSCA lacked the Jackson field office report on Barnes, it may have been difficult for HSCA investigators to challenge their source.[41] Separately, the report notes an anonymous source who was once involved with White Knights terrorist activities in the 1960s. This source argued that the White Knights were a local group who did not operate outside Mississippi. In other words, the source maintained the White Knights could be discounted because they would not have been involved in any attack on King across state lines in Tennessee.[42]

The net effect of these HSCA interviews with unnamed sources was the same as when the FBI cleared Stoner, Barnes, and Bowers for having alibis outside of Memphis on April 4, 1968. Their operating principle—that the Klan was parochial—was just as misleading. It was generally true that most Klans operated within their own states or local jurisdictions, but we have developed extensive information that, especially when it came to murdering Dr. King, the White Knights and members of the Swift network were more than willing to work across state lines. J. B. Stoner had offered to bring his "boys from Atlanta" to kill King and the Reverend Fred Shuttlesworth in

Alabama in 1958. William Potter Gale traveled from California to Alabama to join a plot against King in 1963. A very close associate of White Knight Burris Dunn, who overheard conversations between Dunn and Bowers about King over several years, was confident that, however parochial the White Knights were, they would have made a special exception in working across state lines if King was the intended victim. Informant Delmar Dennis described a specific Mississippi White Knight plot against King in 1965 that would have taken place in Selma, Alabama. Dennis, in fact, told investigative journalist Jerry Mitchell that the White Knights were national in their reach.[43] Indeed, in the relevant time frame, 1967, Elaine Smith, a close friend of L.E. Matthews, told law enforcement that Bowers and Matthews " . . . had been on missions out of the state" of Mississippi.[44]

Part of the problem for the HSCA was their preconceived notion—one shared by many—that the Klan was a bunch of local hillbillies, fractured by internal rivalries, limited in their tactics, and with no particular strategy. With such prejudices, the Klan appears very much like a modern-day inner-city gang. They have their turf that they control, but they do not broaden their activities outside their immediate region. For the most part, this is true, as Patsy Sims amply details in her work on the Klan.

But what the HSCA missed was the power of Wesley Swift's Christian Identity end-times vision to unify key leaders at the top of organizations such as the National States' Rights Party and the White Knights of the Ku Klux Klan of Mississippi. Especially from 1967 to 1969, these men increasingly came together to join forces; Stoner, whose closest associate, Connie Lynch, was a Swift minister, became very active with members of the White Knights in Mississippi starting in 1967. Bowers used Barnes's protégés Tarrants and Ainsworth—members of the Swift Underground—for his bombing campaign in Mississippi in 1967–1968. After Ainsworth's death, Barnes moved to Jackson where he and his wife, Pauline, preached Swift's theology to anyone who would listen. At Barnes's invitation, Gale visited Mississippi on multiple occasions to minister and deliver Swift's message. Imperial Wizard James Venable accepted and embraced a California affiliate of his National Knights of the Ku Klux Klan that was run by one of Swift's closest aides. Joseph Milteer, an associate of Venable and Stoner, traveled the country, meeting with and attending functions organized by Swift's followers. Swift's message had captured the imagination of people like Bowers and Stoner, to the extent that his taped sermons were played at parties across the South. Decades later, Osama bin Laden, through the power of his religious vision, managed to inspire individuals and groups from America to travel and train in Afghanistan and then wage jihad in Somalia, but thirty years earlier, Wesley Swift similarly motivated a group of diffuse adherents in states across America to pursue an end-times race war. And killing King was a fundamental plank in the strategy to induce that race war.

WHAT THE ACADEMICS HAVE MISSED: RELIGIOUS TERRORISM

If the HSCA missed the religious component of a King plot, modern scholars, with their post-9/11 focus on religious terrorism, could help investigators understand the dynamic that may have led to King's murder. Reanalyzing elements of the white supremacist movement in the 1960s in the context of religious terrorism would represent a significant shift for some in the field of terrorism studies, but it might provide valuable insights—not only into the violence surrounding the civil rights movement but also possibly into the modern evolution of current religious terrorist organizations such as Al-Qaeda.

Such a change would not require any kind of revisionist history but a reapplication and reconsideration of what is already known about the origins of certain domestic terrorist groups, what is known about religious terrorism as a concept, and what is already documented concerning the actual acts of violence in the 1960s. Recent scholarship, for instance, has already called attention to the underlying religious motivations of domestic terrorist groups such as the Order and the Aryan Nations who terrorized America in the 1980s and 1990s. They may be seen as extreme outgrowths of the Christian Identity message,[45] but their religious denominations were formed by devotees of Wesley Swift and were modeled on Swift's Church of Jesus Christ Christian, which was created in 1946.

In making such comparisons, one must be careful, as the Swift network in the 1960s was layered on top of, and their goals hidden from, the rank-and-file members of organizations such as the White Knights. But given this limitation, one can still see these groups loosely following the kind of template described by terrorism scholar Dr. Bruce Hoffman in his analysis of religious extremists for the RAND Corporation.

According to Hoffman, religious terrorists are more willing to resort to "indiscriminate violence" than are secular terrorists, for such acts are not only sanctioned in their religious worldview but also necessary "for the attainment of their goals." The White Knights and National States' Rights Party were so violent that even other Klan groups, notably the United Klans of America, sought to distinguish themselves from Bowers's and Stoner's organizations.[46]

Hoffman adds that religious terrorists are less concerned in obtaining the sympathy of outsiders as they are with satisfying the religious impera-tives of their current membership.[47] On this front, the evidence is mixed. Stoner, from the start, attacked Jewish synagogues when this was generally frowned upon by everyday southern reactionaries. Bowers had repeatedly attempted to push the White Knights in an anti-Semitic direction in 1964 and 1965 but with no success. It was not until law enforcement pressure drained the White Knights of most of its rank-and-file membership that Bowers was able to use his inner-circle operatives, some of whom shared the same enthusiasm for Swift's theology, to focus their violent attention on Jews more so than on blacks. It is important to note that for a member of the Christian Identity denomination, all Christian Anglo-Saxon whites are, in essence, their followers. The everyday white is still a "true" Israelite but with a false consciousness; once the race war comes, all these people will "wise up" and battle the forces of Satan.

Thus Bowers and his fellow travelers, while more extreme than any oth-er group at the time, could not, as Hoffman articulates about other religious terrorists, resort to "almost limitless violence against a virtually open-ended category of targets—that is, anyone who is not a member of the terrorists' religion or religious sect."[48] If he killed white Christians, Bowers would not only limit his power and influence over his remaining flock but also literally eliminate potential soldiers in the end-times race war to come.

Finally, and most relevant to a discussion of the King assassination, Hoffman notes that, in contrast to secular terrorists who "regard violence as a way of instigating the correction of a flaw in a system that is basically good or as a means to foment the creation of a new system," religious terrorists instead "seek vast changes in the existing order."[49] We discussed earlier how this connects to a strategy of propaganda of the deed. A thorough analysis shows that the violent activities Bowers sponsored—as well as those Stoner and his followers committed—do not make sense as mere acts of reactionary racism or vigilante terrorism. It doesn't require much prescience to predict that killing four young girls in a church in Birmingham or killing a conservative civil rights figure like Medgar Evers in front of his family would foment strong reactions like a race riot. Such riots would represent the best hope of drawing federal troops into the state and escalating the violence. But federal intervention in state affairs ran counter to the very currents of southern culture. Only diabolical men such as Bowers would want intervention, because it could provoke a race war, the one Wesley Swift prophesied.

THE ARC OF THE UNIVERSE

To a follower of Swift at the beginning of 1968, such a prophecy must have seemed almost at hand. The racial tensions spotlighted during the nonviolent period of the civil rights movement from 1954 to 1965 did not disappear with the passage of the Voting Rights Act. As global economic forces began to take working-class jobs overseas and out of America's ghettos and inner cities, blacks were left with new political rights but even fewer economic opportunities. Frustrations began to fester, and even as Dr. King shifted his focus from political justice to socioeconomic justice, more and more blacks began to gravitate from his larger message of nonviolence to the more militant message of someone like Stokely Carmichael, who famously coined the term "Black Power." It was Carmichael who once said that "Every courthouse in Mississippi ought to be burned down tomorrow, to get rid of the dirt in there, and the filth."[50] To Sam Bowers, who hoped that provocations in Mississippi would erupt in federal intervention, and then reprisals from black militants, Carmichael's words must have been music to the ears. And while blacks did not burn down the courthouses of Mississippi, by 1968, violence was becoming the outlet of choice for many victims of de facto racism.

In 1965 the race riots in the Watts neighborhood of Los Angeles, California, started a trend that would plague America throughout the decade. The next few years saw riots in Chicago, Illinois; Newark, New Jersey; Detroit, Michigan; and dozens of other cities across the country. Some estimates say that in the "long, hot summer" of 1967 alone, there were more than 150 race riots across the country.[51] The civil disorder had changed the entire national security posture of the United States, involving the United States military in domestic intelligence gathering in unprecedented fashion. No longer was the national security infrastructure concerned about communists in Martin Luther King Jr.'s organization; they were focused on identifying black militants.

By 1968 America was a racial powder keg ready to explode, and the fuse of King's assassination pushed the country closer to Swift's dark dream than at any point in the nation's history. It created the waves of violence and rioting that the national security establishment so feared and Sam Bowers and J. B. Stoner so desired. The military and National Guard was deployed in America's cities in ways not seen since the Civil War. As much as structural flaws and philosophical limitations impeded law enforcement's investigation of the King assassination, it must be remembered that the tension in the nation also circumscribed their efforts.

But in the end, just as Senator Bobby Kennedy pacified a crowd on the evening of April 4 in Indianapolis, Indiana, by appealing to King's vision of mutual understanding and racial harmony, it was Martin Luther King Jr. who triumphed, even in death. The riots calmed. Sam Bowers and his ilk largely faded into the background, and the Klan has never approached its level of influence and violence since King's death.

King, whose shift to socioeconomic issues had cost him popularity with white America before his death, has become an icon of righteous citizenship and racial harmony. Few historical figures are as respected across America's increasingly polarized, ideological spectrum. His ideas have been appropriated by President Barack Obama, who keeps a bust of King in the Oval Office, and by Glenn Beck, who held a major event in King's honor. This reverence has even made some of King's contemporaries uneasy, as some commentators have sought to remind Americans that King died on his way to the Poor People's Campaign, after marching in solidarity with union workers.[52]

But if King's ideas about racial justice are celebrated, if his views on economic justice are debated, one of his core goals, legal justice, has until recently largely been ignored. Time and time again, King marched in memory of or eulogized those whose murders shocked the nation into guilt over its larger inequities. King demanded justice for the victims, even as racists plotted to kill the minister on such visits. The names of those victims join King's on the civil rights memorial outside the Southern Poverty Law Center in Alabama as a reminder of those who lost their lives in the civil rights struggle, but also as a sad reminder that so many of their homicides have gone unsolved.

Starting in the 1990s, cultural and structural changes in the South allowed some of these crimes to be prosecuted. Notably, Sam Bowers went to prison in 1998 for the murder of Vernon Dahmer, the killing he ordered in 1966, and Bowers died behind bars forty years after Dahmer. Emboldened by such successful prosecutions, the Justice Department formed a Cold Case Initiative to investigate civil rights violence. To date, it has had very little success. But the Justice Department's renewed efforts lack legitimacy for another reason: They do not include an investigation into the murder of Martin Luther King Jr.[53]

In response to the claims of James Earl Ray's attorney, William Pepper, whose theories had gained favor with some of King's family members, the Justice Department did briefly reanalyze the King assassination in 2000.

Having once again dismissed Ray's improbable Raoul stories, and having found that Pepper's chief witness to a conspiracy, Loyd Jowers, was someone who was clearly motivated by money and not honesty, the Justice Department correctly dismissed Pepper's arguments. Narrowly focused, this effort in 2000 did not examine many of the key outstanding issues in the case.[54]

A renewed effort by the Cold Case Initiative should not simply focus on the material developed in this book but also on crime scene evidence that has never been subjected to the latest forensic analysis. As we detail in Appendix A, with the help of modern technology and with limited effort and expense, the Justice Department could attempt to match several unknown prints recovered in the King case from important items and in Bessie Brewer's rooming house to criminals within their computerized database that stretches back to the 1950s. One important place to start might be the prints recovered from the William Len Hotel, not far from the Lorraine Motel. Staff there pointed the FBI in the direction of two men who had registered at the William Len Hotel on the day of King's murder but who had left abruptly that evening. The investigation revealed that these two men then made a sudden change in their plans, taking a flight out of Memphis to Houston; in both instances these men used two different sets of fake names, preventing the FBI from ever identifying the suspicious characters. But their fingerprints were recovered from the hotel registry, which could today be compared to millions of fingerprints in a matter of seconds by a computer. This is just one of several promising leads, which we detail in Appendix A, that could help solve the King murder.

Such a delayed response to the murder would have satisfied Martin Luther King Jr., who liked to tell audiences frustrated with the pace of social reform that "the arc of the universe is long, but it bends toward justice."[55] Decades have passed since his own murder, but the time has come for a serious pursuit of justice. Digging into the King murder mystery may force us to revisit parts of our history that are uncomfortable or painful to remember. It may disclose oversights or connections to informants that are embarrassing or shocking. It may disclose additional, private information about Dr. King himself, details that remind us of his human flaws but that also remind us of his courage in fighting for justice even in the face of scurrilous rumors aimed at besmirching his character and dignity. But these efforts could not be more uncomfortable and painful, more embarrassing and shocking, than King's murder itself, which deprived the country of a leader who challenged America and Americans, however burdensome it was, to be a better country, to be better human beings. Perhaps it is only through such sacrifice and suffering, as Bobby Kennedy reminded that crowd in Indianapolis, that we truly achieve understanding. "Even in our sleep," he told the audience, quoting the Greek poet Aeschylus, "pain which cannot forget falls drop by drop upon the heart until, in our despair, against our will, comes wisdom, through the awful grace of God."

APPENDIX A

OPEN QUESTIONS

In the final chapter, we explored a number of serious issues with both the King murder investigation and the evidence offered in the prosecution of James Earl Ray. The investigation failed not only to thoroughly deal with the question of conspiracy but also, in fact, to even recognize the nature or existence of a demonstrable, ongoing conspiracy that had been in play against Dr. King for years before his murder. Compromised by an extremely premature declaration that no conspiracy existed and by statements from both the attorney general and FBI firector that a single individual had been involved, the field investigation was hamstrung from its very beginning. Further, the lack of a coordinated analysis of the leads pointing toward conspiracy and the lack of Justice Department involvement or oversight turned the investigation into nothing more than an effort to support the prosecution's case against Ray. And, as we have demonstrated, the evidence against Ray appears to be much more questionable than either the Memphis district attorney or the early writers on the case claimed. Its weaknesses escaped serious discussion largely because of Ray's initial guilty plea, allowing the prosecutor to enter all his evidence with no aggressive challenge from the defense.

While none of that clears Ray of actually doing the shooting and certainly not of being an accessory to a conspiracy, it supports our contention that the actual conspiracy in play may have escaped exposure both in the prosecution of the crime and in the official history of Dr. King's assassination. Up to this point we have worked at presenting a picture of what that conspiracy may have involved, including alternative patsies and even the possibility of a much more dramatic act of violence than that at the Lorraine Motel.

Continuing in that vein, we take this opportunity to introduce additional points that suggest not only that other parties were in Memphis in support of an extended conspiracy, but also that there remain open questions that deserve further investigation. We believe that these questions could be seriously pursued if the King murder were now to be reclassified as an open cold case, in the same manner as other high-profile murders of the civil rights era.

WHO WERE THE MYSTERIOUS GUESTS AT THE WILLIAM LEN HOTEL?

Less than a mile from where King was killed, at the William Len Hotel in Memphis, an intriguing series of events unfolded on April 4, which were brought to the FBI's attention. This led to a mystery that bureau agents were never able to resolve and that the HSCA never addressed. Employees at the hotel reported that two new guests, who had only recently registered that afternoon, suddenly departed around midnight, hours after King was murdered. The guests had checked in during the afternoon of April 4, but left at 12:10 AM on April 5. That behavior seemed quite suspicious to the employees, and they reported it to the FBI, who then tried to identify the individuals and trace their movements.[1]

In attempting to trace the names in the hotel registry—"Vincent Walker" and "Lawrence Rand"—the FBI learned quickly that the names were aliases. The addresses the two individuals provided were also dead ends. The FBI decided to trace the movements of the men in hopes of pinning down their true identities. They interviewed the cab driver who picked up one of the individuals at the hotel. The driver could not help in identifying the man, but his account made the FBI even more suspicious. The cabbie said that this individual directed him to drive to West Memphis, Arkansas, but then redirected the driver to go to the Municipal Airport in Memphis, Tennessee. There, the driver was told to wait while his passenger checked flight schedules. The passenger appeared to also be scouting the airport. Then he told the driver to take him back to the hotel and to wait again; shortly thereafter, the original passenger returned with another male, and together they proceeded to the airport. The FBI was able to determine that the individuals in the cab and at the hotel were one and the same.[2]

The FBI then followed up by checking the airport's records. The records indicated that the two men had in fact purchased tickets to Houston early on the afternoon of April 4. They used different false names, "W. Davis" and "B. Chidlaw," and were booked as a party of two. However, the flight on which they eventually traveled was not the one for which they had reservations. They departed on their flight from Memphis at 1:50 AM and arrived in Houston at 2:50 AM. The story continued with the FBI investigating limousine rides departing from the Houston airport. One driver recalled picking up six passengers in total and dropping a pair off at a building, but the FBI could not say for certain that any of the six were the pair from the William Len Hotel. They searched the hotels the limo driver suggested but found no record of their names in any registry, and the lead died.[3]

At that point the FBI threw up its hands and speculated that the men were probably just common criminals anxious to flee Memphis given the intense police presence that overtook the city after King's murder.[4] That cannot be completely discounted. One of the men did suddenly change destinations in the cab, and they did find their way onto a different flight (from Memphis to Houston) than what they originally intended. However, the FBI had learned that these individuals had already purchased tickets to leave Memphis on the early afternoon of April 4; this suggests that they intended to leave Memphis on short notice even before King was murdered and thus before a police presence would have scared them away. More to the point, even if they were criminals, the FBI failed to appreciate the evidence in their own files suggesting such individuals may have been outsourced participants in a King murder plot. In broad strokes, the men fit the profile of the very "traveling criminals" of the Dixie Mafia who were approached with a King bounty offer. It is possible that a full review of the FBI's and law enforcement's files on LeRoy McManaman and Donalds Sparks could offer valuable clues to "traveling criminals" that might have been brought into a King bounty offer. We have obtained prison records on McManaman, but we have not yet been able to obtain the requested FBI files for either man, even though both are legally available under the Freedom of Information Act guidelines.

Fortunately, a simple alternative to resolving the mystery of the two men may also be available through recourse to modern technology. The FBI collected the fingerprints of these two men from hotel registration cards taken from the William Len Motel.[5] Since neither man could be connected to Ray in 1968, no broad fingerprint search was undertaken—but with today's print databases and computerized fingerprint scanning, the two might still be identified and their associations pursued.

WHO DO THE FINGERPRINTS BELONG TO?

If the FBI is still in possession of the William Len prints, modern forensic technology may be able to help investigators identify the two men who stayed under assumed names but left in a hurry. The U.S. Justice Department has access to a database of digitized prints from millions of donors; individuals who were arrested for or convicted of state and federal crimes—some going back decades. The system, known as the Integrated Automated Fingerprint Identification System (IAFIS), compares digitized prints from unknown contributors to digitized prints from this database of potential suspects. An investigator will take a fingerprint or palm print from a crime scene, scan it through IAFIS, and see if the system generates a pool of potential suspects whose fingerprints appear to match the crime scene prints. Then an actual fingerprint expert will use this much smaller set of computer-generated prints to see if there is, in fact, a legal match. Back in the 1960s, the "traveling criminals" of the Dixie Mafia who went from state to state committing crimes could be comfortable knowing that their fingerprints were not on file with local law enforcement. Now, with IAFIS, a hoodlum arrested in Kentucky may find himself on trial for the home robbery he committed in Delaware. Following 9/11, the database has grown to include millions of prints from suspected or convicted criminals. The database has been used to solve cold cases that go back as far as the 1950s[6] and is so successful that the FBI annually gives an award for the most impressive match.[7]

In principle, this technique can be applied not only to the William Len Hotel prints but also to crime scene fingerprints from every part of the King murder investigation. As part of their investigation, the House Select Committee on Assassinations commissioned a number of independent experts to look at fingerprints recovered from different crime scenes. These included prints from Bessie Brewer's rooming house where Ray allegedly fired the fatal shot, from Ray's white Ford Mustang in which he fled from Memphis to Atlanta, and from the Atlanta rooming house where Ray stayed before and after the King murder. The HSCA experts could not match several of these prints to James Earl Ray or others suspected of involvement in the crime![8] In addition to these prints and the prints recovered from the William Len Motel, the FBI also lifted prints from the receipt found for a dinner for two at Mammy's Shanty in Atlanta;[9] this was found among Ray's possessions, and Ray was coy when discussing it with author William Bradford Huie. Perhaps the IAFIS could determine with whom Ray was consorting in Atlanta.

Moreover, while several prints were said to match Ray's, later research into the examinations showed that some of their experts disagreed as to the certainty of those matches. This new technology could remedy that discrepancy by removing some of the human element with a computer, and it could either confirm that these prints belonged to James Earl Ray or potentially match them to others.

The system is not foolproof; the records for whoever contributed the prints may not be in the system, and the process is subject to human error. Moreover, a match even to a former criminal may be irrelevant in the sense that the criminal may have innocently left fingerprints on previous occasions. For instance, there may have been unrelated criminals who stayed at Bessie Brewer's rooming house. But if a print were to match a close friend of Leroy McManaman (the Leavenworth inmate who was a contact for details about a bounty on King's life), for instance, the implications would be hard to ignore. That possibility alone demands that this simple and cost-effective fingerprint testing be performed.

Unfortunately, the FBI has told us that they do not know where these fingerprints can be presently found. The Shelby County district attorney's office donated a tremendous amount of original material from Ray's trial to the National Civil Rights Museum in Memphis. Additionally, copies of prints may well be at the National Archives and Records Administration at College Park, Maryland. We have spent enough time with the FBI's central headquarters file (available to the public through the National Archives and Records Administration) to be confident that the material is not there, but there are many additional boxes of files that are loosely indexed and may have prints. An even more likely possibility is that Archives II (the National Archives building in College Park, Maryland) possesses these materials in their collection of files from Congress's investigation. (Recall that the FBI presented fingerprint cards to the HSCA experts.) If Congress retained possession of these prints, they would be among the hundreds of thousands of pages of material that is presently being withheld from the public. As it turns out, releasing that material is not nearly as difficult as what was once thought.

WHAT COULD BE DEVELOPED FROM THE HSCA RECORDS?

Many individuals, including senior members in Congress, believe that the HSCA records have been sealed from public release and can only be disclosed by legal fiat or after the seal's expiration date. The prevailing view has been that only a measure such as the President John F. Kennedy Assassination Records Collection Act of 1992, which declassified millions of documents on JFK's assassination, could yield this information. Even we at one time believed that only time or law would yield the estimated square feet of material believed to be held at the archives.

Our research has shown that this is simply not true! In trying to get clarification as to how long it would be before the seal would be lifted, we learned, from sources at the National Archives, that no such HSCA special records seal actually exists. Instead, the records were sealed under the jurisdiction of the Clerk of the House of Representatives, and under these same congressional procedures, the current clerk can release the records at his or her discretion. Thus, only one person stands between these records of the congressional investigation of the assassination of Martin Luther King Jr. and public access. We have contacted the Clerk of the House of Representatives and urged her to release this material; we have yet to receive any response.[10] However, we assume that members of Congress could obtain the release of the records.

That the records have not been released by now should be a matter of public concern. The HSCA material on the JFK assassination has been available for more than a decade—including documents that have obvious national security implications. In contrast, there are no obvious national security issues involved in the King inquiry. So, it stands to reason that the records of Dr. King's murder are entitled to the same public scrutiny. Those who are afraid that it may reveal information about Dr. King's private life ignore several key points. First, the HSCA Final Report gives a clue as to what kind of material would be at the archives and in what amounts. Very little in the HSCA Final Report relates to the FBI's unfortunate surveillance of Dr. King. Secondly, much of what supposedly would be embarrassing to King is already widely known—stories about his personal affairs have been broadly published and discussed, not only in histories of Director Hoover's personal vendetta against King, but also even by King's closest aides. Dr. King's reputation survives, as it should, even in the face of such revelations. While still living, Dr. King was confronted with the "dirt" collected by Hoover's FBI in an attempt to blackmail him into giving up his crusade for social justice. If Dr. King was willing to risk his reputation and dignity to fight for equality, a crusade in which he demanded justice for those slain in pursuit of that end, then how can the files that could bring justice for his own murder be withheld under the pretense of protecting his image?

WHOSE .30-06 FIRED THE FATAL SHOT?

The HSCA also investigated the most fundamental forensic question in the case: Did the rifle found in front of Canipe's Amusement Company fire the slug that killed Martin Luther King Jr.? James Earl Ray clearly bought that rifle in Birmingham, after exchanging a weapon he purchased the day before. Hence the issue of whether or not Ray is innocent of the shooting (as he claims) or guilty of murder (as the official version claims) pivots, to a large extent, on whether or not his weapon matches the slug recovered from King's body. Normally, this would be a simple matter of microscopically matching the unique grooves and striations from the recovered round (produced by imperfections in every firearm as the weapon imparts spin to the projectile) to bullets that have been test-fired from the suspect's weapon. A procedure so common that it is featured on almost every fictional crime show, this, like so many things related to King's assassination, did not yield a simple answer.

Part of the problem owes itself to the power of a .30-06 rifle: A single shot is usually fatal. In the case of the King killing, soft-point mushrooming ammunition was used, specifically a Remington-Peters .30-06 High Velocity, 150 grain, Pointed Soft-Core Core-Lokt.[11] One of the problems with forensic analysis matching a specific rifle bullet to a specific weapon is that higher-velocity bullets are frequently deformed by whatever objects they strike. Unfortunately, that deformity may obscure or obliterate the markings necessary for association with a specific firearm. The FBI ballistics specialist in the King case rendered a finding that "due to distortion and mutilation no conclusion could be drawn that the submitted bullet came from the submitted rifle."[12] The HSCA interestingly neither confirmed nor denied the FBI's claims about the assassination slug. But they found an additional and more perplexing problem. When they test-fired the alleged assassination weapon, they could not find conclusive matches even between the bullets known to have been fired from the same gun. One bullet would not match a bullet fired just moments later from the same weapon. Hence, any further testing between the actual assassination bullet and a test slug was fruitless, as the very basis for any such test was eliminated. This means that there is no solid proof linking the slug that killed Dr. King to the rifle purchased by James Earl Ray.[13] Nor does the physical evidence exclude Ray's weapon, and thus Ray, from assassinating King.

As such, the idea that King was shot by someone else with a different rifle cannot be discounted on the basis of physical evidence. A sophisticated shooter might even use the .30-06 knowing—perhaps from experience in the Medgar Evers murder—that it could leave a distorted slug. If the goal was to frame Ray as the lone assassin, then using the same rifle as the one purchased in Birmingham would make sense. And at least one newly obtained .30-06 rifle was circulating among the White Knights at the relevant time, brought from California by none other than Thomas Tarrants.

Jack Nelson reported testimony from Thomas Tarrants that in March 1968, he had purchased a .30-06 rifle from Wesley Swift in Los Angeles. Nelson added that the purpose of the rifle was to kill Dr. King. Tarrants denied to reporter Jerry Mitchell that he got this rifle to kill King, but he did admit to getting this rifle as a means of introducing himself to Swift. An FBI report, dated after Tarrants's return to Mobile, describes a .30-06 in his possession.[14] At present, the issue of Tarrants's possession of a new .30-06, brought back from California immediately prior to the King murder, is similar to the issue of Tarrants being one of the very first FBI suspects in the murder investigation: It may suggest that Tarrants was being set up as a patsy, it may suggest more complex involvement in the plot, or it may be pure circumstance. We give serious weight to Tarrants's personal remarks to Mitchell. But even if, as appears likely, Tarrants was oblivious to the White Knights' plot against King, one still has to ask, who else had access to that .30-06 rifle? Was it the rifle that Myrtis Ruth Hendricks saw in Deavours Nix's office in John's Restaurant, the one she later described as being placed into a truck by two unidentified men on April 3, 1968? Could it be the actual rifle used in King's murder? We hope that ultimately the location of relevant FBI records and perhaps even the further cooperation of Tarrants might resolve the mystery of the other .30-06.

WAS THE CB RADIO BROADCAST A HOAX?

While attempting and failing to analyze the ballistics of the King shooting, the HSCA also spent a good deal of time evaluating a fake CB radio broadcast that occurred after the shooting of Dr. King. In doing so they effectively debunked a series of Memphis Police statements that the broadcast had

been done by young local ham radio operators. Initially police told reporters that they had the identities of the young men, although no charges were
filed against them for obstruction of justice, nor was the FCC notified. That
explanation turned out to be complete misinformation, raising questions
about police motives. As background for the incident, we quote details of
the HSCA investigation from its summary report:

> At approximately 6:36 PM on April 4, 1968, an unidentified citizens'
> band radio operator in Memphis was heard broadcasting over chan-
> nel 17. He stated he was pursuing a white Mustang driven by the kill-
> er of Dr. King. The CB operator, contrary to lawful radio procedure,
> never identified himself. He announced that he was chasing the white
> Mustang east on Summer Avenue from Parkway Street at a high rate
> of speed and requested a landline to communicate to the police de-
> partment. The broadcast was made about 33 minutes after the first
> announcement over police radio that Dr. King had been shot.[15]

Among many others, Memphis CB operator William Herbert Austein
heard the original broadcast. As he was driving through the intersection
of Jackson Avenue and Hollywood Street, Austein halted a Memphis police cruiser driven by Lieutenant Rufus Bradshaw. Austein relayed the information received from the unknown CB operator to the police, and for
the remainder of the broadcast, Austein received transmissions over the
CB unit in his automobile, and Bradshaw relayed them to Memphis police
headquarters.

Shortly after 6:36 PM, in response to Austein's request, the unidentified operator said that he was pursuing the Mustang east on Summer Avenue from Highland Street. In subsequent transmissions, the operator told
Austein he was accompanied by two white males in a blue Pontiac, and they
were chasing the Mustang east on Summer Avenue from Waring Road. They
then followed the Mustang north on Mendenhall Road from Summer Avenue. At approximately 6 PM, the chase proceeded north on Jackson Avenue

toward Raleigh, a suburb northeast of Memphis, according to the broadcast. At approximately 6:44 PM, the operator reported that he had just chased the white Mustang through a red light at the intersection of Jackson and Stage Road at ninety-five miles per hour.

At this point, Memphis police began to suspect that the broadcast was a hoax. Two units of the Shelby County sheriff's department, stationed at an intersection at the very moment the white Ford Mustang and blue Pontiac were supposed to have passed through, informed the dispatcher they had seen no one.

At approximately 6:45 PM, the unidentified operator broadcast his position as going out Austin Peay Highway and said the occupant of the Mustang was shooting at him. "The CB operator's final broadcast at approximately 6:48 PM, he said he was approaching Millington Road heading to a naval base from Austin Peay Highway."[12]

In its subsequent investigation of this broadcast, the Memphis Police Department concluded it had been a hoax and that the chase had never occurred. The FBI, relying on the field investigation by the Memphis police, concurred.[1]

Further, the HSCA's examination of a map of the route revealed that the chase covered about ten and a half miles from the first transmission at approximately 6:36 PM to the transmission at approximately 6:44 PM that described the blue Pontiac passing through the intersection of Jackson and Stage. For the two automobiles to have covered ten and a half miles in eight minutes, they had to have averaged a speed of seventy-eight miles per hour. A large segment of the alleged route of the car chase was on a busy artery that was, at the time, crowded with rush-hour traffic. Under such conditions, a high-speed chase such as the broadcast described would have attracted considerable attention, caused numerous traffic infractions, and undoubtedly given rise to citizen complaints. The HSCA's examination of Memphis Police Department records revealed no supporting evidence of such a chase on April 4, 1968.

The FBI's and the Memphis police department's investigative records indicated that an eighteen-year-old CB enthusiast was considered the most likely perpetrator of the hoax. Although prosecution was not recommended, Memphis police officers chiefly responsible for the investigation told the committee that the named eighteen-year-old was considered the prime suspect.

The HSCA's investigation into the identity of the broadcaster, although hampered by the individual's refusal to cooperate, revealed that the evidence the Memphis Police Department and the FBI relied on in naming the eighteen-year-old as the suspect was apparently based on an erroneous interpretation of a key witness statement. Additionally, an extensive background investigation of the eighteen-year-old failed to reveal incriminating evidence. Indeed, the committee uncovered specific exculpatory evidence relating to the eighteen-year-old as the broadcaster and the HSCA's own consultants, FCC engineers, doubted that the individual was responsible. Ultimately, the named eighteen-year-old decided to cooperate with the HSCA, and he denied under oath that he made the broadcast.[16]

Additional possible suspects were identified and interviewed in the course of the HSCA's investigation of the CB broadcast. The HSCA also made an effort to pinpoint the broadcast by identifying all operators who had overheard the broadcast and by obtaining technical data concerning their location, their equipment, and the strength of the signal they had received. The committee used FCC engineers in an attempt to identify the broadcaster. As the FCC stated in its report to the committee, however, the interval of ten years made virtually impossible a task that would have been difficult even in 1968. The committee, therefore, was unable to identify the broadcaster.

William Pepper, author of *Orders to Kill: The Truth behind the Murder of Martin Luther King, Jr.,* reported information apparently not given to the HSCA. Memphis police chief J. C. MacDonald reported hearing the CB broadcast completely override local AM radio reception while at his brother's audio shop on Second Street, one block from Mulberry Street (the area of the shooting). That sort of audio interference suggests that the CB unit transmitting the diversion would have to have been in that immediate vicinity—in downtown Memphis, very close to the crime scene.[17]

The HSCA considered several indications that the broadcast was a conspiratorial act. For instance, the broadcaster asked for a landline relay to police headquarters, a request that shows he wanted the information to get to the police and suggests he had more than a simple hoax in mind. Further, the broadcaster attempted to lead police to the northern part of Memphis, while the most accessible route out of town from the vicinity of the Lorraine Motel was to the south, the direction the committee believed James Earl Ray did indeed follow.[18]

Although its failure to identify the broadcaster prevented the HSCA from determining definitively whether the broadcast was in any way linked conspiratorially to the assassination of Dr. King, the HSCA noted several points in support of its conclusion that the fake CB radio call was not a conspiratorial act. First, the broadcast came a full thirty-five minutes after the assassination, so it could not have assisted in the immediate flight of the assassin out of Memphis. Second, a description of the suspected assassin's white Mustang had been broadcast over the police radio at 6:10 PM, so any CB radio operator who had been monitoring police calls would have had the description of the automobile. Third, the broadcaster did not use the best means of penetrating the police network; he used channel 17, one of the lesser-used CB radio frequencies. Consequently, while the identity of the CB radio operator remained undetermined, the HSCA found that the evidence was insufficient to conclude that the Memphis CB radio broadcast was linked to a conspiratorial plot to kill Dr. King.

Our view is that, given the extensive use of CB radio by Klan members, and in particular the White Knights, this incident should actually be considered a type of "fingerprint" indicating that conspirators were indeed in Memphis on April 4, 1968. Our speculation is that events in Memphis were more complex than Ray simply shooting King, running to his Mustang, and driving south. Given that a description of his white Mustang was broadcast on the police channels at 6:10 PM, we have to wonder if a conspirator, perhaps totally unknown to Ray, was monitoring the police band and realized that Ray's vehicle had been described fleeing the crime scene.

The immediate danger would be that Ray would be caught fleeing from Memphis—that he might break down and say something that would kick off a much broader search.

If the CB radio broadcast were not part of an advance plan but rather a reaction to the immediate and unanticipated identification of Ray's car, it makes a great deal of sense. The men involved would have no way of knowing that Memphis police would be totally ineffective in dispatching warnings to neighboring states or setting up roadblocks on interstates or border-crossing side roads.[19] The conspirators' immediate need was to send the Memphis police in the wrong direction, divert law enforcement from Ray, and protect themselves. Making a diversionary CB radio broadcast would only have taken a few minutes to think through, especially in such a "pressure cooker" situation. And the CB radio diversion not only worked, but also was introduced as a key factual element in the disinformation efforts of both Margaret Capomacchia and Sydney Barnes. Given the reality of the CB radio broadcast and Capomacchia's and Barnes's efforts to tie it directly to Thomas Tarrants, one test for this scenario might be to determine if any of the vehicles used by the White Knights' inner circle were equipped with CB radio equipment.

WHO WAS IN THE GREEN CAR LEAVING THE SCENE OF THE CRIME?

The account of a CB radio incident may in fact tie to another underappreciated lead, one first revealed by researcher Philip Melanson in several of his books published in the 1990s. Although the evidence strongly suggests that Barnes and Capomacchia were attempting to relay a false story to the FBI to frame an innocent person, Tommy Tarrants, this does not mean that all the details of their stories were false. Indeed, if there was a concerted effort to frame Tarrants, then the two may have used a combination of truth and fabrication to lend their story more credibility. If so, it is worth remembering that Barnes specifically said that Tarrants's car was used in the CB radio broadcast, implying that Tarrants's green Buick Electra may have been used to divert police. In a "flip" of a common Klan practice of using another person's car to provide their operatives with an alibi, one could easily envision Tarrants's car being used to focus attention on him while he was off in North Carolina with no alibi of his own. This would have been easy, as Tarrants frequently loaned his car to others and shared it with other inner-circle members. Professor Melanson did not comment on, and likely did not know about, the Barnes and Capomacchia reports, nor did he ever mention Tarrants. But his legwork in Memphis may support the idea that there were multiple patsies associated with the King murder.

Melanson did something that Memphis police had simply not done in 1968. He walked the neighborhood around the scene of the shooting. And in so doing, he came across Olivia J. Catling of 375 Mulberry Street. Mrs. Catling lived a half block or so from the scene of the shooting, and although no policeman had ever talked to her, she had something to say.

In April 1968, Olivia Catling knew that Dr. King was staying at the Lorraine Motel near her house; she had thought of walking down to see if she could catch a glimpse of him. On the evening of the shooting, she was cooking supper when she heard a noise she thought was a shot. Dr. King immediately came to mind, and she turned off her stove and ran out the front door and down the street toward his motel. Her daughter, Cheryl, and a friend were in the front yard, and she ran past them. Mrs. Catling mentioned that she ran out ahead of the children but made no further remark about them coming with her, nor did she cite them as witnesses for what she saw.[20]

When she reached the nearest intersection (Mulberry and Huling Avenue), she noticed a man run out of a driveway, which was in fact a dead-end alley. The man, relatively tall and weighing perhaps 180 pounds, jumped into a green car and raced off down the street, turning onto Vance Avenue. Catling described the vehicle as a good-size car, possibly a Chevrolet, because it looked like her husband's Chevy Impala. In her initial statements to Melanson and others, she remarked on seeing police cars in the vicinity of the same street.

Many years later, the Justice Department (assisted by the FBI), having been encouraged by the King family to reexamine the King murder, became aware of Melanson's work and decided to investigate the Catling incident. They ultimately dismissed Catling's account, noting three reasons for that decision. First, Catling had modified her story, stating that police cars were not present at the actual time of her observation. Second, the Justice Department could not get Catling's daughter, Cheryl, to confirm her story. Cheryl said she had heard no shot and figured that her mother must have heard something on radio or television. Finally, the FBI argued that any fleeing assassin (specifically one fleeing from Bessie Brewer's rooming house) would have needed to descend or jump from a very high wall before reaching the car and driving away from the scene, and this did not seem to fit with Catling's testimony.[21]

We have our own issues with the Justice Department's analysis. First, the fact that Catling modified her story should not, by itself, entirely discredit her account. Witnesses frequently confuse or misremember details even days, much less years, after the fact. If she had seen the running man and later seen police in the area, it would be easy enough for the two observations to have merged in her memory.

Second, as to problems presented by the daughter's lack of confirmation, the FBI did not consider Olivia's full story in context. Olivia Catling said she had run to reach the corner within two or three minutes of the shooting. If Cheryl lagged behind, she would not necessarily have seen what her mother saw. And her mother did not say Cheryl had seen the car. Apparently Cheryl and her friend didn't react at all like her mother, but then they were only children at the time and likely did not share Mrs. Catling's awareness of the significance of the events.

Third, the issue of the wall would be a problem for the Catling account— but only if the individual fleeing had indeed been the shooter and had been coming from the rooming house. That was an assumption that solely the Justice Department made, and no alternatives were considered. If the fleeing individual was already at street level in the nearby area, then he never would have had to descend the wall. Or perhaps the man driving away in the green car played some other role than that of shooter.

As to the car in question, certainly a green Chevrolet Impala would appear similar to a green Buick Electra,[22] the kind of car Tarrants was driving at that time and sharing with his White Knights associates. And there are many roles that the individual Mrs. Catling saw might have been playing. Perhaps he was coming to get the rifle from Ray, heard gunfire, and simply fled. Perhaps he was a decoy intending to be seen fleeing the area in a car that would be seen and remembered. And perhaps, while the man scrambled to escape and figure out what happened, he may have used a radio in the green car to monitor police channels and then broadcast a diversion. As we mentioned, it would certainly be useful to know exactly what sorts of radios were in the cars Tarrants and the other White Knight inner-circle operatives used.

We feel Catling's credibility is strengthened by the fact that there is no evidence that she ever tried to promote or in any way profit from her observation either before or after she related it to Professor Melanson.

WAS THERE BOUNTY MONEY SENT TO JACKSON?

In 1967, Donald Nissen, an inmate in Leavenworth penitentiary, was given details of a $100,000 bounty offer involving the surveillance and murder of Dr. King. We have interviewed Mr. Nissen at some length; his criminal history was quite similar to that of other individuals we have discussed. He was a reserved individual who largely kept to himself and had the reputation of being a hardened career criminal. Most important, he had had previously lived in the Atlanta area and, once released, was known to be returning to a job that would require him to be based in Atlanta but also involved extensive travel throughout the South.[23]

Upon his release, Nissen did return to Atlanta but did not stop to meet with the Jackson, Mississippi, contact identified in the bounty offer. Instead, while on his way back to the South, he related the bounty offer to the FBI while being held on check charges in a Texas jail. At that point, the FBI did make inquiries in Jackson, Mississippi, and at Leavenworth penitentiary but remarkably failed to question the original source of the bounty information, LeRoy McManaman.

Upon arriving in Atlanta, Nissen took up his anticipated sales job and within a few months married. Not long after his return to work, a fellow salesman, Floyd Ayers, mentioned that he would appreciate it if Nissen would drop off a package for him in Jackson, Mississippi. Nissen thought nothing of the matter at the time and did the requested favor; at the time he made no connection between that favor and the bounty offer.[24] Not long afterward, while on a visit to his parole officer at the Atlanta Federal Building, he was accosted by an unknown man who seemed to be very upset that he had been talking about the King offer. Nissen took the courthouse confrontation as a real threat, since he was well aware that Leroy McManaman was a dangerous man to cross and realized that his talk with the FBI was now known to McManaman's associates. Clearly these associates included people not only in Jackson but also in Atlanta. Worse yet, Ayers approached Nissen and asked him if he realized what was in the package he had delivered. He then told him it had contained money to pay for the murder of Dr. King. Faced with this combination of events, Nissen left his job and fled Atlanta with his new wife, breaking his parole and moving out of state.[25]

Following the assassination of Dr. King, Nissen seriously considered that the people involved in the bounty offer might well have been involved in the murder. At that point, he recontacted the FBI, turned himself in, and served the prison time that followed from his parole violation. The bureau reinterviewed him at that point. Unfortunately, while (with his permission) we have obtained his full FBI file, it only contains a summary report of that interview and does not include the agent's interview notes. We were unable to obtain the FBI office files that should have contained the reports from the first agent who had been in touch with him. (The relevant field office files are either missing or have been routinely destroyed.)

Based on information from Nissen, we have been able to do some background work on Floyd Ayers, the person who asked that the package (later claimed to be bounty money) be carried to Jackson. It turns out that Ayers was a known member of the Klan and an associate of James Venable, the militant Atlanta Klan leader and colleague of J. B. Stoner. (Both men were named in previous FBI reports of plots to kill Dr. King.) Ayers was a flamboyant individual, a man with a strange history of attempts to contact the King family. In fact, the Secret Service took him into custody during the King funeral because he was falsely posing as an usher at the service. Shortly thereafter, he was caught in an apparent kidnapping attempt of Martin Luther King Sr., the civil rights leader's father.

We have also developed additional information that corroborates Nissen's account of having transported the package to Mississippi. As noted in an earlier chapter, he was able to describe his delivery of the package to a female in Mississippi—a tall woman, possibly in her forties, who worked not in a major office but rather in a building that was much smaller and antebellum in style. In 1967, the FBI located the woman, interviewed her about the story, and in their report described her physical appearance and her real estate home office. Forty years after his delivery of the package, Nissen's description of the woman and her office matched the description the FBI gave in 1967. We feel that is a significant corroboration because Nissen could not have possibly described this woman or her real estate office if he had not met with her. He did not meet her before giving his initial report to the FBI; her description in the FBI files comes from their interview of her. We did not provide Nissen with any documents describing how she looked and such files are not available in the public domain. This lends a tremendous amount of weight to the idea that he delivered a package was to a woman who had a close relationship with the Leavenworth bounty source, LeRoy McManaman.

Another independent source, with a long, documented history of criminal involvement, confirmed that McManaman was a member of the Dixie Mafia tied to the Oklahoma-based Jerry Ray James gang. That source confirmed that his longtime friend (and a notorious contract killer) Donald Eugene Sparks knew and would have worked with LeRoy McManaman.[26] And Sparks himself had, on two separate occasions and in the presence of FBI informants, mentioned that he had been offered a White Knights bounty contract on King's life in 1964. In short, our source for the details of the 1967 King bounty offer named a specific individual (LeRoy McManaman) whom we can demonstrate was in Jackson in 1964 and personally associated with the hit man (Sparks) specifically named in the 1964 White Knights contract offer.

There is still much that could be done to flesh out the bounty story related by Nissen, that indirectly connects to Sparks (who was in prison when King was murdered) and, most importantly, to McManaman. Finding additional files on McManaman and Sparks would be an obvious place to start. Unfortunately, the FBI told the authors that they routinely destroyed McManaman's files within a few years of his death. The authors obtained Sparks FBI Headquarters file via FOIA, but it makes absolutely no mention about the FBI's investigation into his possible role in the King murder case (such material may be in local, field office investigations into the King assassination, for instance those from FBI's Oklahoma Field Office). The authors have also explored the possibility of obtaining files from the Oklahoma State Bureau of Investigation, but those files are closed to the public.

In the absence of relevant files on Sparks and McManaman, the best bet would be for authorities or the Justice Department to locate any surviving individuals from the Jerry Ray James gang who knew the two men and see if they could provide any additional information. Even if Sparks was only connected to the 1964 plot, which may well be likely, he may have provided insight to his fellow traveling criminals related to McManaman's role in that earlier assassination attempt.

The authors have additionally sought Bureau of Prison files related to Donald Nissen's transfer to Sandstone Federal Correction Institute shortly after he was re-incarcerated for having jumped parole. Nissen told the authors that he requested the transfer after having detailed the danger to his life resulting from his inside information on the King murder. Nissen says, and records confirm, that Sandstone Federal Correctional Institution was indeed often used to house federal criminals whose lives would be endangered by other criminals, figures such as senior mafia members. As of this date, the Bureau of Prisons has not provided us with this information.

But there still may be very important information, from the late 1960s, that could corroborate Nissen's story, and provide additional leads in the matter. Perhaps most importantly, an earlier and more detailed account of Nissen's story may exist. Nissen told the authors that not long after the events in question—his memory is not precise on this matter forty years after the fact—he approached the King family, specifically Martin Luther King Sr., the father of the slain civil rights figure, with his account of the bounty offer and the package delivery. Still scared at the time for his life, he made sure the meeting was a discrete affair. He remembers meeting with King Sr., a secretary, and a member of the Atlanta police department. He believes the conversation was taped by, or transcribed by, the secretary who was present. It is likely that, being closer to the event, the details in this account would be more precise and specific. For instance, Nissen is still not one-hundred percent clear as to when he delivered the package to Sybil Eure or when he was told, after that delivery, about what the package contained (e.g. the bounty money.)

The authors have attempted to find this tape or transcript. We contacted the King Center in Atlanta, Georgia. The historian there said that they could not find such a tape or transcript, but she did tell the authors that the material would likely not even be in the archive. For a number of reasons, a significant amount of material from King Sr. has not been transferred to the institution, at least as of November 2009. If this tape (or transcript) could be located, it could provide important confirmation for Nissen's story, and additional details that could help resolve the King murder.

We feel that Nissen's information provides a significant lead, suggesting that some amount of the money raised in Atlanta might have been delivered to Jackson to help seal a contract with either James Earl Ray or some other interested party. In fact, it is possible that money may have even been waiting in Jackson for the shooters, contingent on events in Memphis going strictly according to plan. Ray obviously never collected the money.

GOING FORWARD

Our intention in exploring this material is to reinforce the fact that there are serious open issues in regard to the King assassination: mysterious men in

Memphis who the FBI itself could not trace, unknown fingerprints on evidence in both Memphis and Atlanta, a highly suggestive CB radio diversion, and a report of a fleeing man in a car that resembles one used in White Knights terror attacks. Beyond that, the .30-06 rifle raises unresolved questions, not only whether or not the rifle in custody fired the murder shot, but also whether or not it was the only .30-06 associated with the murder of Dr. King.

And these lingering questions are not simply a matter of errant reports and generic persons of interest. We have provided names of specific individuals that FBI reports confirm were associated with bounty offers on Dr. King, as well as names of individuals who may have moved money from Atlanta to Jackson, Mississippi, for such an offer. These names offer a significant opportunity for inquiry, especially if it were possible to access FBI headquarters and field office files on them and the HSCA investigation files now held by Congress. In our limited contact with Justice Department officials, we got the impression that the King murder is not and will not be reinvestigated in the same fashion that several civil rights cold cases have been. In some instances such decades-old cases have been successfully prosecuted. In others, the investigation uncovered enough facts to give a true picture of the crime even if no prosecution is feasible. We feel that a similar cold case inquiry is owed to Dr. King.

BEING CONTRARY

In the years following the King assassination, the lack of a clear motive for James Earl Ray, as well as contradictions in his story and his own remarks, have led to the proliferation of conspiracy theories. These theories involve a variety of conspirators and motives, and most assume Ray was indeed some sort of patsy, as he claimed. In addition to their investigation of notorious racists and right-wing extremists, the HSCA considered the involvement of the Mafia, the FBI, southern businessmen, and labor unions. Sprinkled throughout their investigation, which included leads from nine major cities, are occasional references to what is easily the most prevalent suspect group in King assassination literature: the American government.

Ray's first lawyer, Arthur Hanes, talked of a great conspiracy, one involving black militants, American leftists, Chinese communists—anybody but the Klan. He said he had called his contacts with the Klan, the White Citizens' Councils, the NSRP, and even the Minutemen, and none of them knew anything about Ray![1]

In the end, Hanes decided that perhaps it was Castro followers who had plotted King's murder, linked to black militants and backed by Castro or Chinese communists. But, regardless of who was involved, Hanes was convinced there existed a giant conspiracy and Ray was simply being used.

Several months before Ray's trial, the Reverend James Bevel of the Southern Christian Leadership Council, a close associate of Dr. King, announced that Ray was innocent and that he had proved other forces had killed Dr. King. Undoubtedly he pictured a different conspiracy than that which Hanes had in mind.[2] At the time, Ralph Abernathy, the new head of the SCLC, supported Bevel's declaration. Abernathy had replaced Dr. King as the leader of the upcoming Poor People's Campaign march on Washington, DC, in 1968. In a rally associated with the march, Abernathy warned that America would rue the day it "got rid" of King because Dr. King intended only to "shake up" America; Abernathy himself was going to "turn it upside down!"[3]

J. B. Stoner was among the first to propose an alternative conspiracy involving the U.S. government. He claimed the assassination was organized through the FBI, but in his version, the whole conspiracy was done to bring national pressure against the states' rights movement and the opposition to integration![4] Ray himself adopted Stoner's view and aggressively supported it, convincing his future supporters (such as attorney Mark Lane and British lawyer William Pepper) of government involvement. Pepper's writings would become instrumental in persuading a large number of people that the United States government had indeed been behind the assassination and that Ray was truly just a patsy.

Various authors, including one of Ray's own brothers, have written at length about the view that elements of the American government were responsible for the murder of Martin Luther King Jr. Theories that point to the involvement of the CIA or to the Army Special Forces have captured the popular imagination. Decades later, a civil case dealing with the murder would link together Mafia figures and Memphis police, working in conjunction with military intelligence. Beyond certain questionable interpretations of sometimes dubiously sourced "government" documents, a number of different points support the case for a government conspiracy:

- reports of "security stripping" by Memphis police, including the last-minute removal of a black Memphis police intelligence officer and black policemen from a firehouse adjacent to the Lorraine Motel

- reports of a military presence in Memphis, including the involvement of covert personnel directly monitoring Dr. King's movements at the Lorraine Motel

- a known police intelligence officer was at the Lorraine Motel prior to the assassination, and this same officer would join the CIA some years later

- the behavior and machinations of Raoul (an individual described solely by Ray) as an agent of the American intelligence community

- travel and use of fake identities by King's alleged killer, James Earl Ray, may have been beyond Ray's capacity as a low-level criminal but fit well with the modus operandi of America's intelligence agencies

- Ray's use of identities (the Eric Starvo Galt alias in particular), which suggests to some a series of coincidences that could only be explained if he was aided by the intelligence community

- the "confession" of Loyd Jowers and the King civil court conspiracy verdict that concluded that Jowers was guilty in a conspiracy to murder Dr. King

- the belief that Dr. King was viewed as a national security threat because of his public opposition to the Vietnam War

- the belief that Dr. King was viewed as a national security threat because of fear over the scheduled Poor People's Campaign march in Washington, DC

In our own work, we have examined each of these issues, as well as the general idea of government involvement in a conspiracy to assassinate King. We have come to believe that many of the theories of government involvement are based in elements that may have appeared mysterious immediately following the assassination but that have been explained through follow-up inquiries in the ensuing years. With regard to the other points, there are strong counterarguments, and we find the general concept of a government conspiracy to be unconvincing. However, we also know that many of our readers may well have come across one or more of these theories. We offer the following information and observations as counterarguments.

WAS SECURITY IN MEMPHIS INTENTIONALLY COMPROMISED?

Talk in Memphis about police "security stripping" generated some of the earliest concerns about a government conspiracy. There were several elements in that story, but one area that drew the most attention had to do with the removal of a police intelligence officer and two black firemen from the fire station adjacent to the Lorraine Motel. The removal of both Officer Redditt and the firemen are often lumped together as equally suspicious, since all the men in question were black. Officer Redditt was known to have expanded on his own concerns as to whether his removal was related to a conspiracy—so much so that the incident was pursued by private researchers such as William Sartor and author Mark Lane. The story was so provocative that it also drew the attention of the House Select Committee on Assassinations, which interviewed Redditt.

As historian Gerald McKnight details in his work *The Last Crusade*, Officer Redditt's removal can be traced to the police being contacted by a McClellan committee investigator who misinterpreted a threat to another officer in Knoxville as being directed at Officer Redditt in Memphis. The investigator's warning both alarmed and diverted Memphis police senior officers.[5]

Unfortunately this seems not to have been an unknown practice for the McClellan committee. A mere month after Dr. King's death, Senator McClellan himself went to Director Hoover with an explosive story that black militants were planning to hijack the Poor People's March in Washington from the SCLC and unleash a "rein of rioting, looting, and armed insurrection." Hoover ordered a full-court FBI press on the intelligence from the senator's investigators (which McClellan claimed to be airtight). The massive FBI follow-up with its own sources produced not the slightest corroboration, and after several weeks (during which McClellan "moved" the location of his key informant from Tennessee to Alabama and finally to Atlanta), the bureau finally managed to locate the source based on contacts within McClellan's committee. It turned out the source was in Mobile, Alabama, and the bureau determined that not only did he want money for his information, but also that he was "completely unreliable."

Separately, the removal of the firemen from the Butler Street firehouse can be traced to their support of the Memphis sanitation strike. But, as the HSCA determined from their interview with Redditt, their removal may have been largely due to a complaint Redditt himself wrote, identifying black firemen in the station as being a potential problem for the police surveillance team assigned to the fire station.[6] It should also be pointed out that two other officers were assigned to surveillance at the fire station. Even though Redditt was removed, the other officer stayed on his assignment, and we have detailed reports from their ongoing observations of the Lorraine Motel.[7]

We previously addressed other aspects of the purported "security stripping" in our chapter on events in Memphis, and Gerald McKnight provides expanded detail on the subject from his own research. Clearly, security for King was different on the April trip than it had been during the years prior. And certainly the situation was far tenser with far less trust of the police department than in earlier years. Still, while there was not a team of law enforcement officers physically with King, the area within a block of the motel was "swarming with police," as McKnight describes. There were two tactical teams and five cars adjacent to the motel, consisting of more than forty officers. In addition, a dozen officers from another tactical unit were taking a break at the fire station at the time of the shooting (less than two hundred feet away), while a replacement intelligence officer maintained surveillance.[8]

We also offered a counterexplanation that makes more sense of the Redditt removal. Under this scenario, the false threat against Redditt was reported to provide justification for a Memphis court to retain an injunction against the sanitation workers' strike. Lawyers for the SCLC were arguing against the constitutionality of the injunction, but a direct threat of violence against law enforcement would have offered the kind of leverage the city of Memphis would need to keep it in place. Given that Dr. King himself felt that a well-managed and effective protest in Memphis was needed to justify the upcoming Poor People's March on Washington, it stands to reason that those who feared the latter would try to sabotage the Memphis strike.

As noted before, the prosegregationist Senator McClellan was actively trying to subvert the upcoming march to Washington, DC, and he was willing to use false stories to achieve that goal. At the same time, his Permanent Committee on Investigations was actively harassing some of the very groups—such as the Mississippi Freedom Democratic Party—who were sourced in the false threat against Redditt. McClellan, whether with the active knowledge of his subordinate Philip Manuel or through using Manuel as an unwitting messenger, would have met two goals with this kind of misinformation: (1) limiting the effectiveness of the Memphis strike and jeopardizing the future march on Washington, DC, and (2) discrediting groups pushing for blacks' civil rights. Of course what may have been intended as just one more dirty trick against Dr. King was superseded by his murder on April 4, 1968.

The advantage of this explanation over the "security stripping to kill King" scenario is that it avoids the very simple problem presented by the latter notion: Absolutely none of the standard police security procedures described previously would have stopped a sniper attack from across the street from the Lorraine Motel (or, for that matter, a sniper attack from any similar distance) at any time during King's time in Memphis. Neither Redditt nor a closer security detail could have prevented someone from shooting King at that distance. Critics might contend that the stripping was aimed instead at protecting the escape of the shooter. But even Ray eluded capture by avoiding a police officer no more than a minute or two after the shooting. And even then, the first officer on the street in front of Ray's rooming house obtained a description of Ray's car, which was broadcast on police radio almost immediately.

WAS THERE A MILITARY PRESENCE IN MEMPHIS?

Several local reports of police spies, federal agents, and military personnel in Memphis area fed suspicions of some sort of government conspiracy immediately following the assassination. Those reports were indeed correct. But what was not known at the time of the King assassination, and what remained highly secret for a number of years, was the extent to which the U.S. government and the U.S. Army were conducting proactive intelligence and riot-control operations.

John Patrick Finnegan details the extent of that activity in *Military Intelligence*. The book is part of the Army Lineage Series compiled by Romana Danysh for the U.S. Army Center of Military History. This work gives us critical background for what was indeed a military and military intelligence presence in Memphis in 1968.[9] When explored in depth, the true motivation of the surveillance—monitoring the threat of race riots—actually undermines the idea that such personnel would be involved in an attack on Dr. King.

The war in Vietnam had led to a dramatic escalation of army intelligence activities on the home front; the U.S. Army Intelligence Command (USAINTC) was formed in 1965, with the mission of conducting operations inside the continental United States. Seven military intelligence groups operated a network of three hundred offices across the country. The army had also merged counterintelligence and investigative and criminal records data to create the Defense Central Index of Investigations, a truly massive domestic intelligence database. Initially, the military confined its attention to its traditional role of investigating individuals applying for military or governmental positions requiring security clearance. However, the escalation of domestic racial violence in the early 1960s led to alerts and instances of deployment of federal troops to maintain order. Army commanders found it difficult to work with civilian intelligence agencies; in particular, they found the FBI to be increasingly uncooperative and unable to provide the sorts of domestic intelligence needed to support potential army deployments. Also, as the involvement of young, black militants became a key factor in race and antiwar riots in the late 1960s, the military determined that FBI personnel were limited in their ability to infiltrate social movements composed of young people.

Early in the 1960s, local commanders in the South were the first to request counterintelligence support. In August 1965, the newly formed USAINTC found itself giving army field intelligence support during the riots in Watts, California. This led to the first national army contingency plan for collecting domestic intelligence. That plan, code-named Steep Hill, was put together early in 1966 and designed for implementation only after deployment of federal troops.

In 1967 Steep Hill was redesignated Garden Plot (Civil Disturbance Operations), and the decision was made to start intelligence collection as soon as it was determined that a civil disturbance might require troop deployment. Steep Hill was reworked to create a preemptive army intelligence collection effort; that version of the civil Disorder Operations plan was first named Rose Hill, changed shortly later to Punch Block. A variety of incidents in major American cities caused the Punch Block plan to be activated and put into operation eight times during the summer of 1966. Civil disturbance intelligence had become an increasing part of the U.S. Army Intelligence's domestic workload.

During 1967 troubles continued in America's cities. Punch Block was renamed Lantern Spike and was activated four times, with troops committed to a major riot in Detroit. Following events in Detroit, deputy secretary of defense Cyrus Vance ordered the army to reconnoiter all major cities for critical vulnerabilities in case troop deployment was ever needed. During 1967 the army faced the fact that it needed to be able to respond not only to major racial disorder but also to an escalation in antiwar protests, some of which were becoming violent. Popular support for the Vietnam War had begun to waver, and tripling the draft for military service had only escalated student opposition. Army intelligence responded to both perceived threats and dramatically escalated its covert collection activities.

In July 1967, President Johnson issued Executive Order 11365, which established a National Advisory Commission on Civil Disorders (commonly known as the Kerner Commission after its chairman, a former army major general and then governor of Illinois). The commission was created following the Detroit violence, and it found that 160 instances of civil disorder had occurred in 128 American cities. In March 1968, the Kerner Commisison's report included a variety of recommendations for expanding the role of the military in responding to domestic civil disorder (including increased training for army and National Guard units), the development of nonlethal weapons and personal protective equipment, and investigation of psychological techniques for reducing tension and improving riot control.[10]

Beginning in the winter of 1967, the Pentagon developed civil disturbance plans for a number of American cities. The plans anticipated civil violence by students, minorities, and even labor unions. Each area of the country had its own subsidiary plans under Garden Plot. For example, Cable Splicer was the plan that covered the western states of California, Oregon, Washington, and Arizona. Each military region was tasked with conducting exercises to develop and practice its individual plans. In May 1968 the California National Guard conducted its first Cable Splicer Training (Cable Splicer 1).[11]

The year 1968 generated numerous Lantern Spike events, one of which officially designated for Memphis. Following violence during the first sanitation workers' strike, the Memphis Lantern Spike deployment (discussed in some detail in a previous chapter) was authorized. That violence and the scheduling of another protest march triggered the activation and deployment of a number of military and military intelligence personnel. These individuals participated in a broad range of civil disturbance preparations, including coordinated planning with local law enforcement. There was also active military intelligence collection in Memphis, eventually including direct surveillance of the Lorraine Motel, where Dr. King was conducting staff meetings. Those meetings included the Invaders, a local militant group of young blacks who were a priority intelligence target for both the police and military. These Lantern Spike activities, including surveillance of the Lorraine Motel from an adjacent fire station, were observed and reported by locals, including firemen assigned to the station.

The early reports and stories of covert government intelligence in Memphis were real. Such activities, however, were not unique and definitely not associated solely with Dr. King. In fact, by April 1968, such activities had been going on in a number of cities across the country for close to two years. Later in 1968, as the Reverend Ralph Abernathy continued Dr. King's Poor People's Campaign, military intelligence expanded these activities, monitoring everything from caravans on the march to Washington, DC, to activities in the capitol itself. Military intelligence agents monitored "every march, every rally, took scores of photos and filed hundreds of reports."[12] Agents copied license plates of cars and buses and investigated their registrations; agents also infiltrated news conferences with phony press passes. Military intelligence would continue and expand their surveillance activities with local police and other government agencies well into the 1970s. Hence, authors who focus on the suspicious nature of military surveillance of King miss the key point: that such surveillance was authorized in order to provide information in the event of an urban riot so that the military could mobilize to minimize any damage—the very kind of damage the country could face in response to King's murder.

WHY WAS THERE AN INTELLIGENCE AGENT WITH DR. KING AT THE LORRAINE MOTEL?

One of the more widely discussed suspicions of the assassination has been that one of the men who rushed to King's lifeless body was an intelligence officer—to be specific, a police intelligence officer working deep undercover. Researchers discovered that the intelligence officer's name was Merrell McCullough, and determined that some years later he became an employee of the CIA. McCullough was an ex-army military policeman and had served in Vietnam before joining the Memphis police in September 1967. His presence at the Lorraine Motel has frequently been used as an argument for government involvement in the assassination. No one doubts that McCullough was a member of Memphis police intelligence and later of the CIA. The problem is that the speculation and sensationalism attached to the story ignores the context of law enforcement's actual activities during the period, including its history with Dr. King.

Dr. King was the subject of government scrutiny by many different agencies for years. The CIA bugged King's hotel rooms.[13] The FBI famously sent tape recordings, allegedly of King having sex, to King's wife, Coretta, in January 1965.[14] The motivation for much of this was the fear that King's movement had been infiltrated by communists; it was sustained and magnified by Director Hoover's personal animosity toward Dr. King. Still, as the decade evolved, the escalating paranoia of national security ensured that King was only one of a number of figures being watched in the charged political climate of the late 1960s. If not for the damage to civil rights, some of these instances, such as the surveillance of John Lennon, would be comical. In other cases, as with the extensive, ongoing surveillance of civil rights figures and Vietnam War protestors, the efforts were motivated by a growing fear of what Professor Gerald McKnight called "domestic Tet Offensive." Surveillance became a general fact of life across the country during this period in history.[15]

There is no doubt that an undercover Memphis police officer, who some years later was employed by the CIA, was one of the first people to reach Dr. King's body on the Lorraine Motel balcony. In 1968 McCullough was assigned to infiltrate the Invader group. They were a target of the FBI's counterintelligence program focused on both black and white militants and were of interest to the Memphis Police Department. Police interest in the Invaders was especially intense in the spring of 1968, as it was felt that the group had played a key role in instigating the violence associated with the first sanitation workers' strike. Police intelligence had been hard at work trying to obtain information about the Invaders and had successfully placed undercover officers inside the group. McCullough had been uniquely effective at infiltrating the Invaders and was even chosen as its "transportation officer." That position allowed him access both to the Invaders and to individuals with whom they were working, including contacts in the SCLC. For example, McCullough had been chauffeuring SCLC leader Jim Bevel around Memphis the afternoon of the assassination.[16] Those intelligence efforts targeting the Invaders and Dr. King had been exceptionally effective. In one instance, law enforcement produced seventeen pages worth of information on an April conference involving Dr. King. This report included specific details on who was in contact with the Invaders and what was discussed. McCullough and an FBI informant within the SCLC also provided detailed information from Dr. King's April 3 meetings.[17]

McCullough had attended a meeting at the Loraine Motel the evening before the assassination and was still there on April 4; actually several of the Invader members were just checking out of the motel that evening after having failed to reach any agreement with Dr. King in regard to their participation in the planned march. The details of all his work with the Invaders are unclear (he also volunteered to work with the SCLC), but McCullough was quite effective in his surveillance, and his efforts resulted in a drug bust that produced charges against a number of the Invader leaders. Indeed, by the end of 1968, the Invader group had virtually disintegrated, and many of its leaders were in jail, were hiding from the law, or had simply gone back to school.

We know these details about McCullough because the rumors about his presence at the scene of the murder led to his investigation by the HSCA.[18] The HSCA's inquiry determined that he had indeed taken a job with the CIA, but only in 1974. McCullough testified that he had no direct relationship with the CIA, the FBI, or any other intelligence agency in 1968.[19] Although that might well have been true, it is also likely that his reports were channeled through Memphis police to cooperating government agencies (routine practice, as we have described), and his success as an infiltration agent would have certainly have been on record.

Given McCullough's background and 1968 police assignment, his presence at the Lorraine Motel is not surprising. For one thing, the Invaders were the individuals suspected of trying to radicalize the black community in Memphis; they were also suspected of the acts that had turned earlier marches and demonstrations into full-scale riots. As Professor McKnight notes, Frank Holloman, former FBI man and head of the Memphis police force, made the gathering of intelligence a top priority for law enforcement, and McCullough, who was young and had a background as a military police officer, would prove to be an excellent candidate to infiltrate suspected radical organizations and seems to have performed very effectively in his assignment.[20]

That McCullough was so close to the scene of the crime is not so surprising, either. The SCLC leadership, including Dr. King, was in ongoing negotiations with members of the Invaders at the Lorraine Motel. The goal was to bring the Invaders into line with a peaceful demonstration, ensuring they did not destroy the planned march. Those negotiations began to break down when Hosea Williams (one of the few SCLC leaders who wanted to incorporate the violent-prone Invaders as staffers in the SCLC) learned that the Invaders were billing Lorraine Motel rooms to the SCLC account.[21] Finding Invaders and their associates (and infiltrators), such as McCullough, in close proximity to Dr. King seems understandable. In fact at the time of the shooting, many of the Invaders were packing up to leave the motel that evening.

Even the most suggestive aspect of the McCullough story, his eventual employment by the CIA, seems not all that surprising in the context of the times. Ironically, the mundane explanation may have its roots in the civil rights movement itself. A 1967 report, undertaken after complaints were registered by a civil rights activist, revealed that there were fewer than twenty blacks among the approximately twelve thousand nonclerical employees of the CIA.[22] By 1972, African Americans constituted 4.9 percent of the CIA workforce. This still did not satisfy black leaders such as New York representative Charles Rangel, who in 1975, publicly called for additional minority hires.[23] This push for more hires came on the heels of the Nixon administration's strong push for affirmative action policies within the federal government. Nixon, one should recall, issued Executive Order 11478, urging federal agencies to offer equal opportunities to qualified minority candidates.

Given his background in the military and his experience as a Memphis police undercover agent, Merrell McCullough clearly was a prime candidate for recruitment. However, there is no evidence that McCullough was working for the CIA while he was in Memphis, nor is it likely that the CIA would openly employ him later if they had used him in such a capacity or knew that he was in any way connected to a government plot to murder King. Indeed, one should wonder why McCullough would have been placed in a job with any government agency if he was directly connected to such a national conspiracy.

WAS THE MYSTERIOUS RAOUL AN AGENT OF AMERICAN INTELLIGENCE?

James Earl Ray maintained that the key to his being used as a patsy, and a key element in a government conspiracy, was a man who called himself "Raoul."[24] Raoul was the man who purportedly recruited Ray, manipulated him over the better part of a year, and then left him hanging in Memphis. We have no primary information on Raoul other than what James Earl Ray provided, so we are left to judge Raoul largely by his alleged actions.

There are serious questions as to whether Raoul even existed. For example, Ray gave multiple descriptions of Raoul to different investigators and authors. Even some of those who see the hand of the government in manipulating Ray have postulated that Raoul was some sort of composite character. In any event, an examination of Ray's interactions with the alleged rogue point away from a connection between Raoul and U.S. intelligence.

Ray stated that he first approached Raoul, a fellow of apparently Latino extraction, in a waterside bar in Montreal, Canada. At the time, Ray was apparently feeling out a variety of people for leads to false identity paperwork. Raoul responded by introducing the possibility of smuggling to develop a relationship that might lead to the needed identity papers.

Ray introduced Raoul as the excuse for many of his activities, right up to the moment of the shooting in Memphis. Raoul had directed Ray to leave Canada and relocate to the South (Raoul wanted him to go to Mobile, but Ray talked him into Birmingham); the relocation was to put him into a better position for smuggling activities across the Mexican border. Over the long run, it appears that New Orleans was to be the preferred contact point for Raoul. Ray stated that he felt that Raoul was keeping tabs on a number of people similar to himself.

Raoul provided Ray with spending money, money to buy a car, and a variety of other things including photography equipment. This was for no apparent or stated purpose other than to haul it around in his Mustang all the way from Birmingham to Mexico, Los Angeles, Atlanta, and finally Memphis. Raoul also arranged smuggling jobs for Ray across both the Canadian and Mexican borders.

After some time, out of contact with Raoul and in Los Angeles, Ray ran short of money and decided to contact Raoul again, calling and then traveling to New Orleans. At that time Raoul told him that he could set him up in a gun-running deal, moving guns through Mexico and eventually landing Ray inside Cuba. Ray thought that sounded good, called New Orleans from Los Angeles, and found that Raoul had already gone to Birmingham, Alabama. He had left word for Ray to meet him there (apparently assuming there was no way Ray was not going to take advantage of the opportunity). This seems a bit problematic given Ray's caution and history of weighing options; it also left the initiative for future contact in Ray's, rather than Raoul's, hands.

Ray did respond, met up with Raoul in Birmingham, and was told they needed to hurry on to Atlanta. Upon getting a room in Atlanta, Raoul asked for a second key and told Ray they would probably be going to Miami soon. A few days later, Raoul returned and told Ray to buy a hunting rifle. Following the rifle purchase, he told Ray to take it to Memphis (where the gun-running deal would apparently be put together). In the end all this left Ray in Memphis, with a rifle, right across the street from where Dr. King was shot. Clearly Raoul had set Ray up as a patsy in the shooting.

For all the above we have only one source, Ray himself. To test this theory of Raoul as part of a government conspiracy we have to accept certain premises:

- The CIA (or some intelligence agency) routinely places recruiting agents in waterside bars in Canada. Those agents scanned for minor criminals who can be used in illegal, deniable, domestic U.S. intelligence operations.

- Intelligence agents tested recruits by having them engage in smuggling operations across the U.S. border. Apparently the

intelligence community had no way to check recruits' back-
grounds or, if it did, was not concerned about recruits who
have routinely bungled their crimes or about recruits who
were escaped convicts, wanted, and on the run.

- While in this "probationary period," recruits were offered living expenses and equipped with various assets in order to hold
them available for future actions; they may actually have been
out of sight for many months, but contacts were maintained
through cutout telephone numbers with relayed messages. The
intelligence community simply assumed that the recruit would
contact agents through cutouts when money was in short supply—apparently such a "light touch" was acceptable even when
the recruit was being considered for a frame-up in a major domestic assassination.

- Beyond its rather questionable techniques in recruiting and
managing key covert assets, the CIA apparently must have
intended Ray to be caught as he had no warning and only
escaped by sheer luck. That would mean that the plot was to
kill Dr. King and leave a patsy with no apparent motive—and
one who could implicate a major agency operative if said person were caught. Of course, to an extent, Ray did implicate
the mysterious Raoul, but his memory became conspicuously
cloudy when it came to providing verifiable details. Ray could
provide the details of every place he stayed, even phone numbers he collected, but remarkably could not remember his and
Raoul's meeting places, much less telephone numbers or other
actual cutout contact points that could be investigated.

- The CIA, the FBI, or military intelligence would frame someone whose lack of an obvious motive would allow for decades

of accusations and speculations—as opposed to framing someone who would raise fewer questions and significantly undermine one of the expanding and potentially dangerous movements these agencies were already attempting to counter and
undermine. In the case of the FBI in particular, they would
also have to avoid trying to implicate the extreme racists that
they had been battling for several years.

- And for those who accept that researchers have actually, as
claimed, located the "real" Raoul (still using that name), they
also have to accept that a deep-cover intelligence agent would
use his true name (and that any intelligence group security
would accept that).

We have researched tens of thousands of pages of documents relating
to CIA activities, including a variety of domestic operations and activities
(some of which cover the actual recruiting procedures and security vetting
of assets). Beyond that, we refer readers to the detailed Justice Department
study and analysis of Raoul. For us, Ray's story of Raoul as some sort of
intelligence "handler" simply does not ring true. We find much simpler and
more consistent, explanations for Ray's behavior, including the fact that he
had used fictitious individuals as similar diversions in attempts to avoid
blame and divert prosecution in previous crimes.

ARE RAY'S FALSE IDENTITIES AND INITIAL ESCAPE EVIDENCE OF A GOVERNMENT CONSPIRACY?

Irrespective of the existence of Raoul, one of the most frequent views concerning a government conspiracy has to do with the perceived elegance of
Ray's escape and his use of a range of aliases and fake documentation. A
prevailing opinion is that Ray was just a dumb convict and must have had
help to get away as he did after such a crime—especially with everyone on
his trail.

We have detailed the facts of Ray's escape at length, showing that it was far from "elegant." In fact, in contrast to Ray's previous prison escapes, his escape from Memphis seems far from planned. His transit through Canada took far longer than most people realize and included one abortive identity theft and a second attempt that produced a passport with a misspelled stolen identity—a fatal detail that eventually got him picked up by customs in London. We have also pointed out that his lack of funds prevented him from getting the tickets that he needed for a truly successful escape and that he even had to commit minor robberies in London just to sustain himself.

However, there is still the issue of seemingly mysterious coincidences in regard to various names Ray used. These coincidences, and the government intelligence agency involvement they suggest, are most thoroughly developed by Professor Phillip Melanson in his book *The Martin Luther King Assassination*. They involve Ray's purported knowledge of several Canadian citizens as well as the fact that one of them, Eric St. Vincent Galt, worked in a Canadian company that handled U.S. defense contracts and held a Canadian security clearance. Several of the men physically resembled Ray and lived in close proximity to each other in Toronto. The argument is that only a government agency such as the CIA could have provided Ray with such names.

We have discussed Ray's use of false names at some length in preceding chapters. Ray himself had a history of using aliases even before he entered the federal prison system. He himself described the research process for assuming the names of dead citizens. As with most career criminals, he also knew how to generate low-level aliases. Ray had done that for himself in Birmingham, as recently as 1967.

As documented in investigative reports, it was well known inside Missouri State Penitentiary that escapees could go to Canada as a destination to obtain such fake identities. George Edmonson, who was once on the FBI's Ten Most Wanted list, and who served in Missouri State Penitentiary at the same time as Ray, specifically pointed to the availability of such identification in Montreal. He said this would have been known to any criminal, including those serving time in Missouri State. He said that there were "floaters" in Montreal's rue Notre-Dame who were part of a pipeline that helped supply fake identification to criminals.

And research by Canadian investigative journalist John Nicol, using newly available Royal Canadian Mounted Police files, suggests the possibility that Ray might have used criminal sources for some of the names he used. While in Toronto, Ray told a police officer who had stopped him for jaywalking that he was staying at "6 Condor Avenue." Investigation revealed that 6 Condor Avenue was home to George Kapakos, an ex-convict who had "several underworld contacts," according to Nicol. This same address was circled on a map Canadian police found among Ray's possessions, along with other circles on the map for the homes of two of Ray's other "living" aliases: Ramon Sneyd and Paul Bridgman.[26]

Using native Canadian criminal contacts would also explain some of the other oddities researchers have pointed to, including Ray's misspelling of the middle name as Starvo. Critics have noted that Ray's supposed mistake appears to resemble the handwriting of Eric St. Vincent Galt, who at one time, spelled his middle name as St. V. with the abbreviating periods appearing as slant or, hence, someone might read it as Starvo. As Ray could not have had access to the handwriting at the time that Galt used this spelling, some authors claim that it must have come from other sources (presumably government intelligence).[27] But criminals would have been just as capable as any intelligence agency of researching and making use of false identities and hence could have misread an actual document from Eric St. V. Galt—even one collected from years before—and misspelled it as Starvo. That certainly makes more sense than the misspelling coming from a U.S. government intelligence file, as some researchers have claimed; such a file would almost certainly have a typed and correctly spelled version of the name.

Ray himself said he went to the Toronto Telegram offices to research names for use as fake identities, but that may be another Ray falsehood. It would have been more likely for him to obtain details at the Office of the Registrar General. He might well have begun simply by first perusing the voter registration rolls (a suggestion Canadian radio personality Brent Holland made). In the late 1960s these rolls were posted on public lampposts, listing the voters by locality, in a way that would have reduced the need for actual physical surveillance and could easily explain the close proximity of Bridgman, Sneyd, Galt, and Willard to one another.

Without doubt, Ray's use of the name Eric Starvo Galt has generated the most questions and discussion. We do not pretend to be able to answer all the issues raised in regard to that name, but certain points stand out.

First, there was no real individual named Eric Starvo Galt (the closest match was an Eric St. Vincent Galt), so it was impossible for Ray to steal or be given a true Starvo Galt identity. What Ray did was use the name Eric S. Galt (a name listed in the Toronto telephone directory) and obtain a driver's license in Birmingham, using the full name Eric Starvo Galt. Because he initially had no Galt identification when he was first in Canada, he had to cross the border using an official (albeit false) identification that included a social security number he had first obtained in the early 1950s. Ray never had any false identification for Eric S. Galt other than the license and car registration that he obtained for himself in Birmingham.

Ray used the Eric Galt alias for several months, from Canada through the United States to Mexico, back to Los Angeles, and finally in Atlanta. He made numerous purchases in that name, used it on an ongoing basis to register at motels and rooming houses, and even subscribed to a correspondence course and continued to change the postal delivery address for materials using the Galt name in the address changes. Since that was the name in which his car was registered, it created a clear trail for the FBI to follow after the King assassination.

Ray used various other aliases during his travels; some of them seem to match individuals he had known in prison or elsewhere as easily as the Canadian names. But, in regard to Canadian names, there is no sign of actual identity theft until after the King assassination. And in that case, there is no doubt that Ray specifically tried to steal two different real Canadian identities in order to obtain a Canadian passport, aborting the first attempt when he determined the person already had a passport. He succeeded on his second effort; however, his penmanship was so poor that the name was misread and misspelled on the actual document, eventually resulting in his being challenged in London customs and taken into custody.

With these points in mind, it is difficult for us to believe that a sophisticated government intelligence network (or even a criminal one for that matter) was supporting Ray. More to the point, those who highlight Ray's aliases face a fundamental contradiction: Ray himself always claimed that he himself fashioned the fake names and aliases. He never blamed the government or Raoul for his use of aliases. If, as some of Ray's defenders claim, he was lying to protect someone else, they would be hard pressed to say that he was covering for the U.S. government or for Raoul. After all, Ray allowed his attorneys to publicly accuse the government, in speeches and books, of involvement in the King murder. Why would he stop short when it came to the issue of fake identification?

WHAT ABOUT LOYD JOWERS AND
THE CIVIL COURT CONSPIRACY VERDICT?

Many of the allegations of a government conspiracy described in this study were introduced in support of a civil court case brought on behalf of the King family in 1999. The lawsuit was brought against Lloyd Jowers "and other unknown co-conspirators." The King family's attorney was William Pepper, long-time investigator of the King assassination and author of a series of books on the murder; Pepper had spent years investigating Jowers, the owner of a Memphis bar and grill adjacent to the rooming house across from the Lorraine Motel.

The lawsuit against Jowers included the basic claim that Jowers had hired the actual King assassin (not James Earl Ray) and that after the shooting he had received and hidden the rifle used by the "real" sniper (who had fired from the bushes across from the Lorraine Motel). Pepper argued the case that a local grocery store owner, Frank Liberto, paid Jowers $100,000 to assist in the plot. Liberto, in turn (according to Pepper), was connected to the Marcello crime family in New Orleans—which in turn had been functioning as part of a larger government conspiracy (primarily involving U.S. military intelligence) to murder Dr. King.[28] Pepper argued for the existence of a long-standing relationship between the FBI, elements of military intelligence, and the Marcello Mafia crime organization. The trial resulted in a decision against Jowers and "other unknown co-conspirators," and many advocates of a government conspiracy in the assassination of Martin Luther King Jr. cite the jury ruling as proof of their beliefs.

As we have detailed in preceding chapters, there are a great many problems with the evidence introduced against James Earl Ray and serious questions about his personal role as the shooter. To the extent that such evidence was presented to the jury in the civil case, it is not surprising to find a verdict of conspiracy in the murder of Dr. King.

However, in regard to the civil trial and a jury's guilty verdict against Loyd Jowers, we have to note a number of concerns, beginning with the fact that Jowers's attorney, Lewis Garrison, all but stipulated that his client was part of the conspiracy, and the King family lawyer stipulated damages of only $100 for the death of Dr. King.[29] It would have been difficult for Jowers to maintain his total innocence, since as early as 1993, following some of his first interviews with William Pepper, Jowers had gone on *Primetime Live* with Sam Donaldson and admitted his participation in a conspiracy. However, in those remarks Jowers also stated that he had no idea the plot involved killing Dr. King and later instructed his lawyer to defend him on that point.[30]

During the 1999 civil trial, Jowers took Fifth Amendment protection in order to preclude further testimony; however, his attorney stipulated that his prior remarks and statements (including the television interview) could be admitted.[31] With that agreement, a verdict of conspiracy against Jowers was virtually inevitable, regardless of the presentation of any further evidence.[32] Given his lawyer's stipulations (representing a virtual admission of guilt), the civil trial proved to be much like Ray's initial trial after his guilty plea—an opportunity to place material in evidence rather than an aggressive legal contest with constant point and counterpoint from two opposing sides. Jowers's lawyer made few challenges other than to points that might personally affect his client and increase his guilt. Perhaps the best illustration of this comes from the amount of objections offered from either side. In what is supposed to be an adversarial process aimed at bringing out the truth, there were almost no objections during the entire course of the trial.

There are also a variety of questions about Jowers's motive in his initial confession in 1993, about his claims overall, and in regard to his fundamental credibility. In his book *An Act of State,* William Pepper discloses that Jowers and a colleague were pressuring witnesses to support his story in hopes that he could sell it for $300,000.[33] That was confirmed in transcripts of conversations between two of the main witnesses to Jowers's alleged involvement. Admitting to involvement in the crime certainly bolstered Jowers's efforts to make money from the resulting publicity. Given that the Memphis district attorney's office continually showed no interest in reopening the King murder, Jowers was in a perfect position to promote such a story and potentially earn money while facing no criminal consequences.

But the problems go beyond Jowers's questionable motives. To Pepper's credit, his own books give ample reason to doubt Jowers's claims of involvement. The biggest issue involves Jowers's original claim that the man he hired to kill (and who actually shot) Dr. King was Frank Holt. However, Pepper cleared Holt of any involvement in King's murder, and Jowers himself later changed the shooter to be a Memphis police officer. And Pepper acknowledged that Jowers "went along with the [story.]"[34]

In fact, as discussed above, Jowers and his colleague Willie Aikens were pressuring witnesses to support the Holt story to make money. If, on the most fundamental point related to his story, Jowers clearly lied, it becomes difficult to credit the rest of his story. Again, Pepper himself acknowledged that Jowers's testimony was "extraordinary for the number of untruths he told" at the civil trial.[35] In the trial presentations, Pepper did not rely exclusively on Jowers's own claims. His main witness to the events of April 4, as they relate to Jowers specifically hiding a rifle at his restaurant, was Betty Spates, one of Jowers's waitresses and apparently his mistress as well. In a secondhand account Spates gave to a Memphis bail bondsman as early as

1969, she implicated Jowers and has since elaborated in great detail on that story. But Pepper affirms that Spates also had significant credibility issues. She signed a primary affidavit in front of two witnesses that specifically denied the core elements of the story she had previously related to Pepper.[36] More recently, another memorandum has been described that reveals that as early as 1969, Spates admitted to prosecutors that she was paid $5,000 to implicate Jowers.[37] The *King v. Jowers* civil trail included a broad mix of material challenging the official evidence and Ray's guilt. It combined Jowers's confession to a conspiracy with a variety of other evidence suggestive of government involvement, including the involvement of Raoul as the primary government agent manipulating James Earl Ray. We have already addressed concerns pertaining to Ray's introduction of Raoul; other credibility issues have to do with how the entire story of Raoul was investigated (long before the 1999 trial).

Part of that problem has to do with the fact that private investigators routinely used hypnosis to "refine" the memory of witnesses, a practice that is widely criticized by memory experts and psychologists because of its tendency to produce false testimony. Compounding this problem was the investigator's decision to use photographs and questionable photo lineups.[38] Both of these procedures—hypnosis and photo lineups—are especially problematic when applied to witnesses who are recalling their stories thirty to forty years after an event, as was true of many of Pepper's trial witnesses.

The most obvious example of how these techniques could pollute an investigation can be seen in the supposed identification of the mysterious Raoul (the lynchpin to many of the trial claims of wider government involvement). The case for Raoul was bolstered by Pepper's claim that his team had identified and located the real "Raoul"—a Portuguese immigrant with the actual first name of Raoul (who has denied all such claims to the Justice Department and others).[39] The main source for that identification was Glenda Grabow, who came forward for the first time in 1993, claiming that Raoul raped her after having become incensed when Grabow displayed a key chain with the pictures of both Martin Luther King Jr. and President

John Kennedy.[40] Raoul was furious because he had been intimately involved in the killing of both men, according to Grabow, having shot Dr. King from the brush across from the Lorraine Motel and President Kennedy from the sixth floor of the Texas School Book Depository. Grabow's story became even more involved after she underwent hypnosis.[41] She involved Lee Harvey Oswald's eventual killer, Jack Ruby, in her story, and eventually would claim that Ruby actually fathered one of her children.[42] Given the dangers of hypnosis in corrupting a witness's testimony, it is not surprising that her affidavit for the King civil trial included extra details that contradicted what John Billings, one of the first to interview her, claimed in his own testimony.[43] Grabow independently identified a picture of Raoul in a photo lineup, shown by Pepper investigator Ken Herman. But Herman's photo lineup violated virtually every standard for forensic identification, stacking the deck against the accused Raoul. There were only six total pictures to choose from, and the picture of Raoul was distinctly different in its contrast and quality from all the other photos. The age difference between Raoul and some of the others in the photo are also obvious and suggestive. [44] Few of the photos come close to matching James Earl Ray's descriptions of Raoul (in age and ethnicity) available from testimony and in books. After a Justice Department review criticized the lineup technique, author Pepper even acknowledged that the selection of photographs had left something to be desired.[45] Also, the Justice Department and individual researchers reviewed the Portuguese immigrant's employment records, which showed that he was working during both the Kennedy assassination and the King assassination.[46]

It is also important to note that virtually none of the issues we have raised were brought up as challenges during the civil trial. Although Jowers's attorney did cross-examine some witnesses, his focus was simply on testimony that related to his client's personal involvement. There was no effort to challenge material being offered in support of the guilt of "other co-conspirators unnamed," which was described by Pepper as an amalgam of the FBI, the Mafia, military intelligence, and the Memphis police.[47] One of the few reporters covering the trial noted that Jowers was not really Pepper's prime concern. His focus was on the "other co-conspirators," and much of the information presented was quite far ranging. There was no legal challenge or objection to the material being introduced in that regard.[48]

This brings us to the final points that have been brought forward to support what seems to be an almost "intuitive" belief that Dr. King would have been eliminated by the American government. There was, and remains, a belief that Dr. King might have been viewed as a national security threat, so dangerous to the nation that the government itself acted against him in some twisted sort of self-defense. Such views seem to be based largely on two assumptions: that King was a potential threat to the success of the Vietnam War, or that King was a potential source of nationwide civil unrest.

WAS KING A THREAT TO THE WAR IN VIETNAM?

Dr. King had not been publicly active in opposing American involvement in Vietnam during its earliest years, but in 1965 he had expressed his concern that it could diminish recent progress on civil rights. However, the SCLC's annual convention failed to endorse Dr. King's 1965 call for an end to the war. Although personally having no doubt about his own opposition to the escalating war, he was very much aware of the risk to the civil rights movement of associating itself with what was then widely perceived as a radical and un-American antiwar movement. (Military intervention to confront communist expansion in Southeast Asia still had broad support at the time.) Throughout 1966, Dr. King refrained from any major focus on foreign policy.[49] It was not until February 1967 that Dr. King firmly and publicly joined the growing opposition to the war with his famous speech "The Casualties of the War in Vietnam." In April of that year, he continued that effort with a major antiwar address at the Riverside Church in New York City, establishing himself as one of the most prominent antiwar spokespersons. During the "Vietnam Summer" that followed, much of his personal agenda consisted of participation in the exploding "peace movement."[50]

But by early 1968, matters had dramatically evolved for both Dr. King and America in general. By that point, King was far from being the most visible or most aggressive leader of the antiwar movement. His own focus on the war had significantly diminished by the spring of 1968, as the nation as a whole began to turn against the war. Before the Tet Offensive in January 1968, articles that featured King and his anti–Vietnam War stance appeared almost twice as often as those that mentioned King in connection with poverty.[51] But during the first three months of 1968, that ratio had shifted dramatically, with his stand on poverty getting the same amount of coverage as his opposition to the war.[52] That change in media coverage reflects King's own priorities. In December 1967, he had announced plans for a massive Poor People's March on Washington. That dramatic change in focus was largely the result of the other major events of the summer of 1967—the wave of racial riots that began in Detroit and Newark and spread to major American cities. The riots were a major shock to Dr. King: He told his closest friends that "there were dark days before . . . but this is the darkest."[53] Something had to be done to address the desperate poverty and hopelessness of the inner cities. He believed the country might not survive another summer of riots. By the end of 1967, Dr. King had turned his attention to poverty as his key issue, as opposed to the Southeast Asian war.

At the end of February 1968, the Gallup Poll had begun to register the first significant difference between those who felt the war was a mistake and those who thought it was justified, with the former enjoying a plurality that would sustain itself for the rest of the war.[54] Antiwar candidate Eugene McCarthy scored a major symbolic win against President Lyndon Johnson in March of that year, and Johnson took the near-unprecedented step of declining to run for a second term after his once-hawkish coterie of "Wise Men" became dovish.[55] Even the Republican candidate Richard Nixon, who represented a party that had turned against the Vietnam War (as a Johnson administration blunder) before the public as a whole did, was pushing for a "peace with honor."[56] Without question, Nixon took his time in ending the war as president and took measures that moved the war in new directions, but he also dramatically reduced the forces on the ground in Southeast Asia and even forced the Vietnamese leadership to accept what eventually became the basis for the actual

American withdrawal. If the supposed "power elite" believed that killing King would extend "their" war on "their" terms, why would they let Nixon kowtow to public opinion any more than Lyndon Johnson?

But far more specifically, now that we now know many of the details of the actual government antiwar intelligence community initiative, including military intelligence activities, we can say for sure that as of 1968, Dr. King was not a primary target of either the CIA's overseas and domestic CHAOS project or the FBI's antiwar program. The FBI did continue its COINTEL-PRO program against King, but though they had expanded their efforts in general to include surveillance of antiwar student groups, they did not view King as a threat in that way.[57] [58]

Neither the army domestic intelligence program nor the FBI's COIN-TELPRO program focused exclusively on antiwar activists; however, the CHAOS (MH/CHAOS) program of the CIA did. President Johnson initiated the program following representations to him by southern congressmen. Those individuals made the case that foreign, communist agents were infiltrating and training members of the antiwar movement (supposedly students were traveling overseas for training in revolutionary tactics) That story seems to have been a reincarnation of an effort conducted by various integration opponents, which had originally portrayed the civil rights movement being covertly organized and incited by communist agents.[59] Unfortunately, President Johnson was under such pressure over the Vietnam War that he accepted the proposition and ordered the CIA to conduct both overseas and domestic intelligence work with the goal of proving communist manipulation of the antiwar effort. Operation CHAOS, which began in 1967, first used overseas CIA assets to monitor the activities and contacts of U.S. citizens traveling abroad. Some sixty CIA officers eventually conducted both physical surveillance and electronic eavesdropping.

But CHAOS quickly expanded, and under both the Johnson and Nixon administrations, its activities included a variety of CIA programs. The CIA's HTLINGUAL mail-intercept program was used to open letters and packages of both individuals and groups placed on a special watch list. Agents posing as student dissidents infiltrated both foreign and domestic targets. Under project MERRIMAC, agents were placed within domestic antiwar and radical organizations, while in project RESISTANCE, college administrators, campus security, and local police identified antiwar activists and student militants—without the need for actual infiltration.[60] In the end, CHAOS was shown to have broadly expanded its targeting, extending to include organizations ranging from the Students for a Democratic Society to the Women's Strike for Peace, the Black Panther Party, Cross World Books, and Grove Press.[61]

But with all the details that eventually did emerge on CHAOS, there is no sign that the CIA or the national security community in general (beyond the efforts of Director Hoover of the FBI) considered Dr. King or the SCLC as a major subversive antiwar threat, or that they targeted King or the SCLC in their intelligence collection or disruption campaigns as they did the broad range of antiwar elements. The American government was indeed paranoid about even the most peaceful opposition to the war, but by 1968 Dr. King's opposition had become only one voice in the growing tidal wave against the war.

However, Dr. King's newest focus, the Poor People's Campaign and its march on Washington, was another story entirely.

THE FBI'S CAMPAIGN AGAINST DR. KING

One man and one agency of the U.S. government were most definitely still targeting Dr. King in 1968: J. Edgar Hoover and the FBI. Readers who wish to fully understand the details of FBI Director Hoover's personal "war on King" should refer to the detailed history by David J. Garrow, *The FBI and Martin Luther King, Jr.,* and Professor Gerald D. McKnight's *The Last Crusade,* and to the historical study available in the American RadioWorks' series on the FBI and Dr. King.[62] In reviewing the documents themselves, it is sometimes bizarrely fascinating to see how the bureau's own intelligence collection was frequently at odds with their analysis, internal discussions, and memoranda (which were clearly driven by Director Hoover's personal views). As early as 1963, the bureau's director of domestic intelligence prepared a seventy-page report for Hoover, showing in great detail that the civil rights movement was not communist controlled and not a subversive threat that should be targeted by the FBI. Hoover personally derided the report and its author. The FBI intelligence director quickly got the message that his career depended on a quick change of attitude, so he proposed exactly what Hoover wanted—an aggressive counterintelligence program targeting the SCLC and Dr. King, a program designed to "knock him off his pedestal" and destroy King's reputation.[63]

The core of Hoover's and the bureau's initial opinion of Dr. King as a domestic security threat was his longtime association with two close advisors, Stanley Levinson and Harry Wachtel, whom the bureau considered to have deep communist ties and felt to be manipulating Dr. King and the SCLC according to a communist agenda. One of the bureau's key assets (Jack Childs, a.k.a. "Solo") convinced the director that Levinson, who did have a record of Communist Party participation, had overtly left the party only to assume a covert role in manipulating the civil rights movement. Levinson, a New York City lawyer, was extremely active with the civil rights movement, had been introduced to Dr. King in 1956, and in 1958 became a close personal advisor to King and heavily involved in SCLC fund-raising.[64]

In January 1962, the FBI brought Levinson to the attention of Attorney General Robert Kennedy and raised the issue of communist influence on King. Kennedy had his administrative assistant pass a warning to King that certain of his associates were in question, but King responded that he had no reason to question the motives of his supporters. RFK escalated the matter, and the White House advisor on civil rights spoke directly to King, who responded that he had more reason to trust Levinson than he had to trust the FBI. With no resolution of the issue, RFK authorized wire taps on Levinson and King. Although the FBI surveillance never confirmed any communist ties, it did show the extent of Levinson's influence on King and helped to confirm Hoover's personal suspicions.[65] From that point on, Hoover began to spread the word that King was very possibly under communist influence, and King was added to the twelve thousand names in the FBI Reserve Index (individuals in a position to influence others against the national interest; these individuals were to be detained in the event of a national emergency). Levinson was carried at a higher threat level than King, being listed on the Security Index, which included members of the Communist Party and similar groups.[66] The Security Index (developed during the Roosevelt administration) was used for individuals who were considered to be active "dissidents"; of the fifteen thousand individuals on the Security Index, some fifteen hundred were African Americans.[67]

Although it was this purported tie to communist influence that allowed Hoover to make King a target of the COINTELPRO program, the depth of Hoover's obsession can be seen in move of the King files to the newer "Black Hate" segment of the program in the late 1960s.[68] Hoover was simply not going to give up his effort to "knock King off his pedestal."

Dr. King's position on the FBI Reserve Index ensured that the bureau's counterintelligence program would target him. That program had been initiated in 1956, focusing on the perceived subversive communist threat of the 1950s. During the early 1960s, Hoover had become convinced that the Communist Party was actively trying to infiltrate and manipulate the emerging civil rights movement. COINTELPRO expansions to cover black civil rights activities occurred in 1960 and 1963. By 1963, the FBI was monitoring not only Dr. King and his SCLC but also the Congress of Racial Equality, the NAACP, the Student Nonviolent Coordinating Committee, and a number of other civil rights groups.[69] During 1964, major escalation of southern racial violence and the Mississippi Burning murders led President Johnson to direct Hoover to expand the program further to include white hate groups such as the Klan. By 1968, in response to escalating race and antiwar rioting, the "New COINTELPRO" target list had virtually doubled in size, broadening to include militant antiwar student and Black Power groups and their leaders. By 1967 more than one thousand agents were involved in daily COINTELPRO activities. The goal of the program was ambitious: "to expose, disrupt, misdirect, discredit, or otherwise neutralize" the targeted organizations. Specific organizations being targeted included the Congress on Racial Equality, the Student Nonviolent Coordinating Committee, the Deacons for Defense and Justice, the Nation of Islam, and the Southern Christian Leadership Conference.[70]

As documented by the "Church Committee" (the U.S. Senate Select Committee to Study Governmental Operations with Respect to Intelligence Activities), COINTELPRO tactics included burglaries, illegal opening and photographing of first-class mail, planting of forged documents to make it appear as if individuals were government informants, anonymous letters to spouses designed to break up marriages, and communications to employers intended to get those individuals fired. The FBI planted news articles and editorials in magazines and newspapers, as well as anonymous letters containing false statements designed to encourage violence between street gangs and the Black Panthers. FBI infiltrators also encouraged violent acts by the groups that they had penetrated, in order to discredit those groups. These revelations made for shocking news in the 1970s. At the time, few understood that these were the same FBI tactics that had been in use since at least 1956!

Although only one of a great many individuals the FBI perceived as a threat, Dr. King received special attention due to Director Hoover's personal animosity for him. That special attention came about as a result of Dr. King's remarks to the media about the lack of FBI intervention in a great many of the violent civil rights demonstrations in the early 1960s. Given Hoover's documented response to any criticism of the bureau, it was inevitable that he would take such comments personally and would use the bureau's resources to discredit King. When FBI surveillance and wiretaps produced no subversive data on Dr. King, it did provide certain material that allowed Hoover to wage a "morals" campaign against King during 1963 and 1964, ending with the notorious letter (and tapes) mailed to King's home and opened by his wife.[71] [72]

Unfortunately we now know that Dr. King was far from being the only victim of such dirty tricks, and he was very likely far from being the last. In fact the record now shows that many of the same tactics were enhanced and widely deployed against both Black Power and antiwar groups from 1967 through 1969. Similar tactics would be used against individuals the COIN-TELPRO targeted until it began to be exposed in 1971.

But by 1968, Hoover's personal vendetta against King had been under-way for some six years, and his constant efforts were beginning to wear on many, both in government and in the media.[73]

Hoover had acted in such an obvious and obsessive fashion that every-one from Attorney General Clark to the national media were beginning to complain about it. Years of feeding exposé material to media outlets had net-ted Hoover no press traction against Dr. King, and that failure most likely resulted in the last-ditch effort of the letter and tapes.

In early 1968, a *Washington Post* story on Hoover alluded to the FBI's efforts to distribute damaging information and to influence press coverage of Dr. King.[74] On January 2, Attorney General Clark denied a new FBI request to gain information on the Poor People's March by setting up wiretaps on the Atlanta SCLC office. On April 2, Hoover again approached Clark about a wiretap, using the violence in Memphis as justification. Clark again turned him down.

Still, Hoover continued his ongoing smear campaign, and the announce-ment of the Poor People's Campaign gave him the grounds to continue it. In February 1968, he circulated a massive backgrounder on King, detailing communist influence and sexual misconduct, including the possibility of King having a mistress. When that produced no response, the FBI generated yet another twenty-one-page report on March 21 and sent it to the president, the attorney general, the CIA, and a host of other government and military offices. At the time of Dr. King's murder, J. Edgar Hoover remained obsessed with Dr. King, but there is little evidence that as of spring 1968 his vendetta was carrying any weight outside his own bureau.[75] That is not to say that many in the government were not very much afraid of black militancy; the riots of 1967 had brought that fear home with a vengeance. But Dr. King was neither the primary figure nor the primary fear of those groups.

By 1968, King had lost his place in Gallup Poll's ten most admired and influential people in America. His position on Vietnam, as well as his sometimes radical stance on poverty (he favored a 300 percent increase in social welfare spending), had alienated him from many once-sympathetic whites, and he was also losing sway with many blacks. The FBI wiretaps and surveillance on his advisors, in particular Levinson, reveal the negative impact of his antiwar position on fund-raising for the SCLC.[76] After 1965, the civil rights movement had splintered between those who favored King's nonviolent civil disobedience and those who favored more militant, even nationalistic aims. A comparison between the frequency of references to King and to the Black Power movement in major articles illustrates this point well. In 1965, when the term "Black Power" first entered the national consciousness, references to King outnumbered references to the phrase by almost 30 to 1; by 1966 that ratio was almost 1.5 to 1. In 1967 and in the first three months of 1968, references to Black Power exceeded references to King by almost 50 percent.[77]

It also has to be repeated that the FBI initiated a "new" and expanded COINTELPRO program in August 1967. President Johnson ordered it following the summer race riots beginning in Detroit and spreading to some sixty-seven cities, in which thirty-two people were killed and some $100 million in damages were sustained. The new COINTELPRO effort was specifically directed toward neutralizing violent black activists. The individuals listed for special attention included H. Rap Brown, Stokley Carmichael, Elijah Muhammad, and Maxwell Stanford.

In the highly recommended book, *Spying on America*, author James Davis interviewed FBI Section Chief George C. Moore. Moore stated that the SCLC really had not fit the new list or the FBI priorities (other than Hoover's), and that the SCLC had been previously investigated for possible communist influence but was not known for "violent propensities," as were the rest of the organizations and individuals. Without commenting on the infamous Hoover campaign on Dr. King, Moore could only offer the comment that it must have had something to do with Dr. King being associated with the SCLC.[78]

It seems clear that the American government did understand the difference between Dr. King and the rising violent black militants of 1969. Even the FBI records illustrate that understanding. That leads us to the one final point that has been presented in support of a government conspiracy to kill Dr. King.

WAS KING ELIMINATED TO PREVENT VIOLENCE?

Dr. King had never been associated with violence. If anything, his lack of militancy had cost him influence with the more militant factions in the movement. In fact, Dr. King was in Memphis the day he was shot because he was trying to demonstrate that nonviolent protest was still an effective formula.

Unfortunately, racial violence was on the upswing, regardless of the successes of civil rights legislation. Dr. King remained one of the strongest forces for peaceful protest, and he provided a strong contrast to increasingly violent antiwar clashes and to black militants such as Stokely Carmichael. In groups ranging from SNCC to the Black Panthers, black militants were claiming that the previous riot in Memphis had proved that the days of nonviolence were over. Dr. King himself had been forced to admit that "nonviolence is a concept now on trial."[79] Surely killing King would only serve to raise the influence of openly militant figures and usher in a time of national violence. The FBI assembled a fifty-man task force focused strictly on Carmichael (to develop criminal charges for incitement to riot), but only after Dr. King's death and the resulting national violence. Any objective analysis would have led to the conclusion that the assassination of Dr. King would produce widespread civil disorder, not prevent it.

Newly released documents and analyses by historians such as Professor Gerald McKnight reveal that the government was well aware of the distinctions between King's pacifist movement and the militant movements such as the Black Panthers. McKnight established that the government prepared a "Rabble Rousers Index" in fear of what they were certain was a small conspiracy in black circles to incite riots.[80] These documents show that what the government feared most was a series of nationwide riots of the kind seen in Watts in 1965 and Newark in 1967 (exactly what followed Dr. King's murder). There was a massive covert effort underway to preempt confrontations that could trigger nationwide violence. By 1967 some fifteen hundred plainclothes military personnel were conducting undercover counterintelligence and surveillance across the country.[81] We see an example of that in the Memphis sanitation strike that attracted King's attention.

Initiated under the military's OPLAN 100 68, a unique domestic plan born out of the late-'60s urban riots and rising black militancy, the Memphis joint-operation military intelligence effort (Lantern Spike) involved a variety of military personnel, the FBI, and the Memphis Police Department. Surveillance was in place on individuals and at meetings even as King arrived on March 28, 1968. Lantern Spike's reports conform to conventional interpretations of the sanitation strike and point out that King-led protests on March 28 and March 29 became violent when agitators began breaking windows and the police clamped down, killing sixteen-year-old marcher Larry Payne and eliciting even greater violence. But the documents also draw distinctions between the militant groups (such as the Invaders) who incited the original violence and the "mature" groups, such as the SCLC, who tamed that violence by April 1. The document also describes the internal dissent within King's movement between those who favored more radical action and those who were still wedded to King's vision of civil disobedience. While the "militant" label had been misapplied in some cases, including to King aide James Bevel, it was never used to describe King himself.[82]

In that sense, the documents illustrate the concern that a handful of black militants could incite widespread violence under the right circumstances. Even the FBI had begun to separate the wheat from the chaff by using a photographic index, created from its computerized Rabble Rouser Index, to identify potential agitators. Using this index, the FBI had cleared Dr. King's Poor People's March organizing committee of any infiltration by the Black Power movement.[83]

From a totally pragmatic viewpoint, while Hoover and southern senators fanned the flames in regard to the Poor People's March, claiming it would bring riots and looting to Washington, the FBI had actively engaged in an illegal and covert, but highly effective, campaign against the march itself. Gerald McKnight details that effort, beginning with an FBI strategy conference in early March 1968 with the sole focus of sabotaging the Poor People's Campaign. As McKnight describes it, the bureau's campaign against the Poor People's Campaign's march was virtually on a "war footing" with extensive rumor and reprisal stories circulated through field offices in every area where the Poor People's Campaign was recruiting participants. The stories ranged from the rumor that gullible participants would be left in DC, stranded, broke, and sick, to the threat that every person involved would lose any government benefits they might be currently receiving.

The bureau even worked with its own paid speakers, as well as with members of the John Birch Society, to place countermarch speakers in areas the SCLC had targeted for recruiting.[84] And the FBI campaign was working. It had taken its toll. And by the end of March 1968, Dr. King was troubled because recruiting was far slower than anticipated and donations had fallen off significantly. The SCLC was facing a serious financial shortfall, and whether or not it would be able to support the march on Washington was becoming a serious question.

What changed the momentum of the movement was Dr. King's murder itself. A dramatic groundswell of donations and volunteers from across the country poured into the effort in response to the assassination.[85] One could claim that this is 20/20 hindsight, save for one fact. Director Hoover immediately realized the consequences of Dr. King's murder, and he expanded the responsibility for the Poor People's Campaign subversion to every single FBI field office, declaring it as one of the principal tasks of the bureau.[86] How could Hoover realize the implications so quickly, but the "power elite" that killed King to prevent that very campaign be so ignorant?

The supposed "power elite," whom critics claim manipulated the machinery of government to murder King while escaping any and all punishment, not only missed the obvious implication for the march on Washington but also could not even stop the Poor People's Campaign. In fact, the march did continue, with stronger support and numbers, under the leadership of the Reverend Ralph Abernathy. In this way, the power elite missed the mark once again, as the files show that Abernathy was viewed, even before the assassination, as more aggressive and more militant than his friend Dr. King.

To believe that the national security apparatus of the United States killed Dr. King is, by deduction, to acknowledge its complete failure in achieving its goals and anticipating the outcomes. It would have completely misread the direction of the civil rights movement, the declining influence that Dr. King had on it, the preassassination strength of the Poor People's Campaign, and the implications his death would have on the supposed goal of preventing urban riots. It would have ignored the information in its very own files that suggested that assassinating King was exactly the wrong thing to do if the goal was preserving domestic civil order. Instead, the assassination of King reinvigorated the Poor People's Campaign, ignited the largest wave of domestic rioting in history, and eliminated the most potent (if less influential) voice against racial violence of any kind. It was the exact opposite of what those in power wanted, but it was exactly what white supremacists like Sam Bowers were hoping for.

SUMMARY

Although we find ample evidence for conspiracy in Dr. King's murder, and ample reason to question the legal process (including the evidence introduced against James Earl Ray), we feel that the majority of open questions suggesting a government-sponsored conspiracy have been addressed and dismissed by research and documents released during the past decades.

Unfortunately, the ongoing focus on a government conspiracy has diverted popular attention and official efforts away from the years of previous attempts by right-wing extremists to kill Dr. King and the leads suggesting a militant racist conspiracy. We urge future historians of the period to provide a more thorough treatment of this sinister side of the 1960s opposition to the civil rights movement. Our hope is that the Justice Department will recognize that there is a significant case for such a conspiracy, and that following such leads could take us down the road to a much more meaningful understanding of Dr. King's murder.

APPENDIX C

PHOTOGRAPHS, KEY PEOPLE AND GROUPS, AND TIMELINE

PHOTOGRAPHS

The Reverend Wesley Albert Swift, from California. Once an active leader in a KKK group, Swift formed the Church of Jesus Christ—Christian in 1946. Under his interpretation of the Christian scripture, Armageddon would come from a race war that would "cleanse" the world of Jews and other minorities. Tapes of Swift's sermons were sent across North America through a mailing list and his message was amplified through a network of traveling ministers. Source: FBI Field Office.

Samuel Holloway Bowers, Jr. The Imperial Wizard of the White Knights of the Ku Klux Klan of Mississippi. Bowers was heavily influenced by the racist message of Wesley Swift. Under his leadership, the White Knights were the most violent Klan group in America in the 1960s according to the FBI. Source: The Mississippi Department of Archives and History.

Sidney Crockett Barnes. An extremist who left Florida for Alabama in the 1960s, Barnes was one of Wesley Swift's most devoted followers. He helped spread the Christian Identity message and the vision of an end-times race war to a number of individuals in the southeast, including to a young Tommy Tarrants, who become a terrorist for Sam Bowers. Files show that Barnes plotted to kill Martin Luther King in 1963 and 1964. Source: Jackson Field Office.

J.B. Stoner, a leader and co-founder for the racist National States Rights Party. Stoner would run on the NSRP ticket as their Vice Presidential candidate in 1964. Alongside Connie Lynch, a minister for Wesley Swift, Stoner inflamed audiences across the country with his message of white supremacy. He was one of James Earl Ray's attorneys.

Thomas Albert Tarrants III, aka Tommy Tarrants, in a mug shot taken after his arrest, in 1967, for possession of an illegal firearm. Tarrants was arrested with Sam Bowers after their vehicle was pulled over for reckless driving in Mississippi. Responsible for several acts of violence in Mississippi, Tarrants was not connected to these crimes until May of 1968. Yet he was inexplicably investigated in connection with the King murder within days of the act. Tarrants rejected the Swift message in favor of traditional Christianity in the 1970s and is now an evangelical minister. Source: Jackson Field Office.

DONALD EUGENE SPARKS

Donald Sparks's 1967 FBI Most Wanted Photo. Sparks was a home burglar and a contract killer in a criminal network that would later be popularized as "The Dixie Mafia." FBI records indicate that Sparks was approached with a bounty contract on Martin Luther King, Jr.'s life in 1964 by the White Knights of the Ku Klux Klan of Mississippi. A member of Sparks's criminal gang would later be connected with a bounty offer, from the same Klan, in 1967. Source: FBI.

Above: Bessie Brewer's rooming house the day after King's murder. It shows extensive brush still present, contradicting the claims by some that the area was cleared immediately after King's murder. Some argue that an assassin may have fired from within the brush rather than from the building itself; others assert that the brush was too thick and thus not an ideal shooting location. Source: Shelby County Registry of Deeds.

Above: The picture shows the rear side of Bessie Brewer's rooming house and, specially, Canipe's Amusement Company. The accused assassin, James Earl Ray, allegedly dropped a bundle of incriminating items, including the murder weapon, in the alcove outside Canipe's. Some argue he was afraid he would confront police officers with the material in hand. Source: Shelby County Registry of Deeds.

Above: The rear of Bessie Brewer's rooming House, the side facing the Lorraine Motel, where Martin Luther King, Jr. was staying. Accused assassin James Earl Ray allegedly fired the shot that killed King from the second floor. Source: Shelby County Registry of Deeds.

Above: The bathroom on the second floor of Bessie Brewer's rooming house. This is where law enforcement and prosecutors believe accused assassin James Earl Ray fired the shot that killed King. Source: Shelby County Registry of Deeds.

Above: The view of the Lorraine Motel from the opening in the second floor bathroom window at the rear of Bessie Brewer's rooming house. A shooter would have had a clear view of King from this vantage point. The markings, indicate the location of King's body (C) and his room (B). Source: Shelby County Registry of Deeds.

Above: View of the rear of Bessie Brewer's rooming house from the second floor of the Lorraine Motel across the street. Source: Shelby County Registry of Deeds.

Above: The green blanket that contained several key pieces of allegedly incriminating evidence, including a rifle and binoculars, found at the alcove in front of Canipe's Amusement Company. The material in this bundle would, over time, lead the FBI to James Earl Ray. Ray would claim that someone else planted the material to frame him. Source: Shelby County Registry of Deeds.

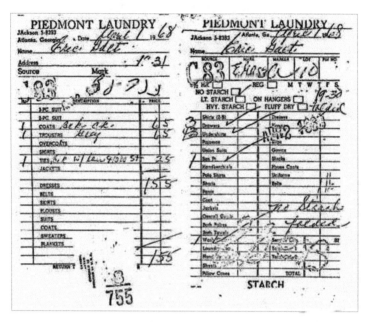

Above: A laundry receipt from the Piedmont Laundry in Atlanta, Georgia, for Eric Galt, James Earl Ray's alias, dated April 1, 1968. This receipt, as well the confirmation from the laundry's owner, presented a dilemma for James Earl Ray and his attorneys. Hoping to avoid the incrimination charge that Ray was stalking King prior to the Memphis murder, Ray asserted that he went to Memphis before King even decided on a return date to lead another sanitation workers' strike. This receipt was strong evidence that Ray first went to Atlanta, King's hometown, and only went to Memphis after King announced his plans. Source: House Select Commitee.

Above: The contents, sans rifle, found wrapped in a green bundle outside of Canipe's Amusement Company. Through diligent work, the FBI was able to trace several of these items to accused assassin James Earl Ray. Source: National Archives.

The Remington Gamemaster 30.06 rifle found in the bundle outside Canipe's restaurant. Authorities claim this was the murder weapon, but ballistics tests were inclusive. The rifle was traced to a gun shop in Birmingham, Alabama, and eventually to James Earl Ray. Ray bought a different weapon the day before but returned that gun for the Gamemaster. The store owner remembered Ray as claiming that he exchanged weapons on the advice of his brother-in-law. Ray claims this was a false reference to Raoul. Source: National Archives.

James Earl Ray's wanted photo, issued by the FBI in their massive manhunt for the alleged King assassin. It was only by the third week of April 1968 that the FBI finally connected Ray to the numerous aliases he used in Memphis and elsewhere. Source: Shelby County of Deeds.

Both of these pictures were separately identified by James Earl Ray as being (or bearing a striking resemblance to) the mysterious figure Raoul, the man who Ray claims manipulated his movements and eventually helped frame him for killing King. The photo on the left is of an individual photographed in Dealey Plaza after President John F. Kennedy's assassination; Ray said this person bore a "striking resemblance" to Raoul. The photo on the right is a passport picture of an individual identified by Ray's last attorney, William Pepper, as being Raoul; Ray positively identified this person as Raoul. The Justice Department, in their 2000 investigation, checked this individual's whereabouts on the day of the King murder and determined he had a firm alibi. In either event, the reader is left to judge for himself if Ray's near-definitive identifications of both pictures as Raoul are mutually exclusive; e.g. if the two pictures could possibly be identified as the same person by Ray. Source: Justice Department.

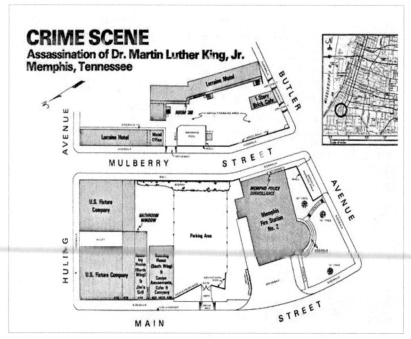

Above: A schematic layout of the crime scene. Source: National Archives.

PEOPLE

Dr. Wesley Swift: A militant extremist and Klan organizer who formed the Church of Jesus Christ Christian in 1946 in Lancaster, California, where he lived, Swift advocated a variation on Christianity that held that Jews were really the offspring of Satan, and that they manipulated other, non-white minorities, into a conspiracy against white Christians. Swift believed the world would be purified of Jews and minorities through a race war. His sermons on these matters, distributed through a network of newsletters and tape recordings, inspired militant white supremacists across the country, including Sam Bowers, J. B. Stoner, Sidney Barnes, Colonel William Potter Gale, and others.

Samuel Holloway Bowers: Bowers was the Imperial Wizard, or leader, of the White Knights of the Ku Klux Klan of Mississippi (WKKKK) in the 1960s. Under Bowers's leadership, the WKKKK became, according to the FBI, the most violent Klan group in America. A devoted follower of Wesley Swift, Bowers was personally responsible for plotting the murders of the three civil rights workers in the Mississippi Burning case, and for ordering the firebombing of the home of voting rights activist Vernon Dahmer in 1966, that resulted in Dahmer's death. He also plotted the murder of farmer Ben Chester White in hopes of luring Martin Luther King Jr. into an ambush if King came to protest the White killing. He was investigated by Congress as a potential suspect in King's murder, but investigators never interviewed him. Bowers was convicted for his role in the Mississippi Burning murders in 1967 and sentenced to ten years in prison; he was not convicted for the Dahmer murder until 1998, when he was sentenced to life in prison. He died in prison in 2006.

Jesse Benjamin "J. B." Stoner: A Nazi aficionado, J. B. Stoner was one of the most active and outspoken white supremacists in America from the 1950s on through the 1970s. Stoner was the legal counsel for the supremacist group the National States' Rights Party and one of its leading voices, running for office under its banner on a number of occasions. With his close associate Conrad "Connie" Lynch, a minister in Wesley Swift's church, Stoner led counter-rallies against King's marches and other similar protests. He was suspected of plotting numerous bombings across the Southeast against black and Jewish targets. He offered a contract on Martin Luther King Jr.'s life in 1958, and was investigated by Congress in the 1970s as a possible suspect in King's murder. He was protected by attorney-client privilege, however, as he was one of convicted assassin James Earl Ray's attorneys in 1968–69. Stoner also had connections to James Venable and Joseph Milteer; some of the leading members of the White Knights of the Ku Klux Klan of Mississippi actively supported Stoner. Stoner was speaking to a several White Knights on the evening of April 4, 1968, when MLK was killed.

James Venable: The longtime leader of the National Knights of the Ku Klux Klan (NKKKK), the second-largest KKK group in America in the 1960s, headquartered in Stone Mountain, Georgia, with subordinate groups across the country as far as California. Venable shared a law office with J. B. Stoner in Atlanta, Georgia. Venable was suspected of plotting to kill Martin Luther King Jr., with Stoner, in 1965. Venable also knew Joseph Milteer and employed Floyd "Buddy" Ayers.

Floyd "Buddy" Ayers: An associate of James Venable, Ayers was, according to one witness, the "bagman" for the King murder, supplying money from Atlanta to Mississippi in connection with a bounty offer on Dr. King. Ayers gained national attention when he infiltrated MLK's funeral in 1968, and then later allegedly tried to kidnap MLK's father.

Joseph Milteer: A rabid white supremacist, Joseph Milteer was an active supporter of the National States' Rights Party, a devoted follower of Wesley Swift, and the founder of his own, independent (racist) political group, the Constitution Party. Independently wealthy, Milteer traveled the country as a salesman, often meeting with other white supremacists, such as James Venable. Milteer is famous for having been secretly caught on tape, two weeks before the assassination of President John F. Kennedy, predicting JFK's assassination with a high-powered rifle from a high-story building. On that same tape, he said that others were plotting to kill MLK. Milteer was in Atlanta, Georgia, when James Earl Ray fled to that city after the murder of Martin Luther King Jr. A confidential source of researcher Lamai Waldron says that Milteer secretly raised the money to kill King in 1968.

Colonel William Potter Gale: Gale was a chief aide to General Douglas MacArthur before returning to the United States and becoming one of the leading white supremacists in the country. He was a minister in the Church of Jesus Christ Christian and formed his own paramilitary group, the California Rangers. In the 1970s, Gale was investigated by Congress as a suspect in the King murder. Congress specifically connected Gale to a King murder plot involving Admiral John Crommelin, Noah Jefferson Carden, and Sidney Crockett Barnes.

Admiral John Crommelin: A WWII naval hero before entering civilian life and becoming one of the major voices of white supremacy in the nation, he was a leading member of the National States' Rights Party and ran on the party's ticket for vice president of the United States of America in 1960. He was also a devoted follower of Wesley Swift. He helped indoctrinate Thomas Tarrants into Swift's worldview. He was also investigated by Congress as a suspect in the King assassination in the late 1970s; he cooperated but denied he had any involvement.

Noah Jefferson Carden: A member of the White Citizens' Council of Mobile, Alabama, a group that led "formal" opposition to the civil rights movement in that city. He was close to Sidney Barnes and also knew Thomas Tarrants. He was investigated by Congress as a suspect in the King assassination.

Sidney Crockett Barnes: A white supremacist from Florida who was forced to flee to Mobile, Alabama, in the early 1960s because he was "too hot" for authorities, Barnes would later become a minister in Wesley Swift's church. He played tapes of Swift for anyone who would listen, and helped indoctrinate many into Swift's cause, including a young Thomas Albert Tarrants III and Kathy Ainsworth. Swift was investigated by Congress as a suspect in the King assassination in the late 1970s (see above). He openly refused to cooperate with the investigation. In 1968, he moved to Jackson, Mississippi, where he was closely associated with a number of men in the White Knights of the Ku Klux Klan of Mississippi, including Danny Joe Hawkins.

Danny Joe Hawkins: A militant member of the White Knights of Mississippi, Hawkins's entire family, especially his father, Joe Denver Hawkins, were known for their extreme hatred of blacks and Jews. Hawkins, along with Tommy Tarrants and Kathy Ainsworth, participated in a series of bombings from 1967 to 1968. On April 4, 1968, the day MLK died, Hawkins was arrested going the wrong way on a one-way street after attending J. B. Stoner's rally in the WKKKK stronghold of Meridian, Mississippi.

Kathy Ainsworth: A young Mississippi schoolteacher who led a double life as one of the chief terrorists of the WKKKK in 1967–68, Ainsworth was raised by her white supremacist mother, Margaret Capomacchia, to hate Jews and blacks, She was very close to Sidney Crockett Barnes, who gave her away at her wedding. Ainsworth joined Danny Joe Hawkins and Tommy Tarrants in a string of attacks against black and Jewish targets in 1967–1968. In one of those attacks, in Meridian, Mississippi, in June 1968, she replaced Danny Joe Hawkins as Tarrants's partner-in-crime, only to be shot and killed in a sting operation. Her mother would later relay supposed inside information to FBI informant Willie Somersett, information related to the King murder that implicated Tommy Tarrants.

Thomas Albert Tarrants III, a.k.a. "Tommy" or "The Man": Tarrants was the self-described chief terrorist for the White Knights of the Ku Klux Klan of Mississippi in 1967–1968. Only in his twenties at the time, Tarrants was already closely affiliated with a number of white supremacist leaders, notably John Crommelin and Sidney Barnes. Having engaged in "petty" acts of racism from his high school days in 1963–66, Tarrants moved to Laurel, Mississippi, in 1967 and convinced Sam Bowers to use him in violent bombing operations directed at black and Jewish targets. He joined forces with Kathy Ainsworth and Danny Joe Hawkins. His participation was unknown to the FBI until late May 1968. In the week prior to King's murder, Tarrants went "underground" to launch a guerilla campaign against the U.S. government. The reporter Jack Nelson includes references that suggest Tarrants may have been considering assassinating MLK, and he was a person-of-interest to the FBI in the immediate wake of King's murder. Tarrants was wounded in the June 1968 sting operation that killed Ainsworth. He was sentenced to thirty years in prison, but was released early after he made a conversion to mainstream Christianity. He is now an active evangelical minister who has renounced his past views and ways. He denies any involvement in the King murder, and the authors believe efforts were made to frame him for the crime.

Donald Eugene Sparks: A major criminal in the 1960s, he was known for burglaries but was also a contract killer. His exploits eventually earned him a place on the FBI's Ten Most Wanted List. He was part of a gang of traveling criminals known as the new James gang, after its informal leader, Jerry Ray James. The group was concentrated in Oklahoma and included his close associate Rubie Charles Jenkins, among others. Law enforcement would later consider the Jerry Ray James gang, and many others like it, as a major criminal threat, and label it the "Dixie Mafia," even though these groups lacked the organization of the Sicilian Mafia and were not all concentrated in the Southeast. The so-called "Dixie Mafia" may have, however, been responsible for more killings than other organized crime groups in the 1970s.

Separate reports say that Sparks was approached with an offer to kill Martin Luther King Jr. by the WKKKK in 1964.

LeRoy McManaman: Described by the FBI as a "big time criminal operator," McManaman was a career miscreant who was known for organizing a string of home burglaries in Kansas and for running an interstate car-theft ring with Rubie Charles Jenkins. Jenkins said that McManaman, who spent considerable time in Oklahoma, was a part of a gang with Jenkins and Sparks. McManaman is alleged to have approached a fellow, soon-to-be-released inmate, Donald Nissen, with a $100,000 bounty offer on MLK's life in 1967. Nissen reported that plot to the FBI, who superficially dismissed it.

GROUPS:

The Church of Jesus Christ Christian (CJCC): This is the ministry formed by Wesley Swift in 1946 that preached an extreme and violent form of Christian Identity beliefs. These included the ideas that Jews were the offspring of Satan and that other minorities were subhuman. A major tenet for the church was the idea that a race war would purify the world, especially of Jews. This ideology continues to have a powerful influence over white supremacists and racist groups to this day.

The White Knights of the Ku Klux Klan of Mississippi (WKKKK): The most violent Klan group in America, led by Samuel H. Bowers, its Imperial Wizard, the WKKKK was formed in December 1963 with members from the Original Knights of the Ku Klux Klan (out of Louisiana) and others in Mississippi. These men were disaffected with the lackluster response to integration in the South, and pushed for greater and bolder acts of violence. At its peak from 1964 to 1965, the White Knights membership may have had reached ten thousand, though by 1968 membership was less than a few hundred. The FBI credits the group with over three hundred separate acts of violence; most notably, the White Knights are credited with killing three civil rights workers in Neshoba County, Mississippi (the Mississippi Burning murders); killing voting rights activist Vernon Dahmer in 1966; and a wave of bombings against black and Jewish targets from the fall of 1967 on through the summer of 1968. Its most notable members, beyond Bowers, included Danny Joe and Joe Denver Hawkins, Burris Dunn, Julius Harper, Alton Wayne and Raymond Roberts, Byron de la Beckwith, Deavours Nix, and L. E. Matthews. Kathy Ainsworth and Thomas Tarrants may have been "informal" members of the group, as some documents describe them as members of the "Swift Underground" who performed terrorist acts on behalf of the WKKKK.

The National States' Rights Party (NSRP): The NSPR was the overt, political face of white supremacy in the 1960s, even as it covertly recruited and inspired groups and individuals to perform acts of extreme violence. Formed by J. B. Stoner and Edward Fields in 1958, the group ran candidates for office, including vicepresident of the United States, although they never received even a small fraction of the national vote. On the other hand, the NSRP was actively involved in some of the most violent acts of resistance to integration in America, acts so extreme that they even offended local Klan groups, such as the United Klans of America in Alabama. The NSRP had its headquarters in Atlanta, Georgia, and then in Birmingham, Alabama, and it focused its activities in the Southeast. Its major publication, *The Thunderbolt*, was a major source of information for racists across the nation.

The National Knights of the Ku Klux Klan (NKKKK): This was, in the 1960s, the second-largest Klan organization in the United States, after the United Klans of America (UKA), in terms of membership. Headquartered in Stone Mountain, Georgia, the NKKKKwas led by Imperial Wizard James Venable. The NKKKK had affiliated groups and Klaverns across the country, including in Ohio and California. Notably, the California Knights of the Ku Klux Klan (CKKKK), formed in 1966 and led by Wesley Swift minister William V. Fowler, were an offshoot of the NKKKK. James Venable spoke to the CKKKK on several occasions in 1967.

The "traveling criminals" or "cross roaders" or "Dixie Mafia": These were loosely knit groups of outlaws willing to commit crimes, especially robbery and theft, across long distances. More of a phenomenon than an official organization, career criminals would join forces in decentralized gangs and work across state lines for major "jobs." Primarily engaged in bootlegging across state lines as some states remained "dry" after Prohibition was repealed in 1934, these criminals expanded their activities in the late 1950s and through the 1960s. This became more and more common as increasingly available phone communication and interstate travel, by plane or over the new interstate highway system, made cross-state activity more possible. The "traveling criminals" were especially active in two regions: the Southeast (stretching from the Mississippi Delta to Florida) and the Great Plains. Not to be confused with the Sicilian Mafia, these criminals lacked a hierarchy and were far less structured than conventional, organized crime syndicates. They were often, at the same time, more bold than the Sicilian Mafia, targeting even law enforcement officials (famously Sheriff Buford Pusser in Tennessee) and federal judges. By the 1970s, this loose-knit coalition was one of the major forces for criminal activity in the United States, with some crediting its members as having committed more actual killings than the Sicilian Mafia. In the late '60s and early '70s, in response to this growing criminal gang, law enforcement began using the shorthand "Dixie Mafia," even though both terms are misnomers.

White Citizens' Councils: These groups were formed, major city by major city, in the 1950s after the *Brown v. Board of Education* decision by the U.S. Supreme Court set the stage for ending segregation; their goal was to "formally" undermine integration. Often comprised of prominent business and civic leaders, they used their influence and resources to outwardly oppose the civil rights movement in a more "respectable" and legal way than that of the Ku Klux Klan. However, many White Citizens' Council members were directly and indirectly tied to more violent groups, such as the NSRP and the KKK, even if those connections were often informal and covert. Joseph Milteer claimed to be an "informal" member of the Atlanta White Citizens' Council, and Noah Jefferson Carden was a member of the Mobile White Citizens' Council. Both men were connected with purported plots to kill Martin Luther King Jr.

Americans for the Preservation of the White Race (APWR): Formed in the mid-1960s in Mississippi, this group was similar to the White Citizens' Councils, in providing an outwardly "civil" response when undermining integration efforts. The group would, for instance, raise money for the defense funds for racists accused of hate crimes or publish newsletters opposing the integration of schools. However, the FBI recognized the APWR as a front for the WKKKK, and its most prominent members and leaders were almost all, to a person, followers of Sam Bowers.

TIMELINE

1946:   The Church of Jesus Christ Christian is founded by former
               Klan organizer Reverend Wesley Swift in Lancaster, Cali-
               fornia.

1957–58:   Wave of bombings of Jewish synagogues across the South-
               east; J. B. Stoner is suspected of planning the bombings, but
               he is never convicted for them.

1958:   The National States' Rights Party (NSRP) is formed in
               Tennessee; J. B. Stoner is its legal counsel. In Alabama,
               Stoner offers to plot the murder of several civil rights lead-
               ers, including MLK, for money.

September   Riots at the University of Mississippi over the admission of
1962:   its first black student, James Meredith, galvanize militant
               white supremacists across America.

May 1963:   King's room at the Gaston Motel in Birmingham is de-
               stroyed by a bomb; almost simultaneously, the home of
               King's King's brother, A. D. King, is destroyed by a bomb.

June 1963:   Assassination of Mississippi NAACP activist Medgar
               Evers by white supremacist Byron de la Beckwith; riots in
               Jackson, Mississippi, erupt following Evers's funeral.

September   Former Admiral John Crommelin, Noah Carden, Sidney
1963:   Crockett Barnes, and former Colonel William Potter Gale,
               all Swift followers, reportedly plot a MLK assassination in
               Birmingham, Alabama. Bombing of the Sixteenth Street
               Baptist Church in Birmingham, Alabama, by Klansmen
               kills four young girls; riots follow.

December
1963:

The White Knights of the Ku Klux Klan of Mississippi (WKKKK) is formed by disaffected Klan members in Louisiana and Mississippi; Sam Bowers is named their Imperial Wizard (leader).

1964:

Reports say Carden, Crommelin, and Barnes continue to plot the murder of MLK. Reports say the WKKKK is pursuing a contract-for-hire murder plot against King involving a criminal killer.

May 1964:

In St. Augustine, Florida, the cottage where King was supposed to have been staying is the target of a machine-gun attack.

July 1964:

The first of several major urban race riots breaks out in New York City. Sam Bowers inspires the murder of three civil rights activists in Neshoba County, Mississippi, in what will be known as the Mississippi Burning killings.

1965:

The FBI receives informant reports that J. B. Stoner and National Knights of the Ku Klux Klan (NKKKK) Imperial Wizard James Venable are plotting to murder MLK. Informant Delmar Dennis informs the FBI of a WKKKK plot to assassinate King in Selma, Alabama.

February
1965:

Swift follower Keith Gilbert plots to kill MLK in Los Angeles.

June 1965:

NKKKK-connected racist Daniel Wagner says he was recruited into a failed plot to kill Martin Luther King, Jr. in Ohio.

August 1965:   Urban race riots in the Watts section of Los Angeles, California, receive national attention.

January 1966:   Voting rights activist Vernon Dahmer dies in Mississippi as a result of a firebombing/shooting attack plotted by the WKKKK and Sam Bowers.

June 1966:   On orders of Sam Bowers, innocent farmer Ben Chester White is killed in hopes of luring MLK into an ambush in Mississippi.

April 1967:   James Earl Ray escapes from the Missouri State Penitentiary in Jefferson City, Missouri.

May 1967:   Soon-to-be released inmate Donald James Nissen is approached by a fellow prisoner with a $100,000 bounty offer from the WKKKK on the life of MLK. James Earl Ray, now an escaped fugitive, visits St. Louis and finds work in Illinois.

June 1967:   Donald Nissen, released from Leavenworth Penitentiary, reveals the $100,000 plot to the FBI. Start of the "Long Hot Summer": urban race riots erupt across America including in Atlanta, Georgia; Boston, Massachusetts; and Tampa, Florida. James Earl Ray flees to Canada in hopes of eventually escaping North America. Nissen is asked by a Klan-connected acquaintance to deliver a package to Jackson, Mississippi; he later learns the package contained money for the King bounty.

July 1967:   Race riots continue across the country.

August 1967:   Failing to escape North America, James Earl Ray returns to the United States, specifically to Birmingham, Alabama. He assumes the false identity of Eric Starvo Galt and purchases a white Ford Mustang.

September 1967:   Despite an FBI crackdown on its operations, the WKKKK begins a months long wave of bombings against black and Jewish targets; the bombings are later attributed to Thomas Albert Tarrants, III.

October 1967:   James Earl Ray moves from Birmingham, Alabama, to Mexico. Sam Bowers and six others are convicted for their roles in the Mississippi Burning murders; Bowers is sentenced to ten years but is released on appeal bond.

November 1967:   James Earl Ray moves from Mexico to Los Angeles, California.

December 1967:   James Earl Ray takes a trip to New Orleans, Louisiana, after visiting the California headquarters of segregationist third-party candidate and former Alabama Governor George Wallace. Donald Nissen violates his parole and flees Atlanta, Georgia, after being threatened by a stranger for talking to authorities. Sam Bowers and Tom Tarrants are arrested in Mississippi for reckless driving; Bowers is acquitted and Tarrants avoids trial.

January 1968:   James Earl Ray moves to a "run-down" part of Los Angeles and stays in the St. Francis Motel.

February 1968:   James Earl Ray pursues the possibility of plastic surgery.

March 1968:   According to the St. Francis Motel manager, Alan Thompson, a mysterious visitor named "James C. Hardin," who earlier had called Ray, visits James Earl Ray. James Earl Ray files a change-of-address card indicating he will move to Atlanta, Georgia, MLK's hometown.

March 17, 1968:   Per reporter Jack Nelson, Tom Tarrants visits the Reverend Wesley Swift in California to get a rifle to kill MLK; Tarrants denies this in 2007.

March 18, 1968:   MLK speaks at a rally for the Memphis Sanitation Workers' Strike.

March 22, 1968:   James Earl Ray shows up in Selma, Alabama, the same day MLK has a speaking engagement. Thomas Albert Tarrants, III, the self-described chief terrorist for the WKKKK, jumps bond and goes "underground" to pursue a guerrilla war against the U.S. government.

March 24, 1968:   James Earl Ray arrives in Atlanta and rents a room in a rooming house in the Peach Tree section of the city.

March 28, 1968:   Ray visits Birmingham, Alabama, and purchases a rifle; on this same day, MLK arrives to lead the Memphis Sanitation Workers in a protest march; the march turns violent, and King returns to Atlanta.

March 29, 1968:   MLK announces he will return to Memphis the following week. Sam Bowers places a phone call to Birmingham, Alabama. In Birmingham, Ray purchases a .243 rifle.

March 30,
1968:

Ray exchanges the .243 for a better, more expensive gun, the Remington Gamemaster 30-06 at the supposed suggestion of his "brother-in-law."

April 1,
1968:

According to records and testimony, Ray returns to Atlanta, Georgia; Ray denies this.

April 2,
1968:

James Earl Ray drives to Memphis, Tennessee.

April 3,
1968:

King returns to Memphis to lead another protest march.

April 4,
1968:

At 6:01 pm, outside the Lorraine Motel in Memphis, Tennessee, a rifle bullet fatally wounds MLK.

ACKNOWLEDGMENTS

This book would not have been be possible without the generous contribution of time, insights, and critiques by a number of individuals. The authors would especially like to thank Jerry Mitchell, the Reverend Ed King, Dr. Gerry McKnight, Dan Christensen, David Boylan, Keith Beauchamp, and Dan Dunn, for their contributions and support of our efforts. We also offer our special thanks for support and encouragement to our family members Lawrence Wexler and Kathy Hancock and to our good friends Debra Conway and Sherry Feister.

The team at Counterpoint Publishing was of tremendous help to the authors. Kelly Winton and Laura Mazer were always available for advice and support. We'd especially like to thank Eric Brandt, who put forth enormous effort to help us through the developmental editing phase, and Charlie Winton, the CEO of Counterpoint, who sacrificed time from a very busy schedule to personally involve himself in the editing process.

We are also grateful to others who were very helpful to our research into the King murder and associated matters. We especially appreciate the comments and contributions of Joy Washburn, Jason Kull, Roanna Elliott, Pat Speer, William Kelley, Dr. Chester L. Quarles, Dr. John Drabble, Rex Bradford, Mark Zaid, Kel McClanahan, Lamar Waldron, Donald Tomasello, Scott Kercher, and Alan Kent.

In addition, a number of individuals provided important information to the authors via interviews. That list includes Janet Upshaw, retired Detective Fred Sanders, and several others who, due the sensitive nature of their comments, we will not identify. Special thanks goes to Donald Nissen, who, for fear for his life, stayed quiet for many years, but who—in the face of those same fears—finally confirmed his own experiences with a White Knight bounty offer on the life of Martin Luther King Jr.

We would also like to express our appreciation to several former FBI agents who were interviewed for this book. Whatever flaws plagued the original FBI investigation into Martin Luther King Jr.'s murder, those problems should be attributed to the bureau's institutional impediments, and to the man who put those structures in place, Director J. Edgar Hoover. Individual field agents commonly worked the case to the best of their ability, producing key investigative reports and data. We feel that their individual work was severely limited by organizational and reporting procedures as well as Director Hoover's own personal biases—including his extreme dislike of Dr. King. The former agents we'd most like to thank for their dialog with us are Stanley Orenstein and Gerard Robinson. The late Jim Ingram was also especially helpful in providing early insights to the authors, and he continued to encourage our research until he passed away.

Likewise, staff members at several institutions were most helpful to our work. We would like to thank the staff of the Civil Rights Museum in Memphis, of the National Archives and Records Administration at College Park, Maryland, of the Record Information and Dissemination Section of the FBI, and of the library research staff at the University of Michigan—especially Julie Herrada, for her relentless pursuit of material from the "Dixon Line."

NOTES

INTRODUCTION

1. Robert F. Kennedy, "Robert F. Kennedy on the Death of Martin Luther King" (speech), April 4, 1968, transcript and Windows Media Audio, Great Speeches Collection, The History Place, last modified July 2010, accessed October 25, 2011, http://www.historyplace.com/speeches/rfk-mlk.htm.

2. Charles Nicholas, "Ramsey Clark," Civil Rights Photos, *The Commercial Appeal*, accessed October 25, 2011, http://gallery.pictopia.com/memphiscom/gallery/6294/photo/8838612/?o=9.

3. Select Comm. on Assassinations, *Summary of Findings and Recommendations*, H.R. Rep., at 3 (1979), National Archives, accessed December 11, 2010, http://www.archives.gov/research/jfk/select-committee-report/summary.html.

CHAPTER I

1. Gerold Frank, *An American Death: The True Story of the Assassination of Dr. Martin Luther King, Jr., and the Greatest Manhunt of Our Time* (New York: Doubleday, 1972) 43 This particular threat was telephoned into American Airlines in Memphis. The FBI focused in on it, alerting Memphis Police, the Shelby County Sheriff, the Federal Aviation Administration, and the 111th Military Intelligence Group. It and other threats against King were kept in a separate headquarters file and not filed within the bureau's main Murder of King/MURKIN file.

2. Keith D. Miller, *Martin Luther King's Biblical Epic: His Final, Great Speech* (Jackson, MS: University Press of Mississippi, 2011). This book offers an extensive treatment of the context and content of King's last speech.

3. Ibid.

4. Martin Luther King Jr., "I've Been to the Mountaintop" (speech), Mason Temple, Memphis Tennessee, April 3, 1968. YouTube video, Adobe Flash audio, and transcript, 5:40, "Martin Luther King, Jr.," American Rhetoric, last modified August 20, 2011, accessed December 2, 2011. http://www.americanrhetoric.com/speeches/mlkivebeentothemountaintop.htm.

5. Philip H. Melanson, *The Martin Luther King Assassination: New Revelations on the Conspiracy and Cover-up* (New York: S.P.I. Books, 1994) 86–88.

6. Select Comm. on Assassinations, *Summary of Findings and Recommendations*, at 282–85 (1979), National Archives, accessed December 11, 2010, http://www.archives.gov/research/jfk/select-committee-report/part-2-king-findings.html#last.

7. Melanson, 86–88.

8. Select Comm. on Assassinations, *Summary of Findings and Recommendations*, H.R. Rep., section 6, Evidence of a Conspiracy in St. Louis, at 359–70 (1979), Mary Farrell Foundation, accessed December 11, 2010, http://www.maryferrell.org/mffweb/archive/viewer/showDoc. do?absPageId=69427.

9. Martin Luther King Jr., *Stride toward freedom: The Montgomery Story* (Boston: Beacon Press, 2010) 125–26. Unfortunately, the lack of serious police interest in investigating this bombing makes it almost impossible to include in any analysis of attempts on King's life. In fact, although the bomb did endanger King's family, it may have been more of an effort at intimidation than at extermination. King was at a regularly scheduled meeting at the time. The strong likelihood that the attack was a response to King's civil rights efforts means that, even if one considers this among the nine plots we analyze, it would not fundamentally change our conclusions.

10. Ibid., 124–25.

11. Seth Cagin and Philip Dray, *We Are Not Afraid: The Story of Goodman, Schwerner, and Chaney and the Civil Rights Campaign for Mississippi* (New York: Nation Books, 2006) 381–82; also Frank, 68; also Don Whitehead, *Attack on Terror: The FBI against the Ku Klux Klan* (New York: Funk & Wagnalls, 1970) 282; also Stephen B. Oates, *Let the Trumpet Sound: A Life of Martin Luther King, Jr.* (New York: HarperPerennial, 1994) 403–4. The sheriff was eventually acquitted of charges relating to the murders of the three young men; however, his deputy (Cecil Price) was convicted as an accessory to the crime. There is a real question as to when exactly this event took place. Notably, historian Stephen Oates supports our version of this account, but Cagin and Dray offer a different account; in *We Are Not Afraid* they write that King made his remarks while attending a commemoration of the Mississippi Burning murders in July 1965, and that the law enforcement officer in question was Deputy Cecil Price and not Sheriff Rainey. For the purpose of this book, when and where the event took place is largely irrelevant to the substance of our work.

12. Diane McWhorter, *Carry Me Home: Birmingham, Alabama; the Climactic Battle of the Civil Rights Revolution* (New York: Simon & Schuster, 2001) 114–15. Shuttlesworth organized Birmingham's first mass voting rights march of black veterans and moved on to push for integration of the city buses. That effort brought six sticks of dynamite to the wall outside his bedroom, blowing him and his mattress out of his church parsonage. The FBI would eventually determine that the key individual involved in the Shuttlesworth bombing was Robert Chambliss. Chambliss would later be connected to both the Sixteenth Street Baptist Church bombing in Birmingham and a bombing attack targeting Dr. King.

13. Ibid., 22. The primary motivation for the attack was legally mandated school integration in Alabama.

14. "White Christian Party Attacks Equality, Purity, Beauty and Religion of the Negroes," *Muhammad Speaks*, last modified September 15, 2010, accessed September 30, 2010, http://www. muhammadspeaks.com/Messenger-vs-KKK.html.

15. McWhorter, 132. The church was attacked with a timed bomb, one consisting of ten to twenty sticks of dynamite. That sort of bomb was clearly not just standard Klan intimidation and harassment but also an attack on a new scale.

16. Ibid., 132–5. Stoner's desire to go after Dr. King is reflected in the fact that he had started negotiations for the Shuttlesworth attack at $5,000; clearly he was giving an incentive for a contract on Dr. King at only $1,500.

17. Pamela Colloff, "The Sins of the Father," *Texas Monthly*, April 2000.

18. McWhorter, 74, 132.

19. Select Comm. on Assassinations, *Summary of Findings and Recommendations*, H.R. Rep., section 6, Evidence of a Conspiracy in St. Louis, at 377, National Archives, accessed December 11, 2010, http://www.archives.gov/research/jfk/select-committee-report/part-2c.html#klan.

20. FBI, "Airtel from SAC Miami to FBI Director re: BAPBOMB, Sidney Crockette Barnes a.k.a. Racial Matters" (March 12, 1964) FBI file. The file contains two FBI follow-up interviews with Barnes pertaining to the 1963/1964 reports. Barnes told the agents that he felt the Sixteenth Street Baptist Church bombing had been done by "niggers," and that he had no personal knowledge of it, although if he had, he would never give it to government agents. He stated he had been playing golf at a local resort, with one of the other suspects (Noah Carden), on the date of the bombing. A separate report, from an FBI informant, reveals the informant's conversations with Barnes after the FBI interviews in which Barnes discussed how he had misdirected the FBI and his concern that the FBI apparently had identified or would shortly identify the men behind the bombing because they already knew that Gale and Cardin were in Birmingham. Barnes also noted that when Carden was arrested on bootlegging charges, one of a number of weapons taken into custody actually belonged to William Potter Gale of California; Carden was holding it for him at his home in Alabama. Carden's name will come up again in this book, associated with the Swift network and its members in North Carolina. The informant reports also note a discussion in which Barnes states that because the primary target (designated as "Coon") had not shown up in Mobile, the point man from Alabama was unable to execute the plan. Barnes also stated that the FBI had way too much information about their plans for targeted Negro leaders and they were going to have to alter their plans.

21. Ibid.

22. Ibid; also FBI, "Teletype from Birmingham to Director, Memphis, Tennessee, New Orleans, Louisiana, and Mobile, Alabama" (April 15, 1968) King Assassination FBI Central Headquarters File, MURKIN 44-38861, section 10, available online at the Mary Ferrell Foundation, accessed September 15, 2010, http://www.maryferrell.org/mffweb/archive/viewer/showDoc.do; jsessionid=9746DB08F0898DE02C0A865E7406C5FC?docId=99574&relPageId=65; also Dan Christensen, "King Assassination: FBI Ignored Its Miami Informer," *Miami*, no. 12 (October 1976), 37–38, available online at Cuban Information Archives, last modified February 23, 2008, accessed September 15, 2010, http://cuban-exile.com/doc_101-125/doc0114.html. See the latter for the redacted names.

23. Michael Newton, *The Invisible Empire: The Ku Klux Klan in Florida* (Gainesville, FL: University Press of Florida, 2001) 170.

24. Patsy Sims, *The Klan*, 2nd ed. (Lexington, KY: University Press of Kentucky, 1996) 135.

25. Ibid., 170.

26. Ibid., 168–69.

27. Taylor Branch, *Pillar of Fire: America in the King Years* (New York: Simon & Schuster, 1998) 325, 339. Several factors point to this having been racially motivated. Branch mentions that the attack occurred amid well-substantiated reports that local Klansmen were trying to kill King while dressed as women (so as to get closer to him). More to the point, the assistant to King who had been staying at the cottage while King was out reported being followed, and his own car windows were shot out on the same day. The shooting occurred just after a particularly hostile

confrontation between civil rights agitators and white reactionaries in the Saint Augustine slave market. The seemingly unavoidable conclusion, therefore, is that this was Klan connected seems unavoidable.

28. Jim Bishop, *The Days of Martin Luther King Jr.* (New York: Putnam, 1971) 342.

29. Paul Hendrickson, "From the Fires of Hate, An Ember of Hope," Style section, *Washington Post*, July 22, 1998, http://www.washingtonpost.com/wp-srv/style/features/dahmer.htm.

30. FBI, "Airtel from SAC Oklahoma City to Director re: Donald Eugene Sparks . . ." (April 24, 1968) King Assassination FBI Central Headquarters File, MURKIN 44-38861-2926; also FBI, "Airtel from Tampa to Director re: Donald Eugene Sparks . . ." (April 18, 1968) King Assassination FBI Central Headquarters File, MURKIN 44-38861-1331.

31. Activities of the Ku Klux Klan Organizations in the United States: Hearings Before the Comm. on Un-American Activities, 89th Cong. at 2936 (February 1 and 7–11, 1966) accessed September 15, 2010, http://www.archive.org/stream/activitiesofkukl05unit/activitiesofkuk-l05unit_djvu.txt.

32. Branch, 412.

33. Ibid., 414, 498.

34. William H. McIlhany, *Klandestine: The Untold Story of Delmar Dennis and His Role in the FBI's War against the Ku Klux Klan* (New Rochelle, NY: Arlington House, 1975) 54.

35. "The News of the Day," *Los Angeles Times*, May 20, 1966. Apparently such a warning to Dr. King would have had to come from the attorney general because FBI director J. Edgar Hoover forbade his special agents from providing King or any of his representatives with information on outstanding threats. One such warning included a March 1965 memorandum from Hoover to the special agents in charge of the Atlanta and Mobile bureau offices relating an anonymous threat to kill King in Selma, Alabama.

36. Gilbert would join Richard Butler, another Swift disciple, in creating what would become perhaps the most well-known white supremacist organization in America, the Aryan Nations. To this day, the Church of Jesus Christ Christian is the religious order associated with the Aryan Nations. Although the Aryan Nations emerged after Swift's death in 1970, the teachings of this church are identical to Swift's theology.

37. FBI, "Report from Miami to Director, Memphis, Birmingham, Kansas City" (May 23, 1968) King Assassination FBI Central Headquarters File, MURKIN 44-38861, section 47, available online at Mary Ferrell Foundation, accessed September 15, 2010, http://www.maryferrell.org/mffweb/archive/viewer/showDoc.do?mode=searchResult&absPageId=1070097.

38. *Activities of the Ku Klux Klan Organizations in the United States: Hearings Before the Comm. on Un-American Activities,* 89th Cong. at 3441–42 (February 1 and 7–11, 1966) (testimony of Daniel Wagner), available online at Internet Archive, USA Government Documents, accessed September 15, 2010, http://www.archive.org/stream/activitiesofkukl04unit/activitiesofkuk-l04unit_djvu.txt. The immediate goals were to use the dynamite to blow up the Ohio offices of the National Association for the Advancement of Colored People (NAACP), the Ohio offices of the Congress of Racial Equality (CORE), and a black mosque presumably from the Nation of Islam. This aspect of the story was corroborated by more than one witness as well.

39. Ibid., 3428, 3441–42. While on the surface the purported assassination scheme seems fanciful—involving the murder of not only Dr. King but also the president of the United States and others—it does seem clear that at least Wagner was serious about the effort. Making the matter

more confusing, and perhaps even more fanciful, is that the scheme included, among Witte's intended victims, her husband and NKKKK higher-up Hugh Morris. Witte apparently wanted to shift allegiances to the Dixie Knights of the KKK and take the rest of the Ohio Klans (from the NKKKK) with her; killing Morris was part of this plan.

40. Ibid. In this light, the connection to NKKKK higher-up Hugh Morris once again becomes important. Morris testified to HUAC and expressed his belief that the Wagner story—including the attempt on his life—was a hoax. This was odd since Morris (according to Wagner and a police informant) found Wagner's efforts to inform him of said plot—done secretly at the behest of the police after Wagner's robbery arrest in 1965—sufficient and noble enough to officially indoctrinate Wagner into the NKKKK. Morris's denial before the HUAC only served to benefit Witte, the woman who tried to kill him. This raises the possibility that information Witte had about the less fanciful $25,000 bounty offer may have served as leverage over Morris. While, according to Wagner, Witte sourced this bounty to the NKKKK in general, it is worth noting that, according to testimony from J. B. Stoner to the HSCA, Morris had offered a $25,000 bounty on King's life. Morris denied this, but Congress found evidence he was speaking about slaying King in 1961.

41. Ibid., 3390 (testimony of undercover informant Bobby J. Stephens).

42. Sims, 248.

43. Ibid., 140, 253. Venable at one point represented Stoner himself when the latter was charged with a bombing in 1958 of an Atlanta synagogue.

44. FBI, Main King File, file 100-106670, section 23, at 11 (1965).

45. Michelle Malkin, "Remembering an American Insurrection," Townhall, September 27, 2002, http://townhall.com/columnists/MichelleMalkin/2002/09/27/remembering_an_american_insurrection.

56. Jerry Mitchell, "The Last Days of Ben Chester White," Clarion Ledger, February 23, 2003, http://orig.clarionledger.com/news/0302/23/m01.html.

47. BBC, "Klansman Gets Life for 1960s Murder," World: Americas, BBC News, August 23, 1998, http://news.bbc.co.uk/2/hi/americas/156290.stm. On orders from Sam Bowers, White Knights firebombed and shot into Dahmer's home; Dahmer was killed and his family narrowly escaped. Bowers was tried four times but was not convicted until 1998. Four other White Knights were convicted at the time for the firebombing, and several more—including Bowers—were convicted for their roles in the Mississippi Burning murders of civil rights workers James Chaney, Michael Schwerner, and Andrew Goodman in 1967. That said, the years 1967 and 1968 were possibly the most violent in the history of the White Knights.

48. FBI, Main King File, file 100-106670, section 32, at 97 (October 1964). The figure of $100,000 is interesting because the HSCA seriously considered that a $100,000 open bounty—sourced to North Carolina but apparently multistate in its reach—was what possibly triggered King's Memphis murder. The full reasons behind the HSCA's consideration of this specific offer are not clear, as Congress sealed its internal records. There are descriptions of a $100,000 North Carolina–based plot in the FBI's King materials.

49. Donald Nissen, in discussion with the authors, November 9, 2009.

50. FBI, Main King File, file 100-106670, section 32, at 97 (October 1964).

51. David Boylan, "A League of Their Own: A Look Inside the Christian Defense League," Cuban Information Archives, last modified March 17, 2006, accessed September 12, 2010, http://

cuban-exile.com/doc_026-050/doc0046.html.

52. Comm. on Un-American Activities, *Para-Military Organizations in California White Ex-tremist Organizations, Part II: National States' Rights Party The Present-Day Ku Klux Klan Move-ment*, H.R. Rep., 90th Cong. 1st Sess. at 63 (December 11, 1967).

53. FBI, "Sidney Crockette Barnes" summary file, at 13 (November 30, 1971). This is a sum-mary file we obtained via the Freedom of Information Act (FOIA).

54. Ibid. Barnes also describes Gale as leading a two-thousand-person armed outfit in anticipa-tion of violence resulting from James Meredith's efforts to integrate the University of Missis-sippi in 1962.

55. FBI, "Teletype from SAC Memphis to Director, Atlanta, Memphis, New Orleans, and San Antonio," Main King File, file 100-106670, section 13, at 14.

56. Ibid. This same report describes King as a target for this newly forming militant group and the mysterious military officer.

57. FBI, James Venable FBI Headquarters File, file 1165004-001, 157-HQ-1628, section 2, at 3 (1967). In fact, Venable made a number of trips to California and spoke at a number of meet-ings. The file shows he was there at least on February 19, April 1, April 20, and April 28–29, 1967.

58. Frederick J. Simonelli, *American Fuehrer: George Lincoln Rockwell and the American Nazi Party* (Urbana: University of Illinois Press, 1999) 121.

59. FBI, "Memorandum from SA Richard F. Kilcourse to SAC Los Angeles," 62-5101 (April 23, 1968).

60. FBI, James Venable FBI Headquarters File, file 1165004-001, 157-HQ-1628, section 1, at 3 (1967).

61. Melissa Fay Greene, *The Temple Bombing* (Cambridge, MA: Da Capo, 2006) 209.

62. FBI, "Memorandum from SA Richard F. Kilcourse to SAC Los Angeles," 62-5101 (April 23, 1968).

63. Wesley Swift, "No Place to Hide" (sermon), March 8, 1965, transcript, Israel Elect of Zion, http://www.israelect.com/reference/WesleyASwift/sermons/65-03-08.htm.

64. "Wesley Swift, Racist Minister, Victim of a Heart Attack in Mexico," *Dixon Line* 7, no. 11 (1970), 1, 14.

65. Comm. on Un-American Activities, *Para-Military Organizations in California White Extrem-ist Organizations, Part II: National States' Rights Party The Present-Day Ku Klux Klan Movement*, H.R. Rep., 90th Cong. 1st Sess. at 63 (December 11, 1967).

66. Michael Stohl, *The Politics of Terrorism*, 3rd ed. (New York: Marcel Dekker, 1988) 557.

67. Ibid., 551.

68. Gus Martin, *Essentials of Terrorism: Concepts and Controversies* (Thousand Oaks, CA: Sage Publications: 2008) 74. Martin does not draw the direct connection to the Klan but it can easily be inferred from his definition.

69. Charles Marsh, *God's Long Summer: Stories of Faith and Civil Rights* (Princeton, NJ: Princ-eton University Press, 1997) 60.

70. Jerry Mitchell, email message to author Stuart Wexler, February 4, 2011.

71. Confidential interview, November 2009. For a number of reasons, we wish to protect the identity of our source.

CHAPTER 2

1. Michael Honey, *Going Down Jericho Road: The Memphis Strike, Martin Luther King's Last Campaign* (New York: W. W. Norton & Company, 2007) 445–46.

2. Ibid.

3. Robert Jewett and John Shelton Lawrence, *Captain America and the Crusade against Evil: The Dilemma of Zealous Nationalism* (Grand Rapids, MI: W. B. Eerdmans, 2003) 169.

4. Michael Barkun, *Religion and the Racist Right: The Origins of the Christian Identity Movement* (Chapel Hill: University of North Carolina Press, 1994) 48.

5. Ibid., 51.

6. Ibid., 177.

7. Ibid., 55.

8. Swift was a major force in popularizing the new "two-seed" (or "seedliner") theory. That view holds that Eve was seduced by the serpent and conceived Cain. Since modern Jews descend from Cain, they are then the literal children of Satan.

9. Barkun, 49.

10. "Doctrinal Statement of Beliefs," Kingdom Identity Ministries, accessed August 5, 2011, http://www.kingidentity.com/doctrine.htm. For those wishing to explore the exact textual foundations for these claims by CI believers, the following excerpt, from the statement of doctrine of one Christian Identity sect, provides biblical references: WE BELIEVE in an existing being known as the Devil or Satan and called the Serpent (Gen. 3:1; Rev. 12:9), who has a literal "seed" or posterity in the earth (Gen. 3:15) commonly called Jews today (Rev. 2:9; 3:9; Isa. 65:15). These children of Satan (John 8:44-47; Matt. 13:38; John 8:23) through Cain (I John 2:22, 4:3) who have throughout history always been a curse to true Israel, the Children of God, because of a natural enmity between the two races (Gen. 3:15), because they do the works of their father the Devil (John 8:38-44), and because they please not God, and are contrary to all men (I Thes. 2:14-15), though they often pose as ministers of righteousness (II Cor. 11:13-15). The ultimate end of this evil race whose hands bear the blood of our Savior (Matt. 27:25) and all the righteous slain upon the earth (Matt. 23:35), is Divine judgment (Matt. 13:38-42, 15:13; Zech. 14:21).

11. Barkun, 195.

12. Ibid.

13. FBI, Project Meggido (1999), available online at CESNUR, http://www.cesnur.org/testi/FBI_004.htm.

14. David Boylan, "A League of Their Own: A Look Inside the Christian Defense League," Cuban Information Archives, last modified March 17, 2006, accessed September 12, 2010, http://cuban-exile.com/doc_026-050/doc0046.html.

15. Barkun, 199.

16. FBI, Project Meggido. Swift's Christian Identity message contained a very specific view of an imminent "end-time": Armageddon. "The view of what Armageddon will be varies among Christian Identity believers. Some contend there will be a race war in which millions will die; others believe that the United Nations, backed by Jewish representatives of the anti-Christ, will take over the country and promote a New World Order. One Christian Identity interpretation is that white Christians have been chosen to watch for signs of the impending war in order to

warn others. They are to then physically struggle with the forces of evil against sin and other violations of God's law (i.e., race-mixing and internationalism); many will perish, and some of God's chosen will be forced to wear the Mark of the Beast to participate in business and commerce. After the final battle is ended and God's kingdom is established on earth, only then will the Aryan people be recognized as the one and true Israel. Christian Identity adherents believe that God will use his chosen race as his weapons to battle the forces of evil. Christian Identity followers believe they are among those chosen by God to wage this battle during Armageddon and they will be the last line of defense for the white race and Christian America."

17. Swift, Wesley. The Wesley Swift Archive, "The Seal of God." Accessed December 22, 2011. http://swift.christogenea.org/content/seal-god-9-22-63.

18. Michael Friedly and David Gallen, *Martin Luther King, Jr.: The FBI File* (New York: Carroll & Graf, 1993) 162.

19. Michael Newton, *The Invisible Empire: The Ku Klux Klan in Florida* (Gainesville, FL: University Press of Florida, 2001) 161. During this period Lynch was accumulating more than seventy-five thousand miles of road travel a year.

20. FBI, Investigative Summary, National States Rights Party (1976).

21. Charles Marsh, *God's Long Summer: Stories of Faith and Civil Rights* (Princeton, NJ: Princeton University Press, 1997) 60.

22. Patsy Sims, *The Klan,* 2nd ed. (Lexington, KY: University Press of Kentucky, 1996) 235, 273.

23. Marsh, 50. This source is one of the best on Bowers; Marsh is the only person known to have obtained a series of formal, in-depth personal interviews with Bowers and to have gained insight into his childhood and development directly from Bowers himself. This series of interviews was conducted in 1994, after Bowers's release from prison and his return to his home in Laurel, Mississippi.

24. Ibid., 52.

25. Ibid., 53.

26. Ibid., 23.

27. Paul Hendrickson, "From the Fires of Hate, An Ember of Hope," Style section, *Washington Post,* July 22, 1998, http://www.washingtonpost.com/wp-srv/style/features/dahmer.htm.

28. Confidential interviews with the authors, June 2009. Source wishes to remain anonymous.

29. William Turner, *Power on the Right* (Berkeley, CA: Ramparts Press, 1971) 100.

30. Ibid., 132–33, 187.

31. Marsh, 50. Marsh quotes a White Knight recruiting poster that begins with the following statement: "the administration of our national government is now under control of atheists who are Bolsheviks by nature. As dedicated agents of Satan, they are absolutely determined to destroy Christian civilization and all Christians."

32. William H. McIlhany, *Klandestine: The Untold Story of Delmar Dennis and His Role in the FBI's War against the Ku Klux Klan* (New Rochelle, NY: Arlington House, 1975) 38–47.

33. Don Whitehead, *Attack on Terror: The FBI against the Ku Klux Klan* (New York: Funk & Wagnalls, 1970) 8.

34. Sims, 134.

35. Johnson, Dana. *The Spark: Student Journal for Social Justice,* "Separation or Death:." Accessed December 22, 2011.

36. Stoner, J. B. Letter to Muslim Convention, February 1957. Quoted in Muhammad, Elijah.

Message to the Blackman in America. Secretarius Memps Publications, 1997, Chapter 139. Accessed from "Nation of Islam, Settlement No. 1."

37. Branch, Taylor. *Pillar of Fire: America in the King Years.* (New York, NY: Simon & Schuster, 1998) 344.

38. FBI, Investigative Summary, National States Rights Party (1976).

39. Office of the Attorney General, Department of Justice, State of California, Report on Private Armies in California, at 1-2 (April 12, 1965). Both Stoner and Fields had actively supported the Columbians, a post-WWII paramilitary group formed in Georgia. The Columbians had actively plotted a takeover of the state of Georgia. Its leaders were arrested, and stores of arms, ammunition, and explosives were seized, along with lists of public officials and private citizens to be exterminated upon the seizure of power in the state.

40. United Press International, *The Bulletin,* July 26, 1966.

41. Associated Press, *The Sarasota Herald Tribune,* November 22, 1966.

42. Diane McWhorter, *Carry Me Home: Birmingham, Alabama; the Climactic Battle of the Civil Rights Revolution* (New York: Simon & Schuster, 2001) 133. Clarence Kelley, head of the Birmingham field office in 1958, who later headed the MLK murder investigation and eventually became FBI director, participated in the sting on Stoner. Kelley and other agents actually observed Stoner's meetings with the police officers conducting the sting, and Kelley was privy to all the technical details of the operation, including the tape-recording of Stoner.

43. FBI, Investigative Summary, National States Rights Party (1976).

44. McWhorter, 132.

45. Melissa Fay Greene, *The Temple Bombing* (Cambridge, MA: Da Capo Press, 2006) 272–73.

46. Ibid., 408. It is not surprising then that, years later during its 1970s King inquiry, one of Congress's on-the-ground investigators expressed views that undermined the House Select Committee on Assassination's final report. Having seen, firsthand, Stoner's skill in avoiding blame for the temple bombing in 1958, former detective Clifford Strickland expressed his firm conviction to author Melissa Fay Greene that Stoner was behind King's murder.

47. McWhorter, 201–3.

48. FBI, "Memo to SAC Jackson; Subj: J. B. Stoner," 157-3082-19 (August 6, 1968). File obtained by the authors via the Freedom of Information Act (herein FOIA).

49. FBI, "Jackson Field Office Report; Subj: APWR Meeting on 6/2/68," 157-3082-10 (June 3, 1968). File obtained by the authors via FOIA.

50. FBI, "Memorandum from SAC Jackson to FBI Director; Subj: Suspended Racial Informant on 6/2/68," 157-3082-18 (July 12, 1968). File obtained by the authors via FOIA.

51. James B. Skewes, "Not Welcome!" *Meridian Star,* May 31, 1968.

52. FBI reports document how the APWR were a known front group for less violent activity on behalf of the White Knights.

53. FBI, "Jackson Field Office Summary Report, Subj: OKKKKOM, Scott County, Miss., NSRP Meeting, Jackson, Mississippi, 4/26/70," 157-10536-16 (April 28, 1968). File obtained by the authors via FOIA; also FBI Main J.B. Stoner File, file 88-86081, section 1, at 16-17. Stoner's connection to Mississippi may have grown stronger on through the 1980s. This can be inferred from the FBI's internal documents related to their 1983 manhunt for Stoner, after he jumped bond following a conviction for a bombing. While he was on the lam, the FBI considered interviewing Stoner's biggest financial supporters. These donors are not listed,

but the majority were located in Jackson, Mississippi, a White Knight stronghold. More importantly, the FBI only considered interviewing one known Klansman to help in their pursuit of Stoner: Sam Bowers. The documents do not explain why the feds felt there was a connection between the two racists, and Stoner would turn himself into the FBI before the manhunt took full shape.

54. Dina Temple-Raston, "An FBI Man's Inside View of '60s America in Turmoil," NPR, *All Things Considered,* radio broadcast narrated by Melissa Block, August 7, 2009, http://www.npr.org/templates/story/story.php?storyId=111659247.

55. FBI, "Memorandum from SAC Jackson to FBI Director; Subj: National States Rights Party," 157-3082-86 (April 8, 1968). File obtained by the authors via FOIA.

CHAPTER 3

1. Joseph Crespino, *In Search of Another Country: Mississippi and the Conservative Counterrevolution* (Princeton, NJ: 2007) 113. It should be noted that, very quietly, the UKA would also pick off White Knights who were dissatisfied with the lack of extreme violence on the part of the White Knights following the Mississippi Burning murders. Under increased pressure from the FBI following the murders, Bowers put a moratorium on major acts of violence until the scrutiny subsided. This ended within a few months. Publicly, however, the UKA still knew that they would drain far more from the White Knight membership rolls by presenting themselves as less extreme and less violent.

2. Comm. on Un-American Activities, *Para-Military Organizations in California White Extremist Organizations, Part II: National States' Rights Party The Present-Day Ku Klux Klan Movement,* H.R. Rep., 90th Cong. 1st Sess. at 163 (December 11, 1967).

3. Jack Nelson, *Terror in the Night: The Klan's Campaign against the Jews* (New York: Simon & Schuster, 1993) 104.

4. Bruce Hoffman, *Holy Terror: The Implications of Terrorism Motivated by a Religious Imperative* (Santa Monica, CA: Rand Publishing, 1993). It is important to note, once again, that the groups we speak of were a hybrid of religiously inspired terrorists at the top of the organization, with vigilante terrorists among the rank and file. Thus Hoffman's criteria apply in loose form to these groups in ways that are not as obvious to, say, Al-Qaeda. Bowers, Stoner, and others had to manipulate their rank and file to accomplish these greater ends.

5. David C. Rapoport, ed., *Terrorism: The First or Anarchist Wave* (London: Routledge, 2005) 192.

6. Ibid.

7. "America's Homegrown Extremists." *Life* (April 8, 2010) 14, http://www.life.com/gallery/27942/image/81674544#index/13.

8. Alan Cullison, "Inside Al-Qaeda's Hard Drive: Budget Squabbles, Baby Pictures, Office Rivalries and the Path to 9/11," *Atlantic,* September 2004, http://www.theatlantic.com/magazine/archive/2004/09/inside-al-qaeda-rsquo-s-hard-drive/3428/.

9. Diane McWhorter, *Carry Me Home: Birmingham, Alabama; the Climactic Battle of the Civil Rights Revolution* (New York: Simon & Schuster, 2001) 427–38.

10. Claude Sitton, "50 Hurt in Negro Rioting After Birmingham Blasts," *New York Times,* May 13, 1963, http://partners.nytimes.com/library/national/race/051363race-ra.html.

11. Associated Press, "Federal Troops Poised to Move Into Birmingham," *Quebec Chronicle-Telegraph,* May 13, 1963, http://news.google.com/newspapers?id=qFg0AAAAIBAJ&sjid=Osw FAAAAIBAJ&pg=2700,2625710&dq=federal-troops&hl=en.

12. Fred Sanders, in discussion with the authors, July 29, 2011.

13. John R. Salter Jr., *Jackson, Mississippi: An American Chronicle of Struggle and Schism* (Hicksville, NY: Exposition Press, 1979) 182-83.

14. Ibid., 190-96, 221, 222.

15. Marcel Dufresne, "Exposing the Secrets of Mississippi Racism," *American Journalism Review,* October 1991, http://www.ajr.org/article.asp?id=1311.

16. Jerry Mitchell, "Evers' Assassin Said Still at Large," *Mississippi Clarion-Ledger,* January 23, 2011.

17. Bobby DeLaughter, *Never Too Late: A Prosecutor's Story of Justice in the Medgar Evers Case* (New York: Scribner, 2001) 211, 162.

18. Ibid., 58.

19. United Press International, "Six Dead after Church Bombing," *Washington Post,* September 16, 1963, http://www.washingtonpost.com/wp-srv/national/longterm/churches/archives1.htm.

20. This same FBI informant, Gary Rowe Jr., was officially praised (by future FBI Director Clarence Kelley) as having excellent connections to both the police and the Klan. Kelley was right in one sense: Rowe was demonstrated to have gotten a pistol permit by showing his Klan membership card.

21. Sara Diamond, *Roads to Dominion: Right-Wing Movements and Political Power in the United States* (New York: Guilford Press, 1995) 152.

CHAPTER 4

1. Charles Marsh, *God's Long Summer: Stories of Faith and Civil Rights* (Princeton, NJ: Princeton University Press, 1997) 64–66.

2. Ibid.

3. Ibid.

4. Ibid.

5. Ibid.

6. Ibid., 72.

7. Patsy Sims, *The Klan,* 2nd ed. (Lexington, KY: University Press of Kentucky, 1996) 17. Sims describes but does not identify a group known only as the "secret six" who plotted to kill King long before Memphis.

8. Diane McWhorter, *Carry Me Home: Birmingham, Alabama; the Climactic Battle of the Civil Rights Revolution* (New York: Simon & Schuster, 2001) 478.

9. Ibid., 491.

10. Ibid., 484. In a show of support for the expelled Cahaba Boys, the head of the NSRP, Edward Fields, held a rally in Cahaba Heights. Only 250 people attended, but J. B. Stoner made the trip from Atlanta to participate.

11. Ibid., 478.

12. Petric J. Smith, *Long Time Coming: An Insider's Story of the Birmingham Church Bombing That Rocked the World* (Birmingham, AL: Crane Hill, 1994) 96–102. Shortly following the Sixteenth Street Baptist Church bombing, a secret meeting was held between various Klansmen and Ala-

bama Highway Patrol regarding Chambliss and others. Following that secret meeting in a Homewood, Alabama, motel room, the Klansmen were picked up for dynamite possession, a charge carrying a maximum jail time of six months. This seems to have helped isolate them from a separate FBI investigation in the Sixteenth Street Baptist Church bombing. Decades later, Alabama attorney general Bill Baxley was able to build a solid case for the Sixteenth Street Church bombing. Several local and extremely violent Birmingham Klansmen were identified. There were also suggestions that they had been motivated by one or more individuals from outside Birmingham. The FBI possessed the information used in the case immediately following the bombing, but Director Hoover refused local field officer requests to provide it to Birmingham prosecutors. Baxley appealed for access to the reports for years, making more than fifteen visits to Washington to appeal to the FBI and Justice Department. He received no response at all until 1975, and then only after a Washington bureau chief of the *Los Angeles Times* threatened to do a story on the FBI's obstruction of justice in the case. Chambliss and others were convicted for the crime in the late 1970s.

13. David Boylan, "A League of Their Own: A Look Inside the Christian Defense League," Cuban Information Archives, last modified March 17, 2006, accessed September 12, 2010, http://cuban-exile.com/doc_026-050/doc0046.html. AWAKE was disbanded in early 1964 along with the Christian Knights of the Invisible Empire.

14. Ibid.

15. Newton, Michael. *The Ku Klux Klan: History, Organization, Language, Influence and Activities of America's Most Notorious Secret Society* (Jefferson, N.C: McFarland, 2006) 110.

16. Activities of the Ku Klux Klan Organizations in the United States: Hearings Before the Comm. on Un-American Activities, 89th Cong. at 3551-52 (February 1 and 7-11, 1966) (testimony of Earl Holcombe). Available online at Internet Archive, USA Government Documents, accessed September 15, 2010, http://www.archive.org/stream/activitiesofkukl05unit/activitiesofkukl05unit_djvu.txt. It is worth noting that Wagner himself was a member of the Black Shirts in Ohio; the men he met in Georgia were also identified as being members of the Black Shirts in that state.

17. Boylan.

18. Report of Detective Lochart F. Gracey, Jr. to Detective Sergeant C. H. Sapp and State Attorney Richard E. Gerstein (April 10, 1963), available online at The Harold Weisberg Archive at Hood College, accessed September 12, 2011, http://jfk.hood.edu/Collection/Weisberg%20Subject%20Index%20Files/M%20Disk/Milteer%20J%20A/Item%2009.pdf. This is a report on the meeting of the Congress of Freedom. Notably, in addition to mentioning Carden, the report mentions Joseph Milteer and Harry Jack Brown, a.k.a. Jack Brown. The report describes Milteer as running an underground "Dixie Clan" out of Georgia that was radical and militant. This group included Brown. This is significant for two reasons. First, as we detail later in the book, author Lamar Waldron says that Milteer was raising money to kill King in 1967–1968. Secondly, several months after this report on the Congress of Freedom, in November 1963, Milteer would tell informant Willie Somersett, on tape, that Brown was trying to kill King. It is in that same, taped conversation that Milteer also predicted that President John F. Kennedy would be killed with a high-powered rifle.

19. James Dickerson, *Dixie's Dirty Secret: The True Story of How the Government, the Media, and the Mob Conspired to Combat Integration and the Vietnam Antiwar Movement* (Armonk, NY: M. E. Sharpe, 1998) 111.

20. Wyn Craig Wade, *The Fiery Cross: The Ku Klux Klan in America* (New York: Oxford Uni-

versity Press, 1998) 72.

21. Activities of the Ku Klux Klan Organizations in the United States.

22. David J. Garrow, ed., St. Augustine, Florida, 1963-1964: Mass Protest and Racial Violence. (Brooklyn, NY: Carlson Pub., 1989) 98; also Don Whitehead, Attack on Terror: The FBI against the Ku Klux Klan (New York: Funk & Wagnalls, 1970) 67.

23. Activities of the Ku Klux Klan Organizations in the United States, 1532.

24. Whitehead, 67.

25. James Oliver Horton and Lois E. Horton, *Hard Road to Freedom: The Story of African America, vol. 2, From the Civil War to the Millennium* (New Brunswick, NJ: Rutgers University Press, 2002) 170.

26. Nick Kotz, *Judgment Days: Lyndon Baines Johnson, Martin Luther King Jr., and the Laws that Changed America* (Boston: Houghton Mifflin Harcourt, 2005) 230.

27. Ibid., 246–47.

28. Jim Ingram, in discussion with the authors, March 2, 2008.

29. Jerry Mitchell, "A Mobster Takes on the KKK," Journey to Justice (blog), *Mississippi Clarion-Ledger,* February 17, 2010, http://blogs.clarionledger.com/jmitchell/2010/02/17/the-lie-that-wont-die-in-the-mississippi-burning-case/.

30. Activities of the Ku Klux Klan Organizations in the United States: Hearings Before the Comm. on Un-American Activities, 89th Cong. at 2936 (February 1 and 7-11, 1966) accessed September 15, 2010, http://www.archive.org/stream/activitiesofkukl05unit/activitiesofkukl05unit_djvu.txt.

31. Jack Nelson, *Terror in the Night: The Klan's Campaign against the Jews* (New York: Simon & Schuster, 1993) 53–54.

32. Ibid., 22.

33. Ibid., 103, 123, 134

34. FBI, Samuel Holloway Bowers, Jr. bureau file, file 157-1654, section 23, at 15 (August 9, 1968). This is a summary file obtained by the authors via Freedom of Information Act (FOIA).

CHAPTER 5

1. Douglas O. Linder, "The Mississippi Burning Trial (U.S. vs. Price et al.)" Famous Trials, University of Missouri-Kanscas City (UMKC) School of Law, last modified October 18, 2011, accessed November 17, 2011, http://law2.umkc.edu/faculty/projects/ftrials/price&bowers/Account.html.

2. *Los Angeles Times,* "Klan Chief Bowers in Mississippi Jail," *Tuscaloosa News,* November 23, 1968, http://news.google.com/newspapers?id=WQMdAAAAIBAJ&sjid=NZsEAAAAIBAJ&pg=7095,4686072&dq=bowers+appeal-bond&hl=en. *Los Angeles Times* provided this article to *Tuscaloosa News.*

3. Jack Nelson, "Mississippi Terrorism Continues: Convicted Klan Chieftain Still Loose," *Tuscaloosa News,* August 1, 1968, http://news.google.com/newspapers?id=kBcfAAAAIBAJ&sjid=N5sEAAAAIBAJ&pg=7101,42353&dq=bowers+appeal-bond&hl=en. *Los Angeles Times* provided this article to *Tuscaloosa News.*

4. FBI, Samuel Holloway Bowers, Jr. bureau file, file 157-1654, section 7, at 46 (July 16, 1965). This is a summary file obtained by the authors via the Freedom of Information Act (FOIA).

5. FBI, Samuel Holloway Bowers, Jr. bureau file, file 157-1654, section 23, at 20 (August 9, 1968). This is a summary file obtained by the authors via FOIA.

6. Jack Nelson, *Terror in the Night: The Klan's Campaign against the Jews* (New York: Simon & Schuster, 1993) 144.

7. Ibid., 24–25.

8. Ibid., 143–45.

9. FBI, Sidney Crockette Barnes summary file, at 17 (November 30, 1971). This is a summary file obtained by the authors via FOIA. One informant in this document notes that Danny Joe Hawkins, Kathy Ainsworth, and Tommy Tarrants were "together in some secret outfit and Barnes and his wife had brainwashed him." Other parts of this same file note that Barnes had more than four hundred tapes on Swift, and that he and his wife were constantly preaching Swift's message.

10. Nelson, *Terror in the Night*, 17–20, 185.

11. Ibid., 136, 152–62.

12. FBI, "Information Concerning Individuals Who Were Formerly Associated with the WKKKKOM, Jones Co., Miss.," 44-1-7169, at 35 (September 15,1970).

13. FBI, "Summary Report of SA Samuel Jennings, White Knights of the Ku Klux Klan," FBI Jackson field office file 157-63, bureau file 157-1552, (February 24, 1969).

14. Ibid., 10.

15. FBI, "FBI Miami Field Office Urgent Teletype to Headquarters, Memphis, Jackson and Mobile" (August 2, 1968) King Assassination FBI Central Headquarters File, MURKIN Miami 44-1854, Memphis 44-1987, Director 44-38861.

16. Ibid.

17. FBI (August 14 1968) King Assassination FBI Central Headquarters File, MURKIN 44-38261-5051

18. "Urgent Teletype from Miami to Director, Jackson, Memphis," section 68 (August 6, 1968) King Assassination FBI Central Headquarters File, MURKIN 44-58861-5021, available online at the Mary Ferrell Foundation, accessed September 15, 2010, http://www.maryferrell.org/mff-web/archive/viewer/showDoc.do?mode=searchResult&absPageId=1131536. The authors have an updated version with the name Henderson and Tarrants revealed.

19. FBI (August 14, 1968) King Assassination FBI Central Headquarters File, MURKIN 44-38861-5017.

20. FBI (August 14, 1968) King Assassination FBI Central Headquarters File, MURKIN File 44-38261-5051.

21. FBI, "FBI Jackson Field Office to FBI Crime Lab" (April 16, 1968) King Assassination FBI Central Headquarters File, MURKIN 44-38861-1170. Tarrants's name was not on this list, as he had not yet been identified as being a violent member of the White Knights of the Ku Klux Klan of Mississippi.

22. Nelson, *Terror in the Night*, 140. The authors have obtained documents that show that Hendrixson was the person noted by Nelson. The similarity in names also makes it likely that the Henderson noted in the Somersett reports was actuality Hendrixson. It should also be noted that Capomacchia had a close friend and contact in North Carolina, Laura Sullinger. Sullinger's residence was also raided in connection with paramilitary activity. Sullinger's husband, Ferris Wood Sullinger, was one of the leading financiers of Swift's movement.

23. Dan Christensen, "FBI Ignored Its Miami Informer," *Miami* magazine, October 17, 1976, 37-38.

24. Confidential Inter-office Memorandum from Lt. Charles Sapp to Col. Walter E. Headley, Chief of Miami Police: "Investigation of Suspects in Assassination of Martin Luther King" (April-August 1968) available online at the Harold Weisberg Archive at Hood College, accessed November 10, 2011, http://jfk.hood.edu/Collection/Weisberg%20Subject%20Index%20Files/S%20Disk/Somersett%20William%20A/Item%2001.pdf. These memos detailed the investigation, using Somersett, that the Miami Police Department sponsored, starting on April 25, 1968. Somersett was asked to visit with and report on many different extremists across the country. On June 11, 1968, Somersett described a visit he had with Sidney Barnes. Barnes detailed the recent bombings in Meridian, Mississippi, and the "young man" who was involved, clearly Tarrants. He told Somersett that the FBI was trying to find Tarrants but could not do it. Barnes said he knew where Tarrants was and wanted Somersett to meet Tarrants. This is fascinating, in light of information developed in this chapter and elsewhere, that Barnes clearly knew that Somersett was a snitch. Barnes would essentially be setting up Tarrants two weeks before the Meridian confrontation with police that killed Kathy Ainsworth and wounded Tarrants, making Tarrants a public figure. The purpose is unclear.

25. Select Comm. on Assassinations, *Summary of Findings and Recommendations*, H.R. Rep., section 6, Evidence of a Conspiracy in St. Louis, at 383–85, (1979) Mary Farrell Foundation, accessed December 11, 2010, http://www.maryferrell.org/mffweb/archive/viewer/showDoc.do?absPageId=69427.

26. Ibid.

27. A Google news archive search shows that the CB radio incident was reported by some prominent newspapers, including *The New York Times,* as possible evidence of a conspiracy. But the total number of articles referencing a "citizens band radio," at least according to an overall archive search, is only fourteen.

28. FBI, "Memorandum from SAC Jackson, to Director" at 2–3 (July 12, 1968). This material was acquired by the authors via FOIA for J. B. Stoner's Jackson field office file. The suspect was arrested at 10:50 PM.

29. FBI, "FBI Miami Field Office Urgent Teletype to Headquarters, Memphis, Jackson and Mobile" (August 2, 1968) King Assassination FBI Central Headquarters File, MURKIN Miami 44-1854, Memphis 44-1987, Director 44-38861. It is clear that Capomacchia is referring to the handful of individuals connected to the bombing of the Blackwell Real Estate office in Jackson, Mississippi.

30. United Press International, "Informer to Be Key Witness in Harper's Trial," *The Times-News,* July 31, 1968, http://news.google.com/newspapers?id=63Q0AAAAIBAJ&sjid=XCQEAAAAIBAJ&dq=robert%20earl%20wilson&pg=2966%2C2180605.

31. FBI, Samuel Holloway Bowers, Jr. bureau file, file 157-1654, section 23, at 15 (August 9, 1968). This is a summary file obtained by the authors via FOIA.

32. Ibid., 12, 15.

33. FBI, Sidney Crockette Barnes summary file (November 30, 1971) This is a summary file we obtained via FOIA. The amiable relationship between Capomacchia and Barnes and others (in the WKKKKOM) is amply documented repeatedly throughout this report.

34. Nelson, *Terror in the Night,* 138-40.

35. Marilyn Stewart, "Former KKK Terrorist Cites C. S. Lewis' Faithful Obedience," *Baptist*

Press, August 9, 2006, http://www.bpnews.net/bpnews.asp?id=23764.

36. Nelson, *Terror in the Night,* 138.

CHAPTER 6

1. Jack Nelson, *Terror in the Night: The Klan's Campaign against the Jews* (New York: Simon & Schuster, 1993) 140.

2. Marilyn Stewart, "Former KKK Terrorist Cites C. S. Lewis' Faithful Obedience," *Baptist Press,* August 9, 2006, http://www.bpnews.net/bpnews.asp?id=23764.

3. Jerry Mitchell, "Murder of Martin Luther King Jr.; Did Klan Have a Role?" *Clarion-Ledger,* December 30, 2007. The authors were a key source for the article.

4. Jim Ingram, in discussion with the authors, June 20, 2009.

5. Nelson, 138.

6. Thomas A. Tarrants, *The Conversion of a Klansman: The Story of a Former Ku Klux Klan Terrorist* (New York: Doubleday, 1979) 2.

7. Nelson, 206–7.

8. Ibid., 45–46.

9. Ibid., 144.

10. Ibid.

11. Ibid., 24–25.

12. Tarrants, 47.

13. Roy Hoffman, *Alabama Afternoons: Profiles and Conversations* (Tuscaloosa: University of Alabama Press, 2011) 117.

14. Tarrants, 49. The use of radio to monitor police broadcasts is of considerable interest in regard to activities in Memphis during the King murder.

15. Petric J. Smith, *Long Time Coming: An Insider's Story of the Birmingham Church Bombing That Rocked the World* (Birmingham, AL: Crane Hill, 1994) 63.

16. Tarrants, 52.

17. Ibid., 2, 52, 55.

18. Ibid.

19. Jerry Mitchell, *The Preacher and the Klansman* (Jackson, MS: Clarion-Ledger, 1998). This is from a thirteen-part series by Mitchell that won national acclaim.

20. Nelson, 136.

21. Ibid., 29.

22. Nelson, 139–41.

23. Edwin King, in discussion with the authors, July 30, 2011.

24. FBI, Samuel Holloway Bowers, Jr. bureau file, file 157–1654, section 7, at 41 (July 16, 1965). This is a summary file obtained by the authors via Freedom of Information Act (FOIA). In one vignette, from November 1964, one informant has Bowers telling some Klansman that "the Klan should fight the Zionists or Jews, whom he believes are a greater threat to this country."

25. Tarrants, 59.

26. Comm. on Un-American Activities, *Para-Military Organizations in California White Extremist Organizations, Part II: National States' Rights Party The Present-Day Ku Klux Klan Movement,* H.R. Rep., 90th Cong. 1st Sess. at 198 (December 11, 1967).

27. FBI, "Memorandum from SA Richard F. Kilcourse to SAC Los Angeles," 62-5101 (April 23, 1968).

28. Nelson, 61–62.

29. Charles Marsh, *God's Long Summer: Stories of Faith and Civil Rights* (Princeton, NJ: Princeton University Press, 1997) 56–59. The level of both Bower's tactical- and strategic-level thinking was on an order of magnitude beyond popular concepts of Klan planning and activities. He implemented measures for sophisticated security, counterintelligence, and covert action teams; he constructed highly compartmentalized operations utilizing outsiders for key attacks. Even his basic "harassment" activities demonstrated a great degree of sophistication. Marsh quotes from Bowers's own instructions to the White Knights: "The Acts (of harassment) themselves shall always appear to aliens as ridiculous and unimportant. Harassment itself should never aim at accomplishing any goal directly. The purpose of harassment is to stir up and fret the enemy, then step back and wait for him to make a mistake, meanwhile preparing calmly and soberly to exploit any mistake that he does make to the maximum advantage." Bowers even provided a list of tools for such harassment, to include roofing nails, sugar, molasses, firecrackers, snakes and lizards, stink bombs, BB guns, slingshots, air rifles, bows and arrows . . . and proper use of the telephone. It was also important for the harassment to be unpredictable in order to maximize the psychological impact. Acts of harassment and even violence would be mixed with days of total calm. On some days members were to harass, other days they would conduct beatings, and on other days they would simply attend civil rights gatherings, standing at the edge of the crowd, sitting in vehicles, just joking and laughing with each other.

30. FBI, "Summary Report of SA Samuel Jennings, White Knights of the Ku Klux Klan," FBI Jackson Field Office file 157-63, bureau file 157-1552, (February 24, 1969). Danny Joe Hawkins is also described as being a member of an "underground hit squad."

31. Nelson, 139.

32. Robert Jewett and John Shelton Lawrence, *Captain America and the Crusade against Evil: The Dilemma of Zealous Nationalism* (Grand Rapids, MI: W. B. Eerdmans, 2003) 170. It was not unknown for members of the radical network to use robberies to finance major operations, including assassinations. Walter Thudy, a Christian Identity leader, described twenty bank robberies, which were used to build a fund to back a campaign of assassinations. "Killing is normally murder . . . theft is theft. But if you are in warfare, those same acts are acts of war. I am at warfare [sic] with the enemies of my country." It should also be noted that following Tarrants's arrest in the aborted bombing attempt, Sidney Barnes made the remark that Tarrants might well be talking to the FBI and could incriminate Barnes in various acts of violence in Mississippi, including robberies.

33. Tarrants, 58.

34. Nelson, 141.

35. John Drabble, "The FBI, COINTELPRO-WHITE HATE and the Decline of Ku Klux Klan Organizations in Mississippi, 1964–1971" *Journal of Mississippi History,* 66.4 (Winter 2004): 353-401. Historian John Drabble's work is an excellent overview of the impact COINTELPRO had on the White Knights of Mississippi (WKKKOM). He is also one of the few experts who noted the influence of Christian Identity beliefs in early WKKKOM ideology, especially on Bowers. He specifically noted the difference between the type of active, militant anti-Semitism seen in a group such as the WKKKOM as opposed to the passive strain of anti-Semitism-rhetoric, not deed-seen in a group like the United Klans of America.

36. Ibid.

37. Nelson, 188–89.

38. FBI, "Summary Report of SA Samuel Jennings, White Knights of the Ku Klux Klan," FBI Jackson Field Office file 157-63, bureau file 157–1552, (February 24, 1969). Details of the sting on Tarrants and Ainsworth are discussed extensively in Jack Nelson's *Terror in the Night* and Don Whitehead's *Attack on Terror*. The Roberts brothers were reportedly pressured to become actual FBI informants and testify in court against Bowers and others. They refused and were said to have taken a large sum of money (collected from local Jewish sources) to provide information and assist in setting up the people who had been conducting Jewish-targeted bombings. FBI records document information from an inner-circle informant stating that a call was made to Meridian, an hour before the abortive bombing, warning that the bombers were on the way and would be there shortly. Interestingly, the same reports also describe Sam Bowers as telling an informant that the Jews were actually going to be financing White Knight activities. As a side note, although the Roberts brothers were reported to have bought a new car, no other sign of their spending the $70,000 payment was ever reported, and there was no apparent retaliation against them, even when it became common knowledge that they had provided information (which led to the confrontation with Tarrants and Ainsworth).

39. Material in Barnes's summary file indicates that he and his wife were much more impressed with Tarrants and believed him to be a far better match for Kathy. They retained that opinion after her marriage.

40. Patsy Sims, *The Klan*, 2nd ed. (Lexington, KY: University Press of Kentucky, 1996) 267. Ainsworth's father was Italian, a circus juggler; her mother a Hungarian dancer. Her parents had separated when Kathy was very young; Margaret Capomacchia lived in Miami, where she did domestic work.

41. FBI, "Airtel from SAC, Jackson to SAC, Charlotte (157-922) Re: Acquisition of Weapons by Racial Extremist Groups" (August 29, 1968), available online at the Harold Weisberg Archive at Hood College, accessed November 10, 2011, http://jfk.hood.edu/Collection/Weisberg%20 Subject%20Index%20Files/G%20Disk/Gale%20Ainsworth%20Byron/Item%2001.pdf.

42. Nelson, 17.

43. Ibid., 143–44, 173.

44. FBI, Sidney Crockette Barnes summary file (November 30, 1971). This is a summary file we obtained via FOIA. Barnes tells one informant that "you'd be surprised how much he [Gale] trusts her [Ainsworth]."

45. Nelson, 29.

46. Ibid., 29–30.

47. FBI, Jackson report of SA Samuel Jennings "Information Concerning Individuals Who Were Formerly Associated with the WKKKKOM, Jones Co., Miss," section 809, at 31–32 (November 15, 1970).

48. FBI, "Memorandum from SA Richard F. Kilcourse to SAC Los Angeles," 62-5101 (April 23, 1968).

49. Mitchell, "Murder of Martin Luther King Jr.; Did Klan Have a Role?"

50. Ibid.

51. Nelson, 61.

52. Ibid., 140.

53. Tarrants, 61.

54. Ibid.

55. Ibid.

56. Nelson, 136, 152–62.

57. FBI, "BH 44-1740. Airtel: SAC Birmingham to Director," report by Special Agents Robert Barrett and William Saucier (April 8, 1968). The information was taken on April 6, 1968, and dictated on April 8, 1968. Under Tarrants's name, reference is made to a file 157-758, which turns out to be a Mobile field office file. The authors attempted to FOIA this information only to learn that Mobile 157-758 file had been destroyed in 1977. It is rare for the FBI to destroy a file while an individual (in this case, Tarrants) is still alive; it also came on the heels of Congress's new inquiry into Dr. King's murder, for which Tarrants's files were requested only a few months after this Mobile file had been destroyed.

58. FBI, "BH 44-1740. Airtel: SAC Birmingham to Director," report by Special Agents Patrick J. Moynihan and Neil P. Shanahan (April 16, 1968). Beckwith was one of the FBI's earliest suspects. They cleared him based on an alibi. In this case, witnesses and records showing he was on a business trip to Jacksonville seem solid.

59. FBI, "Memorandum from SA Richard F. Kilcourse to SAC Los Angeles," 62-5101 (April 23, 1968).

60. Gerard Robinson, in discussion with the authors, September 29, 2011. Robinson knew of Tarrants from his time as a racist rabble-rouser at Murphy High School. It is worth noting that Robinson remembered the integration efforts in Mobile in 1963—and the response at local high schools—as being one of the few other occasions that he was asked to work in the city proper. In that instance, the small field office was stretched thin because of the sheer number of protests and counterdemonstrations at so many high schools. Robinson could not be positive that the search for Tarrants was the one in response to Tarrants jumping bond; however, the context of his comments/recollection made that obvious.

61. Gerard Robinson, in discussion with the authors, October 2, 2011. It should be noted that Robinson seemed more bothered by the Tarrants search in 1968 when he first recollected the incident then in our subsequent interview.

62. Jerry Mitchell, in discussion with the authors, January 2, 2008.

63. John McAdams, "Joseph Milteer: Miami Prophet, or Quitman Crackpot?" The Kennedy Assassination, last modified October 17, 2009, accessed November 11, 2011, http://mcadams. posc.mu.edu/milteer.htm. The accounts of Somersett's reliability in the FBI reports themselves are contradictory. Yes, the FBI had discontinued using Somersett in 1961, but not because he gave unreliable information; rather it was because he risked exposing another important FBI informant. He was also described as someone who was a professional informant, someone who sought financial gain for his services, but the FBI continued to collect information from Somersett. In fact, FBI reports, well after 1961, consistently note that he had "furnished reliable information in the past." Later, by the mid-1960s, Somersett began to provide reports that seemed fanciful, including information about other assassination attempts. By 1967, the FBI claimed he was "unstable" and "prone to exaggeration." Of course, this was also at the same time that account of his taped conversation with extremist Joseph Milteer on November 9, 1963, was first becoming public, and that taping—rightly or wrongly—clearly threatened the FBI's image. Recall that at the same time the FBI was disparaging Somersett in internal records, the Miami PD considered him and continued to use him as one of their most valued informants. As noted throughout in the rest of this chapter, it is likely that Somersett had be-

come more and more unreliable because he was reporting disinformation from individuals and groups who had suspected him as a snitch by 1962. We believe these contradictory accounts offer two implications: (a) one must treat Somersett's reports with a skeptical eye, but on a case-by-case basis, and (b) one must separate Somersett's content from Somersett's motives. In the remainder of the chapter, and the rest of the book, we argue that Somersett, in reporting the King information in 1968, was in fact reliably reporting disinformation.

64. J. B. Stoner to Fred Hockett, May 23, 1962, Digital Collection, Harold Weisberg Archive at Hood College, http://jfk.hood.edu/Collection/Weisberg%20Subject%20Index%20Files/M%20Disk/Milteer%20J%20A/Item%2003.pdf.

65. FBI, "Airtel from SAC Miami to FBI Director re: BAPBOMB, Sidney Crockette Barnes a.k.a. Racial Matters" (March 12, 1964).

66. Ibid.

67. Bill Barry, "Secret Service Mum on Recording Here," Miami News, February 4, 1967, http://news.google.com/newspapers?id=d9UzAAAAIBAJ&sjid=MusFAAAAIBAJ&pg=2271,956298&dq=high-powered+rifle&hl=en.

68. Willie Somersett, "I Charge Robert F. Kennedy with Murder," National Federation of Labor News, March 26, 1967, Cuban Information Archives, accessed November 10, 2011, http://cuban-exile.com/doc_051-075/doc0062p.html; also Dan Christensen, "Assassinations: Miami Link, Part II; Martin Luther King," Miami magazine 27, no. 12 (October 1976), Cuban Information Archives, last modified February 23, 2008, accessed September 15, 2010, http://cuban-exile.com/doc_101-125/doc0114.html. While the title of the RFK piece is inflammatory, there are two things worth keeping in mind. First, the actual text simply charges that RFK was negligent in trying to protect his brother. Somersett's argument assumes that RFK would have even found out about the Milteer report, and there is no evidence that it did. Which brings us to the second major point: Somersett was largely sympathetic with the ideas of the extremists with whom he associated. He was radical in his political beliefs, which is why he was able to ingratiate himself with so many fellow radicals. Somersett, however, did not agree with their violent approach to achieving change, which is why he became an informant.

CHAPTER 7

1. Investigation of the Assassination of Martin Luther King, Jr.: Hearings Before the Select Comm. on Assassinations, 95th Cong., 2nd Session, vol. 5, at 317–18 (November 13–15, 1978), available online at Mary Ferrell Foundation, accessed December 11, 2010, http://www.mary-ferrell.org/mffweb/archive/viewer/showDoc.do?docId=95657&relPageId=321.

2. James Earl Ray, Who Killed Martin Luther King?: The True Story by the Alleged Assassin (New York: Marlowe, 1997) 127–30.

3. William Brandford Huie, He Slew the Dreamer: My Search, with James Earl Ray, for the Truth about the Murder of Martin Luther King, Jr. (New York: Delacorte Press, 1970) 177. It is important to note that Ray maintained the Raoul story even before his plea, to individuals such as Huie.

4. William Pepper, An Act of State: The Execution of Martin Luther King (London: Verso, 2003) 55. The individual, Sid Carthew, came forward after seeing a mock trial of James Earl Ray. But he was coming forward almost twenty-five years after the crime. The timing of his recollection

raises red flags as it stands, but Carthew also had a strong connection to the British Nationalist movement, with its serious strain of xenophobia and racism.

5. Ibid., 198–99. Pepper parrots the line that Ray was simply joking with Huie when he lied in his first alibi tale. But Ray said this to his attorney, Arthur Hanes, as well. He also knew that Huie was in active contact with Hanes. This would mean that Ray was telling a joke to individuals responsible for saving Ray from a possible death sentence.

6. William Bradford Huie, "Why James Earl Ray Murdered Dr. King" *Look* 33, no. 8 (April 15, 1969): 102–12.

7. Select Comm. on Assassinations, *Summary of Findings and Recommendations,* H.R. Rep., section 6, Evidence of a Conspiracy in St. Louis, at 369–70, (1979) available online at Mary Farrell Foundation, accessed December 11, 2010, http://www.maryferrell.org/mffweb/archive/viewer/showDoc.do?absPageId=69427.

8. Petric J. Smith, *Long Time Coming: An Insider's Story of the Birmingham Church Bombing That Rocked the World* (Birmingham, AL: Crane Hill, 1994) 59.

9. Jerry Mitchell, "Murder of Martin Luther King Jr.; Did Klan Have a Role?" *Clarion-Ledger,* December 30, 2007.

10. Confidential interview with the authors, November 2009. The authors wish to protect the woman's identity for a number of reasons.

11. FBI, "Information concerning individuals who were formerly associated with the WKKK-KOM, Jones Co., Miss.," Jackson Report of SA Samuel Jennings, serial 809, at 31-32 (November 15, 1970); also Jack Nelson, *Terror in the Night: The Klan's Campaign against the Jews* (New York: Simon & Schuster, 1993) 139.

12. Activities of the Ku Klux Klan Organizations in the United States: Hearings Before the Comm. on Un-American Activities, 89th Cong. at 2936 (February 1 and 7–11, 1966) accessed September 15, 2010, http://www.archive.org/stream/activitiesofkukl05unit/activitiesofkuk-l05unit_djvu.txt.

13. FBI, "Airtel from SAC Oklahoma City to Director re: Donald Eugene Sparks . . ." (April 24, 1968) King Assassination FBI Central Headquarters File, MURKIN 44-38861-2926; also FBI, "Airtel from Tampa to Director re: Donald Eugene Sparks . . ." (April 18, 1968) King Assassination FBI Central Headquarters File, MURKIN 44-38861-1331.

14. "Donald Sparks, Alias . . ." *Evening Independent,* November 15, 1967, http://news.google.com/newspapers?nid=950&dat=19671115&id=F-4LAAAAIBAJ&sjid=O1cDAAAAIBAJ&pg=5447,2716870.

15. FBI, "Airtel from Tampa to Director re: Donald Eugene Sparks . . ." (April 18, 1968) King Assassination FBI Central Headquarters File, MURKIN 44-38861-1331. The FBI also challenged Knight because he reported the rumor that Sparks was involved in the killing of another wanted fugitive, John Gibson Dillon. Knight claimed that Dillon was killed in Mississippi and then taken to Oklahoma, where his body was found buried in a well. While the details of where the killing took place are not discussed in the reports, the Oklahoma State Bureau of Investigation did cite an informant who said that Rubie Jenkins, Lester Pugh, and others were involved in Dillon's murder. All these men, especially Jenkins, were close to Sparks. In fact, one document, without describing where the murder took place, says that Jenkins was driving a car when someone (not identified) bludgeoned Dillon to death. See Dee Cordry, "Dixie Mafia, Part 2," The State Crime Bureau Journal (blog), October 11, 2009, http://statecrimebureau.

wordpress.com/tag/dixie-mafia.

16. FBI, "Airtel from SAC Oklahoma City to Director re: Donald Eugene Sparks . . ." (April 24, 1968) King Assassination FBI Central Headquarters File, MURKIN 44-38861-2926. The first name for Chambliss is redacted.

17. Ibid.

18. Ibid.

19. Bernie Ward, *Kansas Intelligence Report: The Dixie Mafia* (Topeka, KS: The Office of Attorney General Vern Miller, 1974).

20. Janet Upshaw, in discussion with the authors, December 15, 2010.

21. Ward, 7, 45.

22. Ibid., 31–34. This came from the Assistant U.S. Attorney for the Western District of Tennessee.

23. Ibid., 26–31. Leroy B. McManaman, *Appellant, v. United States of America.* 327 F.2d 21. United States Court of Appeals Tenth Circuit. 28 Jan 1964. As described by S. M. Fallas, district attorney in Tulsa County, Oklahoma: The associations and contacts among these individuals went back to prohibition days, evolved into bootlegging, later using their distribution networks to dispose of properties ranging from high dollar burglaries and residence robberies to stolen vehicles. The bootleggers, with a long period of trial and error, had established a good network including transportation, storage and distribution. They also developed a network of bail bondsmen and lawyers, which were very necessary to their expansion into robbery, burglary, arson and murder. After prohibition and after the general decline of bootlegging, they had to either go straight or use their existing pipelines (infrastructure) for other criminal activity. As an example, Leroy McManaman, of Kansas (who will be discussed at length in regard to an MLK murder contract), was indicted in Wichita in 1948 for illegal transport of over 12,000 gallons of whiskey from Illinois and Nebraska into the dry state of Kansas. The value of the whiskey was over $1,000,000 in 1948 dollars. By 1952, McManaman had moved into armed residential robbery and was sentenced to 2042 years. His parole and pardon after only three years (over adamant objection of the judge involved in the sentencing) was something of a scandal in the state. Shortly after his pardon he was arrested for transport of 54 cases of illegal whiskey. His next arrest, as a resident of Oklahoma, was in partnership with Rubie Charles Jenkins (a close associate of Donald Sparks), for interstate transport of stolen vehicles was an extremely sophisticated operation with false registrations obtained in Alabama. He and Jenkins were also charged with interstate transport of weapons and other crimes of violence. *Leroy B. McManaman, Appellant v. United States of America,* United States Court of Appeals Tenth Circuit, 327 F.2d 21, January 28, 1964 Rehearing Denied February 11, 1964.

24. Ibid., 27–33.

25. Ibid., 18–19, 32.

26. Ibid., 59.

27. Confidential interview with the authors, March 21, 2010. The source wishes to remain anonymous.

28. Ward, 19–20.

29. Ibid., 20–24, 32.

30. FBI, "Alleged Offer of $100,000 by White Knights of the Ku Klux Klan, Jackson, Mississippi, to Anyone Who Kills Martin Luther King." Main King File, file 100-106671, section 73,

at 207–10.

31. Donald Nissen, in discussion with the authors, November 9, 2009. We have had numerous interviews and follow-up interviews with Nissen, and he has never wavered on the core details of his story. In only one instance did he dispute the details reported by the Dallas FBI agents who originally interviewed him. He said the part of the report where the agents claimed he had a relationship with McManaman prior to his stay in Leavenworth was inaccurate. It is not uncommon for agents to misreport details, as they do not record interviews or send verbatim transcripts. Nothing in the criminal histories of either man—McManaman or Nissen—suggest that they could have or did have prior contact.

32. Ibid.

33. Ibid.

34. Ibid.

35. Ibid.

36. Ibid.

37. Ibid.

38. FBI, "Airtel from St. Louis to Director" section 69, at 21 (August 12, 1968) King Assassination FBI Central Headquarters File, available online at the Mary Ferrell Foundation, accessed September 15, 2010, http://www.maryferrell.org/mffweb/archive/viewer/showDoc.do?docId= 99886&relPageId=21.

39. "McManaman Draws Sentence of 20 to 42 years," *Great Bend Daily Tribune,* September 22, 1952; also "Figure in Parole, Pardon Case Here Fined on Liquor Charge," *Great Bend Daily Tribune,* February 26, 1958; also "Indict Wichita Booze Dealer," *Atchison Daily Globe,* September 17, 1948; also various Kansas State newspaper articles in the Atchison Daily Globe, September 17, 1948, and *Great Bend Daily Tribune,* September 22, 1953, and September 26, 1958.

40. FBI, "Re: Alleged Offer of $100,000 by the WKKKKOM to Anyone Who Kills Martin Luther King, Jr . . . ," Jackson Field Office File 157-7990 (July 24, 1967). We obtained these files via the Freedom of Information Act. They contain a number of key reports, including the prison records on Nissen and McManaman. These records confirm they worked at the same shoe factory. They also confirm McManaman's desire to marry Sybil Eure. They also include a handful of informant reports, where the FBI asked informants about a $100,000 bounty offer. These are notable for a few reasons. For one thing, they only asked a handful of informants, when the record indicates that they had dozens of them. Secondly, while none of the informants directly heard of a bounty, one informant said he heard that the White Knights were considering putting out flyers offering a $100,000 bounty on King's life. There is no evidence that any such flyers were ever printed. But this suggests that the White Knights had an expectation of having a large sum of money even when they supposedly were losing funds paying for legal defenses.

41. Leroy B. McManaman 327 F.2d 21. United States Court of Appeals Tenth Circuit. McManaman appealed with Jenkins.

42. Confidential interview with the authors, November 20, 2009. The source wished to remain anonymous, but is considered an expert on the Dixie Mafia.

43. Rubie Jenkins, in discussion with the authors, March 18, 2010. Jenkins was elderly at the time of our conversation, but he was sharp. Jenkins was able, without prompting, to identify McManaman as a "redneck from Kansas." He acknowledged that McManaman was "in our gang," referring to his group with Sparks. He denied knowing anything about the King as-

sassination. We do not have any reason to believe he was ever in the loop from the available evidence.

44. "Pardon Recalls Famed Case Here," *Great Bend Daily Tribune,* August 23, 1957.

45. *Leroy B. McManaman, Appellant, v. United States of America.* 327 F.2d 21. United States Court of Appeals Tenth Circuit. January 28, 1964.

46. Charlie Sutherland, in discussion with the authors, November 5, 2010. Sutherland was the deputy federal marshal for the Southern District of Mississippi. We approached Sutherland because (a) the original June 1967 report to the FBI mentioned that an unnamed federal marshal in Mississippi would be a cutout in the case and (b) Sybil Eure identified Sutherland as her cousin to investigators. Sutherland is confident none of his fellow marshals would have participated as cutouts in the White Knights plot. Sutherland also denies, and we believe him, that he himself was not a part of such a plot. On the other hand, we wonder if the mention of Sutherland to Eure—they were cousins—may have been a password of sorts for the source (or anyone involved in the plot) to signal a wish to become entwined in the bounty plot.

47. FBI, "Re: Alleged Offer of $100,000 by the WKKKKOM to Anyone Who Kills Martin Luther King, Jr . . . ," Jackson Field Office File 157-7990 (July 24, 1967).

48. FBI, "Re: Alleged Offer of $100,000 by the WKKKKOM to Anyone Who Kills Martin Luther King, Jr . . . ," (May 17, 1968) MURKIN 44-38861-396. This document includes a summary of both the 1967 and 1968 interviews with Eure.

49. Ibid.

50. FBI, "Airtel from SAC Kansas City to Director re: Memphis Airtel to Kansas City 8-23-68" (September 10, 1968) MURKIN 44-38861-5161.

51. FBI, "Re: Alleged Offer of $100,000 by the WKKKKOM to Anyone Who Kills Martin Luther King, Jr . . . ," Jackson Field Office File 157-7990 (July 24, 1967).

52. Donald Nissen, in discussion with the authors, November 9, 2009. Again, Nissen has insisted from the start that told FBI agent Wayne Mack about the package delivery in August 1968, after he turned himself in. Nissen has no obvious reason to dissemble, as he has avoided publicity for this story for forty years. Recall that we found him, not the other way around. An explanation for why the package delivery story is not in the August 1968 reports is thus important. Several possibilities present themselves. For one thing, Nissen told us that he requested Special Agent Mack because he and Mack had a unique relationship. While they were on opposite sides of the law, they had friendly interactions with each other. One wonders if Mack, knowing the chances that the FBI could expose an informant to harm by accident—through follow-up interviews with accused perpetrators—may have tried to protect Nissen by sanitizing the account. If so, it didn't work, as the FBI did clearly expose Nissen to potential identification even before the King assassination, through their follow-up interviews at Leavenworth penitentiary. This likely was the reason the mysterious man confronted Nissen in Atlanta in December 1967, the event that compelled Nissen to become parole violator. Nissen also recalls that his car windows were damaged not long after the December threat, something that he still believes was connected to the same event. This is not noted in the record, but Nissen never said he provided this information to the FBI, perhaps because it added little to what he was already saying (or because he himself is still not certain if it was directly related to King issue). One could also imagine the SAC in Saint Louis wanting to protect friends in the Jackson field office from the wrath of FBI director J. Edgar Hoover. Hoover had come down hard on individual agents whose behavior, before, during,

and after the JFK assassination embarrassed the bureau. If it came out that agents in the Jackson office failed to take Nissen's original claims seriously before King was murdered, that certainly could make Hoover just as upset with his underlings. This is all speculative, and the answer may not lie in the FBI sanitizing documents but in the vagaries of human memory. It is worth noting that while Nissen was consistent and sharp in his memory, he also had occasional memory lapses. He was, after all, recalling events that are more than forty years old. Studies by experts such as Elizabeth Loftus show that human memory can be confused by more than just the passage of time. Experts say that people often subconsciously remember events in a way that is acceptable to their ethical and personal worldview at the time of recollection. Nissen at present is a born-again Christian, but he was not in 1968. In August 1968, Nissen's conversation with Wayne Mack about the package delivery could have potentially exposed Nissen—unjustifiably—to criminal prosecution. This is because it should have been obvious to Nissen that when he delivered the package he was delivering it to the woman he identified to the Dallas FBI office in June 1967. In his very first, original report, Nissen identified Eure by name and occupation and location. Nissen was and is a smart individual; once he traveled from Atlanta, Georgia, to Jackson, Mississippi, and gave a package to a real estate agent, he must have realized it was possibly connected to the McManaman plot. He very well may not have known about the contents of the package or the exact purpose of his trip—he denies that he did and we believe him. But Nissen also admitted to us that he should have made the connection to Eure/McManaman at the time of the delivery; without committing to an explanation, he did suggest that he may have been afraid of the consequences of not giving Eure the package, as he never truly said no to McManaman in prison. He feared McManaman's reach, even from prison, and may have just gone along to get along, only to find out just how serious his delivery truly was. His subconscious might want him to have told the full truth to the FBI, but perhaps he did not. Another phenomen noted by memory experts is the concept of confabulation. This is when one memory blends with or distorts another memory. Nissen gave us a very specific account of having gone to Martin Luther King Sr. with information about his son's murder; he said he told King's father about the package delivery. Perhaps he confused his efforts to tell the full story to the King family in his recollection of what he did or did not tell the FBI in August 1968. For information on issues with memory see Stephen J. Lynn and Kevin M. McConkey, *Truth in Memory* (New York: Guilford Press, 1998). On this last front, Nissen was very specific and noted that a secretary may have taped and/or transcribed the meeting. Even then, Nissen insisted that his identity be protected. We have tried to locate the tape, but, according to archivists at the King Center in Atlanta, it is likely that such a tape would be among the many items in the King family possession that have not yet been processed and/or donated to the facility. Finding these tapes and/or transcripts would be very important.

53. The FBI appears to have taken Sybil Eure at her word that her brother was in no way connected to any bounty. There is no evidence that they ever interviewed or investigated him in connection with a King plot.

54. "'Crashed' King Rites; Tries to 'See' LBJ; Quickly Arrested," *Jet* (May 23, 1968) 8–9, http:// books.google.com/books?id=SzgDAAAAMBAJ&pg=PA9&dq=ayers+king+funeral&hl=en&e i=aH_yTPTQLoa8lQfly9jbDA&sa=X&oi=book_result&ct=result&resnum=2&ved=0CDIQ6 AEwAQ#v=onepage&q=ayers%20king%20funeral&f=false.

55. The Reverend John Ayers, in discussion with the authors, November 16, 2010. Ayers had no direct information about any involvement in any plot by his brother to kill Dr. King. But he

did not dismiss the idea out of hand either. He was very helpful in providing information about Floyd's life and connections to James Venable.

56. Chester Higgins, "Hair-Raising Experience: 'Kidnap' Try of King Sr. Foiled; Add More Police Protection," *Jet* (May 2, 1968): 14–19, http://books.google.com/books?id=UTgDAAA AMBAJ&pg=PA14&dq=ayers+king+funeral&hl=en&ei=SYDyTOG0KIH6lwea0JSpDA&sa =X&oi=book_result&ct=result&resnum=4&ved=0CDsQ6AEwAw#v=onepage&q=ayers%20 king%20funeral&f=false. The article mentions Ayers's stay at a mental hospital. Ayers's brother says that this may have been connected to an impulsive, violent temper.

57. Additionally, reports from the Miami Police show that Milteer was, at least as of 1963, leading an underground, militant group that was discussing killing prominent political leaders; one other member of this group, Harry "Jack" Brown, was described by Milteer—on tape in 1963—as actively plotting to kill Martin Luther King Jr.

58. Lamar Waldron with Thom Hartmann, *Legacy of Secrecy: The Long Shadow of the JFK Assassination* (Berkeley, CA: Counterpoint, 2008) 339–40, 500–1.

CHAPTER 8

1. Testimony of James Earl Ray, *James Earl Ray v. James H. Rose,* Civil Action No. C-74-166, U.S. District Court for the Western District of Tennessee, Box 13, OPR FBI, 826–831; also Gerold Frank, *An American Death: The True Story of the Assassination of Dr. Martin Luther King, Jr., and the Greatest Manhunt of Our Time* (New York: Doubleday, 1972) 380.

2. Investigation of the Assassination of Martin Luther King, Jr.: Hearings Before the Select Comm. on Assassinations, 95th Cong., 2nd Session, vol. 5, at 317–18 (November 13–15, 1978), available online at Mary Ferrell Foundation, accessed December 11, 2010, http://www.mary-ferrell.org/mffweb/archive/viewer/showDoc.do?docId=95657&relPageId=321.

3. Defense counsels often strenuously avoid evidence or associations that would suggest conspiracy in cases where an insanity defense is being offered. Examples would include not only the trial of James Earl Ray but also the well-known court cases against Sirhan Sirhan and Jack Ruby. In such cases both the prosecution and defense appear to have a common interest in remaining tightly focused on only the defendant.

4. Frank, 178. FBI agents had interviewed John Ray in his Grapevine Tavern. In addition to offering his opinion on his brother, John Ray also asked, "What's all the excitement about; it's only a nigger?" and added that "King should have been killed ten years ago."

5. Jerry Mitchell, "Ex-wife: James Earl Ray 'Didn't Do Anything for Free,'" Journey to Justice (blog), *Clarion-Ledger,* April 1, 2010, http://blogs.clarionledger.com/jmitchell/2010/04/01/ex-wife-james-earl-ray-didnt-do-anything-for-free. Ray's ex-wife describes his attitude in some detail in a recent interview with Jerry Mitchell. Among other things, she shared the following exchange: When she spoke on the telephone to her husband in prison, he angrily asked, "Why haven't you come to see me?" She replied that she needed $800 to fix the car. Ray said if he did get her some money, he wanted to make sure he got paid back. And if she failed to pay him back, Ray told her he'd have someone come by and shoot up her house. She asked him if he had been drinking or was simply having a bad day. He asked why. "Well, you're starting to sound like somebody who would kill Martin Luther King," she quoted herself as saying. "Yeah, I did it," she quoted Ray as replying. "So what? I never got a trial." Not long after that, a Ku Klux Klan

group marched in the Nashville area on Martin Luther King Jr. Day, calling their celebration "James Earl Ray Day." Anna Ray said she was horrified and called the press, telling them Ray wouldn't approve of this. Not long after that, she said, she received papers from Ray. He wanted a divorce, which was finalized in 1993.

6. William Brandford Huie, *He Slew the Dreamer: My Search, with James Earl Ray, for the Truth about the Murder of Martin Luther King, Jr.* (New York: Delacorte Press, 1970) 1–2.

7. William Bradford Huie, "The Story of James Earl Ray and the Conspiracy to Kill Martin Luther King," *Look* 32, no. 23 (November 12, 1968).

8. Frank, 203.

9. Huie, *He Slew the Dreamer,* 13.

10. Ibid., 3.

11. William Bradford Huie, "Why James Earl Ray Murdered Dr. King," *Look* 33, no. 8 (April 15, 1969): 102–12.

12. Huie, *He Slew the Dreamer.*

13. Frank, 206–10. As a side note, Hanes was also a vetted CIA legal asset; he had been used to arrange payments to members of the Alabama Guard unit who had been killed in covert missions supporting the Bay of Pigs. Hanes offered a number of suspects in a conspiracy associated with Ray: black militants, Chinese communists, Vietnamese agents, and eventually Castro agents. Indeed it seems he offered virtually every sort of sponsor other than racists or Klansmen (stating that he had put out feelers to a number of such people and none of them had any knowledge of James Earl Ray).

14. Ibid., 246. Ray, for instance, told William Bradford Huie that he had come across his name while reading Huie's 1956 *Look* magazine article about the racial murder of Emmett Till.

15. Frank, 249, 357. The question of motive has been a major challenge for virtually everyone writing on Ray. In his early work and follow-up books, William Bradford Huie developed the idea that Ray became obsessed with earning himself a place as America's number one criminal and pictured himself heading the FBI's Most Wanted list. In Gerold Frank's massive book on Ray and the crime, which followed Huie's work, he presented a completely different motive, that Ray had a deep-seated, obsessive hatred of blacks and was fulfilling that hatred in killing Dr. King. As we will see, neither of these theories seems to match Ray's actual behavior during the year and a half prior to the shooting of Dr. King in Memphis—indeed Frank contradicts his own final assessment of motive by describing Ray as having nothing in his lifestyle that indicated any cause, nothing ideological in his makeup, and never doing anything that did not benefit him.

16. Frank.

17. William Pepper, *Orders to Kill: The Truth Behind the Murder of Martin Luther King, Jr.* (New York: Caroll & Graf, 1995) 53–54.

18. Frank, 174.

19. Ibid.

20. John Larry Ray and Lyndon Barsten, *Truth at Last: The Untold Story of James Earl Ray and the Assassination of Martin Luther King Jr.* (Guilford, CT: Lyons Press, 2008) 18–26.

21. Ibid., 25.

22. Walter Elkins, "1st Infantry Division." U.S. Army in Germany, last modified June 26, 2010, accessed November 16, 2010, http://www.usarmygermany.com/units/1st%20Inf%20Div/

USAREUR_1st%20Inf%20Div.htm. This site includes a discussion of unit designations as well as information from a former member of the 7892th Infantry Regiment, the unit John Ray and Lyndon Barsten discussed. The website mentions that unit was brought up to combat readiness and was redesignated the 16th Infantry Regiment (coincident with the 16th Regiment being disbanded in Austria and merged into the 16th Infantry). This history provides examples of at least four other army units designated with four-digit numbers.

23. Frank, 174.

24. Lamar Waldron with Thom Hartmann, *Legacy of Secrecy: The Long Shadow of the JFK Assassination* (Berkeley, CA: Counterpoint, 2008) 475. Waldron cites a *Playboy* magazine interview with James Earl Ray. Ray admitted to dealing drugs in prison but qualified his statement by describing himself as "not a big operator" and referring only to his time in Missouri.

25. Jim Bishop, *The Days of Martin Luther King, Jr.* (New York, Putnam: 1971) 40.

26. Ibid., 91.

27. Ibid., 91–92.

28. Gerald Posner, *Killing the Dream: James Earl Ray and the Assassination of Martin Luther King, Jr.* (New York: Harcourt Brace & Co., 1998) 114–15. Aspects of this particular crime provide a good illustration of Ray's increasing sophistication. In this incident it appears that Ray and his partner planned a legal defense that would minimize their actual sentence if caught—given the serious nature of robbing a post office and thus committing a federal crime. Their defense involved concocting a fictitious individual named McBride, who would have supposedly committed the actual robbery. Ray and his partner would be guilty only of purchasing stolen items from McBride, not of the post office theft. The plan worked for them. They were not seen or identified in committing the robbery and when caught were charged only with illegally passing stolen money orders rather than the robbery of a federal post office. Ray's ability and tendency to shift his crimes to mythical confederates was consistent and at least occasionally successful.

29. Huie, *He Slew the Dreamer*, 10.

30. FBI, "Teletype, Minneapolis to Director, Interview with Paul Bridgeman" (June 7, 1968) MURKIN 4251-4350.

31. FBI, "Interview with Cecil Lillibridge" (April 29, 1968) MURKIN 3503, section 39, at 61–64 and MURKIN 2553-2321, section 25, at 109.

32. Huie, *He Slew the Dreamer*, 87. A decade later, the bartender would tell the HSCA that he did not recall the fight. Huie, however, also interviewed two women in the bar who confirmed it.

33. Interview with Jerry Ray by George McMillian, May 29, 1972. Jerry Ray interviews 1969-1975, Box 5; Trial and Post-Trial materials, McMillian/Southern Historical Collection.

34. Investigation of the Assassination of Martin Luther King, Jr.: Appendix to Hearings Before the Select Comm. on Assassinations, 95th Cong., 2nd Sess., vol. xii, at 204, available online at Mary Ferrell Foundation, accessed December 11, 2010, http://www.maryferrell.org/mffweb/archive/viewer/showDoc.do?docId=99710&relPageId=206.

CHAPTER 9

1. FBI, "Memo from Rosen to Deloach," (August 23, 1968) King Assassination FBI Central Headquarters File, MURKIN 44-38861-512, section 69, available online at the Mary Ferrell Foundation, accessed September 15, 2010, http://www.maryferrell.org/mffweb/archive/view-

er/showDoc.do?mode=searchResult&absPageId=113185

2. FBI, MURKIN 4441, section 56, at 19; MURKIN section 19, at 2151-321, section 19, at 226; MURKIN 2326-2440, section 23, at 245; and MURKIN 4143, section 52, at 55.

3. Select Comm. on Assassinations, Summary of Findings and Recommendations, H.R. Rep., section 6, Evidence of a Conspiracy in St. Louis, at 359–70 (1979), Mary Farrell Foundation, accessed December 11, 2010, http://www.maryferrell.org/mffweb/archive/viewer/showDoc. do?absPageId=69427.

4. Ibid., 365.

5. FBI, Investigative Summary, National States Rights Party (1976).

6. Select Comm. on Assassinations, Summary of Findings and Recommendations, H.R. Rep., section 6, Evidence of a Conspiracy in St. Louis, at 366 (1979), Mary Farrell Foundation, accessed December 11, 2010, http://www.maryferrell.org/mffweb/archive/viewer/showDoc. do?absPageId=69427.

7. Ibid., 366-67.

8. Investigation of the Assassination of Martin Luther King, Jr.: Appendix to Hearings Before the Select Comm. on Assassinations, 95th Cong., 2nd Sess., vol. xii, at 248-49 (September 30, 1968) (interview with Donald Mitchell), available online at Mary Ferrell Foundation, accessed December 11, 2010, http://www.maryferrell.org/mffweb/archive/viewer/showDoc. do?docId=95664&relPageId=252. This reported act by Ray is very similar to a King bounty referral made in Leavenworth penitentiary in 1967, where an inmate knowing of a $100,000 bounty on Dr. King referred it to another inmate who was getting out sooner than he was.

9. William Brandford Huie, *He Slew the Dreamer: My Search, with James Earl Ray, for the Truth about the Murder of Martin Luther King, Jr.* (New York: Delacorte Press, 1970) 17–19.

10. George McMillian, *The Making of an Assassin: The Life of James Earl Ray* (Boston: Little, Brown, 1976) 241.

11. Ibid., 240; also McMillian interviews of Jerry Ray May 10, 1970; May 30, 1972; February 23, 1975; July 7 1975; Box 5, Trial and Post Trial materials, McMillian/Southern Historical Collection.

12. Gerald Posner, *Killing the Dream: James Earl Ray and the Assassination of Martin Luther King, Jr.* (New York: Harcourt Brace & Co., 1998) 131.

13. Huie, 22–26.

14. Select Comm. on Assassinations, *Summary of Findings and Recommendations*, H.R. Rep., section 6, Evidence of a Conspiracy in St. Louis, at 370, (1979) available online at Mary Farrell Foundation, accessed December 11, 2010, http://www.maryferrell.org/mffweb/archive/viewer/ showDoc.do?absPageId=69427.

15. Ibid., 368–69.

16. Ibid., 369.

17. Ibid.

18. Ibid., 22–24.

19. Jim Bishop, *The Days of Martin Luther King, Jr.* (New York, Putnam: 1971) 41-42.

20. Investigation of the Assassination of Martin Luther King, Jr.: Hearings Before the Select Comm. on Assassinations, 95th Cong., 2nd Session, vol. 5, at 313 (November 13–15, 1978), available online at Mary Ferrell Foundation, accessed December 11, 2010, http://www.mary-ferrell.org/mffweb/archive/viewer/showDoc.do?docId=95659&relPageId=317. The HSCA and

the FBI focused heavily on Ray's brothers as suspects. We also suspect that the brothers had more involvement than they have disclosed with James Earl Ray after his escape in 1967. Some of James Earl Ray's references to Raoul may have in fact been references to Jerry Ray. But a reference to a "brother" is simple enough as a cover for just about any contact that one wishes to hide. So while we concede the possibility that they may have been involved at some level with Ray after his escape, there is no solid evidence that ties them to any of Ray's crimes after his escape from Missouri State Penitentiary.

21. Huie, 75.

22. Ibid., 50–78.

23. Ibid., 38.

24. FBI, "Teletype SAC Omaha to Director" (April 10, 1968) MURKIN 1301-421, section 11, at 228.

25. Select Comm. on Assassinations, *Summary of Findings and Recommendations,* at 388 (1979), National Archives, accessed December 11, 2010 available online at Mary Ferrell Foundation, accessed December 11, 2010, http://www.maryferrell.org/mffweb/archive/viewer/showDoc.do?docId=95659&relPageId=392.

26. Gerold Frank, *An American Death: The True Story of the Assassination of Dr. Martin Luther King, Jr., and the Greatest Manhunt of Our Time* (New York: Doubleday, 1972) 294–95.

27. Ibid., 138-39, 173.

28. Ibid., 172.

29. Huie, 110.

CHAPTER 10

1. As with many other pieces of information, the phone calls are suggestive but circumstantial. They came from pay phones where Ray stopped and was attempted to make calls, however the calls cannot be specifically traced to Ray, and information on the telephone numbers themselves is no longer available, other than the fact that they were unlisted numbers in cities associated with King bounty offers. We know that several of the White Knight members in Laurel and Jackson had unlisted numbers, but those records are long gone as of 2010. Thanks to the efforts of researcher Joy Washburn, the Laurel number was traced to a series of classified ads in the *Laurel Leader-Call.* Unfortunately, again, whatever individuals were connected to the ads neglected to leave their names or identifying information, only the otherwise unlisted Laurel number. The ads were mostly for automobiles, some fairly expensive for the time period. It is impossible to tell whether these ads were for wholly legitimate business activities or fronts for something more. The last ad, listed the day after a call from the Texas pay phone, was for a mechanic. That ad was the last time this number appeared anywhere in the public domain.

2. William Brandford Huie, *He Slew the Dreamer: My Search, with James Earl Ray, for the Truth about the Murder of Martin Luther King, Jr.* (New York: Delacorte Press, 1970) 115–19.

3. Ibid., 22–24.

4. Gerold Frank, *An American Death: The True Story of the Assassination of Dr. Martin Luther King, Jr., and the Greatest Manhunt of Our Time* (New York: Doubleday, 1972) 300–301.

5. Ibid., 301. The Montreal World's Fair was known as Expo 77; it had begun in the spring of 1967 and drew a considerable number of U.S. citizens to Montreal and increased traffic across

the U.S./Canadian border.

6. Philip H. Melanson, *The Martin Luther King Assassination: New Revelations on the Conspiracy and Cover-up* (New York: S.P.I. Books, 1994) 31-38. Professor Melanson thoroughly developed and detailed issues regarding the name Eric Starvo Galt. There was no such individual Eric Starvo Galt; however, over a period of years, Eric St. Vincent Galt had signed his full name in an abbreviated fashion that might have lead to St. Vincent being misread as Starvo (his penmanship was rather sloppy; of course that would only apply to signed rather than typed documents). Melanson determined that Eric St. Vincent Galt had begun, over a several-month period in 1966, to change his signature to Eric S. Galt. Melanson felt that would have prevented Ray from seeing (and misreading) a written sample during his trip to Canada in 1967. Melanson speculated on who might have given the name Eric Starvo to Galt, his suspicion was increased by the fact that he thought that Ray himself had only used the Starvo name once, when he leased an apartment in Montreal. This led Melanson to believe that Ray had actually changed his usage of the name to reflect Eric St. Vincent Galt's new signature style. While it is true that Ray routinely signed his Galt alias as Eric S. Galt, he did again use the Starvo name when submitting a driver's license application in Birmingham. It is possible that he was prompted to provide his full name at that point rather than just an initial (it is also possible that Ray felt he should use a full name on legal documents) but his Birmingham use of Starvo rather than the actual St. Vincent middle name seems to confirm that Ray had no knowledge of the true Eric St. Vincent Galt (or that someone had "corrected" his knowledge the name) and suggests that he truly was not trying to steal the identity of Eric St. Vincent Galt. Investigation did locate an Eric S. Galt (the individual's full name was Eric St. Vincent Galt). He lived in Toronto and worked for Union Carbide as a manufacturing inspector for proximity fuses.[7] The FBI further determined that Eric Galt was listed in the 1967 Toronto telephone directory.[8] But there was no actual "Eric Starvo Galt" who was a legal Canadian citizen. Because of that, Ray could not steal the "real" identity of Eric Starvo Galt. Ray was not unfamiliar with the techniques involved with identity theft, as he would demonstrate after the King assassination. But in 1967, Ray would have had a problem if he had tried to steal the identity of the real Eric St. Vincent Galt to obtain a passport, as St. Vincent Galt traveled internationally and already had a passport. Actually there is no evidence that Ray ever held any sort of Canadian identification for either Eric S. Galt or Eric Starvo Galt.[9] Certainly he had none for Eric St. Vincent Galt. It seems logical to view Ray's first use of the name "Eric S. Galt" or "Eric Starvo Galt" as a simple alias of convenience. It is noteworthy only because Ray would use that alias again back in the United States when obtaining a driver's license in Alabama.

7. Ibid., 32–33. Eric St. Vincent Galt was required to have a Royal Canadian Mounted Police security clearance in support of his job; his firm handled work on certain military contracts, and all workers at the Union Carbide Toronto plant underwent periodic security checks. Galt's last RCMP check had been in 1961. Galt worked on contracts for certain military projects and had worked on top-secret proximity fuze. This security aspect of his job led some authors, including Melanson and William Pepper (*Orders to Kill: The Truth Behind the Murder of Martin Luther King, Jr.,* New York: Caroll & Graf, 1995) to propose that his identity was known to U.S. intelligence organizations and was provided to James Earl Ray involving in a sophisticated government conspiracy targeting Dr. King.

8. FBI memo to Director, Memphis (April 18, 1968).

9. Melanson, *The Martin Luther King Assassination,* 20-22, 34-35. There is a possibility that Ray

did consider using the Eric S. Galt name as a true false ID; Ray did write the Canadian Department of Veterans Affairs using that name. Unfortunately neither the actual letter nor any response was ever made available, even though requested. That leaves Ray's motive totally in doubt, and he refused to elaborate on it when questioned. Generally speaking, both the Royal Canadian Mounted Police and other Canadian departments have been very unresponsive in providing Ray and King related documents, citing Canadian privacy and confidentiality laws.

10. Investigation of the Assassination of Martin Luther King, Jr.: Appendix to Hearings Before the Select Comm. on Assassinations, 95th Cong., 2nd Sess., vol. xii, at 252, available online at Mary Ferrell Foundation, accessed December 11, 2010, http://www.maryferrell.org/mffweb/archive/viewer/showDoc.do?docId=95659&relPageId=392. In Los Angeles in December 1967, Ray wrote to the U.S.–South Africa Business Council requesting information about emigration to Rhodesia. His choice of destinations in Africa is corroborated by a variety of his contacts in 1968, after he had successfully left Canada and traveled to Portugal, exploring possible mercenary jobs in Angola.

11. Ray's understanding was a common one for the time; in interviewing other convicts at Missouri State Penitentiary, the FBI determined that there was a general knowledge of how to get Canadian identification, and the descriptions were very much in line with the process Ray followed.

12. Frank, 315.

13. For those who underestimate Ray and overestimate his sincerity, it is necessary to note that while on trial for a 1977 prison escape, Ray met Anna Sandhu, a young courtroom artist. Ray impressed her with his sincerity and his innocence, and within a year the couple married. Anna Ray carried on a media campaign for years until she suddenly filed for divorce in 1990. Anna Ray has publically stated that the reason for the divorce was an argument during which Ray challenged her with a statement that he had indeed killed King and that it was no big deal.

14. Frank, 39. Ray spent about $600 on new clothing and a week's lodging at Gray Rocks; for Ray that sort of spending was something totally unprecedented.

15. Report on Salwyn President John F. Kennedy-Murder of-Assistance to the F.B.I, HSCA Administrative Folder U9, RCMP, available online at Mary Ferrell Foundation accessed September 15, 2010, http://www.maryferrell.org/mffweb/archive/viewer/showDoc.do?docId=10097&relPageId=153. Information provided by Marcell Mathieu of Montreal.

16. Ibid.; information provided by Lise Robilland of Montreal.

17. Philip H. Melanson, The MURKIN Conspiracy: An Investigation into the Assassination of Dr. Martin Luther King, Jr. (New York : Praeger, 1989) 44–50.

18. Kimble had an obvious talent for diverting inquiries well away from his proven Klan associations/drug connections and toward mysterious FBI and CIA sponsors. James Earl Ray used a similar technique to divert investigators toward "Raoul" and his mysterious sponsors.

19. Select Comm. on Assassinations, Summary of Findings and Recommendations, H.R. Rep., at 663 (1979), available online at Mary Ferrell Foundation, accessed December 10, 2010, http://www.maryferrell.org/mffweb/archive/viewer/showDoc.do?mode=searchResult&absPageId=69731.

20. Melanson, The Martin Luther King Assassination, 47–49.

21. Ibid., 49–59.

22. The HSCA discovered no evidence that Kimble himself had smuggled drugs. Based on both his wife's and girlfriend's remarks about his hospital jobs, drug connection, and ready access to cash, it may well be that Kimble focused on obtaining controlled substances and shopped them to others for trafficking. The reporter who most seriously investigated Kimble was able to obtain telephone

numbers called from the phone of one of his Canadian calls; dummy calls determined that the numbers were answered at one bar in New Orleans and five bars in Texas. We speculate that Ray did cross paths with Kimble, a fellow American in Montreal who would have been highly visible in the neighborhood of Ray's apartment, and that Ray left Canada with contact information on fences in New Orleans, Texas, and possibly Miami. He may also have picked up a strong interest in hypnotism from Kimble, who had discussed the subject enthusiastically with one of his Canadian girlfriends and proclaimed its benefits and his own expertise. Ray himself developed a serious interest in hypnotism in 1967; while in Montreal he bought several books on hypnosis. Ray carried the hypnotism books for months; they were with his luggage when he was taken into custody in London following the King assassination. One of the first things he had done upon his arrival in Los Angeles in December 1967 was to locate a Beverly Hills psychologist who specialized in self-hypnosis; Ray started a series of sessions with Dr. Mark O. Freeman early in January 1968.

23. The Royal Canadian Mounted Police conducted an investigation of Kimble via his girl-friend; we have located a copy of the request from FBI headquarters to Ottawa requesting the full results of that investigation; to date, however, there is no indication that those files were supplied to either the FBI or to the HSCA; FBI, "Airtel to Legat Ottowa," King Assassination FBI Central Headquarters File, MURKIN 44-38861, section 73, available online at the Mary Ferrell Foundation, accessed September 15, 2010, http://www.maryferrell.org/mffweb/archive/viewer/showDoc.do?mode=searchResult&absPageId=1132643.

24. John Nicol, "Was the King Assassination 'Triggered' in Canada?" CBC News, last modified January 7, 2009, accessed December 15, 2010, http://www.cbc.ca/world/story/2008/04/28/f-ray-hearings.html. Nicol also cites an HSCA staffer, Melvin Kriedman, as saying that Congress came to believe that Ray was recruited into the plot in Canada.

25. Patsy Sims, *The Klan,* 2nd ed. (Lexington, KY: University Press of Kentucky, 1996) 143.

26. Lamar Waldron with Thom Hartmann, *Legacy of Secrecy: The Long Shadow of the JFK Assassination* (Berkeley, CA: Counterpoint, 2008) 478–79. Waldron discusses the ability of organized crime to generate false identification for its smugglers. Ray actually had no "identity" for Eric Starvo Galt at all until he arrived in Birmingham, Alabama, and that he created himself by buying and licensing a car and obtaining a drivers license all in that name.

27. Investigation of the Assassination of Martin Luther King, Jr.: Appendix to Hearings Before the Select Comm. on Assassinations, 95th Cong., 2nd Sess., vol. xii, at 414 (Interview with James Earl Ray) available online at Mary Ferrell Foundation, accessed December 11, 2010, http://www.maryferrell.org/mffweb/archive/viewer/showDoc.do?mode=searchResult&absPageId=1002963.

28. Interview of Jerry Ray by George McMillian (May 30, 1972), Jerry Ray interviews 1969-1975, Box 5, Trial and Post Trial materials, McMillian/Southern Historical Collection.

29. Investigation of the Assassination of Martin Luther King, Jr.: Hearings Before the Select Comm. on Assassinations, 95th Cong., 2nd Session, vol. i, at 181 (August 14-16, 1978), available online at Mary Ferrell Foundation, accessed December 11, 2010, http://www.maryferrell.org/mffweb/archive/viewer/showDoc.do?mode=searchResult&absPageId=998400.

30. FBI, "Sidney Crockette Barnes" summary file, at 13 (November 30, 1971). This is a summary file we obtained via the Freedom of Information Act (FOIA). The reference to Ray was made to a fellow member of the Americans for the Preservation of the White Race (a White Knights front organization). At the time, both Barnes and the individual he was talking to about knowing Ray were highly trusted couriers for the head of the White Knights (L. E. Matthews, successor to Sam

Bowers). The same source reported that Matthews had remarked on Barnes's claims to have high-level connections in Texas and Alabama as well as on the coasts; Matthews had also described Barnes as being "crazy" in his dedication to Wesley Swift and the Christian Identity mission.

31. Bob Zellner with Constance Curry, *The Wrong Side of Murder Creek: A White Southerner in the Freedom Movement* (Montgomery, AL : NewSouth Books, 2008) 303. Ray had supposedly never been in Pascagoula. He denied he had mentioned Ingalls shipyard to his apartment manager, although it seems a stretch to think the manager came up with the name on his own. Interestingly, Ingalls shipyard, owned by Litton Industries, had been having the same sorts of union integration problems as other southern manufacturers. The Klan was active in baiting white union workers on the subject of union integration; reportedly their most significant success in Mississippi (and the location of the most violent and radical Klan union members) was at the Masonite plant in Laurel, Mississippi. Laurel was the home base for Sam Bowers, leader of the White Knights and the source for multiple King assassination leads pointing to members of the White Knights. The Klan's influence and connections within southern unions and the opposition to equal union benefits for black workers seems not to have received the same attention as other civil rights struggles; however, we do find many of the more violent racists equally involved in attacks on black union organizers. For general reference, see *Black Labor and the American Legal System,* Bureau of National Affairs, Vo. 1, 1977.

32. "1967 Alabama Drivers License Application," Dr. Martin Luther King, Jr. Assassination Investigation, Tom Leatherwood Shelby County Register of Deeds, accessed December 15, 2010, http://register.shelby.tn.us/media/mlk/index.php?p=301967+Alabama+Drivers+License+Application.jpg&album=James+Earl+Ray. This site is helpful in general for original photographs of evidence from the murder trial of James Earl Ray. It is also of note that in 1967, Louisiana was one of the few states that did not maintain previous records for driver's licenses. Whether or not this was part of the wisdom Ray picked up in prison or good advice from more recent acquaintances is a matter of speculation.

33. FBI, "Interview with William David Paisley Jr," MURKIN 1970 2324, section 21, at 70 (April 9, 1968) Galt was now an "Alabama boy"; his car tags and driver's license proved it, and his Mustang even had a Confederate sticker.

34. Huie, 58–59. Interestingly, when the initial (single-speed) camera shipped to him did not match his order (four-speed), Ray wrote and asked for a replacement. The same day he purchased a Polaroid Land Camera for snapshot purposes. He would use that for his initial sex film efforts in Mexico (305).

35. FBI, "Ray Chronological Activities List and Laboratory Examination of Evidence," MURKIN 4143, section 52, at 10.

36. Sims, 40, 81.

37. Waldron and Hartmann, 501. Sutherland's final estate, including his home, real estate, stocks, savings, and physical assets, was valued at approximately $300,000.

38. Ibid., 494-98.

39. Ibid., 497.

40. FBI, "Joseph Milteer: Atlanta FBI Memorandum, Background and Personal History" RIF# 1801004610451 at 24 (December 1, 1963). This is a report from SA Kenneth Williams and Donald Adams.

41. Waldron and Hartmann, 491.

42. Dan Christensen, "FBI Ignored Its Miami Informer," *Miami* magazine, October 17, 1976,

37-38, available online at Cuban Information Archives, December 15, 2010, http://cuban-exile. com/doc_101-125/doc0114.html.

43. Waldron and Hartmann, 510.

CHAPTER II

1. William Brandford Huie, *He Slew the Dreamer: My Search, with James Earl Ray, for the Truth about the Murder of Martin Luther King, Jr.* (New York: Delacorte Press, 1970) 17-69. In this section Huie also reviews circumstantial evidence that Ray had engaged in prior black-market-type smuggling across the Mexican border on his previous visit.

2. Gerold Frank, *An American Death: The True Story of the Assassination of Dr. Martin Luther King, Jr., and the Greatest Manhunt of Our Time* (New York: Doubleday, 1972) 303–305.

3. Ibid., 304–305. Frank provides additional details that portray the fight being with a group of black men and Ray arming himself with his pistol and talking of killing them. This is one of the items for which Frank provides no specific citation. The HSCA pursued this incident, interviewing the woman. She confirmed that there were two black sailors in the bar and that one was drunk, stumbling and touching her as he passed by; she felt Ray had lost his temper because the man had touched her rather than it being a race issue. On the other hand, she really did not know Ray well, and there was a language barrier that prevented her from understanding some of Ray's remarks. The HSCA accepted her statement; given a broader view of Ray's background, however, it seems likely that the racial interpretation was correct and race had indeed been the issue with Ray.

4. George McMillian, *The Making of an Assassin: The Life of James Earl Ray* (Boston: Little, Brown, 1976) 269.

5. Frank, 306.

6. Investigation of the Assassination of Martin Luther King, Jr.: Hearings Before the Select Comm. on Assassinations, 95th Cong., 2nd Session, vol. i, at 184 (August 14-16, 1978), available online at Mary Ferrell Foundation, accessed December 11, 2010, http://www.maryferrell. org/mffweb/archive/viewer/showDoc.do?mode=searchResult&absPageId=998400.

7. James Earl Ray, *Tennessee Waltz: The Making of a Political Prisoner* (Saint Andrews, TN: Saint Andrew's Press, 1987) 59.

8. Huie, 75. Another possibility was that Ray had managed to bring at least some quantity of marijuana into the United States and needed to move it. Huie found a variety of sources who reported that Ray was moving marijuana shortly before his departure; perhaps he did manage to get rid of it all in Mexico and brought in only cash.

9. Gerald Posner, *Killing the Dream: James Earl Ray and the Assassination of Martin Luther King, Jr.* (New York: Harcourt Brace & Co., 1998) 200.

10. Lamar Waldron with Thom Hartmann, *Legacy of Secrecy: The Long Shadow of the JFK Assassination* (Berkeley, CA: Counterpoint, 2008) 540.

11. FBI, Interview with Marie Martin (April 13, 1968) MURKIN 1051-1175, section 9, at 263.

12. Posner, 200.

13. Ray, 21.

14. Don Whitehead, *Attack on Terror: The FBI against the Ku Klux Klan* (New York: Funk & Wagnalls, 1970) 211–13. It is safe to say that hardcore members of the so-called patriot network

realized that the FBI might monitor their mail. Sam Bowers was well aware of that and followed a practice of using coded letters and false names such as Willoughby Smead. In a later chapter we provide an example of letters intercepted and traced that related to warnings to individuals who had been using a militant safe house in North Carolina.

15. Investigation of the Assassination of Martin Luther King, Jr.: Appendix to Hearings Before the Select Comm. on Assassinations, 95th Cong., 2nd Sess., vol. xiii, at 252-53 (March 1979), available online at Mary Ferrell Foundation, accessed December 11, 2010, http://www.maryferrell.org/mffweb/archive/viewer/showDoc.do?docId=95664&relPageId=256. These references contain excerpts of the letter and the results of an FBI interview with Ronald Hewitson, president of the Orange County, California, chapter of the Friends of Rhodesia. Rhodesia was still marred by racial discrimination and apartheid in the late 1960s.

CHAPTER 12

1. Investigation of the Assassination of Martin Luther King, Jr.: Appendix to Hearings Before the Select Comm. on Assassinations, 95th Cong., 2nd Sess., vol. iv, at 143 (November 9-10, 1978) (Narration by G. Robert Blakey, on possible criminal motives of James Earl Ray and playing of tape, interview with Special Agent Dennis LeMaster, March 10, 1979), available online at Mary Ferrell Foundation, accessed December 11, 2010, http://www.maryferrell.org/mffweb/archive/viewer/showDoc.do?docId=95656&relPageId=147.

2. William Brandford Huie, *He Slew The Dreamer: My Search, with James Earl Ray, for the Truth about the Murder of Martin Luther King, Jr.* (New York: Delacorte Press, 1970) 100.

3. Gerold Frank, *An American Death: The True Story of the Assassination of Dr. Martin Luther King, Jr., and the Greatest Manhunt of Our Time* (New York: Doubleday, 1972) 364–65. It should be noted that Frank was an FBI-endorsed author, recommended as the correct person to convey the bureau's successful solution of the case. This followed his first work on James Earl Ray (which was retitled while in progress from *They Slew the Dreamer* to *He Slew the Dreamer*) with a second book dedicated to defending the FBI from accusations that it might itself have been involved in the attack on Dr. King. It should also be noted that neither Frank nor Huie appear to have been aware of or considered the documents and leads currently available. Neither author dealt with the details of prior planned attacks on Dr. King; Huie in particular rejected the idea that the same individuals could have been plotting against Dr. King over any extended period.

4. Investigation of the Assassination of Martin Luther King, Jr.: Appendix to Hearings Before the Select Comm. on Assassinations, 95th Cong., 2nd Sess., vol. xii, at 204 (1979).

5. "States Rights Party Stirring in California," *Los Angeles Times* (April 13, 1965) 16.

6. FBI, "Atlanta Field Office to Director, Miami, Los Angeles, and Birmingham" (May 12, 1968) MURKIN 44-38861-3970.

7. FBI, "Los Angeles Field Office to Director, Miami, Atlanta, and Birmingham" (May 25, 1968) MURKIN: 44-38861-3959. It is difficult to tell from other documents if the FBI ever resolved this odd detail—that JT was running the Birmingham NSRP from Los Angeles. In any event, the document does not say how long JT had served in this role as of 1968, nor did the FBI attempt to verify his statements that he had voluntarily separated from the NSRP before his move to Atlanta. If nothing else, there remains the possibility that he had been closely involved with the Birmingham NSRP headquarters (located approximately fifteen minutes from Ray's room-

ing house) at the time of Ray's arrival in Birmingham.

8. Investigation of the Assassination of Martin Luther King, Jr.: Hearings Before the Select Comm. on Assassinations, 95th Cong., 2nd Session, vol. iii, at 208 (August 18, 1978), available online at Mary Ferrell Foundation, accessed December 11, 2010, http://www.maryferrell.org/mffweb/archive/viewer/showDoc.do?docId=95655&relPageId=208.

9. FBI, "Airtel SAC Houston to FBI Director" (May 3, 1968) King Assassination FBI Central Headquarters File, MURKIN 44-38861-3067, available online at Mary Ferrell Foundation, accessed September 15, 2010, http://www.maryferrell.org/mffweb/archive/viewer/showDoc.do?docId=145175&relPageId=80.

10. Susan Blakeney, email message to authors, March 12, 2010.

11. FBI, "Airtel from Memphis to Director," section 72 (October 25, 1968) King Assasination FBI Central Headquarters File, MURKIN 44-38861-5328, available online at Mary Ferrell Foundation, accessed September 15, 2010, http://www.maryferrell.org/mffweb/archive/viewer/showDoc.do?mode=searchResult&absPageId=1132538.

12. Jerry Ray to authors, April 2010. In his letter, Jerry Ray says that James became aware of Quinn via a fellow prisoner in Tennessee, after James Earl Ray's arrest. It is odd that Quinn, who seems to have had a low profile outside White Knights circles, was the attorney given to Ray by someone else, if indeed James told the truth on the matter. While some of Ray's earliest attorneys were, like Quinn, Klan-connected, they (Arthur Hanes and J. B. Stoner) had much more obvious national reputations and profiles.

13. FBI, "Memo to SAC Jackson; Subj: J.B. Stoner, Serial: 157-3082" (June 7, 1971). File obtained by the authors via FOIA.

14. FBI, "Airtel from SAC, Newark to Director (Attn: FBI Identification Division)" (June 11, 1968), FBI Central Headquarters File, section 59, available online at Mary Ferrell Foundation, accessed September 15, 2010, http://www.maryferrell.org/mffweb/archive/viewer/showDoc.do?docId=99876&relPageId=38. The authors obtained a copy with fewer redactions from the online version from the FBI MURKIN collection at the National Archives II, College Park. The releases include the names of the informants, which we have kept secret, as we do not know if they are alive or dead. Also, the MURKIN file number is hard to read, so we excluded it.

15. Lamar Waldron with Thom Hartmann, *Legacy of Secrecy: The Long Shadow of the JFK Assassination* (Berkeley, CA: Counterpoint, 2008) 510–11.

16. Ibid., 511.

17. FBI, "Airmail from SAC Tampa to Director" (July 4, 1974) MURKIN 44-38861.

18. Janet Upshaw, in discussion with the authors, December 15, 2010. Upshaw, the daughter of the Fulton County jailer, is presently searching through her own notes to see if she can help us identify the prisoners.

19. Waldron and Hartmann 510–511, 545.

20. Because of his White Citizens' Councils affiliations, Milteer was well networked throughout the southern states. White Citizens' Council members including individuals from the Jackson and Laurel, Mississippi, areas had attended Constitution Party conventions in which Milteer participated. In short, Milteer had an extremely broad social network ranging beyond his NSRP, Constitution Party, and Klan affiliations—one that has been extremely difficult to access in detail because of the apparent lack of FBI files relating to Milteer's racist activities. He was clearly known to the bureau, but to date the only files that have emerged relate to the Kennedy

assassination, and virtually none pertain to his association with other subjects. This is difficult to understand because at least one FBI informant clearly identified him as being heavily involved in both racist and potentially violent political activities.

21. William Turner, *Rearview Mirror: Looking Back at the FBI, the CIA and Other Tails* (Granite Bay, CA: Penmarin Books, 2001) 297.

22. Other authors have noted the manager's report; Gerald Posner (*Killing the Dream: James Earl Ray and the Assassination of Martin Luther King, Jr.,* New York: Harcourt Brace & Co., 1998) comments that the FBI conducted a nationwide search and could not locate anyone who fit the story. He also mentions one FBI memo that speculates that the manager was simply trying to cash in on a reward. Currently available documents allow us to delve into the FBI's investigation, which was indeed far more comprehensive and did produce names, photographs, and aliases. Unfortunately there is no sign that the FBI integrated that investigation with the sorts of corroborative information that are available to us now.

23. See for instance FBI teletype from Los Angeles to Director, June 6, 1968; FBI teletype from Memphis to Director, 29 May 1968; FBI teletype from Los Angeles to Director, Memphis, Atlanta, San Diego, Birmingham, Springfield, Las Vegas, Louisville, New Orleans, and Jackson, May 30, 1968; FBI Airtel from Los Angeles, June 10, 1968, among others. These documents are available at the Mary Ferrell online archive, www.maryferrell.org.

24. "Report from SA Dennis LeMaster," Los Angeles 44-1574-D-456 (May 29, 1968), available online at the Harold Weisberg Archive at Hood College, accessed November 10, 2011, http://jfk.hood.edu/Collection/Weisberg%20Subject%20Index%20Files/H%20Disk/Hardin-Ashmore%20Records%20From%20Chip%20Selby/Item%2019.pdf. Thompson claimed that a vagrant who had frequented the area and bars around his hotel was the impetus for his coming forward with the Hardin account. The man had approached Thompson, mentioned a figure similar to Hardin, which triggered Thompson's memory of the collect calls and visit from Hardin. He suggested that the Hardin information might be worth some money but warned Thompson that he had to be left out of the story; Thompson suspected that the man had outstanding issues with law enforcement and wanted no exposure. The FBI put considerable pressure on Thompson to disclose the identity of this third party, and ultimately he did give them the individual's nickname, "Fitz." FBI agents were able to use the nickname to track down the individual (David Fitzwater), who they verified had indeed frequented the bar Ray had habitually visited. The bartender at the Jackrabbit, where Thompson said Fitz overhead Ray talking to Hardin, recalled both Fitz and Ray. But, as Thompson predicted, Fitz definitely wanted nothing to do with the FBI and denied everything except knowing Thompson. The FBI did not press Fitzwater on the subject but instead continued to actively and seriously pursue the Hardin identification for weeks after locating and contacting Fitzwater. We are left to wonder why Thompson would involve Fitz in the first place if he had been making up the story from scratch, or why Fitz simply did not support Thompson's claims if the two had been in collusion.

25. Frank, 79, 99. Ray's path first crossed Dr. King's on the night of March 22 in Selma, Alabama, as King was supposed to speak there that evening. But as often happened, King changed his plans at the last minute and appeared thirty miles away in Camden, Alabama. Initially Ray lied about his Selma stop, saying he had gotten lost between New Orleans and Birmingham. Of course Selma was sixty miles off the freeway between those two cities, so that is at best improbable. When Huie challenged him on the Selma stop, Ray finally admitted that he had gone there because of King.

26. Investigation of the Assassination of Martin Luther King, Jr.: Hearing Before the Select Comm. on Assassinations, 95th Cong., 2nd Sess., vol. ii, at 65-91 (August 17, 1978), available online at Mary Ferrell Foundation, accessed December 11, 2010, http://www.maryferrell.org/mffweb/archive/viewer/showDoc.do?docId=95654&relPageId=65. The operator of Ray's Atlanta rooming house testified that on March 31, Ray had paid in advance for an additional full week's stay in the building, further supporting the view that Ray's trip to Memphis was not something Ray planned by himself.

CHAPTER 13

1. The HSCA did submit reports to Congress finding evidence of conspiracy in both the murders of President Kennedy and Martin Luther King Jr. The committee formally requested that the Justice Department accept their findings and open its own criminal investigation. Congress took no action in either instance, nor did the Department of Justice. James Earl Ray died in April 1998. In December 1999, a civil action against a self-confessed accessory to the King murder a Memphis Court, brought by the King family, resulted in a jury finding that the U.S. government had been involved in the murder of Dr. King. The King family appealed to the Department of Justice to open an inquiry into the death of Dr. King, which it did. In June 2000 a report issued by attorney Barry Kowalski absolved the government from any involvement in the King murder.

2. Investigation of the Assassination of Martin Luther King, Jr.: Appendix to Hearings Before the Select Comm. on Assassinations, 95th Cong., 2nd Sess., vol. ix, at 224, available online at Mary Ferrell Foundation, accessed December 11, 2010, http://www.maryferrell.org/mffweb/archive/viewer/showDoc.do?mode=searchResult&absPageId=1002783.

3. William Brandford Huie, *He Slew the Dreamer: My Search, with James Earl Ray, for the Truth about the Murder of Martin Luther King, Jr.* (New York: Delacorte Press, 1970) 100, 110, 153, 176.

4. Ibid., 110.

5. Gerold Frank, *An American Death: The True Story of the Assassination of Dr. Martin Luther King, Jr., and the Greatest Manhunt of our Time* (New York: Doubleday, 1972) 324–25.

6. Philip H. Melanson, *The Martin Luther King Assassination: New Revelations on the Conspiracy and Cover-up* (New York: S.P.I. Books, 1994) 67. It should also be pointed out that any room on either the first or second floor of the motel would have been a clear shot from the location of the rooming house across the street.

7. William Bradford Huie, "The Story of James Earl Ray and the Conspiracy to Kill Martin Luther King," *Look* 32, no. 23 (November 12, 1968).

8. With this perspective, the murder of Dr. King seems very similar to the blatant, highly visible, and public attack on James Meredith, which occurred during major press coverage of Meredith's Mississippi march and in front of a group of assembled reporters. And in the Meredith case, the shooter apparently never even served time for the attack.

9. David Garrow, *The FBI and Martin Luther King, Jr.: From "Solo" to Memphis* (New York: W.W. Norton, 1981) 185–86.

10. Ibid., 184.

11. Ibid.

12. Ibid., 188.

13. Jim Bishop, *The Days of Martin Luther King, Jr.* (New York, Putnam: 1971) 2. Bishop quotes the Reverend Bernard Lee, King's companion and bodyguard: "Usually Dr. King's personal staff in con-

ference with the hierarchy of the Southern Christian Leadership Conference worked on matters of personal safety weeks ahead . . . sending advance men . . . asking police protection . . . this time there was no advance work. It isn't our style of operation . . . we got no intelligence on Memphis."

14. Ibid., 8.

15. Some authors believe that one of Ray's actual brothers may have encouraged Ray to return the rifle. But evidence for this is circumstantial at best, and we find the evidence for a so-called fraternal conspiracy wanting. David Lifton and Jeffrey Cohen, in a 1977 article, argue that James invented the Raoul story as a cover for one of his brothers' actions. The Lifton/Cohen piece makes much of the fact that witnesses who dealt with James Earl Ray said consistently that Ray referred to meetings with his brother. These became meetings with Raoul when Ray himself retold the story after his 1968 conviction. Lifton and Cohen cited a comment by Percy Foreman, Ray's trial attorney, in which he said that Ray admitted his brother was with him in Birmingham during the gun purchase. William Bradford Huie, however, says that if this happened, Foreman never mentioned it to him. Furthermore, employment records seem to confirm that the brother in question was where he said he was, working in Chicago. Generally speaking, those who had experience with the Ray brothers were skeptical that they had the competence or reliability to be used in a King conspiracy. One brother, in particular, frequently has made statements that implicate James Earl Ray and reveal aspects of a supposed plot, so he is not the kind of person one wants on the inside of a murder conspiracy.

16. Select Comm. on Assassinations, Summary of Findings and Recommendations, at 293 (1979), National Archives, accessed December 11, 2010, http://www.archives.gov/research/jfk/select-committee-report/part-2a.html.

17. There are two plausible reasons that a .30-06 was specified; either or both may have been in play. For example, Sam Bowers was well aware such a weapon was capable of killing a man with a single shot; one of his operatives had used a .30-06 and a single shot to kill Medgar Evers. In the source of that case, a mushrooming bullet was shown to be difficult to match to a given .30-06 weapon. Based on that experience, it was clear that with a .30-06, fingerprints on the rifle, rather than an exact bullet-weapon match, were likely to be the key in any prosecution. It also appears that the White Knights might have been very interested in obtaining that sort of weapon for an act against King. The combination of these factors suggests that the people pulling Ray's strings had something specific in mind, and that when he bought a cheaper (but "wrong") rifle, he was ordered to switch to the .30-06.

18. Frank, 13, 44. Although Ray stated that he had no idea King was in Memphis, a Memphis paper found in his motel room (where he stayed the evening before the murder) contained headline coverage of Dr. King and a photograph of King standing in front of his room on the balcony of the Lorraine Motel. Certainly Ray knew King was in Memphis and he knew exactly where he was staying. The rooming house Ray selected had a full view of the balcony rooms, the first floor rooms, and the motel staircase.

19. Gerald McKnight, *The Last Crusade: Martin Luther King, Jr., the FBI, and the Poor People's Campaign* (Boulder, CO: Westview Press, 1998) 61. It should also be noted that press coverage of King's disastrous March appearance had included observations that he had spent a night at a luxurious "white" hotel. Actually he had been escorted there by police who wanted him far away from the violence. Lieutenant Nichols of the MPD had stayed at the hotel until King and his staff registered and were assigned rooms. Because of the negative press, there was no doubt at all that King would be staying at a "black" motel upon his return.

20. Ibid., 67.

21. Ibid., 68.

22. Ibid., 60, 80. Files on the FBI effort against Dr. King have been released and detailed in a number of books. The most comprehensive of those is David Garrow's *The F.B.I. and Martin Luther King Jr.* (1981). In *The Last Crusade,* Gerald McKnight also points out that the FBI had been escalating its official effort against Dr. King right up to the day of his death and continuously pushing that effort with its media and legislative contacts. Extensive files on that effort first became visible to Congress and the public during the 1970s.

23. Frank, 78–79.

24. McKnight, 68.

25. Ibid., 79–81. McKnight provides a detailed synopsis of the complex security situation surrounding Dr. King's arrival in Memphis for the second sanitation workers' march.

26. Ibid., 67.

27. Ibid., 79.

28. Ibid.

29. Ibid., 76.

30. Ibid.

31. Melanson, 69–70.

32. Ibid., 174–75.

33. Investigation of the Assassination of Martin Luther King, Jr.: Hearings Before the Select Comm. on Assassinations, 95th Cong., 2nd Sess., vol. iv, at 268 (November 9–10, 1978) (Memphis Police Departmental Communication, Inspector Tines to Chief MacDonald, April 4, 1968), HSCA MLK Exhibit F-189, available online at Mary Ferrell Foundation, accessed December 11, 2010, United States Congress. House Select Committee on Assassinations. MLK Report, Volume IV. Washington, D.C.: U.S. Government Printing Office, 1979. http://www.maryferrell. org/mffweb/archive/viewer/showDoc.do?mode=searchResult&absPageId=999995.

34. Ibid.

35. McKnight, 77.

36. Melanson, 175–76.

37. It has been established that the FBI had placed informants within targeted "subversive" groups across the nation as part of COINTELPRO. In Memphis, members of the Invaders group have been reported as being FBI informants and "provocateurs." In order to establish their credentials and be accepted, informants often presented themselves as highly militant and aggressive, inciting illegal acts and participating in them as and part of their intelligence collection. FBI infiltrators and informants inside the Klan took similar tactics; the bureau covered some of their activities in order to maintain their position as informants (Diane McWhorter reviews the details of the career of one such Klan informant/provocateur, Gary Thomas Rowe Jr., at length in *Carry Me Home*). There were obvious problems with this tactic. In some cases informant activities actually provoked additional violence; in other instances other law enforcement infiltrators and informants reported the provocateurs' remarks as absolute fact. Due to the level of fear during this period, even the most radical remarks were often accepted as factual, raising the level of fear and triggering a high degree of law enforcement overreaction. A dramatic example of this occurred later in 1968, in Chicago. In that instance the FBI provided Chicago police with a great deal of information that later turned out to contain little fact and much fiction. In his book *The Bureau: My Thirty Years in Hoover's FBI*, William C. Sullivan itemized

examples ranging from planned sniper attacks on police to firebombing buildings and even the assassination of the mayor of Chicago, the vice president, Senator McCarthy, Roy Wilkins (head of the NAACP), and Edwin King (head of the Mississippi Freedom Democratic Party). While none of these violent acts were attempted (even Sullivan was forced to describe the reports as an intermingling of fact and fiction), the FBI warnings clearly alarmed Chicago's mayor and helped trigger the highly violent police response to a number of initially peaceful demonstrations during the Chicago Democratic convention. We interviewed the Reverend Edwin King, who was present at the Mississippi Freedom Democratic Party meeting that generated the reported threat that seems to have triggered the Redditt incident in Memphis. Edwin King stated that one of the topics of the meeting, in addition to the upcoming DC march, was the march in Memphis. Martin Luther King and his aides had requested that the MFDP, with its well-established tradition of passive nonviolence, assist in keeping the Memphis march nonviolent. Edwin King related that a number of individuals unknown to the MFDP members showed up at the meeting and seemed to engage in a number of side conversations. At the time, the individuals were thought to be from the Invaders in Memphis, although later it was learned that was not the case. Any discussion of threats or contracts was certainly not part of the main MFDP meeting and would have been totally out of character for that group. This leads us to the possibility that the entire Redditt incident may have resulted from the ongoing "dirty tricks" campaign that was being conducted against the civil rights movement and against Dr. King in particular, specifically due to Director Hoover's orders to undermine and prevent the planned DC march.

38. After Action Report, Civil Disorder Operation March 28-April 12, 1968, available online at Mary Ferrell Foundation, accessed September 15, 2010, www.maryferrell.org.

39. Bishop, 34. What was not a mystery was the location of Dr. King's motel and motel room. Media coverage had made that generally known, and TV footage from the evening before the assassination shows King out on the Lorraine Motel's second-floor balcony with the room number 306 visible in the background.

40. Huie, He Slew the Dreamer, 116–17. There has been discussion of the fact that the location of Dr. King's room on a second-floor exterior room placed him in the ideal position for a sniper attack. In considering that point, it should be noted that rooms on both the first and second floors of the motel were visible from Ray's chosen rooming house and that both Ralph Abernathy and the Lorraine Motel owner stated for the record that Dr. King had previously stayed in that same Lorraine room, number 306 (one of the newer and more comfortable rooms) on earlier visits. However, we visited Bessie Brewer's and the Lorraine Motel (now a museum), and from discussion with staff, and his own observations, we do not believe the room that Ray chose to rent— room 5B—had a clear view of room 306. In other words, Ray chose to rent a room before really thinking about whether or not it provided a clear view of King. This suggests that, if Ray chose to shoot King, it was not something he had decided even when he rented the room at Bessie Brewer's just hours before he killed King.

41. Gerald Posner, Killing the Dream: James Earl Ray and the Assassination of Martin Luther King, Jr. (New York: Harcourt Brace & Co., 1998) 273. Posner argues that Ray's room did provide a view of Dr. King, that it is possible that a shot could have been fired from that room, and it would have been a less than ideal shooting position but shooting from inside the bathtub in the common bathroom was also a less than ideal stance and provided far more risk of interruption. After visiting the museum ourselves, we disagree strongly with Posner's notion that room 5B provided even a "less than ideal" perspective on the Lorraine and room 306; in fact it appeared

to us to not have any view whatsoever. There was no agreement to the exact location of the rifle fire from the ear-witnesses in the rooming house. The HSCA attempted to resolve the source of the rifle fire but in the end determined that it could have come from either the opposite buildings or the brush-screened ground-level area behind them—the failure to trace the wound through Dr. King's body and the question about the position of his head at the time of the shooting left the entire matter in doubt. Ray's room provided only a very difficult view of Dr. King's room at the Lorraine, if any view at all, and that would have required Ray hanging out the window to observe. Simple observation would have been easy enough from the common bathroom, which did provide a clear view; however, shooting from inside the bathtub in the common bathroom appears to have been quite a challenge and provided far more risk of interruption. Considerable suspicion has been expressed in regard to reports that the brush behind the rooming house was cleared immediately following the assassination. However, police crime scene photos from the following day show the brush still in place. Those photos and considerable material relating to the Memphis crime scene may be found online at the Shelby Counter Registrar's website, http://register.shelby.tn.us/media/mlk/index.php?album=Crime+Scene.

42. Frank, 84. The police record also shows that an ambulance was ordered at 6:04, arrived at 6:06, and was off to the hospital by 6:09. These observations were noted by Patrolman Richmond, who was observing with binoculars from the fire station.

43. Ibid., 100, 107.

44. Ibid., 347.

45. Melanson, *The Martin Luther King Assassination,* 84–85.

46. Ibid., 98.

47. Mark Lane and Dick Gregory, *Murder in Memphis: The FBI and the Assassination of Martin Luther King,* revised ed. (New York: Thunder's Mouth Press, 1993) 156.

48. Ibid., 154–57.

49. Ibid., 33.

50. Philip H. Melanson, *The MURKIN Conspiracy: An Investigation into the Assassination of Dr. Martin Luther King, Jr.* (New York: Praeger, 1989) 94.

51. "Teletype from Birmingham to Director, Memphis, Tennessee, New Orleans, Louisiana and Mobile, Alabama," (April 15, 1968) section 10, King Assassination FBI Central Headquarters File/MURKIN 44-38861, available online at Mary Ferrell Foundation, accessed September 15, 2010, http://www.maryferrell.org/mffweb/archive/viewer/showDoc.do?mode=searchResult&absPageId=1068700.

52. Judge W. O. "Chet" Dillard, *The Final Curtain: Burning Mississippi by the FBI* (Denver, CO: Outskirts Press, 2007) 41–42.

53. Lamar Waldron with Thom Hartmann, *Legacy of Secrecy: The Long Shadow of the JFK Assassination* (Berkeley, CA: Counterpoint, 2008) 592, 599. In reference to the dropping of the bag, Waldron notes that Scotland Yard detective Alec Eist testified to the HSCA that while in English custody, Ray had remarked that he had to throw away the gun because he had seen a police vehicle or policeman. Also being taken into custody with the rifle would have made a totally concrete case against Ray.

54. The HSCA found that the radio in the Mustang was not working, which would have prevented Ray from even hearing news broadcasts that might have assisted him during his escape.

55. Frank, 157.

56. Waldron and Hartmann, 604–605.

57. Ibid. The letter appears to be a response to a prior communication from Milteer to the correspondent. Dan Christensen, "FBI Ignored Its Miami Informer," *Miami* magazine, October 17, 1976, 37–38.

58. Harvey Edward Lowmeyer had worked in a prison kitchen with James Earl Ray's brother John.

59. John Willard is the name of a Toronto man, living a few miles from the area where Eric St. Vincent Galt, Paul Bridgeman, and George Sneyd lived. Ray definitely did try to steal the identities of Bridgman and Sneyd; he was forced to give up on Bridgman after he staged a prospecting call and found Bridgman already had a passport. He found that Sneyd did not, completed a passport replacement request with information taken from Sneyd's birth notice, and used that name in his travel out of Canada. Unfortunately for him, his writing was so poor that the first passport was misspelled and he had to obtain another—it was having two passports in his possession that brought him to the attention of a customs agent in London and led to his being detained and taken into custody (he was carrying a concealed pistol at the time). Because Ray definitely did work on stealing the identities of Bridgman and Sneyd, it has been argued that the Willard name was also stolen or given to Ray by associates. However, Ray used the name only once, in Memphis, and had no identification for the name at all; it was simply used instead of a name that could be tracked to him (as the Galt identity could), much the same as the use of Lowmeyer's name, which Ray used in his purchase of his rifle. Whether or not the name actually related to Willard of Toronto is speculation; Harvey Lowmeyer is a name found in the United States, as is James Willard.

60. Huie, *He Slew the Dreamer*, 140-46.

61. Ibid.

CHAPTER 14

1. FBI, "Urgent Teletype from Dallas Field Office to Director, Memphis and Jackson," (April 23, 1968) MURKIN 44-38861-1835.

2. Ibid.

3. Ibid.

4. FBI, Samuel Holloway Bowers, Jr. bureau file, file 157-1654, section 23, at 15 (August 9, 1968) This is a summary file obtained by the authors via Freedom of Information Act (FOIA).

5. FBI, "Urgent Teletype from Dallas Field Office to Director, Memphis and Jackson" (April 23, 1968) MURKIN 44-38861-1927.

6. FBI, Samuel Holloway Bowers, Jr. bureau file, file 157-1654, section 23, at 15 (August 9, 1968). This is a summary file obtained by the authors via FOIA.

7. FBI, "44-1-7169 Information concerning individuals who were formerly associated with the WKKKKOM, Jones Co., Miss." (September 15, 1970).

8. FBI, Samuel Holloway Bowers, Jr. bureau file, file 157-1654, section 23, at 15 (August 9, 1968). This is a summary file obtained by the authors via FOIA.

9. Ibid., 21.

10. "Timeline: The 1968 Manhunt for Martin Luther King's Killer," *American Experience: Roads to Memphis* WGBH, PBS: Public Broadcasting Service, http://www.pbs.org/wgbh/americanexperience/features/timeline/memphis-hunt. This website has an excellent and thorough timeline of the manhunt. However, it is more biased to the idea of Ray as a calculating, sole killer

than the authors would prefer.

11. FBI, "Memorandum from McGowan to Rosen" (April 24, 1968) MURKIN 44-38861-2649.

12. FBI, "Airtel from SAC Oklahoma City to Director re: Donald Eugene Sparks . . ." (April 24, 1968) King Assassination FBI Central Headquarters File, MURKIN 44-38861-2926; also FBI, "Airtel from Tampa to Director re: Donald Eugene Sparks . . ." (April 18, 1968) King Assassination FBI Central Headquarters File, MURKIN 44-38861-1331-2926.

13. FBI, "Teletype from Birmingham to Director, Memphis, LA, and Mobile," (April 15, 1968) King Assassination Central Headquarters File, MURKIN 44-38861-1203, available online at Mary Ferrell Foundation, accessed September 15, 2010, http://www.maryferrell.org/mffweb/archive/viewer/showDoc.do?docId=99574&relPageId=64.

14. FBI, "Memorandum from SA Richard F. Kilcourse to SAC Los Angeles," 62-5101 (April 23, 1968).

15. Ibid.

16. Select Comm. on Assassinations, *Summary of Findings and Recommendations,* at 450-51 (1979), National Archives, accessed December 11, 2010, http://www.archives.gov/research/jfk/select-committee-report/part-2e.html. The HSCA noted that the FBI continued to investigate the conspiracy angle after the Galt investigation, even saying to select field offices that "leads concerning any other suspects developed from any source must be given immediate and thorough handling on a top-priority basis." However, the files indicate that many leads were held in abeyance. In addition, as noted elsewhere in this chapter, individuals were dismissed as suspects simply for having alibis outside of Memphis. Most relevant to our discussion was what the HSCA also found, namely that the "FBI files indicate only limited efforts, independent of specific leads, to investigate the possible involvement of extremist organizations such as the White Knights of the Ku Klux Klan of Mississippi or the Minutemen, even though they had demonstrated both a propensity for violence and a clear antagonism toward Dr. King."

17. FBI, "Airtel from SAC Oklahoma City to Director re: Donald Eugene Sparks . . ." (April 24, 1968) King Assassination FBI Central Headquarters File, MURKIN 44-38861-2926; also FBI, "Airtel from Tampa to Director re: Donald Eugene Sparks . . ." (April 18, 1968) King Assassination FBI Central Headquarters File, MURKIN 44-38861-1331-2926.

18. FBI, "Re: Alleged Offer of $100,000 by the WKKKKOM to Anyone Who Kills Martin Luther King, Jr . . . ," (May 17, 1968) MURKIN 44-38861-396. This document includes a summary of both the 1967 and 1968 interviews with Eure.

19. FBI, "Re: Alleged Offer of $100,000 by the WKKKKOM to Anyone Who Kills Martin Luther King, Jr . . . ," Jackson Field Office File 157-7990 (July 24, 1967).

20. Jack Nelson, *Terror in the Night: The Klan's Campaign against the Jews* (New York: Simon & Schuster, 1993) 119–20.

21. Select Comm. on Assassinations, Summary of Findings and Recommendations, at 377 (1979), National Archives, accessed December 11, 2010, http://www.archives.gov/research/jfk/select-committee-report/part-2c.html#klan.

22. FBI, "Airtel from St. Louis to Director" (August 12, 1968) FBI Central Headquarters File, section 69.

23. 18 USC Sec. 241, http://www.law.cornell.edu/uscode/18/241.shtml. Indeed, when the FBI was gearing up for a possible federal prosecution of "Eric Galt"-before they had made the James

Earl Ray connection—they prepared an indictment using this section of the federal code. Ob-viously, the case was never tried on a federal level, only locally in Memphis, Tennessee.

24. Lamar Waldron with Thom Hartmann, *Legacy of Secrecy: The Long Shadow of the JFK Assassination* (Berkeley, CA: Counterpoint, 2008) 571.

25. Department of Justice/Civil Rights Division Referrals; Affidavits, June 1968, available online at Mary Ferrell Foundation, accessed September 15, 2010, http://www.maryferrell.org/mffweb/archive/viewer/showDoc.do?mode=searchResult&absPageId=106673. See affidavit of John Webster De Shazo, a gun store regular who interacted with Ray.

26. Our work with another individual, Jason Kull, with reverse phone and public records searches place the phone within five to ten minutes of driving distance from the gun store.

27. Curt Gentry, *J. Edgar Hoover: The Man and the Secrets* (New York: W. W. Norton & Co., 2001) 662.

28. Select Comm. on Assassinations, *MLK Report Volume 13*, H.R. Rep., section C: Personal relations between the Department and the Bureau, 174–75, (1979) Mary Farrell Foundation, accessed December 11, 2010, http://www.maryferrell.org/mffweb/archive/viewer/showDoc.do?mode=searchResult&absPageId=1004327.

29. Select Comm. on Assassinations, Summary of Findings and Recommendations, at 381–82 (1979), National Archives, accessed December 11, 2010, http://www.archives.gov/research/jfk/select-committee-report/part-2c.html.

30. Ibid., 377–78.

31. Select Comm. on Assassinations, *Summary of Findings and Recommendations,* at 451 (1979), National Archives, accessed December 11, 2010, http://www.archives.gov/research/jfk/select-committee-report/part-2e.html.

32. Select Comm. on Assassinations, Summary of Findings and Recommendations, at 377-78 (1979), National Archives, accessed December 11, 2010, http://www.archives.gov/research/jfk/select-committee-report/part-2c.html.

33. Ibid., 377.

34. Ibid., 382. Ray initially stalled on executing the waiver for Arthur Hanes as well but relented on Hanes. He never waivered for Stoner, however.

35. Ibid., 402. This claim came from Sapp and not from Somersett. Sapp correctly reported that Somersett had heard other rumors, notably a threat by union officials against King owing to King's connection to labor union strikes (e.g. what he was doing in Memphis). We agree with the HSCA that, having looked at the available documentation from Somersett to the Miami PD, it is unlikely he told this story to law enforcement before the assassination. Lietenant Sapp likely just misremembered a story Somersett reported later. Again, it is important to note that Somersett was an informant who simply reported everything he heard, regardless of whether the source for the information was exaggerating or lying or telling the truth.

36. Dan Christensen, "King Assassination: FBI Ignored Its Miami Informer," *Miami,* no. 12 (October 1976), 37–38, available online at Cuban Information Archives, last modified February 23, 2008, accessed September 15, 2010, http://cuban-exile.com/doc_101-125/doc0114.html. See the latter for the redacted names.

37. FBI File No. 62-117290: section 10, at 16, available online at Mary Ferrell Foundation, accessed September 15, 2010, http://www.maryferrell.org/mffweb/archive/viewer/showDoc.do?docId=146430&relPageId=14. The HSCA requested all relevant material on Tarrants (and

others) in January 1978. The FBI, in their FOIA response to us, said they had routinely destroyed the relevant file, Mobile Field Office File 157-758, in 1977.

38. Jerry Mitchell, "Murder of Martin Luther King Jr.; Did Klan Have a Role?" *Clarion-Ledger,* December 30, 2007.

39. FBI, "SA Ronald Johnson and SA Lester Amann interviews with Sidney C. Barnes" (September 30, 1968) Jackson Field Office File 157-51.

40. FBI, "Sidney Crockette Barnes" summary file, at 13 (November 30, 1971). This is a summary file we obtained via the Freedom of Information Act (FOIA)

41. Select Comm. on Assassinations, *Summary of Findings and Recommendations,* at 377 (1979), National Archives, accessed December 11, 2010, http://www.archives.gov/research/jfk/select-committee-report/part 2o.html.

42. Ibid., 378. One wonders if the sources on Barnes and the source on the White Knights are one in the same. There is an example of at least one individual who had connections to all the relevant parties (e.g. Barnes, Carden, and the White Knights).

43. Mitchell, "Murder of Martin Luther King Jr."

44. FBI, "Information concerning individuals who were formerly associated with the WKKKKOM, Jones Co., Miss.," Jackson Report of SA Samuel Jennings, serial 809, at 31–32 (November 15, 1970).

45. Bruce Hoffman, *Holy Terror: The Implications of Terrorism Motivated by a Religious Imperative* (Santa Monica, CA: RAND Corporation, 1993), http://www.publicgood.org/reports/holywar3.htm.

46. Ibid.

47. Ibid.

48. Ibid.

49. Ibid.

50. Taylor Branch, *At Canaan's Edge: America in the King Years, 1965–68* (New York: Simon & Schuster, 2006) 486.

51. Ernest Cashmore, *Encyclopedia of Race and Ethnic Studies* (London: Routledge, 2003).

52. Michael Eric Dyson, *April 4, 1968:Martin Luther King, Jr.'s Death and How It Changed America* (New York: Basic Civitas Books, 2008).

53. Jerry Mitchell, "Two-Thirds of 124 Civil Rights Cold Cases Closed," Journey to Justice (blog), *Clarion-Ledger,* December 4, 2011, http://blogs.clarionledger.com/jmitchell/2011/11/07/only-third-of-124-civil-rights-cold-cases-still-open.

54. United States Department of Justice, "United States Department of Justice Investigation of Recent Allegations Regarding the Assassination of Dr. Martin Luther King, Jr." (June 2000), http://www.justice.gov/crt/about/crm/mlk/part1.php.

55. Wolfgang Mieder, "Making a Way out of No Way": *Martin Luther King's Sermonic Proverbial Rhetoric* (New York: Peter Lang Publishing, 2010) 212.

APPENDIX A

1. MURKIN 44-38861-3050/FBI Central Headquarters File, Section 68: July 31, 1968 Airtel from SAC, Memphis to Director, available online at Mary Ferrell Foundation, accessed September 22, 2010, http://www.maryferrell.org/mffweb/archive/viewer/showDoc.do?docId=99885&relPageId=29.

2. Ibid.

3. Ibid.

4. MURKIN 44-38861-3051/FBI Central Headquarters File, Section 68: 8 Aug 1968 Memorandum from Rosen to DeLoach, available online at Mary Ferrell Foundation, accessed September 22, 2010, http://www.maryferrell.org/mffweb/archive/viewer/showDoc. do?docId=99885&relPageId=44.

5. Ibid.

6. Leung, Rebecca. "The Ghosts of El Segundo." 48 Hours Mystery. CBS News, 7 May 2009, accessed August 22, 2011, http://www.cbsnews.com/stories/2005/07/05/48hours/main706303. shtml. The reporter details a case where the murder of two police officers in 1957 was solved, thanks in large part to the IAFIS system.

7. "FBI - Latent Hit of the Year - Cold Case Files." Cold Case Files - Know your Cold Cases from SpotCrime, accessed online December 9, 2011, http://coldcase.posterous.com/fbi-latent-hit-of-the-year.

8. United States Congress. House Select Committee on Assassinations. Final Report. Washington, D.C.: U.S. Government Printing Office, 1979, accessed online, December 11, 2010, http://www. archives.gov/research/jfk/select-committee-report/part-2a.html.

9. Federal Bureau of Investigation. "Memorandum from SAC Atlanta to FBI Director Subject: MURKIN" (April 19, 1968).

10. Wilhelm, Kristen. "HSCA Records." Message to Stuart Wexler. 21 Apr 2011. Email.

11. Huie, William Bradford. He Slew the Dreamer: My Search, with James Earl Ray, for the Truth about the Murder of Martin Luther King. N.Y.: Delacorte Press, 1970, 114.

12. Newton, Michael. The King Conspiracy. (Los Angeles: Holloway House, 1987) 84–85.

13. United States Congress. House Select Committee on Assassinations. Final Report. Washington, D.C.: U.S. Government Printing Office, 1979. http://www.archives.gov/research/jfk/select-committee-report/part-2a.html

14. Nelson, Jack. Terror in the Night. (New York, NY: Simon & Schuster, 1993) 139.

15. United States Congress. House Select Committee on Assassinations. Final Report. Washington, D.C.: U.S. Government Printing Office, 1979. http://www.archives.gov/research/jfk/select-committee-report/part-2c.html#citizen.

16. Ibid.

17. Pepper, William. Orders to Kill. (New York, N.Y.: Carroll & Graf, 1995) 207–208.

18. United States Congress. House Select Committee on Assassinations. Final Report. Washington, D.C.: U.S. Government Printing Office, 1979. http://www.archives.gov/research/jfk/select-committee-report/part-2c.html#citizen.

19. Posner, Gerald. Killing the Dream: James Earl Ray and the Assassination of Martin Luther King, Jr. (NY: Harcourt Brace and Co., 1998) 36. No all-points bulletin was issued to any bordering state and contrary to standard guidelines no roadblocks were set up at major roads out of the city. The police dispatcher blamed this failure on "massive confusion and the huge volume of radio traffic."

20. "MLK Consipiracy Trial Transcript—Volume 4." Wayback Machine, January 14, 2009, accessed August 22, 2011, http://web.archive.org/web/20090409100812/http://www.thekingcenter.org/news/trial/Volume4.html. The original trial was housed at the King center site but is presently not available. The authors obtained this via the Wayback Machine, a site that archives

web pages.

21. United States Department of Justice. "Investigation of Recent Allegations Regarding the Assassination of Dr. Martin Luther King, Jr.," accessed August 22, 2011—see Part (b) Accounts of a man fleeing after the shooting. < http://www.usdoj.gov/crt/crim/mlk/part3.htm.

22. Whitehead, Don. *Attack on Terror* (New York, NY: Funk & Wagnalls, 1970) 292.

23. Federal Bureau of Investigation. "Main King File: File Number: 100-106671, Section 73, Alleged Offer of $100,000 by White Knights of the Ku Klux Klan, Jackson, Mississippi, to Anyone Who Kills Martin Luther King,") 207–210.

24. Confidential source. Interview by authors, on November 9, 2009, In interviews with one of the authors, Nissen conceded the possibility that he made the connection at the time. This would be because he identified woman and her real estate practice in the original 1967 interview with the Dallas Field Office. Hence, it would be tough to reconcile his delivering a package to a female real estate manager without him drawing the connection in his own mind. The acknowledged the possibility that he did would have been reluctant to reveal this to law enforcement as it could indirectly implicate him. However, it is important to note that (a) the source is describing events forty years after the fact, (b) the available FBI accounts make no reference to the package delivery story whatsoever, and (c) the woman worked out of her home, which even to this day, surprised our source.

25. Ibid.

26. Confidential source. Interview by authors on January 9, 2010.

APPENDIX B

1. Frank, Gerold. *An American Death: The True Story of the Assassination of Dr. Martin Luther King, Jr. and the Greatest Manhunt of Our Time* (New York, NY: Doubleday, 1972) 208–210, 245.

2. Ibid, 357.

3. McKnight, Gerald. *The Last Crusade: Martin Luther King, Jr., the FBI, and the Poor Peoples Campaign* (Boulder, CO: Westview Press, 1998) 73, 108.

4. Frank, 399.

5. McKnight, Gerald, 77–78.

6. United States Congress. House Select Committee on Assassinations. *MLK Report, Volume IV*. Washington, D.C.: U.S. Government Printing Office, 1979. http://www.maryferrell.org/mffweb/archive/viewer/showDoc.do?docId=95656&relPageId=234

7. United States Congress. House Select Committee on Assassinations. *MLK Report, Volume XII*. Washington, D.C.: U.S. Government Printing Office, 1979 http://www.maryferrell.org/mffweb/archive/viewer/showDoc.do?docId=99710&relPageId=206 also McKnight, 75. There is also little doubt that Redditt's interpretation and elaboration of his experience contributed to considerable conspiracy speculation. However, in his public HSCA testimony Redditt was presented with evidence which forced to recant on certain remarks he had made to author Mark Lane and to acknowledge that his own complaint might have forced the removal of the black firemen as well as to clarify that his assignment was surveillance (not security) and to acknowledge that one officer remained at his post even after his removal. He was also offered the

opportunity for an open ended expansion on issues he felt suggested a conspiracy but declined. HSCA Report Vol. IV, pp. 230-236. Later, in a follow on interview with James DiEugenio, Redditt reportedly stated that his entire HSCA appearance had been a sham and a farce, that he was taken into an extended interview prior to his testimony and actually given a set of "canned" questions and answers that were to be given for the public record. However it should also be noted that historian McKnight describes Redditt as an accomplished self-promoter who seriously damaged the reputation of earlier investigator and author Mark Lane—completely misrepresenting virtually everything Lane had attributed to him (McKnight, 75) McKnight points out that it was generally known in the community that Redditt was a "police spy" and that he had been distrusted, hated, and even threatened by many in the black community prior to the events of Dr King's visit, concluding that the suspicions Redditt had surfaced have indeed been resolved for the "fair minded" and for the historic record (McKnight, 77).

8. McKnight, 73–75

9. Finnegan, John Patrick. Center for Military History of the United States Army. Lineage Series (Washington, D.C.: United States Government, 1998) 154–159.

10. Morales, Frank, "U.S. Military Civil Disturbance Planning—The War at Home," *Covert Action Quarterly*, 69 (2000).

11. "Context of 'Winter 1967-1968: Pentagon Establishes Civil Disturbance Plans Garden Plot and Cable.'" The History Commons Online, n.d. http://www.historycommons.org/context.jsp?item=gardplotestab&scale=2#gardplotestab.

12. McKnight, 124–125.

13. HSCA Segregated Collection/Surveillance on Iden C/. RIF# 104-10125-10199, accessed online at Mary Ferrell Foundation, http://www.maryferrell.org/mffweb/archive/viewer/showDoc.do?docId=28702&relPageId=1.

14. McKnight, 77.

15. It may be difficult for modern readers to appreciate the pervasiveness of the paranoia in those times, however one of the authors (Hancock) remembers university campus police taking photographs of students simply sitting on the campus grass in a passive protest over the cancellation of a controversial campus speaker—the photos were used to create a photo album of suspected campus radicals (nobody was supposed to walk or sit on the grass so obviously the students were radicals). University faculty shouted at each other in public meetings over even such minor events and some were terminated because of their support for freedom of speech. In another instance, at another university, he recalls an antiwar march being funneled through a single-file, walled channel, so that uniformed city police could intimidate students by taking individual photographs of some thousands of people in the march. And those instances represent only the most trivial and overt forms of surveillance and intimidation of the late 1960s.

16. McKnight, 71-72.

17. Ibid, 71.

18. DiEugenio, Jim and Pease, Lia. *The Assassinations*, (Los Angeles, CA.: Feral House, 2003) 516–518

19. Researchers have questioned this but it is clear that he was working for the Memphis Police. His reports were undoubtedly shared with the FBI and possibly other agencies but given his deep undercover position it seems likely that his personal contacts were very constrained.

20. McKnight, 81.

21. Branch, Taylor. *Canaan's Edge: America in the King Years* (New York, NY: Simon & Schuster, 2006) 737–738, 760, 765.

22. Marchetti, Victor and Marks, John. *The CIA and the Cult of Intelligence* (New York, NY: Knopf, 1974) 238.

23. "Rangell Charges CIA with Bias in Hiring Practices," *Jet*, February 27, 1975, 8.

24. The authors note that both the spellings Raoul and Raul have been applied to Ray's self-described handler; Ray never saw a signature from the man so any position on spelling would be speculative—the authors have generally chosen to stick with Raoul although both treatments appear in both books and government documents.

25. United States Department of Justice. "Investigation of Recent Allegations Regarding the Assassination of Dr. Martin Luther King, Jr." "Raoul and His Alleged Participation in the Assassination" http://www.usdoj.gov/crt/crim/mlk/part5.htm.

26. Nicol, John. "Canadian Connection to the Martin Luther King Assassination." CBC News, April 3, 2008. www.cbc.ca/news/world/story/2008/04/28/f-james-earl-ray.html.

27. Melanson, Philip. *The Martin Luther King Assassination* (New York, NY: S.P.I. Books, 1994) 36.

28. Pepper William, *Orders to Kill* (New York: Carroll Graf, 1995) 319, 332, 420.

29. DiEugenio, Jim and Pease, Lia, *The Assassinations* (Los Angeles, CA.: Feral House, 2003) 508.

30. DiEugenio, and Pease, Lia, 494. It should be noted that not virtually nobody, including King family members, believed Jowers in regard to his having no idea of an act specifically against Dr. King. However that position did allow him to present himself as an accessory to a conspiracy but an unknowing accessory in murder, one who could not be charged directly in the killing of a specific individual, Dr. King.

31. Pepper, William, *An Act of State* (New York, NY: Carroll & Garf, 1995. London, G.B.: Verso, 2003) 38.

32. While no criminal case was brought against Jowers based on his 1993 television "confession," its use in a civil case certainly placed him in a very difficult legal position. Clearly the decision to proceed against him for the claim of only $100 was a best-case scenario for him at that point in time. Indeed it may explain why both counsels agreed to a stipulation that the interview could be used in civil court despite Jower's decision to stand on his Fifth Amendment rights and offer no court testimony.

33. Pepper, *Act of State,* p. 31.

34. Ibid., 100

35. Pepper, *Orders to Kill,* 38.

36. Ibid, 384.

37. Pepper, *Act of State,* 214.

38. In the investigation of Raoul, photographs shown to witnesses included such people as Carlos Marcello and Carlos Bringuier, individuals who had figured prominently in both investigations and numerous books relating to the Kennedy assassination. Marcello was a well known New Orleans Mafia chief and had been arrested in NYC in 1966. In 1968 he was sentenced for assaulting a federal officer—after a lengthy legal battle he entered a federal penitentiary time in 1970. Marcello's age and physical description were nothing like Ray's description of Raoul and clearly Marcello was not working waterside bars in Canada recruiting small-time smugglers in 1968. His

inclusion in the photo showing raises serious questions about the selection of photographs for the "photo-lineup."

39. Pepper, *Act of State*, 57-58.

40. United States Department of Justice. "Investigation of Recent Allegations. Regarding the Assassination of Dr. Martin Luther King, Jr." http://www.justice.gov/crt/about/crm/mlk/part5.php.

41. Posner, 305–306

42. United States Department of Justice. "Investigation of Recent Allegations. Regarding the Assassination of Dr. Martin Luther King, Jr." http://www.justice.gov/crt/about/crm/mlk/part5.php

43. Ibid.

44. Grabow's introduction and reference to the Kennedy assassination in her story certainly could have implications for her identification as well. If any individual had simply followed the Raoul story per James Earl Ray, been familiar with the Kennedy assassination (as seems to be the case with regard to Grabow), or looked closely at the photo spread, they could have deliberately or unintentionally selected the Raoul picture due to its differences from all the other photos—many of which are quite familiar to anyone who has read newspaper coverage or books on the Kennedy assassination investigations.

45. United States Department of Justice. "Investigation of Recent Allegations. Regarding the Assassination of Dr. Martin Luther King, Jr." see attachment 9, copy of photo array provided by Dr. Pepper. Readers can reach their own opinion as to the fairness of the photo array by viewing it online at http://www.justice.gov/crt/crim/mlk/jpg9.php.

46. DiEugenio and Pease, 512. In his writing on the Justice Department re-investigation following the Jowers civil trial, Jim DiEugenio expresses the opinion that the Justice Department's work on the individual identified by William Pepper as Raoul makes "a powerful case that this particular Raoul was not involved in the assassination." Readers who wish to pursue alternative opinions in support of a government conspiracy should refer to *The Assassinations* for its presentation and commentary on that view.

47. Ibid., 492.

48. Douglas, Jim. "King Conspiracy Exposed in Memphis." *Probe Magazine* Spring 2000, http://www.ratical.org/ratville/JFK/MLKconExp.html. Actually Pepper described a conspiracy extending beyond the FBI, organized crime figures, military and other intelligence agencies and Memphis police. He asserted that all parties involved were acting as agents of the economic powers (the "establishment") who feared the economic impact which King represented. There is no arguing the fact that Dr. King's focus on basic economic rights for all citizens, involving a redistribution of massive amounts of national income to the poor, was a dramatic call to action. Dr. King felt that it was the only solution for the spiraling riots and civil violence. However, the cold fact is that "the establishment" as reflected in Congress and its legislative actions, had already effectively stonewalled even minor preliminary initiatives of that nature and would continue to do so. Beyond that, both Congress and the President were moving to establish an aggressive counter intelligence and covert action campaign (New Cointelpro and Chaos) on a breadth and scale never before seen in America; it would continue well into the 1970s. By 1968, President Johnson's "Great Society" effort and programs had been gutted both by Vietnam War spending and by political right-wing reaction to the violence in the cities. Professor McKnight summarizes that political reality

and swing to Congressional conservatism in some detail in *The Last Crusade* (18–22). However, what is clear is that the "establishment" was very much in fear of further violence in the cities, and particular of the violence that the Poor People's March might bring to Washington, DC As we illustrate in this book, that fear was not particularly associated with Dr. King, it was associated with the much more aggressive black militants who it was felt might take advantage of the march. And that fear did indeed generate a massive FBI and intelligence effort against the Poor People's Campaign and it both continued and escalated after Dr. King's death.

49. McKnight, 11–12.

50. Ibid., 17.

51. Google News advanced archive search, search terms "Martin Luther King" and "Vietnam," from 1/67 to 12/67, yields 912 hits." Google News advanced archive search, search terms "Martin Luther King" and "Poverty" for same period yields 257 hits; for "Martin Luther King" and "poor" yields 268 hits. Search date March, 20, 2010.

52. Google News advanced archive search, search terms "Martin Luther King" and "Vietnam," from 1/68 to 3/68, yields 166 "hits." Google News advanced archive search, search terms "Martin Luther King" and "Poverty" for same period yields 74 hits; for "Martin Luther King" and "poor" yields 140 hits. Search date March, 20, 2010.

53. McKnight, 18.

54. Gibbons, William Conrad, *The U.S. Government and the Vietnam War* (Princeton, N.J.: Princeton University Press, 1986) 24, fn.

55. Willbanks, James H, *The Tet Offensive: A Concise History* (New York; Chichester: Columbia University Press, 2008) 75.

56. "News Behind The News," *Sacramento Modesto Bee*, February 25, 1968.

57. Davis, James K. *Spying on America—The FBI's Domestic Counterintelligence Program* (New York, NY: Praeger Publishers, 1992) 33–34. In its earliest years the program was focused on the Communist Party as well as any groups which were felt to be fellow travelers. The tactics were quite well developed by the 1960s when they were applied to a much broader range of groups. Estimates are that approximately 40 percent of the FBI's activities involved sending anonymous, inflammatory material to groups and individuals. Special agents would also notify employers, prospective employers, and credit bureaus. Pressure was brought on to bear on colleges, universities and other institutions to remove suspected individuals from teaching positions or any other positions of authority. By 1968, Hoover moved into a virtual crisis mode, monitoring all forms of dissent and proactively using a tool kit of "dirty tricks" against both individuals and groups. FBI COINTELPRO tactics included break-ins for obtaining and photographing records, safecracking, mail opening, microphone plants, phone taps, trash inspection, infiltration, falsely labeling individuals as informants, forcing IRS inquiries, anonymous letters alleging infidelity, using provocateurs to incite inter-group violence and intervening with employers to fire targeted individuals. Actually, all those activities had been in practice since at least 1956, when Director Hoover had reviewed them with President Eisenhower in a National Security Council meeting; the council (including the Attorney General Herbert Brownell) had endorsed the bureau's tactics. Readers seeking an in depth study of the COINTELPRO program and its tactics should read *Spying on America* by James Kirkpatrick Davis. In addition, by 1968 the bureaus "racial intelligence" collection was at its peak, not only targeting militant black groups but the Klan and even the Jewish Defense League.

58. Ungar, Sanford, *FBI: An Uncensored Look Behind the Walls* (Boston, MA: Atlantic-Litte, 1965) 138–140

59. Garrow, David, *The FBI and Martin Luther King Jr.* (New York, NY: Penguin Books, 1985) 24–25. One of the only pieces of "evidence" offered in the claim of communist sponsorship for the civil rights movement was a photograph taken during a ceremony at the Highlander Folk School in Tennessee. That school had been a major target of Klan and White Citizens Councils for years due to its being one of very few integrated schools in the south. The photograph, taken in 1957, showed Dr. King in a crowd of people, one of whom was Abner Berry, a correspondent for the *Daily Worker*. The photograph was taken by an "undercover" agent for the Georgia State segregation commission and distributed widely for several years as evidence of communist influence of the civil rights movement. Despite a concerted effort by anti-integration activists to associate Dr. King with communists, up to 1961 the FBI no significant file on King. Apparently even the FBI found nothing credible in the "Highlander" story. A memo written to Hoover at the time of the Freedom Rides stated that King "had not been investigated by the FBI".

60. Theoharis, Richard, *The Central Intelligence Agency: Security Under Scrutiny* (Westport, CT: Greenwood Publishing Group, 2006) 49, 175, 195, 203, 322.

61. Rockefeller, Nelson, *Report to the President by the Commission on CIA Activities Within the United States* (New York, NY: Manor Books, 1975), 142–144. The organizations, named in the report of the Rockefeller Commission included: Students for a Democratic Society (SDS); Young Communist Workers Liberation League (YCWLL); National Mobilization Committee to End the War in Vietnam; Women's Strike for Peace; Freedomways Magazine and Freedomways Associated, Inc.; American Indian Movement (AIM); Student Non-Violent Coordinating Committee (SNCC); Draft Resistance Groups (U.S.); Cross World Books and Periodicals, Inc.; U.S. Committee to Aid the National Liberation Front of South Vietnam; Grove Press, Inc.; Nation of Islam; Youth International party (YIP); Women's Liberation Movement; Black Panther Party (BPP); Venceremos Brigade; Clergy and Laymen Concerned About Vietnam.

62. "The FBI's War on King," *King's Last March*. American RadioWorks. http://americanradioworks.publicradio.org/features/king/d1.html

63. McKnight, 1–2.

64. Garrow, 40–43.

65. Ibid., 44–47.

66. Ibid., 49.

67. Davis, James K. *Spying on America—The FBI's Domestic Counterintelligence Program* (New York, NY: Praeger Publishers, 1992) 98.

68. Ibid., 41.

69. Ibid.

70. Ibid., 100–101.

71. Garrow, 73–75 and 94–111.

72. Ibid., 125–126.

73. Ibid., 74–75. As early as 1962 FBI domestic intelligence reports had described King as "knowingly, willingly and regularly" taking guidance from communists. Copies of the analysis containing that description were sent by Hoover to the Attorney General, the White House, the Secretary of State, the CIA, and the military services. Attorney General Robert Kennedy considered the report very unfair and forced Hoover to recall it.

74. Ibid., 184–186.

75. McKnight, 81. In his work on Dr. King's Poor People's campaign, historian Gerald McKnight details several aspects of the FBI's ongoing campaign against King during 1968, concluding that if Hoover had indeed planned to eliminate King, he would have not continued, and even escalated such efforts—and he certainly would have destroyed the extensive records which demonstrate his own personal animosity toward King.

76. While Hoover was portraying King as being manipulated by his communist advisors in opposition to the Vietnam war, transcripts of King's calls and meetings actually reveal that those same advisors being cited in Hoover's warnings were cautioning King on his stance, advising him to go slow and stressing the negative impact on public support and fund raising This pro video yet another Instance of Hoover forcing his staff to ignore the actual data which they were collecting—in favor of his own personal attitude.

77. Google News advanced archive search, search terms "black power" registers 168 hits in 1965, 2820 hits in 1966, 4520 hits in 1967, and 990 hits from 1/68 to 3/68. Google News advanced archive search, search terms "Martin Luther King" for same periods yields 4420 hits, 3290 hits, 2620 hits and 618 hits respectively. Search date March, 20, 2010.

78. James Fitzpatrick Davis, spying on America (Westport CT: Greenwood Publishing Group, 1992). This book is essential reading in regard to the history of FBI counter intelligence as well as the various aspects and methods of the Cointelpro programs. It provides detailed reviews of activities conducted against both groups and individuals.

79. Bishop, Jim. *The Days of Martin Luther King Jr.* (New York, NY: Putnam, 1971) 13

80. McKnight, 93–94.

81. Dickerson, James, *Dixie's Dirty Secret* (Armonk, N.Y.:M.E. Sharpe, 1998) 134. Domestic counter-intelligence activities were conducted under Lantern Spike.

82. *Operation Lantern Spike.* The Mary Ferrell Foundation, online at http://www.maryferrell.org/mffweb/archive/textsearch/advancedResults.do?queryStr=|Lantern Spike|&systemDocType=GOVTDOC&docId=99575.

83. McKnight, p. 96

84. Ibid., 26–28.

85. Ibid., p. 84 .

86. Ibid., 84–85.

INDEX